941.14

The Hebridean Traveller

The Hebridean Traveller

DENIS RIXSON

Birlinn

First published in 2004 by
Birlinn Limited
West Newington House
10 Newington Road
Edinburgh EH9 1QS

www.birlinn.co.uk

ISBN 1 84158 294 8

British Library Cataloguing-in-Publication Data
A catalogue record for this book is available from the British Library

Typeset by Hewer Text Ltd, Edinburgh
Printed and bound by Creative Print and Design, Ebbw Vale, Wales

Contents

List of Plates

List of Figures

Acknowledgements

I owe a great deal to the staff of Highland Council Library Service and in particular to Sue Skelton of Inverness Reference Library and Andrina Gammie of the Library Support Unit. As always they have been patient and indefatigable in chasing down my endless requests. I also thank Margaret Macdonald of The Museum of the Isles, Armadale, Skye, for her invaluable help with a reference in Stobie's Map of the Macdonald Estate.

I am very grateful to the following individuals and organisations for permission to quote from their works: The University of St Andrews for extracts from *Scotichronicon*; Dr G. Broderick for extracts from his translation of *The Chronicles of the Kings of Man and the Isles*; Professor D. Thomson for a translation from his book *An Introduction to Gaelic Poetry*; The National Archives of Scotland for extracts from V. Wills, *Reports on the Annexed Estates*; Oxford University Press for extracts from *Edward Lhuyd in the Scottish Highlands 1699–1700*; The New Statesman for part of Philip Johnstone's poem *High Wood* which first appeared in 'The Nation' magazine; Boydell & Brewer Ltd for 'How the First Helandman of God was maid' from *Poetry of the Stewart Court* by Hughes and Ramson; the Scottish History Society for extracts from *Highland Papers (Vol IV)*, *Calendar of Scottish Supplications to Rome 1418–1422* and *Calendar of Scottish Supplications to Rome 1423–1428*; The School of Scottish Studies Archives, University of Edinburgh, for extracts from *Tocher* (36–7).

Permission was sought to reproduce Plate 4 (National Library of Ireland), but no reply was received by the time of going to press.

Note

For a number of the earlier sources, principally of the sixteenth century, I have given the contemporary English version (Bellenden for Boece, Dalrymple for Leslie) immediately followed by a literal transcription. I have adopted a policy of minimal change in all 'translations' from Scots. All I have done is modernised spellings, leaving words and grammar intact even when archaic. I have only substituted modern text where the meaning is otherwise unclear.

Leslie

In 1578, John Leslie, bishop of Ross, produced a ten-volume book on the 'Origin, manners, and history of the Scots. To which is added a new and accurate description of the districts and islands of Scotland, with a true topographical table of the same'. He included a map, a topographical review of the Highlands and Hebrides and a section dealing with their ancient customs.

Within about a decade of its completion, Leslie's Latin text was translated into Scots by Father James Dalrymple, a monk of Ratisbon. In turn this was carefully edited by E.G. Cody and published by the Scottish Text Society in 1884–5. Cody compared Dalrymple's translation with the Latin original, expanded contractions and noted all departures. In the extracts here, Cody's amendments are placed in square brackets, my own in round brackets.

Pont

There are two descriptions of the Highlands and Islands in Macfarlane's Geographical Collections (Vol II) which I have ascribed to Timothy Pont. Sir Arthur Mitchell, Macfarlane's editor, suggested, in 1907, that the second of these (p 509 ff) was largely the work of Timothy Pont. He also drew attention to its similarity to another description printed earlier in the same volume (p 144 ff). From close comparison of the two I am convinced they share a common original in notes made by Timothy Pont, probably in the period 1585–1610. Through later copying, mis-copying and interpolation they have come to appear as they do in Macfarlane. However, proof would require a chapter in itself and since not everybody may be presently convinced as to Pont's authorship I have subscribed these extracts 'Pont(?)'.

Introduction

T his book is about early travellers in the West Highlands and Hebrides. Why? Because travellers' accounts are often the only records we have. Writing any history of this area faces a critical handicap – that so few early documents survive which can be said to be native. Our meagre Dark Age records come largely from the Irish annals, even if some of these may be based on lost Iona sources. From the early mediaeval period we have scattered references in the Norse sagas and the Chronicles of Man. From the later mediaeval period we have a single surviving Gaelic charter and the Gaelic histories given by the Macvurich family in the Book of Clanranald, and by Hugh Macdonald of Sleat.

We have no surviving records from the monasteries of Iona, Saddell, Oronsay or Ardchattan. There was nothing approaching a town or a university anywhere in the West Highlands or Hebrides. Given this paucity of evidence from within the area we have to look without. Our richest sources are the public records of Scotland, supported by the archives of the principal Highland families, particularly the Campbells of Argyll. We have a great many documents which relate to land-ownership in the Highlands, as well as frequent references in the official records whenever Highland interests came into conflict with Lowland. Unfortunately the latter are always loaded with an institutional bias.

To a government based in Edinburgh, English-speaking and Lowland-oriented, the Highlands and Hebrides represented a distant, alien and dangerous region. Its distinctive culture deserved only disparaging or antagonistic notice. It had to be tolerated, since it could not be overwhelmed, but it was usually denied legitimacy – as were other peripheral regions like Wales, Cornwall and Brittany. The objective may not always have been military conquest, which was costly to impose and maintain, but it was certainly cultural subjection and absorption. We have therefore an almost complete absence of native records and a heavily biased set of Lowland Scots records. In order to get beyond these partial views we should survey the various travellers' accounts that have been transmitted to us. Can they give us new facts and insights? This book is a vehicle for that journey.

I have assembled materials from a variety of travellers between earliest times and about 1800. For the early period I have avoided all discussion of the location of 'ultima Thule'. Most likely this was Iceland but it distracts from our purpose of reviewing the Highlands and Hebrides. This area was certainly on the edge of the habitable world but what it was called is less important than what visitors knew and wrote about it.

I have chosen 1800 as a convenient end-date because the modern tourist industry really got under way during the nineteenth century. The development of roads and canals had opened Britain up during the latter part of the eighteenth century. During the nineteenth century steamers and railways carried the process further. As standards of living improved, and the means to travel became more widespread, so the number of people visiting the Highlands and Islands increased steadily. What started as a trickle in the late eighteenth century became a flood a hundred years later. Not everywhere was equally affected. Bute is closer to Glasgow than St Kilda but both islands felt the effects of tourism. Some areas saw their economies transformed, for others it was just a welcome boost during the summer.

As the nineteenth century progressed so the hunting, shooting and fishing industry also took off. Shooting lodges sprang up all over the Highlands. On many estates deer replaced sheep. Oligarchs from commerce and industry bought a chunk of the Highlands to indulge themselves and their friends for a few weeks in summer. This process was to transform the Highlands and is not yet complete. Nowadays there may not be so many coming to hunt and shoot but others come instead to look at wildlife or enjoy their holiday homes and retirement cottages.

With the visitors there was a corresponding growth in travel literature, i.e. books and guides written specifically for the traveller. The earliest accounts, written between 1770–1820, give us the rationale. I have chosen some of these to illustrate particular themes. As the nineteenth century continued there was a geometric progression in literary output. At the risk of stereotyping, much of this lays itself open to parody. In a work entitled something like 'My sojourn in the Northern Hills' the happy author sets out to describe how on one memorable day he bagged a hundred snipe/woodcock/waterfowl before breakfast, followed by a brace of salmon in the forenoon and a twelve–pointer by sunset. The ghillies (Angus/Donald/Ewen), were trusty and reliable; the ponies were stocky and steadfast; whilst the wives and dogs were faithful. Today, for better or worse, such literature has less appeal.

From the historian's point of view the other problem about such 'literature' is that it is more about the visitor than the visited. Not only was there a subconscious assumption that the reader would be more interested in the sportsman's trophies than the area's culture or history, but there also was, and is, an underlying economic bias or imbalance of power. The area's lack of resources, of wealth, people and industry, have made it more vulnerable than most to the demands of the visitor. There is a danger that future developments in the Highlands and Hebrides will be decided on the basis of the desires and wishes of wildlife organisations and summer migrants rather than of local communities.

A tourist industry did not exist in the Highlands and Hebrides until after the

political and economic subjugation of the area in the years following Culloden. Before this the Highlands appeared a dangerous and anarchic wilderness, the home of continuous rebellion from 1689–1747, an area where the
king's writ had scarcely run for centuries before. After Culloden there was a
short and brutally effective process of military 'pacification'. The estates of
many leading rebels were confiscated and administered by the government
until the 1780s. By 1773 Samuel Johnson felt secure enough to visit the
Hebrides and met with warm and generous hospitality. Within the next forty
years the Highlands had their own tourist guide books.

From then till now there has been a constant stream of travel literature
reflecting the interests and preferences of the writers. Men and women have
come here to lose, and find themselves; to paint or draw, compose, reflect,
climb and dream. They have brought with them their own prejudices and
preconceptions and often what they tell us is more about themselves than the
culture or people they are visiting. I have chosen therefore to end with the
work of Mrs Murray, a redoubtable stravaiger who visited the area at the very
end of the eighteenth century, who showed a firm no-nonsense sympathy to
Highlanders and who consciously laid out guides for others to follow. Such
visitors were too interested in what they found to want to change it. Sadly that
isn't always the case today.

Early visitors to Scotland came for a variety of reasons and the chapters of
this book reflect this. I give here a brief outline which will explain *the logic of
the book's structure*. These reasons are not necessarily sequential in time,
many are concurrent.

Firstly there were political, military or diplomatic reasons. The kingdom of
Man was the political authority in the Isles, though not the Highlands, from
1079–1266. It was treated as a distinct political unit and we have a certain
amount of correspondence with the nation states of Scotland, England and
Norway. Even after the collapse of the kingdom of Man, the Lords of the Isles
maintained diplomatic relations with the English court until their own demise
nearly three hundred years later. The kings of England assembled material of
a military value in their long campaign to subjugate Scotland – the work of
John Hardyng in providing information for a land invasion is a good example
of this. The kings of Scotland assembled similar material in their long
campaign to subjugate the Highlands – Alexander Lindsay's rutter being a
matching example at sea. Diplomats visiting Scotland tell us what they knew,
heard or thought of the Highlands. In the years before the Union of Crowns
the area posed such problems for the internal stability and governance of
Scotland that we have a great many references by Lowland Scots. From the
Civil Wars until Culloden the Highlands and Hebrides represented a direct
military and political threat to the stability of the whole of Britain and this also
is reflected in contemporary reports.

Then there was the church. The church was the greatest institutional
sponsor of travel to, from and within the Highlands and Hebrides. It was also

a good record-keeper. As a result we have a great deal of Papal material from the earliest records in the thirteenth century. After the Reformation this changes in quality and quantity but we then find the records of the various Roman missions which attempted to keep Catholicism alive in the area. The Protestant church proved an equally vigorous researcher and record-keeper. Many of the most important reports about the Highlands and Islands were written either by ministers or specifically at the behest of the Church of Scotland. We have the internal reports of Dean Monro and Martin Martin, the external reviews of Timothy Pont and John Walker, Webster's population survey in 1755, and the great Statistical Accounts in the 1790s and 1840s.

There were the commercial or economic reports. It is difficult to separate these from the political and military cloaks they often wore, but a distinct and important reason for visiting the area was to establish its economic potential. Such motives became important from the latter part of the sixteenth century; the whole reason for the colony of Fife Adventurers in Lewis was to tap the supposedly vast riches of the area. Sometimes, as in the case of Captain Dymes in 1630, Thomas Tucker in 1656, John Walker in 1764, or John Knox in 1786, researchers were dispatched to the area specifically to establish the facts. In the case of Dean Monro I have no doubt the value of his report as an indication of the area's wealth was one of the reasons why it was copied and preserved. The fact that Buchanan chose to include it in his *History of Scotland* was the highest contemporary accolade. In addition, whatever the particular intent of such reports they often reveal more in the telling. The accounts of Monro, Martin Martin and Dymes contain a great deal of economic data but are especially valuable because they contain so much by-the-way or anecdotal material.

Whether the reasons were political, military, ecclesiastical or commercial all such commentaries and itineraries were incomplete without a map. The mapping of the Highlands and Islands presents particular difficulties. Not only are they remote but the surveys need to be done both by land and sea. Most travellers did not bring their own boats with them which left them dependent on local goodwill. Moreover, in this area more than most, they were greatly dependent upon the weather. So whilst scattered Hebridean islands appear on maps from the 1240s it is not until John Elder's map of c. 1543 that order descends on the perceived chaos. Unsurprisingly this knowledge was drawn from within the Gaelic world, a fact not generally recognised since it really only saw the light of day through Mercator who probably did not know his ultimate source. The mapping and charting of the Highlands and Islands cannot be viewed independently of the literary sources but it deserves a chapter to itself.

Another reason for travelling, which is very ancient, but which largely escapes the notice of historians, is sport. In early days the kings and nobility of Scotland travelled to the Highlands and Hebrides to enjoy the chase. Admittedly this did not involve great numbers of people and it only took place at certain times of year, but it was an ancient and high-status activity. Our evidence for this in early times is partial and sketchy but we should not see the Victorian fever for hunting as something new. Hunting, hawking, fowling and fishing were old pursuits in this area. Unfortunately the scale of the late Victorian and Edwardian obsession with hunting has rather obscured its earlier history. The Highlands are replete with draughty old shooting lodges; their entrance halls stuffed with trophies. The growth of deer forests in the last decades of nineteenth century transformed the Highland economy and drove sheep out of the glens from which, a hundred years before, the sheep had driven people. Some still pay a fortune to kill a stag or net a salmon but whilst locally important on some estates stalking is not as critical to the Highland economy as it once was.

Finally there is tourism. Samuel Johnson's sensational tour of 1773 was the equivalent of a pop or movie star promotion today. It was as if the mass media of the literary world suddenly focused on the Hebrides. Of course we cannot hold him solely responsible; there were lots of ancillary factors which helped locate the Highlands and Islands on the British and international horizon. There were Ossian and Mendelssohn and Sir Walter Scott. There was a mountain landscape or an island seascape for anyone and everyone; there was a dramatic vista for the Romantic, a dark grotto for the Goth; an unopened cairn for the antiquarian, secret knowledge for the mystic. It seemed that whatever people came looking for they could find, whether they had brought it with them or no. It was a field day, not just for the geologist and naturalist, but for the artist and musician, the folklorist, the historian and the storyteller.

We are still living the effects of this wave of interest. Nevertheless, although tourism does not have an agenda of military conquest or political suppression, although it may not intend cultural demise or economic weakness, its effects can be devastating and insidious. It disguises how this area once appeared, even what it once was. The tourist industry's version of Highland history is, for many people, all the Highland history they will ever know. It threatens to become all of Highland history. This book tries to show, through the reports of early travellers, more of what was once the essential nature of the Highlands and Islands.

It is useful to remind ourselves of this as we try to regulate the effects of the visitor today. It would be ironic if the Highlands and Islands fell victim to the consequences of tourism; if the area became a parody of itself. It would be sad if Highlanders became the projection of others, a stereotype of the beliefs and fictions of outsiders. I do not for a moment doubt that their characters are strong enough to withstand this. What worries me more is that their economic opportunities become so restricted that the battle is lost in demographic terms. If nobody can make a living here, except as they are permitted by outside interests, then there will be no local language or culture to preserve. The danger comes from the conservationist and the wildlife organisations rather than the day-tripper. The latter may leave litter but also leaves the area culturally intact and financially improved. The former wields unseen power and influence, acquires land, controls policy, restricts opportunity and so bleeds the people out. Too often these quangoes escape democratic control or even oversight.

Anybody who has dealt with numbers of tourists will have found, depressingly quickly, how stereotypes match expectations. Visitors want, and pay for, pictures of Highland cattle, the Loch Ness Monster, pipes, tartan, shortbread, oatcakes and whisky. But then these are sometimes the very things that bring them here in the first place. What attracts people are not the diversities and complexities they don't yet know, but the simple certainties they do. This has always been the case and we can also look at some of the stereotypes and enticements that existed in former times. Remoteness always favours invention; ignorance spurs the imagination. The Hebrides were always remote and most Europeans were ignorant of their inhabitants. What was written about them included a degree of wild speculation, a great deal of plagiarism and some utter nonsense. But the marvels and curiosities of the Highlands and Hebrides were retailed endlessly down the centuries. I have trailed a few of these to give a flavour of visitor expectation and what passed for knowledge elsewhere.

Issues of personal comfort and security always concern the traveller and since these feature so often in early accounts I have allowed room for them here. It was difficult for visitors to overlook these when discomfort and danger loomed large. Of course it was useful to other travellers to know the pitfalls in front of them but often it was because the poor put-upon traveller simply wished to complain or get his own back. Whether or not a visitor slept well gives little insight into the host culture, more of the tolerance and character of the writer. However, travel in former times was physically very demanding and we do find additional information about the area by following this line of enquiry. Issues of habit and hospitality; food and drink; expense; the state of the roads and the ferries; objects of curiosity and diversion; all add to our understanding of this distant space and time.

Finally there is travel literature as literature. Some of these travellers were self-consciously writers. They wished to impress their readers with their literary skills as well as their travel experience. This is more true of the period after about 1773 when Johnson and Boswell were pioneers on what became a well-worn trail. We do have 'literary' works from earlier periods. Franck's extraordinarily florid prose stands out as a labour of industry and also as a labour. Mrs Grant of Laggan, Samuel Johnson, James Hogg were all known for their literary achievements. John Leyden wrote his letters from the Highlands to Sir Walter Scott. Edward Daniel Clarke was deeply influenced by Samuel Johnson's prose on Iona. Ever since then writers and poets have been ten-a-penny, nay sometimes more.

We should also weigh how well some of these travellers knew their subject.

Samuel Johnson left Inverness on 30 August 1773 and returned to Oban on 22 October. He published an account of his travels on the basis of the experiences of less than eight weeks. Boswell did the same. Yet Johnson's work is probably as well known as that of Martin Martin who spent much of his life in the area. We know that Martin Martin's book was a great favourite of the young Samuel Johnson although the older man was disparaging of Martin's style. From our point of view issues of style are less important than what he tells us of contemporary Highland culture. On that basis Martin Martin is one of our single most important literary sources. But equally we should not dismiss Samuel Johnson because his knowledge was of necessity shallow. That caustic and cantankerous wit saw deeply, thought potently and judged objectively. His evidence is important.

This work, therefore, is not a history of travel in the Hebrides. It is a collection – part anthology, part review – of travellers' reports, comments, judgements, jokes, anecdotes and soliloquies. It is neither comprehensive nor complete. It is not definitive. It follows certain tracks, others remain untraced. It retails what some of the many visitors to the Highlands and Hebrides have written about their experiences. But in collecting these under certain themes I would like it to be more than what Burt called a 'parade of reading'. It uses selected quotations to try and open windows on an earlier world. It is weighted in favour of the West Highlands and Hebrides although occasionally drawing material from elsewhere. It is also weighted in favour of materials from the pre-Culloden era when Highland culture was still largely intact.

Through such a medium we too can travel, widely in space and time, even crossing a dimension of culture. As in any voyage we do not see every shore or visit every port; some horizons do not open, some views remain shrouded. But the literature of travel is the great interface between Highland culture and the rest of the world. In the absence or shortage of other material it is an indispensable window on knowledge.

Chapter 1

Perceptions of the Highlands

B efore we discuss the reality it is necessary to look at the perceptions.
Historical data is seldom raw and unprocessed. The pen is informed by
memory and belief as well as the eye. It is essential to look at the intellectual
and cultural background of the presenter in much the same way as we would
when watching a television programme today. There is the truth, and then
there is the truth as it is currently being presented.

Travellers' perspectives of the Highlands cannot be taken in isolation. All
travellers have preconceptions; they come burdened by the cultural baggage
of their countries of origin. They inherit bias, they learn prejudice. The
grounds may be physical, religious, cultural or linguistic. They may take a
national framework or they may be specific to a particular region or class of
people. Minds may be set by preconceived ideas or beliefs. I am not going to
give a detailed examination of changing historical perceptions of the Hebrides, nor even the cultural background of each visitor. Instead I am just going
to draw attention to the fact that the former have a history and each of the
latter a context. Here we just acknowledge these multiple frameworks; the
views of individuals will be examined in the chapters that follow.

Apart from the Romans and the Vikings few of the early travellers to the
Hebrides were from outside the British Isles. Pytheas the Greek, (actually
from the Greek colony of Massilia or Marseilles in Southern France) *may*
have visited the Hebrides c. 320 BC. Certainly the Roman fleet sailed round
Britain. But from the departure of the Romans (c. AD 400) to the arrival of
the Vikings (c. AD 800) most travellers to the Hebrides were native or Irish.
From these early times we have only the haziest details. The region was at
the periphery of the known world. Little was reported and the worst was
easily imagined. As far as classical accounts of the Hebrides are concerned I
am going to take shelter behind Buchanan, the great sixteenth-century
historian:

> *It now remains that I say something concerning the islands, that part of the
> British history which is involved in the greatest confusion. Setting aside,
> therefore, the more ancient writers, from whom it is impossible to extract any
> information, I shall follow the writers of our own time, upon whose accuracy
> and veracity more reliance may be placed . . .*
>
> *Those are called the Western isles which are spread over the Deucaledo-
> nian sea, on the west side of Scotland, from Ireland almost to the Orcades.*

The British historians, of the last and the present age, commonly style them the Hebrides, certainly a new name of whose origin no trace can be found among ancient writers. In that part of the ocean some place the Aebudae, or Aemodae; but they are at so much variance among themselves, that they scarcely ever agree in situation, number, or name. Strabo, to begin with the oldest, may perhaps be excused for having followed uncertain report, that part of the world not having then been sufficiently explored. Mela enumerates seven Hemodae, Martianus Capella as many Acmodae, Ptolemy and Solinus five Aebudae, and Pliny seven Acmodae, and thirty Aebudae. I shall retain the name most frequently used by the ancients, and designate the whole of the Western Islands Aebudae. Their site, relative condition, and produce, I shall describe from more recent and more certain authority; following chiefly Donald Monro, a pious and diligent man, who went over the whole of them himself, and minutely inspected them in person. (G. Buchanan, *Rerum Scoticarum Historia*, 1582, translated by J Aikman)

Thomas Pennant was more scrupulous and discussed ancient views of the Hebrides at length, before also concluding: '*From all that has been collected from the ancients, it appears, that they were acquainted with little more of the Hebrides than the bare names.*' (T. Pennant, *A Tour in Scotland and Voyage to the Hebrides*, 1772.)

During the Viking period the Hebrides were visited as never previously. They were convenient stopping points on the route between the Northern Isles and the Viking enclave in Dublin. During this period Hebridean society was itself in a state of complete flux. There had been so much Norse immigration that the islands were known as Innsegall, or the Strangers' Isles, and the people who lived there as the Gall-Gaidhil or Foreign-Gaels. To the Irish chroniclers these men had a reputation even more fearsome than the Vikings themselves. Unfortunately, apart from some scraps in the sagas and the Irish annals, there are few surviving records that tell us anything about the area or its inhabitants.

After 1266 the Hebrides returned to Scotland and from now on the most important visitors were Scottish. They were important because of their number, their proximity, and the fact that they represented the political and military authority of Lowland Scotland. Their common perspective requires us to look, in general terms, at the long and troubled relationship between the kingdom of Scotland and the Highlands and Islands.

The Highland Line

The Highland/Lowland divide was, in the past, regarded as the fundamental rift within Scotland. This has often been given a physical definition. The

'Highland Line' is drawn on maps to include an area that stretches from Kintyre in the south-west, skirting north of Glasgow to the region of Stonehaven on the East coast. From there it runs north, excluding a narrow strip of coastland, all the way to Caithness. Physically, the Highlands include at least half of Scotland.

This arbitrary physical division is, arguably, even less important than the perceived cultural or linguistic one:

> *The manners and customs of the Scots vary with the diversity of their speech. For two languages are spoken amongst them, the Scottish and the Teutonic; the latter of which is the language of those who occupy the seaboard and plains, while the race of Scottish speech inhabits the highlands and outlying islands. The people of the coast are of domestic and civilized habits, trusty, patient, and urbane, decent in their attire, affable, and peaceful, devout in Divine worship, yet always prone to resist a wrong at the hand of their enemies. The highlanders and people of the islands, on the other hand, are a savage and untamed nation, rude and independent, given to rapine, ease-loving, of a docile and warm disposition, comely in person, but unsightly in dress, hostile to the English people and language, and, owing to diversity of speech, even to their own nation, and exceedingly cruel.* (Skene, *John of Fordun's Chronicle of the Scottish Nation*, c. 1380)

> *The Lowlands are so-called by way of comparison, and as they relate to the Highlands I just spoke of. Not but that the mountains here are both numerous and lofty . . . Yet, considering its neighbourhood to the Northern Provinces, whose mountains are more contiguous and of greater number, it may (in some measure) justifie the distinction; though I should chuse rather to make the difference between 'em on the account of the language, garb, humour, and spirit of the people, than the strict etymology of the word or situation of the country.* (Thomas Morer in Hume Brown, *Early Travellers in Scotland*, 1689)

This conceptual boundary is more difficult to define and has itself a history. Unlike the physical boundary it has shifted over time. A map of the linguistic and place name evidence would show that Gaelic, brought by the Scots from Ireland in the fifth century, became established over most of what is now Scotland. The primary exceptions were the extreme south-east (Lothian), the extreme north-east (Caithness), and the Northern Isles. This linguistic dominance matched the political success of the Dalriadic Scots and the eclipse and decline of the native Picts and Britons. However whilst the Dalriadic Scots achieved political success in creating the kingdom of Scotland in the ninth century, their linguistic dominance was soon under attack from English spreading from the south and east of the country. This process has been going on ever since and has involved centuries of friction, competition and mistrust. To a degree language and culture were coterminous. Burt writes of the people of Inverness:

> *but the natives do not call themselves Highlanders, not so much on account of their low situation, as because they speak English.*
>
> *This rule whereby to denominate themselves, they borrow from the Kirk, which, in all its acts and ordinances distinguishes the Lowlands from the Highlands by the language generally spoken by the inhabitants, whether the parish or district lies in the high or low country . . .*
>
> *What I am saying must be understood only of the ordinary people; for the gentry, for the most part, speak our language [English] in the remotest parts of Scotland.* (Edmund Burt, *Letters from a Gentleman in the North of Scotland*, late 1720s)

and of the differences between Highlanders and Lowlanders:

> *In England the name of Scotsman is used indiscriminately to signify any one of the male part of the natives of North Britain; but the Highlanders differ from the people of the low country in almost every circumstance of life. Their language, customs, manners, dress, etc., are unlike, and neither of them would be contented to be taken for the other.* (Edmund Burt, *Letters from a Gentleman in the North of Scotland*, late 1720s)

> *Under the denomination of highlander are comprehended in Scotland all that now speak the Erse language, or retain the primitive manners, whether they live among the mountains or in the islands: and in that sense I use the name.* (Johnson, *A Journey to the Western Islands of Scotland*, 1773)

There is a proverbial Gaelic saying about the great hatred of the Lowlander for the Gael which sums up the Gaelic perception of this relationship. Certainly the antagonism and rivalry has often been bitter and acute. This book is not about that relationship and whether such perceptions are accurate or fair, but they should be borne in mind when reviewing the accounts of Scottish travellers to the Hebrides. The conflict between Highlander and Lowlander was cast in bitter terms by protagonists of both cultures. Here follows an anonymous poem from the Bannatyne Manuscript which gives the Lowland perspective. It dates to before 1568:

> *How the First Helandman of God was maid*
> *Of ane Horss Turd in Argylle, as is said*
>
> *God and Sanct Petir was gangand be the way*
> *Heiche vp in Ardgyle quhair thair gait lay,*
> *Sanct Petir said to God, in a sport word,*

'Can ye nocht mak a heilandman of this horss tourd?'
God turnd owre the horss turd with his pykit staff
And vp start a helandman blak as ony draff.
Qwod God to the helandman,
'Quhair wilt thow now?'
'I will doun in the lawland, Lord, and thair steill a kow.'
'And thow steill a cow, cairle, thair thay will hang the.'
'Quattrack Lord of that? For anis mon I die.'
God than he lewch and owre the dyk lap
And owt of his scheith his gowlly owtgatt.

Sanct Petir socht this gowly fast vp and doun,
yit cowld not find it in all that braid rownn.
'Now', quod God, 'heir a marvell. How can this be
That I sowld want my gowly, and we heir bot thre?'
'Humff,' quod the helandman and turnd him abowt
And at his plaid nuk the guly fell owt.
'Fy', quod Sanct Petir, 'thow will nevir do weill
And thow bot new maid sa sone gais to steill.'
'Vmff, quod the helandman, and swere be yon kirk,
'Sa lang as I may geir gett to steill will I nevir wirk.'
(Adapted from *Poetry of the Stewart Court*, Hughes and Ramson)

(How, it is said, God made the first Highlander – out of a horse turd in Argyll.

God and Saint Peter were going by the way
High up in Argyll, where their road lay,
Saint Peter said to God, in a joking manner,
'Can you not make a Highlander out of this horse turd?'
God turned over the horse turd with his pointed staff
And up sprang a Highlander as black as any dregs.
Said God to the Highlander
'Where are you going now?'
'I am going to the Lowlands, Lord, there to steal a cow.'
'And you steal a cow, man, there they will hang thee.'
'What matter, Lord, of that? I must die sometime.'
Then he laughed and leapt over the dyke
And from his sheath removed God's dirk.

Saint Peter sought this knife all up and down,
Yet could not find it in all that wide space.
'Now', said God, 'here is a marvel. How can this be
That I should miss my knife, and we here are only three?'
'Humff,' said the Highlander and turned him around.

And from his plaid fold the knife fell out.
'Hey', said Saint Peter, 'you will never do well
If you, just new made, so soon goes to steal.'
'Hmmph', said the Highlander, and swore by yon kirk,
'So long as I may get gear to steal I will never work.')

The poem nicely epitomises the cultural backdrop for the Lowland view. The Highlander was lazy and untrustworthy, shiftless and faithless, and by nature a thief. That this became part of Lowland lore is suggested by Burt's censure: '*But I cannot approve the Lowland saying, viz., "Show me a Highlander, and I will show you a thief" '*. (Edmund Burt, *Letters from a Gentleman in the North of Scotland,* late 1720s.)

There is plenty of evidence that the dislike was fully reciprocated. In 1543–44 John Elder argued that at least the Highlanders kept their word:

And howbeit the babalonicall busscheps and the great courtyours of Scotland repute the forsoide Yrishe Lordes as wilde, rude, and barbarous people, brought vp (as they say) without lerninge and nourtour, yeit they passe theame a greate deale in faithe, honestie, in policy and witt, in good ordour and ciuilitie; ffor wher the saide Yrische Lordes promises faithe they keipe it truely . . . Therfor, and pleas your Highnes, like as the saide bussheps and ther adherentis repute ws rude and barbarous people, euen so do we esteme theame all, (as they be,) that is to say, ffals, flatteringe, fraudelent subtile, and covetous. (Collectanea de Rebus Albanicis)

(And howbeit the Babylonical bishops and the great courtiers of Scotland repute the forsaid Irish [Gaelic] Lords as wild, rude, and barbarous people, brought up (as they say) without learning and nurture, yet they pass them a great deal in faith, honesty, in policy and wit, in good order and civility; for where the said Irish Lords promise faith they keep it truly . . . Therefore, and please your Highness, like as the said bishops and their adherents repute us rude and barbarous people, even so do we esteem them all, (as they be), that is to say, false, flattering, fraudulent, subtle, and covetous.)

In 1689 Thomas Morer gives a nice twist to the Highlanders' reason for theft:

Once or twice a year, great numbers of 'em get together and made a descent into the Lowlands, where they plunder the inhabitants, and so return back and disperse themselves. And this they are apt to do in the profoundest peace, it being not only natural to 'em to delight in rapine, but they do it on a kind of principle, and in conformity to the prejudice they continually have to the Lowlanders, whom they generally take for so many enemies.

We are dealing here in generalisations and it may be argued that these are irrelevant when looking at the contributions of individual travellers. It could be claimed that the truth will be revealed, not by examining some conceptual cultural interface, but through the myriads of unique physical and emotional contacts between visitors and their hosts. However not all travellers were equally open-minded and in the great river of historical literature it still makes sense to speak of prevailing currents and a direction of flow. Putting each account into its context helps us to understand, and make allowances for, each contributor's limitations. It also heightens our appreciation of the more generous-hearted and tolerant observers. Travellers like Taylor, the poet, stand out for their decency and objectivity.

This then was the common rumour about the Highlands. That they were distant, and difficult to access, was hard fact. That they were savage and barbarous was easy to imagine. The Highlands and Islands were culturally distinct and so presented a challenge to the culture of Lowland Scotland. This threat was always latent, as between all competing cultures, occasionally open and military. It is not until the work of Dean Monro and Martin Martin that we see the Highlands through Highland eyes. Most of the time our view of the Highlands is from a hostile Lowland perspective.

As an example of the strength of cultural division let us look briefly at the issue of intermarriage. Intermarriage is perhaps the most effective way in which the barriers between different cultures can be broken down. Where it does not succeed between the parties themselves then it often succeeds through their offspring.

Intermarriage

Intermarriage has long been a tool for healing family, dynastic, tribal and racial divisions. This is why it is such a powerful and emotive political issue. Those who oppose it want to preserve what they see as 'purity'; those who promote it often wish to unite more than the two individuals involved. In the light of the cultural schism between the Highland and Lowland worlds one or two quotations may help us gauge the importance of this issue in the past. First of all marriage has always been used as a political tool to unite feuding families – as instanced in this Papal dispensation:

30 May 1393
To the Bishop of Sodor. Faculty to dispense Hector Macgileeom, donzel, and Mor, daughter of Calen Cambel, damsel, of Sodor and Argyll dioceses, from the impediment to marriage arising from the third and fourth degrees of consanguinity. Notwithstanding their knowledge of this impediment, they have espoused themselves to be married, without subsequent consummation, in order to establish peace and harmony among their families and friends,

whereas until now there have only been wars, dissensions, murders and other
grave scandals. (Papal Letters to Scotland – Clement VII, Scottish History
Society)

or in 1447:

To the bishop of Argyll. Mandate, at the petition of John de Lorn, layman, and
Fingola de Insulis, of his diocese (containing that they are natives of the extreme
parts of the realm of Scotland and inhabit those parts, which are utterly wild
and whose inhabitants are commonly called 'black Scots'; that they, not in
ignorance that they were related in the second and third degrees of kindred and
the third and third degrees of affinity, committed fornication and had offspring;
and that they desire to marry, in order to assuage the grave strifes and discords
which have arisen in consequence between their parents, relatives by kindred
and affinity and their friends), after imposing penance for incest, to dispense
them to marry, decreeing the said offspring and that to be born of the marriage
legitimate. (Calendar of Papal Letters, vol X, pp 336–37)

Another letter illustrates a reluctance to marry across the Highland/Lowland
divide; in this particular case it was used as an excuse to overcome a problem
of consanguinity. The church had elaborate rules regarding marriage between
those within certain degrees of kindred and affinity. Difficulties could only be
overcome by papal dispensation.

February 1366
To the Bishop of Argyle. Mandate, if the facts be as stated, to dispense John
son of Colun Cambel, donsel, and Mariota daughter of John Cambel,
damsel, to intermarry, seeing that by reason of the diversity of dialects
between the highlands (in which the said John and Mariota dwell) and the
low lands of Scotland those inhabiting them rarely do so, and that by reason
of the continued war and pestilence in the said realm there is such a dearth of
nobles that it is hard for them to marry except within the prohibited degrees,
in which condition are the said John and Mariota, they being related in the
fourth degree of kindred. (Calendar of Entries in the Papal Registers, Papal
Letters, vol 4)

On the national and international stage intermarriage was a crucial diplomatic
tool to cement or broker alliances. In fact a marital union was suggested by
John Major as a way of implementing political union within Britain. After a
long commentary on the internal divisions between the Scots and English he
goes on to reflect:

Those wars are just which are waged in behalf of peace; and to God, the Ruler
of all, I pray, that He may grant such a peace to the Britons, that one of its

*kings in a union of marriage may by just title gain both kingdoms – for any
other way of reaching an assured peace I hardly see. I dare to say that
Englishman and Scot alike have small regard for their monarchs if they do
not continually aim at intermarriages, that so one kingdom of Britain may be
formed out of the two that now exist. Such a peaceful union finds continual
hindrance in each man of hostile temper, and in all men who are bent upon
their private advantage to the neglect of the common weal. Yet to this a
Scottish or an English sophist may make answer: 'Intermarriages there have
been many times, yet peace came not that way.' To whom I make answer,
that an unexceptionable title has never been in that way made good.* (J.
Major, 1521, in Hume Brown, *Scotland before 1700*)

John Elder, in his letter to Henry VIII in 1543–44, was also in favour:

*Consideringe also what ease and quiettnes, what wealth and ryches we
shulde haue in Scotland in few yeares, yf now after our said noble Kynges
decese, Prynce Edowarde, whom God preserue, your Maiesties naturall
sonne and heare of the noble empyr of England, shuld, as he shall by the
grace of God, marye our younge Queyne of Scotland. (Collectanea de Rebus
Albanicis)*

(Considering also what ease and quietness, what wealth and riches we
should have in Scotland in few years, if now after our said noble King's
decease, Prince Edward, whom God preserve, your Majesty's natural
son and heir of the noble empire of England, should, as he shall by the
grace of God, marry our young Queen of Scotland.)

But, as Major himself acknowledged, there were always those who preferred
distinction and division. At the very end of the sixteenth century we find the
following proposal amongst the documents concerning the Fife Adventurers:

Articlis to be contracted amongst the Societie of the Lewis.
(Number 10 reads)
*Na mariage or uther particular freindschip to be be any of the Societie,
without consent of the haill, with any Hyland man.*
(Register of the Privy Council XIV, pp cxxix–cxxx)

(Articles to be contracted amongst the Society of the Lewis.
No marriage or other particular friendship to be by any of the Society,
without consent of the whole, with any Highland man).

Burt comments on the lack of intermarriage between Highlanders and
Lowlanders:

The marriages of the chiefs and chieftains are, for the most part, confined to the circuit of the Highlands; and they generally endeavour to strengthen their clan by what they call powerful alliances. As to the lower class of gentry and the ordinary people, they generally marry in the clan whereto they appertain.

All this may be political enough, i.e. the chief to have regard to the Highlands in general, and his followers to their own particular tribe or family, in order to preserve themselves a distinct people; but this continues them in a narrow way of thinking with respect to the rest of mankind and also prevents that addition to the circumstances of the whole, or part of the Highlands, which might be made by marriages of women of fortune in the Lowlands. This, in time, might have a good effect, by producing a union, instead of that coldness, to say no more, which subsists, at present, between the natives of those two parts of Scotland, as if they bore no relation one to another, considered as men and subjects of the same kingdom, and even the same part of it.

But to return to the marriages of the Highlanders there are many of the Lowland women who seem to have a great liking to the Highland men, which they cannot forbear to insinuate in their ordinary conversation. But such marriages are very rare; and I know but one instance of them, which, I must confess, will not much recommend the union of which I have been speaking. (Edmund Burt, *Letters from a Gentleman in the North of Scotland*, late 1720s)

In Kintyre, which was subject to immigration from Ayrshire in the early seventeenth century, there was long a tradition of separation between the Highland and Lowland communities. The Lowlanders had a separate church and married amongst themselves – although no doubt language played a part in such decisions. These distinctions took many years to erode. At the end of the eighteenth century Pennant wrote of the Lowland families in Kintyre: *'These still keep themselves distinct from the old inhabitants, retain the zeal of their ancestors . . . but are esteemed the most industrious people in the country.'* (T. Pennant, *A Tour in Scotland and Voyage to the Hebrides*, 1772.)

Such facts only reinforce Thomas Morer's perception that the divide between the Highland and Lowland worlds was cultural rather than physical.

Intermarriage is where separate cultures collide and unite. The business of physical union is a microcosm of all the other possible unions, political, religious, economic, linguistic and cultural. Marriage is only one of many different interfaces, but a crucially important one. But as these unions have their proponents so they face opposition. Some would prefer division. Even a society that thinks itself tolerant and civilised faces a basic logical problem here. How do you protect diversity, which many of us would argue is a good thing, without maintaining division?

Although we are looking at this issue in the context of the Highland/Lowland divide it is universal and timeless, perhaps never more relevant than now. It is not long since apartheid or 'separate development' was the order of the day in South Africa, not much further back to the Nazis and their Aryan supermen. Technical progress with genetics, the science of eugenics, the possibility of tinkering with the genes of animals and humans, have all given new slants on old problems. Phrases like 'ethnic cleansing' and 'genetically modified' have passed into general usage.

These are just new variations on an old debate. Early historians of Scotland were as much concerned with declining standards as we are with exam results. They looked back, as we do, to a golden age where yet earlier Scots personified the virtues. They had agendas too, agendas which may seem simpler but which contain, in nascent form, elements which recur now. Their language provides certain clues. In any debate today the use of certain words like 'purity' and 'miscegenation' would immediately set alarm bells ringing in the minds of the hearer. These are emotive codes that have often been used as a clarion call for some form of supremacist movement. For earlier Scots historians the terms 'degeneracy' and 'effeminacy' performed a similar function although the context was then more mainstream. We shall look at such agendas in the next chapter.

Reputation

Travellers' accounts are also important for establishing the changing 'reputation' of the Gael to the outside world. This was only partly decided by the actions of Gaels themselves. The 'truth', then as now, was as it was reported. Travellers' tales fed back into the consciousness of the outside world, particularly that of Lowland Scotland. In turn this 'reputation' informed all future travellers and their accounts. It set their fears and expectations. It also meant that the first contact that most English or Continental visitors had with the Highland world was actually the Lowland view of it. There was an international understanding that there were two kinds of Scots. The Highlanders were 'wild' Scots, Gaelic-speaking and savage, in contrast to the more civilised, English-speaking, 'domestic' Scots. This Lowland filter was hardly a favourable introduction to the world of Gaeldom.

> *The wild Scots live in the manner of the Scythians, they are ignorant of the use of bread; when they are hungry they outstrip a stag in swiftness of foot, overtake it and kill it, and so sustain life: they eat the flesh raw, only squeezing out the blood.* (Peter Swave, 1535, in Hume Brown, *Early Travellers in Scotland*)

Now whilst we can understand how these myths arose they are, actually, pure hokum. Highlanders ate oats and barley just like everyone else in Scotland – in fact over the centuries they proved strikingly devoted to grain crops, however poor the return. It was only when the use of potatoes became widespread during the eighteenth century that they became less single-minded. The differences were just in their preference for oats and the way they prepared their meal.

Although some men in places like the Kalahari can actually outrun their prey (by virtue of stamina rather than swiftness), I doubt this often succeeded against a red deer, trapping being the preferred method. Certainly Highlanders at a pinch would have eaten meat raw – who wouldn't if they were starving – but there is plenty of evidence, both archaeological and documentary that they seethed the deer instead.

The peoples of outlying regions such as Scotland and Ireland were often endowed with characteristics of unspeakable savagery. Certainly some of the practices of a remote and marginal economy will appear cruel to a richer society that regards itself as more civilised. There is however an element of tabloid journalism involved here. A screaming headline would sell a book as well in mediaeval times as now and there has always been a taste for the ghoulish and macabre. Some of Gerald of Wales' material in his twelfth-century *History and Topography of Ireland* give the impression of a Victorian freak show. When dealing with such 'history' we must filter out the ferocity of the language and a deal of invention.

Bishop Leslie, who had acquaintance with Highlanders, explains how they used to cook oxen when on campaign and lacking their ordinary utensils:

> *For cheiflie in tyme of weir quhen to the feildes to karie pottis, panis, and vthir kitchine veshels, thay thot hauie and molestful, in place of potis and sik seithing vessielis, the painches of ane ox or ane kow thay vset cheiflie. Gif necessitie vrge, this day thay take the hail meklewame of ane slain ox, thay turne and dicht it, thay fill it partlie with watir partlie with flesche, they hing it in the cruik or a sting, eftir the maner of a pott, and sa thay kuik it verie commodiouslie vpon the fyre.* (Dalrymple's translation in E. Cody (ed.), *Leslie's History of Scotland*, 1578)

> (For chiefly in time of war when to the fields to carry pots, pans, and other kitchen vessels, they thought heavy and molestful, in place of pots and such seething vessels, the paunches [stomachs] of an ox or a cow they used chiefly. If necessity urge, [to] this day they take the whole greatwomb [greater stomach] of a slain ox, they turn and clean it, they fill it partly with water partly with flesh, they hang it in the crook or a sting [forked pole], after the manner of a pot, and so they cook it very commodiously upon the fire).

Franck offers a rather more charged version of the same practice in his *Northern Memoirs* (1656/7): '*So from thence we travel into Cathness, and the country of Stranavar; where a rude sort of inhabitants dwell, (almost as barbarous*

as Canibals) who when they kill a beast, boil him in his hide, make a caldron of his
skin, browis [broth] *of his bowels, drink of his blood, and bread and meat of his*
carcase.'

It is easy to see how such an account might be exaggerated and emboidered.
Thomas Kirk was not above a little improvement in pursuit of literary frisson:

> *Their cruelty descends to their beasts, it being a custom in some places to feast*
> *upon a living cow, they tye in the middle of them, near a great fire, and then*
> *cut collops of this poor living beast, and broil them on the fire, till they have*
> *mangled her all to pieces; nay, sometimes they will only cut off as much as*
> *will satisfie their present appetites, and let her go till their greedy stomachs*
> *call for a new supply; such horrible cruelty as can scarce be parrallel'd in the*
> *whole world.* (Thomas Kirk (1679) in Hume Brown, *Early Travellers in*
> *Scotland*)

The reality was much more mundane. An officer in Cumberland's army
commented: '*When they Bleed their Cattle, which is generally twice a Year, they,*
with great Care, preserve the Blood, which they mix with Oatmeal to eat, and is
esteemed by them a most nourishing Dish.' (*A journey through Part of England*
and Scotland, 1746.)

In 1769 Pennant writes of the occupants of a shieling by Glen Tilt: *Their*
food oatcakes, butter or cheese, and often the coagulated blood of their cattle spread
on their bannocks.' (T. Pennant, *A Tour in Scotland* 1769.)

And three years later of the parish of Gairloch: '*The cattle are blooded at*
spring and fall: the blood is preserved to be eaten cold.' (T. Pennant, *A Tour in*
Scotland and Voyage to the Hebrides, 1772.)

At the end of September 1784, Monsieur Faujas de Saint Fond, a French
geologist, was staying with the Macleans of Torloisk in Mull. He paid a great
deal of attention to food and table-customs: '*At four o'clock, they sit down to*
dinner. Here is the menu of the meal which I noted exactly in my journal . . .
2. Black pudding made with bullock's blood and barley flour, seasoned with
plenty of pepper and ginger . . . (Faujas de Saint Fond, *A journey through*
England and Scotland to the Hebrides in 1784.)

Today we may not prepare black pudding in quite the same way but we still
eat it. Old habits died hard in some of the remoter islands which probably
helped fuel a reputation for savagery:

> *I have been assured, that in some of the islands the meaner sort of people still*
> *retain the custom of boiling their beef in the hide; or otherwise (being destitute*
> *of vessels of metal or earth) they put water into a block of wood, made hollow*
> *by the help of the dirk and burning; and then with pretty large stones heated*
> *red-hot, and successively quenched in that vessel, they keep the water boiling*
> *till they have dressed their food.* (Edmund Burt, *Letters from a Gentleman*
> *in the North of Scotland*, late 1720s)

There is a passage of J.L. Buchanan's which implies that boiling meat in the hide was not unknown at the end of the eighteenth century: '*Nay, I spoke with a man who saw the thief boiling a bag full of meat with a gentle fire held below, while he constantly rubbed the bottom with grease, fastened to a stick, to keep it from burning.*' (Buchanan, *Travels in the Western Hebrides from 1782 to 1790.*)

Burt had never been to the Western Isles but he was sensible enough to see how rumour exaggerated:

> *For I confess I never was in any one of them, though I have seen several of them from the mainland . . . But these islands are so remote and unfrequented, they are a very proper subject for invention; and few, I think, would have the curiosity to visit them, in order to disprove any account of them, however romantic.* (Edmund Burt, *Letters from a Gentleman in the North of Scotland,* late 1720s.)

For others, though, ignorance was the mother of invention – as Jorevin de Rocheford demonstrates in 1661. He writes of Scotland:

> *It is bordered on the west by the Ebudes* [Hebrides] *Islands, and divers other small islets, which are at the entrance of an almost infinite number of great gulfs advanced into the kingdom, which they furnish with fish, in abundance. But the country is so mountainous and so ingrateful in some places, that it is not worth cultivation; and the cold so intense as scarcely to permit grain to ripen . . . I know very well that the northern part of this kingdom, beyond the river Tay, is almost uninhabited, on account of the high mountains, which are only rocks, where there is no want of game in great quantities; but there grows but very little corn . . . It is said, that there are certain provinces on that side of the country, where the men are truly savage, and have neither law nor religion, and support a miserable existence by what they can catch.* (Jorevin de Rocheford, in Hume Brown, *Early Travellers in Scotland*)

This Continental view of the Highlands in the seventeenth century is the literary equivalent of early mediaeval maps of the area. Jorevin de Rocheford knew little more about the Highlands and Hebrides in 1661 than Matthew Paris in the 1240s. If he had, he would have known that the problem for farmers on the west coast was not the cold but the wet, that they had laws and religion, just not those favoured by Lowland Scotland, and that within a century they were going to suffer from overpopulation. He was only right about their poverty.

More threatening though, was the Highlanders' reputation for violence. Without going into the long military tradition of Highlanders we can recognise that this, in itself, was a factor any traveller had to take into account. Document after document demonstrate how heavily armed the Highlanders were, their affection for their chief, their vicious clan wars, and their hardiness in battle. Such attributes by no means equate with violence towards strangers because the Highlands have an equally long tradition of hospitality; but we can understand how such an equation might form in the mind of the visitor! Add a little scaremongering or poetic licence and the damage was done.

> *The nobility and gentry Lord it over their poor tenants, and use them worse than gally-slaves; they are all bound to serve them, men, women, and children; the first fruits is always the landlord's due. Those of his own name that are inferior to him, must all attend him (as he himself must do his superior, of the same name, and all of them attend the chief) if he receives a stranger, all this train must be at his beck armed as aforesaid; if you drink with them in a tavern, you must have all this rubbish with you; and if you offend the laird, his durk shall be soon sheathed in your belly, and, after this, every one of his followers, or they shall suffer themselves that refuse it, that so they may be all alike guilty of the murder . . .*
>
> *What strange butcheries have been committed in their feuds, some of which are in agitation at this day, viz, Argill with the Macclenes, and Macdonnels about Mula [Mull] Island, which has cost already much blood, and is likely will cost much more before it will be decided; their spirits are so mean, that they rarely rob, but take away life first; lying in ambuscade, they send a brace of bullets on embassy through the travellers body, and to make sure work, they sheath their durks in his lifeless trunk, perhaps to take off their fine edges, as new knives are stuck in a bag pudding.* (Thomas Kirk – 1679, in Hume Brown, *Early Travellers in Scotland*.)

Now this highly coloured scene was painted by someone who was bilious towards Scots in general and Highlanders in particular. However there were other visitors who gave a more charitable view. John Taylor, the poet, visited Scotland in 1618. He was moved to verse in the epilogue to his book of travels:

> *I vow to God I have done Scotland wrong,*
> *(And (justly) 'gainst me it may bring an Action)*
> *I have not given't that right which doth belong,*
> *For which I am halfe guilty of detraction:*
> *Yet had I wrote all things that there I saw,*
> *Misjudging censures would suppose I flatter,*
> *And so my name I should in question draw,*
> *Where Asses bray, and pratling Pies doe chatter:*
> *Yet (arm'd with truth) I publish with my Pen,*
> *That there th'Almighty doth his blessings heape,*
> *In such aboundant food for Beasts and Men;*
> *That I ne're saw more plenty or more cheape.*
> (John Taylor, *The Pennyles Pilgrimage*, 1618)

After the Union of Crowns, contacts between the different parts of the United Kingdom became more frequent. The Commonwealth period must have acquainted a lot of English soldiers with the Highlands. As we shall see later, both Captains Franck and Burt wrote sympathetically of the area. However, Martin Martin was well aware that the Highlands had a problem with image:

> *I am not ignorant that foreigners, sailing through the Western Isles, have been tempted from the sight of so many wild hills that seem to be covered all over with heath, and faced with high rocks, to imagine that the inhabitants, as well as the places of their residence, are barbarous; and to this opinion, their habit, as well as their language, have contributed. The like is supposed by many that live in the south of Scotland, who know no more of the Western Isles than the natives of Italy, but the lion is not so fierce as he is painted, neither are the people described here so barbarous as the world imagines . . . The inhabitants have humanity, and use strangers hospitably and charitably. I could bring several instances of barbarity and theft committed by stranger seamen in the isles, but there is not one instance of any injury offered by the islanders to any seamen or strangers.* (Martin Martin, *A description of the Western Islands of Scotland*, c. 1695)

We can find some support for this statement in the treatment meted out to the crew of a boat from Lubeck which was shipwrecked off the Isles. In the Register of the Privy Council we read of a Letter of Council dated 28 November 1627 which says:

> *Whairas ane shippe of Lubecque callit Sanct Laurence, laidnit with salt, being laitlie upoun her dew course frome Spaine toward the toun of Lubecque, she wes by contrarious winds drivin upoun the northwest iles of this kingdome whair she wes brokin and her whole laidning exposied to the injurie of the sea, the equippage of the shippe by the providence of God being preserved, and by favour of the commander of the iland whair thay susteaned shipwracke thay wer sent heere to the burgh of Edinburgh. And whairas now they ar to make thair addresse home as they may best find the commoditie of passage, these ar thairfoir to will yow and every ane of yow whome these presents doe concerne to assist thir poore strangers* [whose names then follow].

As we shall see in later chapters such civilities were not extended to Scots fishermen in the same area at the same time – but then the latter were competitors rather than objects of charity. Nevertheless the Highlanders *appeared* fierce. David Bruce reports the reputation of Barra about 1750:

> *About two Leagues to the South of South Uist lyes Barra, an Island about 5 Miles long and three Broad, it belongs to a Family of the McNeils. This being the Southmost of that long Row of Islands which lye in a very Open and*

Boisterous Sea, Ships and other Vessels have been often thrown by Tempests upon it whose Crews the Inhabitants are said to have Murdered that they might secure the Goods and Wrecks to themselves; (Lang, *The Highlands of Scotland in 1750*)

But this is contradicted by Walker's view of Coll. He is talking of the scarcity of wood on the island: '*They have little, but what they obtain from Shipwrecks, and with this indeed, they are but too well supplied. The unfortunate Sufferers are sure of being treated with the greatest Honour and Humanity by the Inhabitants, but when the thing happens, the timber of the ship becomes a very convenient Windfall.*' (McKay, *Walker's Report on the Hebrides*, 1764 and 1771.)

Johnson was later to praise Highland civility and hospitality but he seems to have entertained some doubts before his visit. Boswell records that:

'*From an erroneous apprehension of violence, Dr Johnson had provided a pair of pistols, some gun-powder, and a quantity of bullets: but upon being assured we should run no risk of meeting any robbers, he left his arms and ammunition in an open drawer, of which he gave my wife the charge.*' (Boswell, *The Journal of a Tour to the Hebrides*, 1773.)

However he was still a little nervous. On the way to Glenshiel the party stopped to refresh their horses. Johnson sat down on the grass and conceived the idea of his book. His musings encapture the anxiety of any traveller about to enter a new and remote region without any of the known and accustomed securities of his homeland.

We were in this place at ease and by choice, and had no evils to suffer or to fear; yet the imaginations excited by the view of an unknown and untravelled wilderness are not such as arise in the artificial solitude of parks and gardens, a flattering notion of self-sufficiency, a placid indulgence of voluntary delusions, a secure expansion of the fancy, or a cool concentration of the mental powers. The phantoms which haunt a desert are want, and misery, and danger: the evils of dereliction rush upon the thoughts; man is made unwillingly acquainted with his own weakness, and meditation shews him only how little he can sustain, and how little he can perform. There were no traces of inhabitants, except perhaps a rude pile of clods called a summer hut, in which a herdsman had rested in the favourable seasons. Whoever had been in the place where I then sat, unprovided with provisions and ignorant of the country, might, at least before the roads were made, have wandered among the rocks, till he had perished with hardship, before he could have found either food or shelter. (Johnson, *A Journey to the Western Islands of Scotland*, 1773.)

Highlanders had their own take on the question of barbarism. Johnson commented favourably on how well they spoke English. He goes on:

*By their Lowland neighbours they would not willingly be taught; for they
have long considered them as a mean and degenerate race. These prejudices
are wearing fast away; but so much of them still remains, that when I asked a
very learned minister in the islands, which they considered as their most
savage clans: 'Those,' said he, 'that live next the Lowlands.'* (Johnson, *A
Journey to the Western Islands of Scotland*, 1773)

On this basis the good minister would not have been surprised to read the
following from the apparently civilised and accessible island of Islay in 1798:

*This Meeting, with every feeling of humanity for the distressed Sufferers, who
have the misfortune to be shipwrecked on the coast of this Island, have to
regret that numbers of the Country people, shaking off all fear of God, or
regard to the laws, are in the constant practice against every rule of Christian
charity, or hospitality, of resorting in numbers to the shores, where strangers
have the Misfortune of being shipwrecked, and that for the sole purpose of
plunder; which practice this Meeting hold in the greatest abhorrence, and now
declare their disapprobation of; and in order, as much as possible, to remedy
the evil, this Meeting not only collectively, but individually, pledge themselves to use their utmost exertions, not only for the preservation of the
property of the individuals, who may have the Misfortune to be wrecked on
these coasts, but also for bringing to condign punishment all and every such
persons as may be found plundering from wrecks: And in order this resolution
of the Gentlemen of Islay may be made as public as possible, the Clerk is
hereby required to send an Extract of this Minute to the Ministers of the
different parishes of the Island, to be affixed on the Church doors, that none
may pretend ignorance, and it is hoped that the Ministers, for the sake of good
order, will explain these resolutions to their parishioners from the pulpit.*
(Ramsay, *The Stent Book and Acts of the Balliary of Islay, 1718–1843*)

It is difficult to form objective judgements when we only have opinions from
the two opposite poles of Lowlander and Gael. All the more valuable therefore
is the evidence of Edward Lhuyd, the great antiquarian, who travelled to the
Highlands in 1699. Lhuyd was a Welshman who was alive to English
antipathy towards his own country and language and not at all unsympathetic
to the distinctive language and culture of the Highlands. Moreover he had a
position of some status and independence as Keeper of the Ashmolean
Museum in Oxford. Lhuyd's journey and findings have been examined
by J.L. Campbell and D. Thomson in *Edward Lhuyd in the Scottish Highlands*.
Before he visited Scotland, Lhuyd had heard disquieting reports of the
Highlands. He wrote in 1697:

*I must beg your further trouble of enquiring of Dr Grey or Dr Wallace
whether they have heard of any Gentleman or Clergyman amongst ye*

Highlands anything studious of their own Language and the Antiquities of their countrey; as also whether we may travail there with safety, provided we can be well recommended. As for course fare and hard lodging we are proof, being but an other sort of Highlanders our selves: but if it be the manner of the Countrey (as some tel me) to knock men in ye head even for a threadbare suit of cloaths, I shall easily bridle my Curiosity. (R.T. Gunther, *Life and Letters of Edward Lhwyd,* 1945)

In the event he had no need to curb his curiosity for in December 1699 he wrote:

In this kingdom our travels in the High-lands were through Cantire [Kintyre], *Argyle, and Lorn, besides the Isles of Mac y Chormic* [Eilean Mor], *Mul, and y Columb Kil* [Iona] . . . *In the High-lands we found the people every where civil enough; and had doubtless sped better as to our enquiries, had we the language more perfect.* (Campbell & Thomson, *Edward Lhuyd in the Scottish Highlands,* pp xvi–xvii)

In January 1700 he reaffirmed this:

we found a great deal of Civility and kindness as well in the highlands as the Lowlands And tho, the highlanders be represented both in England & Ireland Barbarous and Inhospitable we found (th)em quite otherwise, the Gentlemen, men of good sense and breeding and the Com(m)ons a subtil inquisitive people and more civil to Strangers in directing them the way (the mean occasion we had of their kindness) than in most other Counties, The main cause of their being reputed Barbarous I take to be no other than the Roughness of their Countrey as Consisting very much of barren mountains and Loughs and their retaining their antient habits Custom and Language on which very account many Gent(lemen) of good sense in England Esteem the . . . Welsh at this day barbarous & talk so much of wild Irish in this Kingdom (Campbell & Thomson, *Edward Lhuyd in the Scottish Highlands,* p 6)

In March of the same year Lhuyd wrote that he had been:

amongst the Hebrides, and other highlands of Scotland with whom their neighbours seem to have less commerce than they have with either of the Indies. They are nothing so barbarous as the Lowlanders and English commonly represent them; but are for what I could find a very hospitable and civil people: and the main reasons of the contrary character I take to be their adhering too much to their antient customs, habit and language; whereby they distinguish themselves from all their neighbours; and distinctions always create mutual reflections. (Campbell & Thomson, *Edward Lhuyd in the Scottish Highlands,* p xx)

Burt said much the same:

> *The Highlands are but little known even to the inhabitants of the low country of Scotland, for they have ever dreaded the difficulties and dangers of travelling among the mountains; and when some extraordinary occasion has obliged any one of them to such a progress, he has, generally speaking, made his testament before he set out, as though he were entering upon a long and dangerous sea voyage, wherein it was very doubtful if he should ever return. But to the people of England, excepting some few, and those chiefly the soldiery, the Highlands are hardly known at all: for there has been less, that I know of, written upon the subject, than of either of the Indies; and even that little which has been said, conveys no idea of what a traveller almost continually sees and meets with in passing among the mountains; nor does it communicate any notion of the temper of the natives, while they remain in their own country.* (Edmund Burt, *Letters from a Gentleman in the North of Scotland*, late 1720s)

as did Samuel Johnson:

> *to the southern inhabitants of Scotland, the state of the mountains and the islands is equally unknown with that of Borneo or Sumatra . . . They are strangers to the language and the manners, to the advantages and wants of the people, whose life they would remodel, and whose evils they would remedy.* (In Campbell & Thomson, *Edward Lhuyd in the Scottish Highlands*, p xxi)

Lhuyd did not venture north of Argyll which was controlled by the pro-government Clan Campbell. Whether he would have said the same of Inverness-shire is uncertain. They had very differing reputations:

> *we must steer our course by the North Pole, and relinquish those flourishing fields of Kintire and Innerary; the pleasant bounds of Marquess Argile, which very few English-men have made discovery of, to inform us of the glory of the Western Highlands, enrich'd with grain, and the plenty of herbage. But how the Highlander will vindicate Bowhider and Lohabbar, with Reven* [Ruthven] *in Badanoch, that I know not; for there they live like lairds, and die like loons, hating to work, and no credit to borrow, they make depredations, so rob their neighbours.* (R. Franck, *Northern Memoirs*, 1656/7)

While Kirk says of Loch Ness:

> *A little further we came to the Lough: it is about two miles broad and twenty-five miles long. It is remarkable that this Lough . . . never freezes; and if a horse's fetlocks be hung with icicles, this water thaws them*

immediately. About the further end of this Lough are great fir-woods, but they are so full of rogues that we durst not see them: none dare pass the Highlands without a guard of ten or twelve, at the least. (T. Kirk, *Tours in Scotland 1677*)

By the eighteenth century many parts of Scotland were becoming more settled. The bloody family vendettas and internecine feuds of earlier times seemed to be fading into memory. Unfortunately, some Highlanders retained a notorious reputation as cattle-rustlers. There is a manuscript report in the British Library (published by Lang as *The Highlands of Scotland in 1750*) which surveys the Highland clans from a military and political perspective. It was probably written by David Bruce who acted as a government agent after Culloden. The section concerning Knoydart would intimidate most travellers:

In all the Countries I have yet travel'd through the People Live by their own Labour and Industry and are no more given to Theft than the Lowland Countries, but as I proceeded on the Coast Southward I came to Knoidart which is a perfect Den of Thieves and Robbers. Glengarry is Proprietor of this Country and it is inhabited by his Clan who are all Papists. The Inhabitants of this Country have been ever Wild Rapacious and a plague and Disturbance to their Neighbours, but they have within these few years exceeded their ordinary Bounds which was Occasioned thus: Coll McDonald of Barisdale, Cousin Germane to Glengarry, took up his Residence here as a place of undoubted Security from all Legal Prosecutions, he entered into a Confederacy with McDonald of Lochgarry and the Camerons of Loch Arkeg with some other as great Villains in Rannoch, a part of Perthshire. This famous Company had the Honour to Methodize Theft into a Regular Trade, they kept a number of Savages in Dependance upon them for this purpose whom they Out-hounded upon the Sutherlands, Rosses, Munroes, and McKenzies to the North, the Frasers, McIntoshes, Grants, Roses of Kilra-vock, Brodies, Gordons, Farquharsons, Forbeses, and Ogilvies to the East; and the Shires of Perth, Stirling, Dunbarton, and Argyle to the South. When the Thieves were Successful these Gentlemen had a Dividend of the Spoil of their own making; but if they returned Empty handed the fellows were at no Loss, as they forced their Provisions wherever they travelled, and every one who laid in their way thought himself very fortunate if they Required no more, for which reason they seldom failed to be plentifully Supplied with the best the Country afforded, and if at any time it happened that one of them met his Deserts at the Gallows by the Vigilance of the Neighbouring Clans, which very rarely happened, the whole Tribe to which the Thief belong'd never fail'd to Embrace the first Opportunity of having (as they term it) Blood for Blood.

and of Glengarry:

> *It is observed of Thieves in other parts of the Country, especially the Camerons, that they are very Hospitable and Civil to Strangers, but the People of Glengarry are of quite a Different Disposition, Churlish and Inhospitable to the last Degree, and never admit a Stranger within their Doors. In short they are the very Dregs and Refuse of Mankind and it is no small Reproach to Great Britain to have allowed such a Sett of Villains to trample upon the Laws for so many Ages. They have ever been the Plague of their Neighbours, except for about Eight Years which proceeded from a Pannick they had Received from Oliver Cromwell, during which time they remained perfectly Honest. And since Parties of His Majesty's Forces have been stationed here and in other Corners remarkable for Theft, by the Care and Prudence of General Bland, the Country has enjoy'd more Quiet than it has done for 40 years before.*

There can be little doubt that the military presence, heavy and unwelcome though it was, helped to consolidate the new political settlement:

> *The People of these Wild Countries could never believe that they were Accessible 'till the King's Forces Scoured them after the Battle of Culloden which was a prodigious Surprize to the Inhabitants. The Common people, tho' Papists, Curse their Prince and Chiefs together, as they are sensible that all their Calamities are owing to them.* (David Bruce in Lang, *The Highlands of Scotland in 1750*)

This scouring also worked by sea where the ships of the navy brought reprisal parties to scattered islands in a manner not seen since Viking times. In 1750, David Bruce regarded the islanders as more civilised than those on the mainland west coast. He was not alone. The Rev. Donald MacQueen, who spent much time with Johnson and Boswell, wrote an appendix for Pennant in 1774. He too regarded islanders as more civilised than those on the opposite mainland, partly because they saw more visitors. When discussing cattle-theft he wrote:

> *This transaction happened on the mainland, where dark woods, extensive wastes, high-forked mountains, and a coast indented with long winding branches of the sea, favoured the trade. These were strongholds, little frequented by strangers, where the ancient practices and prejudices might be preserved to the last periods of time, without some such violent shock as that of the year 1745. The islanders yielded much earlier to the arts of peace and civility.* (Rev. Donald MacQueen, 1774, Appendix to Pennant)

Pennant visited western Inverness-shire in 1772 and commented on the enormous social changes wrought by and since Culloden.

> *There is not an instance of any country having made so sudden a change in its morals as . . . the vast tract intervening between these coasts and Loch Ness. Security and civilization possess every part; yet thirty years have not elapsed since the whole was a den of thieves, of the most extraordinary kind. They conducted their plundering excursions with the utmost policy, and reduced the whole art of theft into a regular system. From habit it lost all the appearance of criminality: they considered it as labouring in their vocation; and when a party was formed for an expedition against their neighbour's property, they and their friends prayed as earnestly to heaven for success, as if they were engaged in the most laudable design.*
>
> *The constant petition at grace of the old highland chieftains, was delivered with great fervor, in these terms: 'Lord! Turn the world upside down, that christians may make bread out of it'. The plain English of this pious request was, That the world might become, for their benefit, a scene of rapine and confusion.* (T. Pennant, *A Tour in Scotland and Voyage to the Hebrides*, 1772)

Its most notorious practitioner was:

> *the celebrated Barrisdale, who carried these arts* [of stealing] *to the highest pitch of perfection: besides exerting all the common practices, he improved that article of commerce called the black-meal to a degree beyond what was ever known to his predecessors. This was a forced levy, so called from its being commonly paid in meal, which was raised far and wide on the estate of every nobleman and gentleman, in order that their cattle might be secured from the lesser thieves, over whom he secretly presided, and protected. He raised an income of five hundred a year by these taxes: and behaved with genuine honor in restoring, on proper consideration, the stolen cattle of his friends . . .* [Whilst] *observing a strict fidelity towards his own gang; yet he was indefatigable in bringing to justice any rogues that interfered with his own.* (T. Pennant, *A Tour in Scotland and Voyage to the Hebrides*, 1772)

The loyalty which the clans of the north-west showed to the Jacobite cause did nothing to endear them to Lowland Britain. Four armed uprisings in less than sixty years were bound to heighten fears and exaggerate dangers. Their 'disaffection' from the church and the established order, coupled with their perennial practice of cattle-theft left ample scope for prejudice. Visiting the Highlands during these troubled times was not for the faint-hearted. As David Bruce said in 1747, they were 'not certain when we lay down but our throatts might be cutt before morning'.

With hindsight Culloden was the watershed. Military defeat was followed by reprisal, subjugation and the removal of judicial power from the Highland chiefs. Economic changes over the coming century were to remove more of their influence over the lives of their clansmen. By about the 1770s the situation had been transformed. For more than two centuries since the Highlands and Hebrides have been cast as victims.

Though much maligned for some of his severer castigations of things Highland this process can be traced back at least as far as Samuel Johnson's tour in 1773. Both he and Thomas Pennant, who visited in 1772, comment repeatedly on the civility and hospitality of the Highlanders. Johnson himself seems to have been scrupulous over manners. Boswell writes: '*After dinner, as the ladies were going away, Dr Johnson would stand up. He insisted that politeness was of great consequence in society.*' (Boswell, *The Journal of a Tour to the Hebrides*, 1773.)

Such a man would appreciate the strength and integrity of Gaelic society. He would understand its elaborate structure, its mannered courtesies. Pennant did not perhaps have Johnson's perceptiveness but gives us plenty of examples of kindness and consideration. On his first tour he writes of the courtesy and self-confidence of Highlanders: '*hospitable to the highest degree, and full of generosity: are much affected with the civility of strangers, and have in themselves a natural politeness and address, which often flows from the meanest when le(a)st expected . . . I fear they pity us; but I hope not indiscriminately.*' (T. Pennant, *A Tour in Scotland*, 1769.)

On his second he tells of Skye: '*Take leave of several gentlemen, who, according to the worthy custom of these islands, conveyed us from place to place, and never left us till they had delivered us over to the next hospitable roof, or seen us safely embarked.*' (T. Pennant, *A Tour in Scotland and Voyage to the Hebrides*, 1772.)

With such compliments in print, visitors would not be restrained by the old fears and anxieties. Since then tourism has gone from strength to strength. The military hardiness of the Highlanders, begrudgingly admired from mediaeval times, was another key to the reintegration of the Highlander into the British body politic. Their performance in the British army from the late eighteenth century led quickly from pride to political rehabilitation. The whole sorry saga of clearance and emigration have meant that the horns around the Highland head have been replaced by a comely halo. For the purpose of making objective judgements it may be just as damaging.

By the late eighteenth century the Highlands no longer posed a military or political threat whilst increasing awareness of the economic problems of the area cast Highlanders in the role of victims. Mass emigration from the 1770s, the potato famine of 1846–47 and its associated publicity, then the reports of the Napier Commission and the Deer Forest Commission opened the eyes of the rest of Britain to the poverty and misery of the people. Countless travelogues have developed this since. The Highlander is now seen in a far different light. Newspaper articles, radio and television reports adopt a sympathetic, almost reverential tone. A Celtic glow adorns every account. The problems of the Highlands and Hebrides are seen through a journalistic prism which distorts in a new way.

Of course this prejudice is not necessarily any more 'true' than previous perceptions – but how times have changed. The irony is that Scotland now has a brand image that is closely associated with Highland garb, music and culture. The ubiquitous tourist icon is a kilted piper in a Highland glen. The image that would have horrified and frightened the 'civilised' Scots of mediaeval times is now used to charm and suborn their descendants. The objective remains the same, to secure a flow of resources from richer to poorer, but today it is achieved more subtly. Where before cattle were stolen, now a brand is sold.

The above quotations illustrate the changing 'reputation' of the Gael. This 'reputation' informed all travellers and their accounts. It will be further revealed as we read some of these.

Chapter 2

Historians and their agendas

I n a book about travellers' evidence it is necessary to justify the inclusion of extracts from the work of historians. The reason is simply that the latter often included the former, or unacknowledged abstracts from them. We have no mediaeval or earlier accounts by travellers in the Hebrides. We only have some snippets of evidence which often do no more than give us some detail about the physical environment. Usually they tell us little about the culture or beliefs of the inhabitants.

Scottish historians, though, do give general evidence about the Highlands and Islands. Some, as Fordun, just list the islands and their attributes. Others, such as Boece, use the issue as a peg on which to hang a moral soliloquy. Leslie, as a bishop of Ross, wrote with a good deal of sympathy and understanding. Buchanan paid Dean Monro the ultimate compliment of including Monro's account of the isles in his own published History. In all cases I have no doubt that they drew from a public fund of knowledge built up by travel and contact over many generations. In addition they received information from Highlanders themselves. Boece quotes a Sir Duncan Campbell of Argyll on a terrible monster afflicting the area. From Boece the story passed into Holinshed and so into history or myth.

Historians were important as movers and shakers, as opinion-formers, as spin-doctors. They had a role analogous to journalists and television presenters today. They were the intellectual elite. Nobody was a professional historian; they had other jobs but also wrote history. Bower was an abbot, Leslie a bishop, Major and Buchanan taught. These historians had varying agendas so it is not as if they were necessarily even-handed. Many axes have been ground on the whetstone of history. Within the Highlands they have been sharpened for the sake of clan or family, language, culture and religion. Purpose, for an historian, is often as important as content, indeed it often sets the content. We can see this by looking at a few quotations from the group of historians who burst into print in the sixteenth century.

John Major, whose history was published in 1521, stands in contrast to some later historians of the sixteenth century – Boece, Leslie and Buchanan – who praised the Highlanders as symbols of ancient Scottish virtue. Major wrote from a Lowland perspective:

> *Further, just as among the Scots we find two distinct tongues, so we likewise find two different ways of life and conduct. For some are born in the forests*

and mountains of the north, and these we call men of the Highland, but the others men of the Lowland. By foreigners the former are called Wild Scots, the latter householding Scots. The Irish tongue is in use among the former, the English tongue among the latter. One-half of Scotland speaks Irish, and all these as well as the Islanders we reckon to belong to the Wild Scots. In dress, in the manner of their outward life, and in good morals, for example, these come behind the householding Scots – yet they are not less, but rather much more, prompt to fight; and this, both because they dwell more towards the north, and because, born as they are in the mountains, and dwellers in forests, their very nature is more combative. It is, however, with the householding Scots that the Government and direction of the kingdom is to be found, inasmuch as they understand better, or at least less ill than the others, the nature of a civil polity. One part of the Wild Scots have a wealth of cattle, sheep, and horses, and these, with a thought for the possible loss of their possessions, yield more willing obedience to the courts of law and the king. The other part of these people delight in the chase and a life of indolence; their chiefs eagerly follow bad men if only they may not have the need to labour; taking no pains to earn their own livelihood, they live upon others, and follow their own worthless and savage chief in all evil courses sooner than they will pursue an honest industry. They are full of mutual dissensions, and war rather than peace is their normal condition. The Scottish kings have with difficulty been able to withstand the inroads of these men . . . Our house-holding Scots, or quiet and civil-living people – that is, all who lead a decent and reasonable life – these men hate, on account of their differing speech, as much as they do the English. (John Major in Hume Brown, *Scotland before 1700*)

Major laboured under a notion that had persisted since classical times – that people who lived in the far north were mentally slower, fiercer in battle and also more comely. '*Aristotle observes in the sixth book of his Politics that southern peoples excel the northerners in intelligence, and that, on the contrary, northerners have the advantage in warlike virtue. In northern nations, therefore, we need not expect to find craftiness in war, or guile.*' (John Major in Hume Brown, *Scotland before 1700*.)

And again: '*To the people of the North God gave less intelligence than to those of the South, but greater strength of body, a more courageous spirit, greater comeli-ness.*' (John Major in Hume Brown, *Scotland before 1700*.)

Bower elaborates on this when discussing a ferocious battle in Strathnaver in 1431:

It was a matter of astonishment to many that they attacked each other with such spirit that no one protected himself with the help of flight so as to save his life. This is explained by the fact that our fellow-Scots across the mountains, living as they do on the border or boundary of the world, experience little of

*the scorching summer heat or the sun's blaze by which the blood as a friend of
nature might be dried up: it is for this reason that, compared with the other
nations of the world, they have been found to be naturally more stout-hearted.
Vegetius in his De Re Militari Book 1, Chapter 3 writes right to the point
when he says: 'It is an established fact that everywhere some men are born
faint-hearted and some energetic; yet one nation surpasses another in war,
and it is the open expanse of sky which contributes most often to robustness of
spirit as well as of body, for it is said that all nations which are close to the
sun, being dried up with excessive heat, have greater mental awareness, but
less blood, and in consequence do not have the self-possession and confidence
for fighting, because those who know that they have very little blood are
afraid of being wounded. On the other hand northern peoples who are far
from the fires of the sun, are in deed more headstrong, yet with an overflowing
and lavish supply of blood are eager for fights. New recruits (i.e. fighting men)
therefore should be selected from the more temperate regions; such men have a
good supply of blood available so that they treat wounds and death with
contempt, and they cannot lack the practical good sense which both maintains
discipline on active service and is of great service when it comes to advice in
battle.'* (Bower, *Scotichronicon*, vol 8, Book XVI, ch 17)

Major also pointed up an issue that was ducked by later sixteenth-century
historians, namely that Lowlanders, admittedly because they had something
to lose, were willing to place themselves within the framework of a society
where relations between individuals were governed by rules, not force. The
Highlanders, in his view, had no property to lose, instead lived off the
property of others, and so found civilised life uncongenial. Despite the status
and reputation of later historians like Boece and Leslie it is the views of Major
we find echoed in the eighteenth century. In truth, though, each generation
favours or resuscitates the historians it needs. Their experience of the
Highlanders during the period 1640–1750 probably meant that the rest of
Britain shared Major's jaundiced view of them. After the Highland threat had
receded so we could refind those ancient virtues of simplicity, honesty and
integrity. Truth, like beauty is always in the eye of the beholder.

Hector Boece, whose *History* was published in 1527, claimed that he had
been asked by certain Scottish noblemen to show how their ancestors had
lived. This he would do, despite the fact that it would surely draw upon him
the wrath of various magnates. His agenda was to compare the simple,
virtuous old with the rank, luxurious new. With this conceit as motive Boece
went gleefully to task:

*And, thairfore, I intend, first, to schaw, quhat maneris hes bene amang our
eldaris, baith in time of weir and peace; and be quhat ingine, wisdome, and
chevelrie, thay have debatit aganis sa mony strong ennimes, howbeit thair
ennimes come oftimes in this realme with maist dangerus incursionis: and,*

finalie, we will schaw, how the notable strenth, vigour, and soverane virtew failyeit ay the mair amang thaim that thay declinit fra the temperance of thair eldaris: quhill at last it is cumin to thir dayis, in quhilkis we leif in gret tranquillite; howbeit the samin is mair be benevolence and sleuth of our nichtbouris, than ony manlie prowis of our self. Now will I schaw, the schortest way I may, how we, in thir present dayis ar drownit in all maner of avarice and lust. Yit I belief that sic men as ar of severe life, following the temperance of thair eldaris, sall rejose to heir the honourable maneris of thair eldaris; utheris that ar of mair brutall and vicius life, seing thair vices taxit with sic dishonour, sall dres thaim plesandlie to revert fra thair evil and schamefull dedis to better life. First, I suppone, that the thing that I say, in repreving the corruppit maneris of the warld now present, be nocht takin in repreif of every man; bot allanerlie to sik men that leiffis with intemperance: for sik men deservis mair repreif than I may gif thaim at this time. And gif ony man findis his bile opnit for purgatioun be me, that he hide nocht his infirmite, bot erar seik the best remeid he may, to amend his life. (Hector Boece in Hume Brown, *Scotland before 1700*)

(And, therefore, I intend, first, to show, what manners have been among our elders, both in time of war and peace; and by what ingenuity, wisdom, and chivalry, they have debated against so many strong enemies, howbeit their enemies came often into this realm with most dangerous incursions: and, finally, we will show, how the notable strength, vigour, and sovereign virtue failed ever the more among them that they declined from the temperance of their elders: until at last it has come to these days, in which we live in great tranquillity; howbeit the same is more by benevolence and sloth of our neighbours, than any manly prowess of ourselves. Now will I show, the shortest way I may, how we, in these present days are drowned in all manner of avarice and lust. Yet I believe that such men as are of severe life, following the temperance of their elders, shall rejoice to hear the honourable manners of their elders; others that are of more brutal and vicious life, seeing their vices taxed with such dishonour, shall address them pleasantly to revert from their evil and shameful deeds to better life. First, I suppose, that the thing that I say, in reproving the corrupt manners of the world now present, be not taken in reproof of every man; but only to such men that live with intemperance: for such men deserve more reproof than I may give them at this time. And if any man finds his bile opened for purging by me, that he hide not his infirmity, but rather seek the best remedy he may, to amend his life.)

Boece's premiss was moral decline. Scottish vigour and independence were formerly maintained by a virile and spartan masculinity. The fact that the latter had so drastically fallen away was an implicit threat to the former. One of the principal causes of the current degeneracy was physical luxury or surfeit:

Our eldaris, howbeit thay wer richt virtewis baith in weir and peace, wer maist exercit with temperance; for it is the fontane of all virtew. Thay wer of temperat sleip, meit, and drink, and sic refectionis as wer preparit with litill laubour or cost. Thair breid wes maid of sic stuf as grew maist esalie on the ground. Thair vitallis wer nocht siftit, as we do now, to mak thaim delicius to the mouth; bot wer all ground togidder under ane forme. The flesche maist frequent amang thame, wes othir wild flesche, won on the fellis be thair hunting, quhilk maid thaim of incredible strenth; or ellis it wes of thair awin tame bestial, specially beif, as we do yit in our dayis: howbeit we ar richt far different fra the use and custome of all uthir nationis. The steirkis, quhen thay ar bot young velis, ar othir slane, or ellis libbit to be oxin, to manure the land; bot the quiokis war nevir slane quhill thay wer with calfe, for than thay ar fattest, and maist delicius to the mouth. The common meit of our eldaris was fische; nocht for the plente of it, bot erar becaus thair landis lay oftimes waist, throw continewal exercition of chevelry, and for that caus thay leiffit maist of fische. Thay disjunit airly in the morning with smal refectioun, and sustenit thair liffis thairwith quhil the time of sowper; throw quhilk thair stomok was nevir surfetly chargit, to empesche thaim of uthir besines. At the sowper thay war mair large; howbeit thay had bot ane cours. Quhen thay kest thaimself to be mery, thay usit maist aqua vite; nocht maid of costly spicis, bot of sic naturall herbis as grew in thair awin yardis. The common drink that thay usit was aill; and, in time of weir, quhen thay lay in thair tentis, thay usit nocht bot watter. Ilk man had als mekill mele as micht suffice him for the day, and maid breid thairof at the fire; on the samin maner as the Romanis did, specialy Antonius Caracallus, Empriour. Thay had sendill flesche in thair campis, bot gif it war won be pray of ennimes. Thay eit, for common, flesche half raw; for the saup is maist nurisand in that maner. Attoure, thay had ay with thaim ane gret vessell, wrocht full of butter, cheis, mele, milk, and vinacre, temperit togidder; be quhilk thay saiffit thair liffis mony dayis fra extreme hungar, soukand the jus and humouris thairof, quhen na vittallis, throw incursionis of ennimes, micht be found. And, howbeit thay had peace with thair ennimes, thay sufferit nocht thair bodyis to be corruppit with sleuth; bot wer exercit othir in continewall hunting; for in that game was gret honour amang our eldaris; or ellis thay had exercition of rinning, sum times fra the planes to the montanis, and fra the montanis to the planis; or ellis thay war exercit in wirsling, or uthir corporall exercition. Thay had thair hedis ay cowit, as the Spanyeartis usis; but ony bonet or cover, les than thay war trublit with infirmite. Nane of thame, throw ithand cowing of thair hedis, grew beld. Thay yeid commonly bairfutit; and, gif thay had ony schone, thay dippit thaim first in the watter or thay put thaim on, specialy in winter quhen maist schill and persand stormes apperit, that thair sollis, quhilkis war hardin with the hetis of the semer and snawis of winter, suld be the mair abil to sustene laubour. Thair abulyement was not maid be motion of insolence, bot erar efter the general gise of the cuntre. Thair hois war maid of smal lint or woll, and yeid nevir above thair kne, to make thaim the mair waldin and sowpill. The mantillis that thay usit in winter wes maid of gros woll; and in semer wes maid of small and finest woll that thay micht get. Thay slepit on benkis, or bonchis of stra, bot ony cover; and lernit thair sonnis, fra thair first yeris, to eschew eis, and to sleip on the samin manner. Ilk moder wes nurice to her awin barne. It was ane suspition of adultre aganis ony woman, quhare hir milk failyeit. The wemen thocht thair barnis war not tender nor kindly to thaim, bot gif thay war nurist als weill with the milk of thair breist, as thay war nurist afore with the blude of thair wambe. Attoure, thay held that thair barnis war degenerat fra thair nature and kind, gif thay war nurist with uncouth milk.

(Our elders, howbeit they were right virtuous both in war and peace, were most exercised with temperance; for it is the fountain of all virtue. They were of temperate sleep, meat, and drink, and such refections [meals] as were prepared with little labour or cost. Their bread was made of such stuff as grew most easily on the ground. Their victuals were not sifted, as we do now, to make them delicious to the mouth; but were all ground together under one form. The flesh most frequent among them, was either wild flesh, won on the fells by their hunting, which made them of incredible strength; or else it was of their own tame beasts, especially beef, as we do yet in our days: howbeit we are right far different from the use and custom of all other nations. The stirks, when they are but young veals, are either slain, or else gelded to be oxen, to manure the land; but the heifers were never slain until they were with calf, for then they are fattest, and most delicious to the mouth. The common meat of our elders was fish; not for the plenty of it, but rather because their lands lay often waste, through continual exercise of chivalry, and for that cause they lived mostly on fish. They breakfasted early in the morning with [a] small meal, and sustained their lives therewith until the time of supper; through which their stomach was never excessively burdened, to hinder them from other business. At the supper they were more expansive; howbeit they had but one course. When they cast themselves to be merry, they used mostly aquavitae; not made of costly spices, but of such natural herbs as grew in their own yards. The common drink that they used was ale; and, in time of war, when they lay in their tents, they used nought but water. Each man had as much meal as might suffice him for the day, and made bread thereof at the fire; in the same manner as the Romans did, especially Antonius Caracallus, Emperor. They had seldom flesh in their camps, unless it were won by prey of enemies. They ate, for daily fare, flesh half raw; for the sap is most nourishing in that manner. Besides, they had always with them a great vessel, wrought full of butter, cheese, meal, milk, and vinegar, mixed together; by which they saved their lives many days from extreme hunger, sucking the juice and matter thereof, when no victuals, through incursions of enemies, might be found. And, howbeit they had peace with their enemies, they suffered not their bodies to be corrupted with sloth; but were exercised either in continual hunting; for in that game was great honour among our elders; or else they had exercise of running, sometimes from the plains to the mountains, and from the mountains to the plains; or else they were exercised in wrestling, or other physical exercise. They had their heads always cropped, as the Spaniards do; without any bonnet or cover, unless they were troubled with infirmity. None of them, through continual cropping of their heads, grew bald. They went commonly barefoot; and, if they had any shoes, they dipped them first in the water before they put them on, especially in winter when most chill and piercing storms appeared, that their soles, which were hardened with the heats of the summer and snows of winter, should be the more able to sustain labour. Their dress was not made by motive of insolence, but rather after the general guise of the country. Their hose [stockings] were made of small linen or wool, and went never above their knee, to make them the more manageable and supple. The mantles that they used in winter were made of coarse wool; and in summer were made of small and finest wool that they might get. They slept on benches, or bunches of straw, without any cover; and learned their sons, from their first years, to eschew ease, and to sleep in the same manner. Each mother was nurse to her own bairn. It was a suspicion of adultery against any woman, where her milk failed. The women thought their bairns were not tender nor kindly to them, unless they were nourished as well with the milk of their breast, as they were nourished before with the blood of their womb. Besides, they held that their bairns were degenerate from their nature and kind, if they were nourished with strange milk.)

After painting this picture of hardiness – of life, diet and clothing – Boece continues with a hymn to masculinity:

Thay war sa accustomit with ithand pine and laubouris, that thay curit nothir the fervent heites of the semer, nor yit the schil frostis in the winter. Thay travelit maist on thair fute; and, in the time of weir, thay had thair cariagis and vittallis turst with thaim on thair hors: and, quhen dangeir occurrit, thay refusit na maner of besines nor laubour that micht pertene to forsy campionis. Gif it hapnit thaim, be mischance, to be vincust; thay fled with sic spede to the montanis, that na horsmen micht ouirtak thaim. The injure done to ony ane of thaim, was repute sa common to thaim al, that thay wald nevir evoid the displeseir thairof out of thair hertis, quhill the samin war recompansit with the blude of thair ennimes. He that wes maist noble, desirit erest to fecht in the wangard, quhare his vassalage and manheid micht be maist knawin. The nobillis and commonis contendit quhay suld be maist faithful to othir; and quhen the capitane, throw his fers spreit and hardines, apperit in ony extreme dangeir of ennimes, all the band that was of his opinion, ruschit sa fersly to his defence, that othir thay deliverit him out of that present dangeir, or ellis all at anis lois thair lives with him. The sepulturis of all nobillis war decorit with als mony hie stanis, rising about the same, as he had slane afore of ennimes in his life. He that was found in the army but flint and furisine, or but his swerd beltit fast to his sidis, was schamefully scurgit; and he that sald his swerd, or laid it to wed, was degradit of auctorite, and banist, as unworthy creature, out of thair cumpany. He that fled in time of battall, or departit fra the army without command of the capitane, was slane, but ony dowme, quhare evir he micht be apprehendit; bot his gudis war gevin to his sonne. The wemen war of litil les vassalage and strenth than was the men; for al rank madinnis and wiffis, gif thay war nocht with child, yeid als weill to battall as the men. Als sone as the army was passand forthwart, thay slew the first levand beist that thay fand; and nocht allanerly baithit thair swerdis with the blude thairof, bot taistit the samin with thair mouth, with na les religion and faith, than thay had bene than sicker of sum felicite following. Gif thay saw thair awin blude in battall, thay grew nocht astonist bot, boldin in maist brime fury, set thaim to revenge the samin. In all battallis assailyeit be thaim, thay socht nevir victory be treason, falset, nor slicht; and thocht ay degrading to thair nobilite, to vincus thair ennimes with ony othir thing bot force of fechting. Thay held it for gret febilnes to revenge ony displeseir, hatrent, or slauchter, be treason; attour, sencerite and simpilnes was equaly honorit amang thaim all. Quhen thay war to pas on thair ennimes, ilk man yeid, as we do now, upon his awin cost, except sa mony as war wagit.

(They were so accustomed with constant pain and labours, that they heeded neither the fervent heats of the summer, nor yet the chill frosts in the winter. They travelled mostly by foot; and, in the time of war, they had their baggage and victuals trussed with them on their horse: and, when danger occurred, they refused no manner of business nor labour that might pertain to strong champions. If it happened [to] them, by mischance, to be vanquished; they fled with such speed to the mountains, that no horsemen might overtake them. The injury done to any one of them, was reputed so common to them all, that they would never remove the displeasure thereof out of their hearts, until the same were recompensed with the blood of their enemies. He that was most noble, desired first to fight in the vanguard, where his vassalage and manhood might be most known. The nobles and commons contended who should be most faithful to [the] other; and when the captain, through his fierce spirit and hardiness, appeared in any extreme danger of enemies, all the band that was of his opinion, rushed so fiercely to his defence, that either they delivered him out of that present danger, or else all at once lost their lives with him. The burial-places of all nobles were decorated with as many high stones, rising about the same, as he had slain before of enemies in his life. He that was found in the army without flint and fire-iron, or without his sword belted fast to his sides, was shamefully scourged; and he that sold his sword, or laid it to pledge, was degraded of authority, and banished, as (an) unworthy creature, out of their company. He that fled in time of battle, or departed from the army without command of the captain, was slain, without any trial, wherever he might be apprehended; but his goods were given to his son. The women were of little less vassalage and strength than the men; for all rank (of) maidens and wives, if they were not with child, went as well to battle as the men. As soon as the army was passing forward, they slew the first living beast that they found; and not only bathed their swords with the blood thereof, but tasted the same with their mouth, with no less religion and faith, than (if) they had been then surer of some felicity following. If they saw their own blood in battle, they grew not astonished but, emboldened in most fierce fury, set themselves to revenge the same. In all battles undertaken by them, they sought never victory by treason, falsehood, nor sleight; and thought (it) always degrading to their nobility, to vanquish their enemies with any other thing but force of fighting. They held it for great feebleness to revenge any displeasure, hatred, or slaughter, by treason; besides, sincerity and simplicity was equally honoured among them all. When they were to pass on their enemies, each man went, as we do now, upon his own cost, except so many as were waged.)

Swept along by the fervour of his argument Boece then moves to a very extreme position on how such hardiness and masculinity has to be maintained. In order to prevent degeneracy society has to be ruthless:

He that was trublit with the falling evil, or fallin daft or wod, or havand sic infirmite as succedis be heritage fra the fader to the son, was geldit; that his infeckit blude suld spreid na forthir. The wemen that was fallin lipper, or had ony othir infection of blude, was banist fra the cumpany of men; and, gif scho consavit barne under sic infirmite, baith scho and hir barne war buryit quik. All dronkattis, glutonis, and consumers of vittallis mair than was necessar to the sustentation of men, were tane, and first commandit to swelly thair south of quhat drink thay plesit, and incontinent thairefter was drownit in ane fresche rever. Forthir, howbeit thay had na administratioun of justice in time of weir, yit sic justice was ministerd in time of peace, that oftimes thay war ouir severe in thair punition; for thay knew weil, fra thair pepil wer drawin fra battall to peace, thay suld be gevin to sa mony enormiteis, that the samin micht nocht be dantit but gret punition. For the pepill war of sic nature, als sone as thay knew thaimself gilty of ony offence committit aganis the kingis majeste or commounweill, thay set thaim to rais divisioun amang the gret princis of the realme: nochtheles, quhen thay ar tretit with soft and moderat empire, thay ar found richt humane and meke pepil, richt obeysand to reason; and nocht allanerly kepis thair faith efter the reason of thair contract, bot gevis ane gowpin, or ellis sum thingis mair abone the just mesure that thay sell. This consuetude is sa straitly kepit, that gif the samin be nocht done, the biar will nocht stand to the contract of merchandice.

(He that was troubled with the falling evil [epilepsy], or become daft or mad, or having such infirmity as succeeds by heritage from the father to the son, was castrated; that his infected blood should spread no further. The woman that was fallen leprous, or had any other infection of blood, was banished from the company of men; and, if she conceived child under such infirmity, both she and her bairn were buried alive. All drunkards, gluttons, and consumers of victuals more than was necessary to the sustenance of men, were taken, and first commanded to drink their fill of what drink they pleased, and immediately thereafter were drowned in a fresh(water) river. Further, howbeit they had no administration of justice in time of war, yet such justice was ministered in time of peace, that often they were over severe in their punishment; for they knew well, once their people were drawn from battle to peace, they should be given to so many enormities, that the same might not be daunted without great punishment. For the people were of such nature, as soon as they knew themselves guilty of any offence committed against the king's majesty or commonwealth, they set themselves to raise division among the great princes of the realm: nonetheless, when they are treated with soft and moderate rule, they are found right humane and meek people, right obedient to reason; and not only keep their faith after the reason of their contract, but give a handful, or else some things more above the just measure that they sell. This habit is so strictly kept, that if the same be not done, the buyer will not stand to the contract of merchandise.)

After making his call for social eugenics and firm government Boece identifies Highlanders as the surviving standard-bearers of the old virtues:

Thay usit the ritis and maneris of Egyptianis, fra quhome thay tuk thair first beginning. In all thair secret besines, thay usit not to writ with common letteris usit amang othir pepil, bot erar with sifars and figuris of beistis maid in maner of letteris; sic as thair epithafis, and superscriptioun abone thair sepulturis, schawis: nochtheles, this crafty maner of writing, be quhat sleuth I can not say, is perist; and yit thay have certane letteris propir amang thaimself, quhilkis war sum time vulgar and commoun. Forthir, thay that spekis with the auld tongue of that cuntre, hes thair asperatioun, thair diptongis, and thair pronunciation, better than ony othir pepill. The commonis ar nocht exercit thairwith; bot allanerly thay that dwellis in the hie partis of the land: and, becaus thir men hes thair langage mair eloquent and propir than the commonis hes, thay ar callit poetis; and makis poetis, effering to thair eruditioun and science, with mony gret cerimonyis. Beside mony craftis and science, quhilkis thay have translatit in thair awin toung, thay profes maist the science of medcinary, and ar richt excellent in it; for thay knaw the nature of every herbe that growis in thay cuntreis, and curis all maner of maledyis thairwith. Heirfore I say, thair is na region in the warld sa barrant nor unfrutfull, be distance fra the sonne, bot, be providence of God, al maner of necessaryis to the sustentatioun of man, may be gottin plesandly in it, gif thair war sic pepill that culd laubour it, effering to the nature thairof. Nochtheles, as our eldaris, quhilkis dwelt continewally merchand with the realme of Ingland, lernit the Saxonis toung, be frequent jeoperdeis and chance of battall, sustenit mony yeris aganis thaim; sa the pepill, now present in Scotland, hes tint baith the langage and maneris of writing usit sum time be our eldaris, and hes now ane new maner of writingis and langage: howbeit, the Hieland hes baith the writingis and langage as thay had afore, mair ingenius than ony othir pepill. How may thair be ane greter ingine, than to make ane bait of ane bull hid, bound with na thing bot wandis? This bait is callit ane currok; with the quhilk thay fische salmond, and sum time passis ouir gret rivers thairwith; and, quhen thay have done thair fisching, thay beir it to ony place, on thair bak, quhare thay pleis. Bot we wil return to the maneris of our anciant freindis. (Hector Boece in Hume Brown, *Scotland before 1700*)

(They used the rites and manners of Egyptians, from whom they took their first beginning. In all their secret business, they used not to write with common letters used among other people, but rather with ciphers and figures of beasts made in manner of letters; such as their epitaphs, and writing above their tombs, shows: nonetheless, this crafty manner of writing, by what sloth I cannot say, is perished; and yet they have certain letters proper among themselves, which were sometime vulgar and common. Further, they that speak with the old tongue of that country, have their aspiration, their diphthongs, and their pronunciation, better than any other people. The commons are not exercised therewith; but only they that dwell in the high parts of the land: and, because these men have their language more eloquent and proper than the commons have, they are called poets; and make poems, according to their erudition and science, with many great ceremonies. Beside many crafts and science, which they have translated into their own tongue, they profess most the science of medicine, and are right excellent in it; for they know the nature of every herb that grows in those countries, and cure all manner of maladies therewith. Therefore I say, there is no region in the world so barren nor unfruitful, by distance from the sun, but, by providence of God, all manner of necessities for the sustenance of man, may be gotten pleasantly in it, if there were such people that could labour [at] it, according to the nature thereof. Nonetheless, as our elders, which dwelt continually bordering with the realm of England, learned the Saxon's tongue, by frequent jeopardies and chance of battle, sustained many years against them; so the people, now present in Scotland, have lost both the language and manners of writing used some time by our elders, and have now a new manner of writing and language: howbeit, the Highlands have both the writings and language as they had before, more ingenious than any other people. How may there be a greater ingenuity, than to make a boat of a bull hide, bound with nothing but sticks? This boat is called a currach; with the which they fish [for] salmon, and sometimes pass over great rivers therewith; and, when they have done their fishing, they bear it to any place, on their back, where they please. But we will return to the manners of our ancient friends.)

Boece's monologue is a lecture read by every generation to its successors. We need the old vigour, the old asceticism, the old simplicity. What makes it relevant to our story is that it was the Highlander who was held up as the epitome of ancient virtues. Intriguingly, Boece throws in a couple of extra facts about the Gaelic-speaking Highlanders – that they were particularly skilled in medicine and making currachs. Boece also tries to date this change, this falling off from a former grace:

Be chance of sindry seasonis, specialy about the time of King Malcolme Canmore, al thingis began to change. For quhen oure nichtbouris, the Britonis, war maid effeminat be lang sleuth, and doung out of Britane be the Saxonis in Walis, we began to have alliance, be proximite of Romanis, with Inglismen; specially efter the exterminatioun of Pichtis: and, be frequent and daily cumpany of thaim, we began to rute thair langage and superflew maneris in oure breistis; throw quhilk the virtew and temperance of our eldaris began to be of litil estimation amang us. Than we war gevin, efter the arrogance and pride of Inglismen, to vane glore and ambution of honouris, and began that time to seke new names of nobilite; howbeit, afore thay dayis, he was maist nobil, that was decorit mair with virtew than riches, confiding mair in his awin dedis, than in ony dedis of his eldaris. Than began, in Scotland, the maneris of Dukis, Erlis, Lordis, and Baronis; for afore thay dayis, the principall men of Scotland under the king war callit Thanis, that is to say, Gadderaris of the Kingis malis; and war ay rewardit be the king, as thair faith and virtew deservit.

(By chance of sundry seasons, specially about the time of King Malcolm Canmore, all things began to change. For when our neighbours, the Britons, were made effeminate by long sloth, and driven out of Britain by the Saxons into Wales, we began to have alliance, by proximity of Romans, with Englishmen; specially after the extermination of Picts: and, by frequent and daily company of them, we began to root their language and superfluous manners in our breasts; through which the virtue and temperance of our elders began to be of little estimation among us. Then we were given, after the arrogance and pride of Englishmen, to vainglory and ambition of honours, and began that time to seek new names of nobility; howbeit, before those days, he was most noble, that was adorned more with virtue than riches, trusting more in his own deeds, than in any deeds of his elders. Then began, in Scotland, the ranks of Dukes, Earls, Lords, and Barons; for before those days, the principal men of Scotland under the king were called Thanes, that is to say, Gatherers of the King's rents; and were always rewarded by the king, as their faith and virtue deserved.)

So much then was the fault of the English! But, in addition, one of the main reasons for current decadence was surfeit or luxury. Boece warms to his theme:

But now I beleif nane hes sic eloquence, nor south of langage, that can sufficiently declare, how far we, in thir present dayis, ar different fra the virtew and temperance of our eldaris. For quhare our eldaris had sobriete, we have ebriete and dronkinnes; quhare thay had plente with sufficence, we have immoderat cursis with superfluite; as he war maist noble and honest, that culd devore and swelly maist: and, be extreme deligence, serchis sa mony deligat coursis, that thay provoke the stomok to ressave mair than it may sufficiently degest; throw quhilk we ingorge and fillis our self, day and nicht, sa full of metis and drinkis, that we can nocht abstene, quhill our wambe be sa swon, that it is unabil to ony virtewis occupation. And nocht allanerly may surfet dennar and sowper suffice us, abone the temperance of oure eldaris, bot als to continew our schamefull and immoderit voracite with duble dennaris and sowparis; throw quhilk mony of us ganis to na othir besines bot to fil and teme our wembe. Attour to continew this schamefull intemperance, abone the necessar sustentation of nature, we geif us to sic unhappy laubour, that na fische in the see, nor foule in the aire, nor best in the wod, may have rest; bot socht heir and thair, to satisfy the hungry appetit of glutonis. Nocht allanerly ar winis socht in France, bot in Spainye, Italy, and Grece; and, sum time, baith Aphrik and Asia socht, for new delicius metis and winis, to the samin

effect. Thus is the warld sa uterly socht, that all maner of droggis and
electuaris, that may nuris the lust and insolence of pepill, ar brocht in
Scotland, with maist sumptuus price, to na les dammage than perdition of the
pepill thairof: for, throw this immoderat glutony, our wit and reason ar sa
blindit within the presoun of the body, that it may have no knawlage of
hevinly thingis; for the body is involvit with sic clowdis of fatnes, that,
howbeit it be of gud complexioun be nature, it is sa opprest with superflew
metis and drinkis, that it may nothir weild, nor yit ouir the self; bot,
confessand the self vincust, gevis place to all infirmiteis, quhill it be miserably
distroyit: as apperis be sindry experience. For mony of our pepill, in remot
and in maist cauld region, ar strikin oftimes with maist vehement fever, thair
inwart bowellis blesand as thay war in ane ithand fire; quhilkis cumis of sic
spicery and uncouth droggis, brocht out of remot cuntreis in this regioun.
Utheris of thaim ar sa swollin, and growin full of humouris, that thay ar
strikin haistely deid in the poplesy; and, howbeit thay recover for ane schort
time efter, thay ar bot ane deid pepill; levand, and buryit in sepulture,
havand bot ane schadow of life. The young pepill and barnis, following thir
unhappy customis of thair faderis, gevis thameself to lust and insolence,
havand all virtuus occupation and craftis in contemptioun; and, becaus thay
ar lang customit and hantit thairwith, quhen time occurris of weir to defend
the cuntre, thay ar sa effeminat and soft, thay pas on hors as hevy martis;
and ar sa fat and growin, that thay may do na thing in compare of the
soverane manheid of thair eldaris. Als sone as thay ar returnit hame, becaus
thair guddis ar not sufficient to nuris thame in voluptuus life and pleseir of
thair wambe, thay ar gevin to all maner of avarice; and othir castis thame to
be strang and maistrifull thevis, or ellis sewaris of dissention amang the
nobillis.

(But now I believe none have such eloquence, nor completeness of
language, that can sufficiently declare, how far we, in these present
days, are different from the virtue and temperance of our elders. For
where our elders had sobriety, we have inebriety and drunkenness;
where they had plenty with sufficiency, we have immoderate curses with
superfluity; as (if) he were most noble and honest, that could devour
and swallow most: and, by extreme diligence, search (for) so many
delicate courses, that they provoke the stomach to receive more than it
may sufficiently digest; through which we engorge and fill ourselves,
day and night, so full of meats and drinks, that we cannot abstain, until
our womb be so swollen, that it is incapable of any virtuous occupation.
And not only may surfeit dinner and supper suffice us, beyond the
temperance of our elders, but also to continue our shameful and
immoderate voracity with double dinners and suppers; through which
many of us achieve no other business but to fill and empty our stomach.
Besides to continue this shameful intemperance, beyond the necessary

sustenance of nature, we give ourselves to such unhappy labour, that no fish in the sea, nor fowl in the air, nor beast in the wood, may have rest; but sought here and there, to satisfy the hungry appetite of gluttons. Not only are wines sought in France, but in Spain, Italy, and Greece; and, sometimes, both Africa and Asia sought, for new delicious meats and wines, to the same effect. Thus is the world so utterly sought, that all manner of drugs and electuaries, that may nourish the lust and insolence of people, are brought into Scotland, with most sumptuous price, to no less damage than perdition of the people thereof: for, through this immoderate gluttony, our wit and reason are so blinded within the prison of the body, that it may have no knowledge of heavenly things; for the body is wrapped with such clouds of fatness, that, howbeit it be of good complexion by nature, it is so oppressed with superfluous meats and drinks, that it may neither manage, nor over-come(?) the self; but, confessing the self vanquished, gives way to all infirmities, until it be miserably destroyed: as appears by sundry experience. For many of our people, in [a] remote and most cold region, are stricken often with most vehement fever, their inward bowels blazing as (if) they were in a constant fire; which comes of such spicy and strange drugs, brought out of remote countries into this region. Others of them are so swollen, and grown full of humours, that they are struck hastily dead in the apoplexy; and, howbeit they recover for a short time after, they are but a dead people; living, and buried in sepulchre, having but a shadow of life. The young people and bairns, following these unhappy customs of their fathers, give themselves to lust and insolence, having all virtuous occupation and crafts in contempt; and, because they are long accustomed and used therewith, when time occurs of war to defend the country, they are so effeminate and soft, they pass on horse like heavy cattle; and are so fat and overgrown, that they may do nothing in comparison to the sovereign manhood of their elders. As soon as they are returned home, because their goods are not sufficient to nourish them in voluptuous life and pleasure of their womb, they are given to all manner of avarice; and either set themselves to be strong and masterful thieves, or else sowers of dissension among the nobles.)

Certain themes stand out from Boece's history. The Highlander represented an ideal, although it would be interesting to know if this was the result of Boece's personal experience or just the logical conclusion his crusade against luxury drew him to. Many Lowlanders who lived near the Highlands regarded their neighbours as less than perfect. To Boece the Highlander was the archetypal noble savage, the noble *Scottish* savage. He stood for the old ways – the old language, manners, customs, costume and machismo. Boece may not have had this last word in his lexicon but it would have suited him perfectly. He wanted a simple, straightforward, honest, virile warrior. The repeated use of words such as gluttony, effeminacy, degeneracy, indicate his unconscious goals.

Boece was by no means alone in his horror of luxury and surfeit. Although austerity and simplicity became part of the essential nature of Protestantism there were plenty of voices raised within the pre-Reformation church against the luxurious lifestyles of contemporary clerics. Boece's history was political in that he used conservatism as a tool as he railed against the affluence of his day.

Leslie too has a section dealing with old Scots manners, – 'chiefly of those who live in the Highlands and Hebrides'. Here he praises those who made a virtue of necessity – literally:

> *The Scottis . . . quhithir it was in peace or weir [did not fritter away their life] in curious cheir, and thair lyfe in daintie and diligat disches, or in taisting fyne wines . . . Bot thair kair and trayuel was hail in this to sustein thayr bodies commodiouslie and weil, of sik fude as thay mycht haue of the grunde, and thair thirst to slokne . . . wt sik drink as [wells or streams] gaue thame thay vset gladlie and wt gude wil. Sum vset breid of ry, sum of quheit, sum of peise or beanes, bot not few of ates, as this or that ground gaue in gretter abundance. Grettest delyte thay had in oxin flesche, and in [veal] evin sa, and [these sometimes when they were running with blood] . . . because then thay war mair sappie and bettir than, to the nurishment of the body. Oxne, [calves], scheip, or Gait gif sum tymes war in wanting, not so much with capons, pliueris and vthiris sik kind of cheir vset thay, bot fishe of q[uhi]lke thay had in abundance . . . thay satisfiet thair hungir sueitlie: Nocht be the day was lycht, nathir at noneday bot at evin only thay first prepaired the table, and that verie scharpe and skairs, quhen al thair lyfe nathing they hated mair than gluttonie, assuiring thame selfes that sik sobrietie in meit and drink and sik maner of fair and cheir war mair proffitable athir to restore to thair health seik and waik, or quha war not seik and waik to make freshe and stark, quhilke throuch lang experience and vsse thay had leired, quhen amang thame war verie few seiknessis, bot of age al departed this lyfe. (Dalrymple's translation in E Cody (ed.), Leslie's History of Scotland, 1578)*

(The Scots . . . whether it was in peace or war [did not fritter away their life] in curious cheer, and their life in dainty and delicate dishes, or in tasting fine wines . . . But their care and travail was wholly in this to sustain their bodies commodiously and well, of such food as they might have of the ground, and their thirst to slake . . . with such drink as [wells or streams] gave them they used gladly and with good will. Some used bread of rye, some of wheat, some of peas or beans, but not (a) few of oats, as this or that ground gave in greater abundance. Greatest delight they had in oxen flesh, and in [veal] even so, and [these sometimes when they were running with blood] . . . because then they were more sappy and better then, to the nourishment of the body. Oxen, [calves], sheep, or Goat if sometimes were in wanting, not so much with capons, plovers and other such kind of cheer used they, but fish of which they had in abundance . . . they satisfied their hunger sweetly: Not when the day was light, neither at noon but at evening only they first prepared the table, and that very sharp and scarce, when all their life nothing they hated more than gluttony, assuring themselves that such sobriety in meat and drink and such manner of fare and cheer were more profitable either to restore to their health [the] sick and weak, or [those] who were not sick and weak to make fresh and strong, which through long experience and use they had learned, when among them were very few sicknesses, but of age all departed this life.)

As Boece, so Leslie ties these spartan characteristics of the Highlanders to their fitness for military campaigns:

Amang thame this was thair maner, the gretter of digrie and the nobiller of blude that ony of thame war, in the weiris he was formest, and gaue the first brasche in the feild, and set first on the ennimie: and this he did to moue and inflame his cumpanie to stand stoutlie, & wtout feir to gang fordward. the men of weir throuch his exemple, the scharplier walde sett upon the ennimies, and thair awne bodyes sett for the body of thair capitane, and frome danger him defend, and from al perrel of lyf him preserue. for as we said afoir, thair prince or capitane, ze naturallie, as it war thay helde in sik reuerence, that for thair cause or at thair command, thay walde venture thair awne lyfe to quhatsaevir danger or death albeit nevir sa bittir. Thay war not now vphaldne to the weiris on the Kings waiges, bot nurissed and brocht vp in the hous, and thair sustentatione to the feild was brocht out of the hous; quhilk thay vset sa moderatlie and wt sik sobrietie, that thay walde leid a lang lyfe frie frome al seiknes [sucking some small relish of butter, milk, or cheese, mixed with meal].

(Among them this was their manner, the greater of degree and the nobler of blood that any of them were, in the wars he was foremost, and gave the first attack in the field, and set first on the enemy: and this he did to move and inflame his company to stand stoutly, and without fear to go forward. the men of war through his example, the sharper would set upon the enemies, and their own bodies set before the body of their captain, and from danger him defend, and from all peril of life him preserve. for as we said before, their prince or captain, he naturally, as it were they held in such reverence, that for their cause or at their command, they would venture their own life to whatsoever danger or death, albeit never so bitter. They were not now upheld to the wars on the King's wages, but nourished and brought up in the house, and their sustenance to the field was brought out of the house; which they used so moderately and with such sobriety, that they would lead a long life free from all sickness [sucking some small relish of butter, milk, or cheese, mixed with meal].)

Moreover these virtues were characteristic of the Highlanders at peace as well as war:

Gif ony tyme thay had frie frome the weiris, that in peice thay mycht leiue, thay spendit it nocht in ydlenes, or vanitie. and in ald wyfes fable, bot thay thocht best to make the members of thair body mair firme, stable, and sure, and to fortifie thame selfes, to spend that tyme in rinning, fenceng wt swordes in the barresse; and in werstling: and that with age thay mycht that natural courage and strainth in thame make mekle quicker and abler, the verie wylde beistes [they often hunted on foot with a dog] . . . Quhairof proceidit that the les thay war gyuen to voluptuous and fleshlie pleisouris.

(If any time they had free from the wars, that in peace they might live, they spent it not in idleness, or vanity and in old wives' fables, but they thought best to make the members of their body more firm, stable, and sure, and to fortify themselves, to spend that time in running, fencing with swords in the lists; and in wrestling: and that with age they might that natural courage and strength in them make much quicker and abler, the very wild beasts [they often hunted on foot with a dog] . . . Whereof [it] proceeded that the less they were given to voluptuous and fleshly pleasures.)

The Highlanders had their own child-rearing skills:

This maner of way thay vset to bring vp thair bairnes. first to exercise thame in schoteng arrowis, neist in casteng dartes, thaireftir in feiding horses, and prouoiking thame to rinn, and last in handling of waiponis exerce thame with all diligence to propone wnto thame famous and preclare exemples of men of renoume, quhais futstepis thay mycht follow, the fade and inimitie borne toward thair parents to instil in the hartes of thair barnes, that quhen thay cam to perfectione the scharplier thay mycht persue thame: albeit in this thay war worthie of al correctione, that thay war sa vehementlie sett to reuenge: for gif ony discorde or diskyndnes had fallin amang thame, was eftir nevir clein forzhet, na nocht quhen thay war deid, quhen the barnes zit alyue nocht only war ennimies to the perents, bot, except thay gaue a manifest and ane euident sygne and takne of peace and luue, with a deidlie fade, hatred and Invie, thay persekuted and pursuet the hail stok and familie perteining to the sam parents, baith barnes and oyes, and sa this deidlie faid was nevir put in the buke of obliuione.

(This manner of way they used to bring up their bairns; first to exercise them in shooting arrows, next in casting spears, thereafter in feeding (or fighting) horses, and provoking them to run, and last in handling of weapons, exercise them with all diligence to propose unto them famous and illustrious examples of men of renown, whose footsteps they might follow, the feud and enmity borne toward their parents to instill in the hearts of their bairns, that when they came to perfection the sharper they might pursue them: albeit in this they were worthy of all correction, that they were so vehemently set to revenge: for if any discord or unkindness had happened amongst them, [it] was after never clean forgot, no not when they were dead, when the bairns yet alive not only were enemies to the parents, but, except they gave a manifest and an evident sign and token of peace and love, with a deadly feud, hatred and envy, they persecuted and pursued the whole stock and family pertaining to the same parents, both bairns and grandchildren, and so this deadly feud was never put in the book of oblivion.)

Their clothing was modest, functional and fetching:

Thair cleithing was til necessitie, and nocht til decore, maist conuenient ay to the weiris; for thay al vset mantilis of ane forme, baith the Nobilitie and the commone people, excepte that the Nobilitie delyted mair in coloured claith and sindrie hewis . . . Thir sarkis the mair potent amang thame vset to smeir with saffroune, bot vthiris wt a certane fatnes, and this thay did to keip thame cleine from al filthines . . . Bot the cleithing of the women with thame was maist decent. for thair cotes war syd evin to the hanckleth, wyd mantilis abone, or playdes all embroudiret artificiouslie; bracelets about thair armes, iewalis about thair neck, broches hinging at thair halse, baith cumlie and decent, and mekle to thair decore and outsett.

(Their clothing was for necessity, and not for decoration, most convenient always to the wars; for they all used mantles of one form, both the Nobility and the common people, except that the Nobility delighted more in coloured cloth and sundry hues . . . These shirts the more powerful among them used to smear with saffron, but others with a certain fat, and this they did to keep them clean from all filthiness . . . But the clothing of the women with them was most decent, for their coats were hung as far as the ankle, wide mantles above, or plaids all embroidered artificially; bracelets about their arms, jewels about their neck, brooches hanging at their throat, both comely and decent, and much to their adornment and outset.)

While the men were models of sturdy simplicity:

> *al thair kair was to excel in glore of weirfair and victorie, thair labour and*
> *hail studie baith in peace and weir was ay sett thairto, gyueng thame selfes, in*
> *a maner, haillie to that exercise.*
>
> *Na men war les diligate than they, les leicherous, and mair abhored*
> *voluptuous plesour. of quhilk by al that we haue said, this may be ane evident*
> *takne, that thair heid, zoung nor ald, thay neuir couered in the nycht. oft*
> *quhen thay restit, thair heid thay laid vpon the bair erth, or at leist vpon a*
> *greine turfe, or sum of the greiner bent or raschis, or than a grosse seck spred*
> *vndir thame.*

(all their care was to excel in glory of warfare and victory, their labour
and whole study both in peace and war was always set thereto, giving
themselves, in a manner, wholly to that exercise.

No men were less delicate than they, less lecherous, and more
abhorred voluptuous pleasure, of which besides all that we have
said, this may be an evident token, that their head, young nor old,
they never covered in the night. Oft when they rested, their head
they laid upon the bare earth, or at least upon a green turf, or some
of the greener bent [grass] or rushes, or then a coarse sack spread
under them.)

Leslie, who, as bishop of Ross, may have had considerable acquaintance with
Highlanders, joins Boece in praising their conservatism.

> *Behaulde now the maneris, wt quhilkes the Scottis of ald war induet, bot*
> *quhy say I of ald? quhen thay, quha this day wt vs speik the ald scottis toung,*
> *planelie haue the selfe sam maneris. for quha this day ar, haue hithirto keipet*
> *the institutiounis of thair elderis sa constantlie, that nocht onlie mair than 2*
> *thowsand zeirs thay haue keipet the toung hail vncorrupte; bot lykwyse the*
> *maner of cleithing and leiueng, that ald forme thay vnchanget aluterlie haue*
> *keipet.*

(Behold now the manners, with which the Scots of old were endowed,
but why say I of old? when they, who this day with us speak the old Scots
tongue, plainly have the selfsame manners; for who this day are, have
hitherto kept the institutions of their elders so constantly, that not only
more than 2 thousand years they have kept the tongue wholly un-
corrupt; but likewise the manner of clothing and living, that old form
they unchanged all utterly have kept.)

Leslie refuses to regard the Highlanders as somehow a race apart. They are
not wild and barbarous and foreign. Instead they are the very embodiments,

the repositories, of ancient Scottish virtues – not least because they have proved more constant to the Catholic faith.

> *For quhen thay reid the ald Scottis. quhais futstepis thay zit follow in the hilandes of Scotland, was not elegant and ornat in their cleithing, nor honest in thair maneris; quha, quhen as thay write sik wordes, thay accuse the hail scottis men, not considering that gif ane thing was not praisworthie in thame, or in ane sorte; many things by that thay haue worthie of singular prais.*

(For when they read [that] the old Scots, whose footsteps they yet follow in the Highlands of Scotland, were not elegant and ornate in their clothing, nor honest in their manners; when they write such words, they accuse the whole Scottish people, not considering that if one thing was not praiseworthy in them, or in one sort; many things besides that they have worthy of singular praise.)

George Buchanan, whose *History of Scotland* was published in 1582, quoted Dean Monro in full on the Hebrides but wrote a few paragraphs by way of introduction. These contain observations similar to those of Boece and Leslie:

> *In their food, clothing, and in the whole of their domestic economy, they adhere to ancient parsimony. Hunting and fishing, supply them with food. They boil the flesh with water poured into the paunch or the skin of the animal they kill, and in hunting sometimes they eat the flesh raw, merely squeezing out the blood. They drink the juice of the boiled flesh. At their feasts they sometimes use whey, after it has been kept for several years, and even drink it greedily; that species of liquor they call bland, but the greater part quench their thirst with water. They make a kind of bread, not unpleasant to the taste, of oats and barley, the only grain cultivated in these regions, and, from long practice, they have attained considerable skill in moulding the cakes. Of this they eat a little in the morning, and then contentedly go out a hunting, or engage in some other occupation, frequently remaining without any other food till the evening.*
>
> *They delight in variegated garments, especially striped, and their favourite colours are purple and blue. Their ancestors wore plaids of many different colours, and numbers still retain this custom, but the majority, now, in their dress, prefer a dark brown, imitating nearly the leaves of the heather, that when lying upon the heath in the day, they may not be discovered by the appearance of their clothes; in these, wrapped rather than covered, they brave the severest storms in the open air, and sometimes lay themselves down to sleep even in the midst of snow.*
>
> *In their houses, also, they lie upon the ground; strewing fern, or heath, on the floor, with the roots downward and the leaves turned up. In this manner they form a bed so pleasant, that it may vie in softness with the finest down,*

while in salubrity it far exceeds it; for heath, naturally possessing the power of absorption, drinks up the superfluous moisture, and restores strength to the fatigued nerves, so that those who lie down languid and weary in the evening, arise in the morning vigorous and sprightly. They have all, not only the greatest contempt for pillows, or blankets, but, in general, an affectation of uncultivated roughness and hardihood, so that when choice, or necessity, induces them to travel in other countries, they throw aside the pillows, and blankets of their hosts, and wrapping themselves round with their own plaids, thus go to sleep, afraid lest these barbarian luxuries, as they term them, should contaminate their native simple hardiness. (G. Buchanan, *Rerum Scoticarum Historia*, 1582, translated by J. Aikman)

Here again we meet the themes of simplicity, hardiness and manliness. For a contemporary French perspective we can turn to Nicolas de Nicolay:

Those who inhabit Scotland to the south of the Grampian chain, are tolerably civilized and obedient to the laws, and speak the English language; but those who inhabit the north are more rude, homely, and unruly, and for this reason are called savages (or wild Scots). They wear, like the Irish, a large and full shirt, coloured with saffron, and over this a garment hanging to the knee, of thick wool, after the manner of a cassock. They go with bare heads, and allow their hair to grow very long, and they wear neither stockings nor shoes, except some who have buskins [boots] made in a very old fashion, which come as high as their knees.

Their arms are the bow and arrow, and some darts [light javelins], which they throw with great dexterity, and a large sword, with a single-edged dagger. They are very swift of foot, and there is no horse so swift as to outstrip them, as I have seen proved several times, both in England and Scotland. (Nicolay d'Arfeville, 'Navigation of King James V of Scotland' in *Transactions of Iona Club*, 1834)

What we see in the Scottish historians of the sixteenth century is the age-old conflict between asceticism and luxury, want and plenty. It is an issue laden with moral dilemmas, as old as man, and the preoccupation of the world's principal religions. The arguments still run. As recently as the 1960s and 1970s the ideal for the youth of the richest and most technologically advanced nations on earth was to reject material wealth, to pad around barefeet in faded jeans, to use flowers as adornment and symbol, to affect languidity and leisure. The materialistic, fashion-conscious youth of today have come a long way from this but asceticism will surely resurface. Men and women will ever fluctuate between the age-old dichotomies; between surfeit and sufficiency, sloth and industry, lust and celibacy, indulgence and abstention. In all human societies want and plenty have coexisted; the tensions between them give us our shifting moral frameworks.

But, whatever Boece's rose-tinted view of the Highlanders, did their ideals match his? His much-vaunted economy may, from their point of view, have been a child of necessity rather than choice. The issue is too large for this book and must be answered from within Gaelic culture but we can indicate arguments for and against.

On the one hand there was a powerful monastic tradition of asceticism. During the so-called Dark Ages there is plenty of evidence for the strength of eremitic monasticism on the west coast and neighbouring mainland. The Irish missionary saints are associated with vigour, hardiness and simplicity, with enduring trial and hardship for the sake of the faith. On the other hand there is plenty of mediaeval evidence from the Highlands and Islands that the churchmen of the west shared the vices of mediaeval churchmen everywhere. Papal documents are full of accusations of simony, lust, avarice and squandering monastic resources. Since most of the evidence reflects the extremes of asceticism or indulgence it is difficult to know at what point between them the truth usually lay.

It is the same with the secular world. On the one hand the Gaelic poetic tradition was unashamedly aristocratic in flavour – for both audience and patron. Here we find unbridled praise of food and drink, feasting and luxury. Wine, cards, music, plenty, – these are stock items in Gaelic praise-poems; not perhaps what Boece himself would have favoured. On the other it may be that the use of such language suggests that the norm was precisely the opposite, that most Highlanders lived lives of stark poverty and simplicity, and were fascinated by a literature of unashamed luxury. The evidence from Martin Martin and later commentators reinforces the view of a marginal economy whose occupants always lived on the edge of starvation. Moreover there are hints that Boece had fellow-minded conservatives within the Gaelic world. In the famous *brosnachadh* or incitement to battle written for the Earl of Argyll just before the battle of Flodden in 1513 the last verse runs:

Attack the Saxons in their land,
awake! MacCailein, understand,
O golden-haired one, that a fighter
profits much by sleeping lighter.
> (D. Thomson, *An Introduction to Gaelic Poetry*, London, 1977)

The military aspect of Highland society, the need for watchfulness, did not sit well with feasting and cheer. Sections in Monipennie's *Scots Chronicles* deal nicely with this issue and demonstrate why it concerned so many Scots. Sensual pleasures such as gluttony are reproved because from there it is but a short step to effeminacy and military weakness:

Donaldus quintus . . . began his reign . . . in the year of Christ 854 . . . a
vicious and odious king, his people made effeminate by his vices and sensuall

pleasures; his nobles admonished him to reform his evil life, he continued still
without reformation. (*Monipennie's Scots Chronicles*, p 69)

Such conduct could only presage unmitigated disaster, viz. defeat by the
English! Initially Donald had overcome the English, Britons and Picts at
Jedburgh but:

Donald, right insolent after this victorie, came to the water of Tweed with his
armie, and found two ships laden with wines and victuals, which were taken
and parted amongst his warriours. King Donald was given to such voracity
and lust of his wombe, (the whole camp using the same), and being full of
tavernes, brothels, and whores, followed dicing and carding, with contention,
killing one another.

The result, of course, was that the English: *'came suddenly on the Scots, and*
killed twenty thousand, being without armour, full of wine and sleep.'
In sum the English conquered much of Southern Scotland whilst Donald
was eventually imprisoned by his nobles and killed himself. This was the
quintessential cautionary tale for Scots!
The concerns of these sixteenth-century historians continued into the
seventeenth century where we find Taylor, the poet, echoing Boece's praise
of things Highland from the same moral base. He is discussing the moderation
and self-sufficiency of the Highland lairds whom he met during his visit of
1618:

In Scotland, beyond Edenborough, I have beene at houses like castles for
building; the master of the house his beaver being his blue bonnet, one that will
weare no other shirts but of the flaxe that growes on his owne ground, and of
his wives, daughters, or servants spinning; that hath his stockings, hose, and
jerkin of the wooll of his owne sheepes backes; that never (by his pride of
apparell) caused mercer, draper, silkeman, embroyderer, or haberdasher to
breake and turne bankerupt: and yet this plaine home-spunne fellow keepes
and maintaines thirty, forty, fifty servants, or perhaps more, every day
releeving three or foure score poore peeple at his gate: and besides all this, can
give noble entertainement for foure or five dayes together, to five or sixe Earles
and Lords, besides Knights, Gentlemen, and their followers, if they bee three
or foure hundred men and horse of them; where they shall not onely feede but
feast, and not feast but banket. This is a man that desires to know nothing so
much, as his duty to God and his King, whose greatest cares are to practise
the workes of piety, charity, and hospitality: he never studies the consuming
art of fashionlesse fashions; he never tries his strength to beare foure or five
hundred acres on his backe at once, his legs are always at liberty, not being
fettered with golden garters, and manacled with artificial roses, whose weight
(sometime) is the reliques of some decayed lordship. Many of these worthy

housekeepers there are in Scotland, amongst some of them I was entertained;
from whence I did truely gather these aforesaid observations. (Taylor, *The*
Pennyles Pilgrimage)

Phrases in the above passage suggest Taylor may have had the Laird of Grant
in mind because earlier in the text he describes being entertained in this
chieftain's house.

There stayed there foure dayes, foure Earles, one Lord, divers knights and
gentlemen, and their servants, footmen and horses; and every meale foure
longe tables furnished with all varieties: Our first and second course being
threescore dishes at one boord; and after that alwayes a banquet: and there, if
I had not forsworne wine till I came to Edenborough, I thinke I had there
dranke my last.

Taylor paints a picture where the chief embodied the best of both worlds. He
could provide plenty, without ruining himself. In the long run this was to
prove unsustainable in a Highland context. Within the next three centuries
there would be plenty of examples of Highland chiefs running up huge debts
because they lived beyond their means. Many of them, or their successors,
then had to sell off lands that had been in their family's hands for centuries.
    This debate is timeless. In any society, at any time, there is the issue of what
to spend on the lily, what on the loaf of bread. Taylor touches on perennial
dilemmas, consumption against restraint, display against modesty, fashion
against utility. His metaphor was that a piece of clothing might require the
produce of hundreds of acres to sustain. It is the same today. A designer dress
or bauble might be worth a year's income to someone at the bottom of the
earnings ladder. What is telling is that Taylor was reporting on a climate of
opinion he must have met in Scotland. This attitude, this horror of display
had been there in Boece's day, it was there with early monasticism, it is always
there. But in a world of scarce resources it is also prompted by common sense.
Some families contributed to their own downfall by their inability to cut their
cloak according to their cloth.
    In 1628 William Lithgow plays the same tune:

And in a word, the seas of Scotland and the isles abound plentifully in all kinds of
fishes, the rivers are ingorged with salmon, the Highland mountains overclad
with fir trees, infinite deer, and all sorts of other bestial; the valleys full of pasture
and wild fowl, the low-laid plains inriched with beds of grain, justice all where
administered, laws obeyed, malefactors punished, oppressors curbed, the clergy
religious, the people sincere professors, and the country peaceable to all men.
    The chief commodities whereof, transported beyond sea, are these: wheat,
corns, hides, skins, tallow, yarn, linen, salt, coal, herrings, salmon, wool,
keilling [cod]*, ling, turbot, and seaths. And last, and worst, all the gold of the*

kingdom is daily transported away with superfluous posting for court, whence they never return any thing, save spend all, end all; then farewell fortune. So that numbers of our nobility and gentry now become, with idle projects, down-drawers of destruction upon their own necks, their children, and their estates; and posting postilions, by dissolute courses, to enrich strangers, leave themselves deservedly desolate of lands, means and honesty for ever: doing even with their former virtue, long continuance, and memory of their noble ancestors, as Mr Knox did with our glorious churches of abbacies and monasteries (which were the greatest beauty of the kingdom), knocking all down to desolation; leaving nought to be seen of admirable edifices, but like to the ruins of Troy, Tyre, and Thebes, lumps of walls, and heaps of stones.

So do our ignoble gallants, though nobly born, swallow up the honour of their famous predecessors, with posting foolery, boy-winding horns, gormandizing gluttony, lust, and vain apparel; making a transmigration of perpetuity to their present belly and back. (William Lithgow in Hume Brown, *Scotland before 1700*)

The fact that Lithgow uses exactly the same conceit as Taylor, the metaphor of wearing rents on your back, suggests they were not alone in their concerns. Beneath Lithgow's emphatic language and love of alliteration we can detect the familiar themes of a nobility living beyond its means and the bleeding of capital from rural areas.

This last was an important issue for the Highlands. As towns and industry grew so the Highland and Lowland economies fell out of kilter. In the Middle Ages it would be difficult to point to a drain of resources from Highlands to Lowlands. Highland nobles might journey to the city and waste their money at court but by the same token the king and other nobles would come to the Highlands for great hunting events. For the most part though Highland nobles raised and spent their rents locally. This had also been the case with the Scottish kings. Don Pedro de Ayala writes in 1498:

They do not remain long in one place. The reason thereof is twofold. In the first place, they move often about, in order to visit their kingdom, to administer justice . . . The second reason is, that they have rents in kind in every province, and they wish to consume them. While travelling neither the king nor any of his officers have any expenses, nor do they carry provisions with them. They go from house to house, to lords, bishops, and abbots, where they receive all that is necessary. The greatest favour the king can do to his subjects is to go to their houses. (Don Pedro de Ayala in Hume Brown, *Early Travellers in Scotland*)

This summarises the relationship between the nobility and their followers. Much rent, particularly in the Highlands and Islands, was paid in kind, and needed to be consumed on the spot. What Ayala said of the king could equally be said of any of the great nobles or chiefs: '*He is in want of nothing, judging from the manner in which he lives, but he is not able to put money into his strong boxes.*' (Don Pedro de Ayala in Hume Brown, *Early Travellers in Scotland*.)

Over the centuries the Highlands failed to develop any large-scale industries or centres of population to match the fleshpots of the south. There was also a trend for landowners to convert their rents from kind to cash. The latter was moveable and as a result wealth started to drain inexorably away. This process effectively worsened economic conditions in the Highlands and later commentators reflect this concern. Some of the most telling analyses come, not from historians, as in the sixteenth century, but from visitors who had an eye to the economic problems and prospects of the area. In 1786 John Knox came up the west coast on a survey for the British Fisheries Society. At the beginning of his report he gives a 'General description of the West Highlands and Hebride Isles'. He concludes:

> *Thus we find that the Highlands, besides supplying home demands, exports fish, black cattle, horses, sheep, timber, bark, lead, slate, and kelp; to which may be added sundry articles of less importance, as skins, feathers, oil.*
>
> *The aggregate amount of these exports is surely sufficient to procure the necessary articles of grain, and various utensils in iron, steel, timber, etc. wherewith to improve their lands, extend their fisheries, furnish themselves with decked vessels, and erect more comfortable dwellings.*
>
> *Such are the specific wealth and the specific wants of the Highlands. But as the value of its natural produce, by sea and land, is almost wholly absorbed by the great landholders, and by many of them spent at Edinburgh, London, Bath, and elsewhere; as the people are thus left more or less at the mercy of stewards and tacksmen, the natural resources of the country, instead of a benefit, become a serious misfortune to many improveable districts. Those who, by their education and their knowledge of the world might diffuse general industry, and raise a colony of subjects, useful to their king, to their country, and to themselves, are the very persons who glean these wilds of the last shilling, and who render the people utterly unqualified for making any effectual exertions in any case whatever.*

The curse of absentee landlords has long afflicted the Highlands. What Knox makes clear is that it is not just the owners who absent themselves, but the rents also. Robert Somers visited Arisaig in 1847, the year after the dreadful potato blight. His letters were published in book form in 1848. He found that most families were trapped in abject misery and he summarises what had become of the relationship between landlord and tenant by the mid-nineteenth century. This was the culmination of a process that had been developing for hundreds of years:

There is no work whatever going on upon the estate. Lord Cranstoun and his factor are both absentees. The one lifts the rent, and the other carries it off and consumes it; and this comprehends the whole of the relation between landlord and tenant in Arisaig . . .

The land rental of Arisaig is somewhere about £1,200 per annum. The population is 1,250. A pound per head is the relative proportion of rent and population in Skye, and some of the most destitute districts of the West Highlands. The population must necessarily be very poor on an estate where there is a human being for every pound which goes into the pocket of the landlord. Very probably Lord Cranstoun receives a larger share of the annual produce of Arisaig than the whole 1,250 souls put together. To make up his rent the people toil, and save, and stint themselves – living upon the scantiest and poorest fare, and scraping together every farthing they can lay their fingers upon, from one year's end to another. It must be obvious to the most superficial thinker, that a fund accumulated by so many hands, and at the expense of so many sacrifices, must be designed to discharge some very important functions, and that the prosperity of the district in which it is raised must depend very essentially upon the manner in which it is expended. A wise and reflecting landlord would feel an awful responsibility as that tribute was laid term after term upon his rent-table. He would see in it the laborious savings of the people, and in himself the banker to whose trust these savings were committed, to be laid out in a way by which they would both be made available for the relief and employment of the people, and be returned periodically with interest to his coffers. It is only by viewing rent in this light, and applying it accordingly, that the proprietor of such a place as Arisaig can discharge his duty, or the population be saved from distress. Rent, in such a community, forms the whole of that surplus produce, of which Malthus has observed, that it is 'the great source of national power and happiness.' There is no surplus produce in any other hands than the landlord's. The people consume all that remains of the annual produce above the landlord's rent, and would consume a great deal more if it could be obtained. Rent is therefore the only saving, the only capital, by which employment can be given in addition to what is already going on, and, consequently, by which the present population can either be relieved from their difficulties, or provision be made for the natural increase of their numbers . . . But Lord Cranstoun looked upon the matter in a different light. He regarded his Highland estate as simply entitling him to a wider round of pleasure; and in the fashionable saloons of London this English nobleman has squandered in a few hours of luxury, without a grudge, the hundreds which cost the poor people of Arisaig a year of toil and privation to collect. (R. Somers, *Letters from the Highlands*, 1848)

Both Knox and Somers demonstrate a real understanding of the Highland problem. It was an economy of scarce resources, not a society with a surplus to export. The removal of any surplus as rent was to bleed the economy dry. Such issues have troubled many later visitors to the Highlands, not least because of the moral dilemmas posed. For two centuries the focal points of debate were landlord power, clearance and emigration. Today there has been a shift of emphasis towards land reform but precious little evidence of any restoration of the Highland economy. Take away the various forms of subsidy, overt and concealed, and there is very little profit-generating economic activity along the west coast.

The irony is that nowhere did the problems of landlordism become more acute than the Highlands – despite the fact that Boece and others pointed to the Highlands as a model of restraint and conservatism. As the centuries unrolled so the economic imbalance between Highland and Lowland societies became ever more acute. The Highlands had no new sources of wealth. They lacked industry and commerce. They had no towns, no traders. Yet the Highland magnates aped their southern cousins and frittered away their Highland rents in southern fleshpots.

Besides, Boece, Leslie, Taylor and Lithgow had never really understood the importance of conspicuous consumption in the Highlands. Highland chiefs had a position to uphold and were very conscious of it. When they were not, their bards and seannachies reminded them. So, in later centuries we find Highland chiefs using up their tenants' rents in flamboyant display, none appearing more ridiculous than Alasdair Ranaldson Macdonell of Glengarry. Where his ancestors had engaged in great deer-hunts of the kind that Taylor described, so Glengarry mounted contests which included tearing a cow apart with bare hands. This larger-than-life figure endeared himself to Sir Walter Scott who is supposed to have modelled the character of Fergus Mac-Ivor upon him. The narrative may have been fine, but the practice was disastrous, as, ironically, Glengarry eventually learned.

Why do these historians matter?

Boece was immensely influential. His original work in Latin only spoke directly to a small cultured elite in Britain and Europe, but it was an elite which held the ears of all the most potent princes. In 1536 John Bellenden's translation into Scots was published and Boece could reach a wider audience within his own country. William Cecil, counsellor to Elizabeth I, had a copy of the Latin edition which now belongs to the National Library of Scotland. During the period of Cecil's ownership, this critically important volume was probably read by Laurence Nowell, an English antiquarian employed in Cecil's household. Nowell drew the first really accurate map of Scotland, almost certainly on the basis of a map sent by John Elder to Henry VIII.

In the margins of the same book is found the symbol of the pointing hand, a symbol associated with John Dee, the internationally renowned astrologer of

Elizabeth I. It has been claimed that John Dee may have been Mercator's unknown informant for his eight-sheet map of Britain published in 1564. Mercator's mapping of Scotland, like Laurence Nowell's, seems to owe much to Elder's work but is less accurate for the west coast lochs, Lochaber and Loch Linnhe. Certainly Mercator quotes Boece several times in his marginal notes and cartouches. Mercator's maps then took a longer lease on life in the copies made by his friend Ortelius for his great Atlas in 1573. Ortelius also quotes Boece.

Boece became immensely influential in Continental Europe due to the fact that his work was translated into French by Nicholas de Nicolay, Cosmographer to the French king. This was the same Nicholas de Nicolay who had a copy of Alexander Lindsay's Scottish rutter, along with a little chart of Scotland, both of which he published in 1583. The Nicolay who was succeeded as French Cosmographer Royal by André Thevet; the same Thevet who drew the first individual Scottish island maps for his projected 'Grand Insulaire'.

Through Boece therefore the world of the Highlands and Islands was brought home to the political and intellectual elites of Britain and France. The area now had a place in the literary and cartographic consciousness of Europe. It was at last on the map. Perhaps the best demonstration of this is just to compare Matthew Paris's map of Scotland with that of Nowell or Mercator. The Highlands and Islands are no longer a vacant space. (See Figures 2 & 5.)

Boece's view of the Highlanders must have permeated the literary and intellectual consciousness of Europe's educated elite. Whether it affected the vast majority of non-literate Scots is another matter. They were much more likely to be influenced by their everyday experiences, especially if they lived in an area which perennially suffered at the hands of the Highlander. Cattle-raids, theft, seizure of fishing-gear, these were the troubled interfaces between Highland and Lowland culture. Practical experience would lead Lowlanders to doubt Boece's contention that Highlanders were old virtue personified.

But historical argument crept into the public consciousness. This may have been particularly true in the Highlands where history and genealogy were culturally important. John Elder, who disliked bishops, offered an alternative Highland creation myth:

which too Yrische wordes, Albon, that is to say, Scotland, and Albonyghe, that is to say, Scottische men, be drywyne from Albanactus, our first gouernour and kynge. Which diriuacion . . . the papistical, curside spir-itualitie of Scotland, will not heir in no maner of wyse, nor confesse that euer such a kynge, namede Albanactus, reagnede ther. The which dirivacion, all the Yrische men of Scotland, which be the auncient stoke, can not, nor will not denye . . . But our said bussheps . . . drywith Scotland and theame selfes, from a certane lady, namede Scota, which (as they alledge) come out of

Egipte, a maraculous hot cuntreth, to recreatt hir self emonges theame in the cold ayre of Scotland, which they can not afferme be no probable auncient author. (John Elder, 1543–4, in *Collectanea de Rebus Albanicis*, p 27)

(which two Irish [Gaelic] words, Alba, that is to say, Scotland, and Albanaich, that is to say, Scottish men, be derived from Albanactus, our first governor and king. Which derivation . . . the papistical, cursed spirituality of Scotland, will not hear in no manner of wise, nor confess that ever such a king, named Albanactus, reigned there. The which derivation, all the Irish men of Scotland, which be the ancient stock, cannot, nor will not deny . . . But our said bishops . . . derive Scotland and themselves, from a certain lady, named Scota, which (as they allege) came out of Egypt, a miraculous hot country, to recreate herself amongst them in the cold air of Scotland, which they cannot affirm by no probable ancient author.)

Part of the reason why Highlanders felt superior to Lowlanders was their reading of history:

Lastly, they have an adherence one to another as Highlanders, in opposition to the people of the low country, whom they despise as inferior to them in courage, and believe they have a right to plunder them whenever it is in their power. This last arises from a tradition, that the Lowlands, in old times were the possession of their ancestors. (Edmund Burt, *Letters from a Gentleman in the North of Scotland*, late 1720s)

The moral issues raised by these early historians surface and resurface through the centuries. They are still relevant today. Politicians, clergymen and journalists cast about for historical data to support their arguments. Historians still give moral lectures and read lessons from the past. People are still troubled by the tensions between want and plenty, poverty and luxury. For most of the world resources remain scarce.

These two opposites, fasting and feasting, scarcity and surfeit, run through Highland culture like every other. We see the legacy of asceticism in the starkness and simplicity of Presbyterian churches and the uncompromising Christianity of some of the Western Isles. The unadorned stone walls, the simple unfurnished interiors, have no room for the luxuries they associate with Rome. The harsh ascetic forms of Christianity still have their appeal. St Columba is still regarded as a heroic saint.

These are not tensions that can be fully resolved, ever. What is important from our point of view is that the Highlands were perceived, by Hector Boece, an immensely influential Lowland historian, to embody the ancient virtues of hardiness and asceticism. Whether they were as he saw them is quite a different matter, as is the issue of whether or not they thought of themselves in this way. Here I merely wish to air his perception, the reality is more difficult to know.

We can ask ourselves if Boece was right. Was the Highlander happy with being a noble savage? Was he content with frugality and parsimony? Were his virtues decided by need or knowledge? Yes, the Highland economy might have been self-sustaining for longer if rents had not been exported, if chiefs had stayed resident. But cultures do not remain isolated. They collide with each other, their belief systems are constantly under assault, their economic structures continually challenged. The tectonic plates of human societies behave as they do in the natural world. If and when Highlanders were presented with the choice, frugality or plenty, which would they opt for, then or now?

The answer *now* is given by every generation of children leaving Highland schools and gravitating to the city for the bright lights and lucrative jobs. Only a tiny fraction choose austerity. The answer *then* is partly given by a nice anecdote in Martin Martin's *Description of the Western Islands* in which he describes the reaction of a St Kildan who was taken to Glasgow:

Upon his arrival at Glasgow, he was like one that had dropped from the clouds into a new world, whose language, habit, etc, were in all respects new to him; he never imagined that such big houses of stone were made with hands; and for the pavements of the streets, he thought it must needs be altogether natural, for he could not believe that men would be at the pains to beat stones into the ground to walk upon. He stood dumb at the door of his lodging with the greatest admiration; and when he saw a coach and two horses, he thought it to be a little house they were drawing at their tail, with men in it; but he condemned the coachman for a fool to sit so uneasy, for he thought it safer to sit on the horse's back. The mechanism of the coach wheel, and its running about, was the greatest of all his wonders . . .

When they carried him into the church, he was yet more surprised, and held up his hands with admiration, wondering how it was possible for men to build such a prodigious fabric, which he supposed to be the largest in the universe. He could not imagine what the pews were designed for, and he fancied the people that wore masks (not knowing whether they were men or women) had been guilty of some ill thing, for which they dared not show their faces. He was amazed at women wearing patches, and fancied them to have been blisters. Pendants seemed to him the most ridiculous of all things; he condemned periwigs mightily, and much more the powder used in them; in fine, he condemned all things as superfluous he saw not in his own country. He looked with amazement on every thing that was new to him . . . He was amazed to think how they could be provided with ale, for he never saw any there that drank water . . . He thought it foolish in women to wear thin silks, as being a very improper habit for such as pretended to any sort of employment. When he saw the women's feet, he judged them to be of another

shape than those of the men, because of the different shape of their shoes. He
did not approve of the heels of shoes worn by men or women.

Martin Martin's account reads strangely like an allegory. It is as if he had
deliberately placed one of Boece's noble Highland savages, full of hardy
simplicity, in the setting most calculated to upset his moral equilibrium.
Martin's final sentence gives the lie to Boece's crusade. Apparently the St
Kildan: '*longed to see his native country again, and passionately wished it were*
blessed with ale, brandy, tobacco and iron, as Glasgow was.'

This almost amounts to a confession. With the exception of iron, Boece
would not have favoured those items chosen by the St Kildan. Like the St
Kildan 'he condemned all things as superfluous he saw not in his own
country'. Unlike the St Kildan, Boece would not let himself be suborned
by foreign luxury. Travel had taken the St Kildan to Glasgow. There he had
eaten of the fruit of the Tree of Knowledge and it would eventually destroy his
Eden. Boece was a lone voice. Few societies successfully remain spartan.

Despite the story of the St Kildan, Martin Martin also endorsed the myth of
the simple, hardy Highlander:

Their simple diet contributes much to their state of health, and long life . . .
They are to this day happily ignorant of many vices that are practised in the
learned and polite world. I could mention several, for which they have not as
yet got a name, or so much as a notion of them.

The diet generally used by the natives consists of fresh food, for they seldom
taste any that is salted, except butter. The generality eat but little flesh, and
only persons of distinction eat it every day and make three meals, for all the
rest eat only two, and they eat more boiled than roasted. Their ordinary diet
is butter, cheese, milk, potatoes, colworts, brochan, i.e., oatmeal and water
boiled. The latter taken with some bread is the constant food of several
thousands of both sexes in this and other isles, during the winter and spring;
yet they undergo many fatigues both by sea and land, and are very
healthful . . .

There is no place so well stored with such great quantity of good beef and
mutton, where so little of both is consumed by eating. They generally use no
fine sauces to entice a false appetite, nor brandy or tea for digestion; the purest
water serves them in such cases. This, together with their ordinary exercise,
and the free air, preserves their bodies and minds in a regular frame, free from
the various convulsions that ordinarily attend luxury. There is not one of
them too corpulent, nor too meagre . . .

The people of these isles . . . are very temperate, and their diet is simple
and moderate in quantity and quality, so that their brains are not in all
probability disordered by undigested fumes of meat or drink. (Martin
Martin, *A Description of the Western Islands of Scotland*, c. 1695)

For all that, it is difficult to reconcile Martin Martin's picture with the numerous eighteenth-century accounts of poverty and degradation. However, later visitors also give plenty of examples of Highland hardiness:

> *I have seen in their Huts, when I have been walking, and forced to retreat thither for shelter from the Rain, their Children, sometimes many in a Hut, full of the Small-Pox, and at their Heighth, they having been lying, and walking about in the Wet and Dirt, the Rain at the same time beating through the Thatch with Violence; so that I used to get from one End of the House to the other to keep dry; but it was all in vain, the Rain soon following me. These Children at the same time seemed hearty, drinking Whey and Butter-Milk; Wet and Cold, with the Inclemency of the Weather, and yet do well! (A journey through Part of England and Scotland, 1746)*

The same author paints a delightful picture of local children collecting fruit on the way to Fort Augustus:

> *We are surpriz'd by a Parcel of almost naked Boys and Girls, coming upon sight [of] us, down some craggy Rocks of a Mountain to sell us Whortle Berries, or the Vaccinia Nigra of Virgil, which they gather in almost every Part of these Mountains in prodigious Quantities. They sold to every one of us near a Mutchkin-full for a Baubee, and they chiefly live on the Fruit, when they are gathering them on the Mountains: By Means of the great Stain they give, their Mouths and Hands are dy'd in a frightful Manner. These are mighty agreeable Fruit to the Taste. (A journey through Part of England and Scotland, 1746)*

Burt often comments on the resilience of Highland travellers. He also reflects that this hardiness or stoicism was partly due to necessity. In a land of meagre resources there was no help but to be long-suffering. Luxury ate away at this – and he could see its effect on Highland soldiers: '*On the other hand, it is observed that the private men of the independent Highland companies are become less hardy than others, from their great pay (as it is to them), the best lodging the country affords, and warm clothing.*' (Edmund Burt, *Letters from a Gentleman in the North of Scotland*, late 1720s.)

Many Highlanders must have been aware of how they were viewed by Lowlanders. They were sometimes guilty of political spin on their own behalf. Burt makes it clear that the Highlanders were both aware of and deliberately contributed to their own reputation for hardiness. This was simply a form of psychological warfare but could not be expected to convince a man like Burt who had a deal of good sense and long association with the army. He refers to these ploys as 'Gasconades' by analogy with similar boasts of the Gascons:

> *One of these Gasconades is, that the Laird of Keppoch, chieftain of a branch of the McDonalds, in a winter campaign against a neighbouring laird, with*

whom he was at war about a possession, gave orders for rolling a snowball to lay under his head in the night; whereupon his followers murmured, saying, 'Now we despair of victory, since our leader is become so effeminate he can't sleep without a pillow'. (Edmund Burt, *Letters from a Gentleman in the North of Scotland*, late 1720s)

An eighteenth-century account of Rum gives us another example of the contrast between ancient thrift and modern indulgence:

As for Corn, there is no more of it raised, than what serves the People for Bread a few Months in Winter. During all the Summer, they live entirely upon animal Food, and yet are healthy and long lived. The year before I was there, a man had died in the Island aged 103, who was 50 years of Age before he had ever tasted Bread; and during all the Remainder of his long Life, had never eat of it from March to October, nor any other Food, during that part of the year, but Fish and Milk; which is still the Case with all the Inhabitants of the Island. I was even told, that this old man used frequently to remind the younger People, of the simple and hardy Fare of former Times, used to upbraid them with their Indulgence in the Article of Bread, and judged it unmanly in them to toil like Slaves with their Spades, for the Production of such an unnecessary Piece of Luxury. (John Walker, *Report on the Hebrides*, 1764)

The old man seems to contradict himself in upbraiding the young for working so hard at self-indulgence, but we catch his drift. Eigg, another small island community, provides further evidence that the famous Highland hardiness was the product of necessity rather than choice.

In former times . . . the people of Eigg, taught by their necessities, were bold cragsmen. But men do not peril life and limb for the mere sake of a meal, save when they cannot help it; and the introduction of the potatoe has done much to put out the practice of climbing for the bird, except among a few young lads, who find excitement enough in the work to pursue it for its own sake, as an amusement. (Hugh Miller, *The Cruise of the Betsey* (Written in 1845))

But equally there were always those who looked over their shoulder at the old frugality. In 1784 Faujas de St Fond commented on the 'commodious' house which Maclean of Torloisk (Mull) had built himself 'in the modern style':

On my asking, why he suffered to remain standing upon the place a kind of large cottage built of dry stones, covered with thatch, or rather heath, and lighted by two narrow windows, which scarcely allowed the daylight to enter.

'It was there,' Mr Maclean answered me with emotion, 'that I was born. That is the ancient habitation of my fathers; and I feel inexpressible regard for this modest site, which reminds me of their virtues and frugal life.' (Faujas de Saint Fond, *A journey through England and Scotland to the Hebrides* in 1784)

What preserved the Highlands in the past was isolation, distance and rumour. Travel has been one of the engines for removing these barriers, opening up choice, threatening the Highland way of life. Freedom to choose has drained the Highland economy; only a small number of people opt for a poorer standard of living, or simply opt out. We may decide that the Highlands offer a richer style of life, a better environment for our families, or for retirement, but our children will probably decide to escape again.

Effeminacy and degeneracy

Beside the issue of surfeit lies the more morally perplexing one of effeminacy. In moral terms luxury is less troubling. Most of us still fulminate against luxurious display. The media trumpet our disgust at 'fat-cat' pay-offs, delight in the despoliation of some petty dictator's pleasure-palace. Yet, at the very same time, every lifestyle magazine and television programme lays before us, in elaborate detail, the designer home we must aspire to. However, despite such blandishments, simplicity and modesty still occupy the moral high ground. We may envy, we may emulate, but our moral attitudes remain largely intact.

The other issue raised by Boece and the early historians is more difficult. Here are Thomas Morer's remarks on how the Lowland Scots have fallen away from their ancient virtues:

We take the Lowlanders to be a Medley of Picts, Scots, French, Saxons, and English, as their language and habit insinuate, which is the reason why the Highlanders, who look on themselves to be a purer race, cannot affect 'em; but on the contrary deal with 'em as a spurious degenerate people. And indeed the Lowlanders abate much of that true courage anciently and deservedly given their forefathers. Whether it be that they degenerate in their kind, or become soft and effeminate by their daily converse with politer nations, we know not; but certain it is, they fall short of their ancestors' spirit (whether Picts or Scots), and in case of a breach, the Highlanders think it advantage enough if they have only these men to fight with. (Thomas Morer, 1689, in Hume Brown, *Early Travellers in Scotland*)

Key words like 'effeminate' and 'degenerate' may not have had the loaded content for Morer that they have today but such conservatism lurches dangerously to the right. An appeal to things 'ancient' and 'pure' can soon be hijacked by those who wish to promote some form of eugenics. An appeal for temperance is morally neutral, not so a crusade against effeminacy and degeneracy. On this basis Boece and Morer would have looked in horror at London and the other great cultural and racial melting-pots. Yet the truth is that they are among the most economically dynamic societies on earth.

The language used by Boece and Morer has been used by many others since. Many Highlanders must have adopted this notion of racial purity: '*The Highlanders are exceedingly proud to be thought an unmixed people, and are apt to upbraid the English with being a composition of all nations.*' (Edmund Burt, *Letters from a Gentleman in the North of Scotland*, late 1720s.)

At the end of his description of the Hebrides, Thomas Pennant uses the figure of a ghost to paint a picture of a benign Highland patriarchy:

> *The ancient Native, full of the idea of the manly look of the warriors and friends of his youth, is lost in admiration at the degenerate progeny: feature and habit are changed; the one effeminated, the other become ridiculous by adopting the idle fashions of foreign climes: lost to the love of their country, lost to all the sweet affections of patriarchal life!* (T. Pennant, *A Tour in Scotland and Voyage to the Hebrides*, 1772)

In the same way the theme of the hardiness of the northerner, as opposed to the weakness of the southron, has never really died. A few years later the Rev. John Lane Buchanan writes of the exploits of two Hebridean soldiers in India: '*Two great chiefs from the Hyperborean Islands of the Hebrides, making war on the shores of India, present a picture of the present extended intercourse among nations, and of the natural sway that hardy have over effeminate climates.*' (Buchanan, *Travels in the Western Hebrides from 1782 to 1790*). Another contemporary minister writes:

> *The time may perhaps not be far distant, when, enervated by luxury, and sunk in effeminacy, the more refined inhabitants of the South will yield to the hardier sons of the North, the seat of empire and the emporium of trade, for which their natural resources, their personal strength and vigour of mind, and perhaps local advantages, so much qualify them.* (Rev Alexander Downie, Minister, Parish of Lochalsh, *Old Statistical Account*, 1791–99)

The issues that concerned Boece and his fellow historians recur through all the time and space of human history. They are with us still. All those who go back to the country – to live a simpler life, to return to their roots, to find themselves, to reconnect; from eighth-century monasticism to twenty-first century escapism; all are grappling with the dilemmas posed by Boece. The irony is that now it is surplus that allows more of us to afford and affect simplicity. A fortune made in a city permits us to play at farming, watch wildlife, weave, spin, paint, draw, pot, sculpt or do any one of the myriad back-to-the-wild, back-to-our-roots ideas we may have nurtured since we left the Garden of our childhood. We can indulge our mental and emotional wants on the basis of physical plenty.

Historians as myth-makers

We should recognise the importance of historians, then and now, as myth-makers. The sixteenth-century historians like Boece projected concepts of purity, asceticism and manliness onto the Highlanders. But these virtues were foisted upon them by outsiders, only some of whom knew much about the area. It is a welcome relief to turn from the prejudice and spin of some of these sixteenth-century polemicists to the straightforwardness and honesty of natives like Monro and Martin, of visitors like Pennant and Johnson.

Many historians share, with rural communities, an innate conservatism. They are deeply imbued with an affection for, and, as they think, a knowledge of, the past. An all-too-common theme amongst them is a sense of loss, of loss through change. Seldom is this loss expressed for some primitive back-breaking technology. Few of us would choose to wash in an icy well on a December morning rather than wallow in warm water. The loss is usually focused on some simpler, less frenetic, lifestyle; where the bonds of community and family felt stronger; where cooperation was valued above competition; where neighbours helped each other. Indeed they may well paint an idyll that never existed or project their own myths upon the past. The next step is to use their history as a vehicle for their hopes and aspirations, their political objectives.

This sense of loss emanates from the writings of early historians like Boece and Leslie. They projected the Highland male as an ideal warrior – the Highland female remains largely unnoticed. In a way we live with that myth still. The Highlanders don't, they have not been able to. For a very long time now they have been buying into the Lowland dream. The economy of Lowland Britain has, since at least early mediaeval times, been stronger, more vibrant, more aggressive, more attractive. Lowland communities have grown and prospered, towns and cities have flourished, trade has expanded. The demand for resources and people have sucked in raw materials and economic migrants from the surrounding areas. This process has been going on for centuries but we really only see it at work in the West Highlands and Hebrides since Culloden. Highlanders have bought into the economic model of Lowland Britain. Some have been driven by ambition, greed or fear; most out of hope or aspiration for their children. But they have been steadily deserting the Highland economy for the Lowland for the last three hundred years. All that is left of the former is a rump of crofting, fishing, forestry, whisky, and tourism.

The relationship is symbiotic. Some from Lowland Britain have bought into a Highland dream. People move here for aesthetic reasons, a simpler life-style, security, the social cohesion of small communities. They stay for a few, in a few cases many, years. Unfortunately, this is a one-generation purchase; their children do not stay to continue a community any more than local children do. They drift away to the wider world of opportunity. Meanwhile some locals return to spend their declining years but essentially a self-sustaining Highland society no longer exists. There is a shadow, buoyed by government employment, subsidy, the rich or the wildlife organisations. In each generation these complementary centrifugal and centripetal tendencies are at work. Some are thrown out, by chance, or choice, or circumstance, to the periphery, but the force of economic gravity is always stronger and so people are drawn inexorably towards the centre.

Today's visitors, journalists, politicians and opinion-formers mould the economy and society of the Highlands in a way that Boece never could. He made a mythical figure of the Highlander but the Highlander remained intact. Today, many important decisions about the future of the Highlands and Islands are made outwith the area. Policies about fishing and the environment, about wildlife and exploitation, are made by a mix of eurocrats, national governments, quangoes and wildlife organisations. Often these are in accordance with the sensibilities of a largely urban population who have little knowledge of the Highlands and Islands, who bear it no ill-will, and have some vague notion of wanting to preserve it.

This sort of preservation usually involves the death of the subject. The area shares characteristics with other remote communities in Northern Scandinavia, Iceland, Greenland and Northern Canada. Modern urban sensitivities restrict opportunities for locals to harvest their natural resources. Most people do not mind the slaughter of cows, sheep, poultry, pigs or fish, but object strongly if it be whales, seals or wild birds. Visitors play their part in this. Outside influence over economic development in the Highlands threatens the sustainability of local communities. Objections to new roads may be overruled, but objections to quarries and windfarms are proving more effective.

A distorted view of the past contributes to this. Most visitors probably know little about the Highlands and Islands beyond Culloden and the Clearances. John Prebble did a wonderful job opening up these events to a wider public but unfortunately most literature stops there. If people knew for how many centuries the island communities depended upon harvesting their natural resources of seals, whales, fish, geese and seabirds would they adopt the same attitudes to protecting these species regardless of their numbers? We cannot hold historians solely responsible for the current obsession with the Jacobites and the Clearances. But land reform is not the only economic issue in the area and outside disapproval of Highland economic development needs to be recognised. Nimbyism in the Highlands is often not-in-the-back-yard of my favoured holiday destination or retirement home. There is a danger that deliberately or accidentally we will lock the Highlands into a past that is actually a projection of the present. This is implicit in every tourist brochure, every visitor and heritage centre, every objection to economic initiative on the grounds that it will destroy a piece of the area's history or threaten its environment.

The conservationist agenda is a potential death-knell. Wilderness Scotland is, by definition, promoted for the sake of wildlife not people. If it was peopled it would not be a wilderness. Yet this is a travesty of history. The Highlands have always been a peopled landscape. The fact that many glens are now empty, the fact that former habitation sites are now so overgrown or forested that we no longer recognise them, does not make this any less true. The Highlands were not desolate, they were populated, and to project this image of wilderness is a distortion of the past and another reason why history matters. Britain, or Brussels, may decide to turn the Highlands and Islands into a playground for the urban leisured class, but let it do so in the light of informed public opinion.

Chapter 3

Political, military, diplomatic

T he last chapter gave a general overview of the 'reputation' of the Highlands and Islands, who set it, how, when, and why it mattered. This chapter deals more specifically with the information provided by travellers who were sent to the area for political, military or diplomatic purposes. In order to place these in context it is necessary to sketch the overall political background.

Before the tourist industry got underway in the latter part of the eighteenth century there were only a very few reasons why people travelled to the Highlands and Hebrides. The first of these was political. For much of its history the area was politically attached to larger and more powerful entities centred elsewhere. Relations had to be maintained with these neighbours, alliances fostered, aggressions resisted.

We know nothing about the political complexion of the Highlands and Islands in prehistoric times. Our first hard information comes from the Irish annals. The Irish Scots migrated across the North Channel into Argyll and the southern Hebrides before AD 500. They seem to have dominated the west coast south of Ardnamurchan by the time the Vikings arrived c AD 800. The situation in the Northern Hebrides and opposite mainland is less certain since we do not know if the Scots had achieved control here prior to the arrival of the Norse. Certainly a Pictish dynasty seems to have flourished in Skye in the seventh century and may also have controlled the west coast from Glenelg northwards. During the chaotic period of the Norse invasions we only have the vaguest information but, although political control may have been fragmented to begin with, the earldom of Orkney seems to have dominated by the end of the tenth century.

This changing political relationship with outside powers did involve some travel to and from the Hebrides. According to the Annals of Ulster, King Aidan made an expedition from South Argyll to the Orkneys in 580 or 581. The Pictish kings of Skye travelled to Ireland in 668, probably looking for political and military assistance. In 733 a Dalriadic fleet under Flaithbertach sailed to Ireland where many of them were slaughtered. Countless Viking ships sailed through the Minches in the ninth and tenth centuries. The earls of Orkney relied on local henchmen such as Earl Gilli of Coll who travelled to Orkney to marry Earl Sigurd's sister at the end of the tenth century.

One of our earliest catalogues of Hebridean islands comes in a poem by Bjorn Cripplehand who was celebrating Magnus Bareleg's violent descent in

1098. Bjorn is keen to show the extent of Magnus's overlordship and takes us on a blood-soaked trip south through the Hebrides, listing the subjugated islands as he goes:

> The fire over Lewis
> Played high in the heaven;
> Far fled the folk;
> The flame rose from the houses.
> The prince went through Uist
> With fire; and the bonders lost
> Wealth and life; the king
> Dyed his sword red in blood.
> He sated the eagles' hunger
> And harried far about Skye.
> The glad wolf battened his teeth
> In blood, on Tiree.
> The maidens south in the isles
> Got sorrow from the lord of Grenland.
> The foe of the Scots harried,
> The folk in Mull fled.
> To the level Sanda the sharp
> King brought the shield of war.
> There was smoke over Islay, where the men
> Of Magnus increased the burning.
> South of Kintyre the folk
> Sank down beneath the swords;
> The wise lord of victory
> Then felled the dwellers of Man.
> (Monsen, Heimskringla)

The poem is not literal. The image of wolves feeding on the corpses of a battlefield would no doubt go down well with Bjorn's audience. Wolves there certainly were in Scotland, but it is most unlikely there were any on Tiree.

From about 1079 a kingdom of the Isles had been created which although centred on the Isle of Man was really a collection of little island fiefdoms. Central control was always difficult to exercise over a widely-scattered archipelago like the Hebrides. On several occasions the Chronicles of Man refer to the approval, or not, of the *principes insularum* [the island chiefs] which suggests a certain practical federalism. The military expedition of Magnus Bareleg in 1098 reasserted Norwegian overlordship. This continued, at least nominally, until 1266, although the kingdom of the Isles was split internally by Somerled's usurpation of Argyll and the southern Hebrides in the mid-twelfth century.

The nominally independent kingdom of Man and the Isles had to maintain good relations with its more powerful neighbours. We have correspondence which indicates embassies to and from England and Norway. Such visits might even include a military contingent. In Heimskringla there is a reference to King Godfrey of the Hebrides being present, with 1500 men, in a battle between King Ingi and Hakon in 1161. From the late twelfth century the Kingdom of Man and the Isles came under increasing pressure from the expanding power of Scotland. This was felt in Bute before the end of the twelfth century and Argyll suffered one, possibly two, Scottish invasions in the 1220s. Kings Alexander II and III wanted to reabsorb the Hebrides. Hakon of Norway did not want to lose them. The Hebrideans were caught in the middle.

Alexander II brought a military expedition west in 1249 but died in Kerrera before he could force the issue. However, a political showdown was only deferred. Between the 1220s and about 1266 there seems to have been a great deal of coming and going between the Hebrides and Norway. The Hebrideans sent their petitions and grievances east, while Norway sent decisions and expeditions west.

From Eirspennill's Hakon Hakon's son's Saga for the year 1224: '*After that, king* [Hakon] *went to Bergen. Then Gillecrist, and Ottar, Snaekoll's son, and many Hebrideans, came to meet him there, from west beyond the sea: and they had many letters concerning the needs of their lands.*' (Anderson, *Early Sources*, II, p 455.) And 1226: '*Thorstein said also that many men had come from west beyond the sea to meet the king. And when king Hakon came to Bergen, he found there . . . Simon, bishop of the Hebrides, and abbot of the holy island. The king decided first the cases of those who had come from the west.*' (Anderson, *Early Sources*, II, p 461.) And then 1229: '*This summer, great dispeace was reported from the west beyond the sea, from the Hebrides.*' (Anderson, *Early Sources*, II, p 464.)

The Macsorley under-kings of the Hebrides (John Macdougall and Dugald Macruari) were with King Hakon in Bergen in the summer of 1248. Both remained in Norway for the winter. Each wanted to be king over the Northern Hebrides (Lewis and Skye) which remained in the control of the kings of Man and not in that of Somerled's family.

From Eirspennill's Hakon Hakon's son's Saga of the years 1247–8: '*Then came from the west, from the Hebrides, Harold, king of Man, son of Olaf, Godfrey's son . . . Then came from west beyond the sea John* [Macdougall], *Duncan's son, and Dugald* [Macruari], *Ruadri's son; and they both endeavoured after this, that the king should give them the title of king over the northern part of the Hebrides.* (Anderson, *Early Sources*, II, p 548.)

Travelling to and from Norway was dangerous. In 1248 the King of Man and his new Norwegian bride were lost at sea:

Harald son of Olaf, King of Man and the Isles, left Norway with his wife, daughter of the King of Norway, and with . . . Laurence, Bishop-Elect of Man and the Isles, as well as with many other noblemen around the Feast of

St Michael the Archangel [29 September] *in his desire to return home. When he was approaching the coasts of Shetland a severe storm arose and he was shipwrecked and drowned with his entire retinue.* (G. Broderick, *Chronicles of the Kings of Man and the Isles.*)

Safe-conducts might seem mundane but they were very necessary. In 1249 John Macdougall of Lorn was caught in a conflict of loyalties between the king of Norway and the king of Scotland. For his Hebridean possessions he owed allegiance to the former, for his mainland possessions to the latter – who was putting intense political pressure on him to make a choice. Before agreeing to meet Alexander II of Scotland, John Macdougall extracted some guarantees. These are mentioned in Eirspennill's Hakon Hakon's son's Saga: '*King Alexander sent word to king John, that he wished to meet him. But this meeting did not take place before four earls in Scotland had pledged their faith [to John] that he should go in truce from that meeting.*' (Anderson, *Early Sources*, II, p 555.) John was wise to be circumspect. Later kings of Scotland proved less than honourable when they had Highland chiefs within their grasp.

In 1263 Hakon, King of Norway, arrived off the west coast of Scotland with a huge fleet to demonstrate that he would defend the Hebrides by force if necessary. Fitful negotiations were carried on between Hakon and Alexander III of Scotland. These are described in Frisbok's Hakon Hakon's son's Saga:

King Hakon had caused a list to be made of all the islands that he claimed for himself, to the west of Scotland; and the king of the Scots had named those that he would not let go: they were Bute, and Arran, and the Cumbraes; but about the rest there was little [conflict] between the claims of the kings. (Anderson, *Early Sources*, II, p 623.)

Hakon's action represents a new departure. In Chapter 2 of the Orkneyinga Saga, and also in Magnus Bareleg's Saga, islands were defined in terms of whether or not you could sail a boat between them and the mainland. Such catch-all definitions were handy since the alternative was to compose a list of every isle and islet, which, in the case of the Hebrides, Orkneys and Shetland Isles would include many hundreds of names. The problem with a catch-all definition was that it lay open to interpretation and King Magnus Barelegs took advantage of this in 1098. Heimskringla, Magnus Bareleg's Saga, describes the negotiations between Magnus and the king of the Scots. They: '*made peace between them, to the effect that king Magnus should possess all the islands that lie to the west of Scotland, all between which and the mainland he could go, in a ship with the rudder in place.*' (Anderson, *Early Sources*, II, p 112–13.)

Magnus then used this definition to include Kintyre by having himself drawn across the isthmus at Tarbert in a boat with the rudder fixed. Kintyre was only connected to the rest of Scotland by a narrow neck of land and Magnus' act took on a legendary quality. It was of such symbolic importance that Bruce felt constrained to repeat the operation in order to reclaim Kintyre for Scotland about 1315.

In the case of Hakon we see a more bureaucratic approach. Hakon had a list of islands made, so that none would be inadvertently omitted. Apparently Alexander agreed to most of the list, disputing only the islands east of Kintyre in the Firth of Clyde. These had probably already fallen into Scottish hands since the Stewarts seem to have been well-established in Bute before 1200. However this was the sticking-point for Hakon. No doubt he realised he had to draw the line somewhere or his empire in the west would be slowly eroded. Accordingly he made a stand at the very edge, between Cumbrae and Ayrshire – whence we have the 'Battle' of Largs. By the middle of the thirteenth century the King of Norway was aware of the inadequacy of catch-all definitions. Lists became important, to avoid doubt or ambiguity. Hakon's list does not survive, but we do have later lists of the Scots and the Papacy.

There was a skirmish at Largs, but no decisive battle, and after suffering in the autumnal gales the Norwegian fleet had to return home. Hakon died in Orkney and his successor Magnus chose to sell off a set of islands that were expensive to maintain and of dubious benefit. The earl of Ross mounted a raid on Skye in 1264, not least to remind Hebrideans of who they now had to fear. With the Treaty of Perth in 1266 the Isles were ceded to Scotland. Political control was nominally exercised from Edinburgh, as it has been ever since. Edinburgh, however, is far away and the area achieved a degree of political autonomy under the Lordship of the Isles which lasted from after the Wars of Independence until 1493.

After the Norse lost the Isles in 1266 the only visitors during the early mediaeval period were Scottish or English. Certainly during the Wars of Independence we can suppose that English ships reached some of the southern Hebrides. We have letters from Angus of Islay to King Edward 1 dated 1292 and 1297. In these he names the islands of Islay, Skye, Lewis and Bute, as well as the mainland of Kintyre. Edward I's officials must have maintained a correspondence with Angus and we can assume some of their ships and captains ventured north from the shelter of the Irish ports. (The crossing from Ulster to Kintyre is only about fifteen miles.)

Even after the tide of war had turned in favour of the Scots, Edward II remained an active supporter of John Macdougall of Lorn. So for a period of at least thirty years the English chancery must have had relatively good information about the Hebrides, from its own sources and its Highland allies. R.A. Pelham suggested that the Gough map of Britain (c. 1360) derived partly from information assembled by Edward I's officials during the Wars of Independence.

Robert Bruce established a powerful base at Tarbert in North Kintyre, (Kintyre and Islay were the heartland of the Macdonald lordship), but after his reign Scottish control was only felt intermittently. Norse influence was now non-existent and English influence negligible. The most frequent foreign contact was with Ireland. The area was largely left to its own devices until the final forfeiture of the Lordship of the Isles about 1493. Relations with the Scottish realm became very troubled. Pro-government clans like the Campbells increased in power and influence at the expense of the Macdonalds and later the Macleans. James IV was aggressive and proactive towards the Hebrides, James V took a fleet there to overawe the islanders in 1540. There was an attempt to restore the lost Lordship of the Isles in 1545 which ended with the death of Donald Dubh, the claimant. This was the last occasion on which the clans of the west Highlands and Islands behaved with any degree of unity. The decline of Highland economic and military power relative to the rest of Britain took place over a long period. The process of political and military annexation, which had begun by 1200, was not completed until after Culloden in 1746.

Associated with these political events there must have been a great many embassies coming and going; a great many messages passing to and from the Highland world. There were formal treaties with the English in 1461 and 1545. There was communication with both English and Irish in Ireland. Along these channels must have passed news and reports about the Highlands and Hebrides. Unfortunately we know very little about such traffic. We have a number of safe-conduct passes. We may find a payment from an English king for a suit of armour to the king of Man or for a cleric to visit the Lord of the Isles. We have a few dates and some facts associated with them, virtually nothing in the way of personal impressions of the land, the people or the culture. The following quotations give an idea of this largely hidden traffic: '*Olave King of Man and the Isles has a safe conduct to come to England with his retinue, to secure peace between himself and Reginald his brother; to last for fifteen days after Michaelmas next. Westminster, 12 April 1228*' (Bain, *Calendar of Documents relating to Scotland*, I, p 182.)

Just occasionally we learn the names of some of those who were less exalted. We have a draft safe conduct, written in French at Arundel, and dated 8 September 1302: '*until All Saints next for Adam le Chapeleyn . . . Rachel de Argeil, Katerine de Argeyl, Padok de Argeyl . . . Lucas de Argeyl . . . They were with Marie, queen of Man, who died at London, and are now returning home.*' (*Calendar of Documents relating to Scotland*, Vol V, No 290)

Rachel and Katherine were probably both from noble families in Argyll and had travelled in the entourage of the queen of Man. By such means the women of Argyll would have had at least some information about the wider world.

The King [Edward II] *to Alan bishop of Inchegall. At the request of Henry de Beaumont, gives him leave to make a visitation of the outer isles of his see, enjoining him to use all means to secure the obedience of their inhabitants to himself. York, 26 June 1312.* (Bain, *Calendar of Documents relating to Scotland*, III, p 55)

5 October 1336
Safe conduct for John of the Isles, and men of his family, his servants and horses, until the Feast of St Andrew next to come. (Rotuli Scotiae I, p 464)

The King [Edward III] commands the release of the vessel and goods of the Bishop of Man, his liegeman, arrested in the port of Lowystoff . . . on his voyage to Rome, by men of that port and Great Yarmouth, on 'irrational' pretexts. Tower of London, 17 December 1340 (Bain, *Calendar of Documents relating to Scotland*, III, p 246)

Fiat for safe conduct for a year for James Skrymiour 'chivaler' of Scotland, with 18 horsemen in his company, to pass and stay in England, and ship for abroad at any port he pleases, and return to his country. Westminster, 12 March 1396–97. (Bain, *Calendar of Documents relating to Scotland*, IV, p 103)

(The Skrymgeour family held lands in Glassary, Argyll.)

Safe conduct and special protection and safeguard to Ector Maclean of Scotland, son of the sister of the Lord of the Isles coming to the King's presence with two servants horse or foot, to speak with his liege lord the King of Scotland, by the King's leave, till Christmas next. Worsop, 18 August 1405. (Bain, *Calendar of Documents relating to Scotland*, IV, p 144)

2 June 1411
Fiat for safe conduct for a year for John Lyon chaplain of the Lord of the Isles of Scotland, and six other persons with horses, etc. to come to the King's [Henry IV] presence and return as often as they please. (Bain, *Calendar of Documents relating to Scotland*, Vol IV, No 806)

In May 1424 Henry VI of England held some Scottish hostages in 'Foderingay' castle under treaty with the King of Scotland. One of these was 'Duncan lord of Argyll'. In July 1424:

Dunckane Cambelle askys a sauff counduyt for these men: Archebauld Cambelle, Walter Clerk, John of Knok', and Morys Neelsoun, coniunctly and severally with 4 servantys with thaym with . . . hors and harneys and all other goodes whatever they be; and alswell that it be not nedefull to thaym to schawe ther counduyt but if it be askyt. (Bain, *Calendar of Documents relating to Scotland*, IV, p 197)

If Alexander III made a list of his newly-acquired island territories in 1266 it is lost. Our first detailed account of the area is found in a chapter in John of Fordun's *Chronicle of the Scottish Nation* dating to about 1380. This data was also used by Walter Bower in his *Scotichronicon*, composed in the 1440s. Whoever was Fordun's source had a degree of knowledge about the Hebrides and had either travelled among them himself or collected information from other travellers. There is a small amount of additional material in Bower which I have placed in bold. Problematic modern identifications are in square brackets.

The Islands of Scotia . . .

There are also many islands, both great and small, at the back of Scotia, between it and Ireland, separated from the Orkneys by a great intervening firth; and the names of some of these are as follows :-

Beginning first from the south, there is an island, formerly called Eubonia, now Man, whose prince is bound to furnish to his lord, the king of Scotland, ten piratical galleys, as often as shall be necessary; besides other regal services. Here is the episcopal see of Sodor.

Arran, where are two royal castles, Brethwyk [Brodick], *and Lochransa.*

Helantinlaysche [Eilean Lamlash or Holy Island]

Rothesay, or Bute, where there is a fair and impregnable royal castle.

Great Cumbrae, a rich and large island.

Little Cumbrae, renowned for sport, but thinly inhabited.

Alesay [Ailsa Craig]

Bladay [Pladda off Arran]

Inch Marnoch, where there is a monastic cell. [Inchmarnock off Bute]

Aweryne [Sanda off Kintyre], *where is the chapel of Saint Sannian,* [Ninian], **(Adomnan)**, *and a sanctuary for transgressors.*

Rachryne [Rathlin], *distant only six miles from Ireland.*

Gya [Gigha].

Helant Macarmyk [Eilean MacCormaig or Eilean Mor], *where is also a sanctuary.*

A large island called Ile [Islay], *where the Lord of the Isles has two mansions, and the castle of Dounowak.* [Dunyveg]

Helant Texa [Eilean Texa], *with a monastic cell.*

Colonsay, with an abbey of canons-regular.

Dura [Jura], *twenty-four miles long, with few inhabitants, but affording very good sport.*

Scarba, fifteen miles long, where there is a chapel of the Blessed Virgin, at which many miracles are performed. Beside this island rushes down the mighty whirlpool of Corrievrekan.

Lunga

Luing

Shuna,

Great Seil

Little Seil

Helant Leneow [Eilean na naomh], *that is, the Isle of Saints, where is a sanctuary.*

Garveleane [Garbh-eilean or Garvelach], *near the great castle of Donqu-honle* [Dun Chonnell], *at a distance of six miles out at sea from the other islands.*

Mull, where are two castles, Doundowarde [Dun Duart] *and Dounarwyse* [Dun Aros].

Out at sea, at a distance of four miles from Mull, is Carneborg [Cairn-burgh], *an exceeding strong castle.*

Hycolumbkil, or Iona, where are two monasteries, one of monks and the other of nuns. There is also a sanctuary there.

Saint Kenneth's Island [Inchkenneth]. *His parish church is there.*

Kerrera

Lismore, where is the episcopal see of Argyll at Lismore.

Coll.

Schonay [Shuna], ***four miles (long) in Lorn***

Tiree, where there is an exceeding strong tower, and great plenty of barley.

Helantmok [Eilean Muick or Muck], *that is, the Isle of Swine.*

Barra, where there is a chapel of the Holy Trinity.

Uist, thirty miles long, where whales **(seals)** *and other sea-monsters abound. There is also the castle of Benwewyl* [probably Borve Castle in Benbecula].

Rum, a wooded and hilly island, with excellent sport, but few inhabitants.

Fuleay [?]

Assek [?]

Skye, *thirty miles long*

Lewis, *sixty miles long*

Hirth [St Kilda], *the best stronghold of all the islands.*

Near this is an island twenty miles long, where wild sheep are said to exist, which can only be caught by hunters. [Flannan Isles according to Monro]

Tyreym [Eilean Tioram in Moidart suggests Skene]

Thorset, where there is a very strong tower. [Thurso]

Stroma, near the whirlpool of the Orkneys.

Durenys, [Durness] *where, at midsummer, the sun is visible at night, not shining, indeed, but as it were piercing through the gloom.*

These above-mentioned islands, as well as many others, lie scattered about in the sea, on the western confines of Scotia, between it and Ireland; and some of these, to the north-west, look out upon the boundless ocean; whence it is believed that the inhabited world is bounded by this region of Scotia.

(W.F. Skene, *John of Fordun's Chronicle of the Scottish Nation*)

Despite the fact that this information was available within Scotland during the fourteenth century it was not successfully disseminated without, or, if it was, it was not regarded as important. Here we can draw a contrast with a poem by John Hardyng who spent time in Scotland during the reign of James I. In some ways his poem is the literary equivalent of his map in the

British Library since it intended to provide logistical information for an invading English army.

How the maker of this booke reporteth the distaunce and miles of the tounes in Scotland, and ye waye how to conveigh an armie as well by lande as water, into the chiefest partes thereof . . .

> *Nowe to expresse unto your noble grace*
> *The verie waye bothe by sea and land,*
> *With the distaunce of tounes and every myles space,*
> *Through the chefest parte of all Scotland,*
> *To conveigh an armie that ye maye take in hand,*
> *Herafter shall folowe in as good ordre as I maye,*
> *The true discripcion, and distaunce of the waye.*

Hardyng's verses take us on a journey round the main Scottish cities with continual reference to the logistical line of supply by sea. In the course of thirty-two seven-line verses Hardyng mentions dozens of places in the south and east of Scotland but his contibutions about the north and west take up no more than five lines:

> *Over all the mountaynes, drye mosses and wete,*
> *Wher the wild Scottes do dwel, than passe unto,*
> *That is in Mare and Garioth also,*
> *In Athill, Rosse, Sutherland, and Chatnesse,*
> *Mureffe* [Moray], *Lenox, and out ysles I gesse.*
> (John Hardyng in Hume Brown, *Early Travellers in Scotland*)

Hardyng's verse is the literary equivalent of his map. The Out Isles are featureless, far removed from the heart of Scotland, separated by a wash of sea. He either knew nothing about the north-west and Hebrides or regarded the area as of no political or military significance. However his verses introduce us to another important reason for gathering information about the Highlands and Islands – for military purposes.

Military sources

For at least four hundred years Highlanders found employment fighting in Ireland, either for Irish chiefs against each other or against the English. We know of these gallowglasses (*galloglaich* = foreign warrior) from Irish and English sources. G.A. Hayes-McCoy has dealt with the Irish evidence very thoroughly in his *Scots Mercenary forces in Ireland* and I do not propose to do more than refer to it here. During the Middle Ages this employment helped sustain large numbers of birlinns, or galleys, which were used to take Hebrideans to Ireland and, upon occasion, to the Northern Isles. These vessels underpinned all communications in the West Highlands and Islands and I have dealt with them in *The West Highland Galley*. The above subjects concern Highlanders travelling *from* the west coast of Scotland but here I propose to concentrate on the evidence of those who travelled *to* the area.

The military perspective is not important in itself – usually we know very little about early expeditions – but because military planners required logistical information for the areas of campaign. The military option provided the stimulus for report and reconnaissance, the drawing up of maps, the planning of supply. We shall see in the chapter on cartography how important an incentive these military requirements became. The author of the Gough Map, John Hardyng, John Elder and Lawrence Nowell, were all providing cartographic evidence that would be valuable to the military and political planners.

Our evidence from the mediaeval period is rather piecemeal. The relationship between the Lords of the Isles, who were used to an almost sovereign autonomy in the west, and their nominal overlords the Kings of Scotland, was perennially troubled. In 1411 there was a pitched battle at Harlaw. In 1455, the House of Douglas, then engaged in a bitter trial of strength with King James II of Scotland, tested the possibility of a Hebridean alliance. William Douglas was slain in Stirling castle and the Auchinleck Chronicle describes a visit from his brother, James, to the Lord of the Isles in Knapdale. An alliance between two of the strongest peripheral forces in Scotland boded ill for central authority.

Item, the 12 day of May, James the brother of Earl William of Douglas that was slain in the Castle of Stirling come to Knapdale, and spake there with the Earl of Ross and Lord of the Isles, and made them all right great rewards of wine, clothes, silver, silk and English cloth and they gave them mantles again. (Auchinleck Chronicle, p 54)

The Lords of the Isles also looked to England for support and in 1461 signed the Treaty of Westminster-Ardtornish. This became one of the reasons for their eventual forfeiture but during the attempt to restore the Lordship in 1545 they again looked for an English alliance. Part of the background to this is given in a long letter from John Elder to Henry VIII in 1543–44:

Moreouer, heringe and seinge what loue and fauour the valiaunt Yrishe lordes of Scotland, other wayes callid the Reddshankes, (excepte the Erll of Argyll, which is ravisshide onelye from the opinioun of the rest, be the Cardinall and his busschops, becaus he is novrisshed and brought vp in ther bosomes, and lyis vnder ther wynges), beris vnto your said Maiestie, of whois princely magnanimitie, Salomonicall wysdome, and sapience, and heroicall

humanitie and beneuolence, now syns the death of our said lord naturall and Kynge, is euer ther communicacion, and euer ther reasonynge:
(Collectanea de Rebus Albanicis)

(Moreover, hearing and seeing what love and favour the valiant Irish [Gaelic] lords of Scotland, otherwise called the Redshanks, (except the Earl of Argyll, who is ravished only from the opinion of the rest, by the Cardinal [Beaton] and his bishops, because he is nourished and brought up in their bosoms, and lies under their wings), bear unto your said Majesty, of whose princely magnanimity, Solomonical wisdom, and sapience, and heroic humanity and benevolence, now since the death of our said lord natural and King, is ever their communication, and ever their reasoning.)

And now Elder gets to the point:

Sene they heire and vnderstand, how mercifully, how graciously, and how liberally your noble Grace hath vsed, orderide, and dealide with the lordes of Irland, ther nyghboures, which haue continewid so many yeares rebellis; perdonying and forgyving theame ther offences and trespasses; creating of them, some erlis, some lordes, and some barons; rewarding theame more like princis then erlis and lordis, with gold, siluer, and riches; and sending theame home agane with gorgious indumentis, and rich apparell . . . Your noble Grace haithe many good hartis emonges the forsaide Yrische Lordes of Scotland, bicaus they vnderstand and heire how mercifully and how liberally (as I haue saide) your Highnes haith orderide the Lordes of Ireland.

(Since they hear and understand, how mercifully, how graciously, and how liberally your noble Grace hath used, ordered, and dealt with the lords of Ireland, their neighbours, who have continued so many years rebels; pardoning and forgiving them their offences and trespasses; creating of them, some earls, some lords, and some barons; rewarding them more like princes than earls and lords, with gold, silver, and riches; and sending them home again with gorgeous endowments, and rich apparel . . . Your noble Grace hath many good hearts amongst the forsaid Irish Lords of Scotland, because they understand and hear how mercifully and how liberally (as I have said) your Highness hath ordered the Lords of Ireland.)

Elder's summary encapsulates the oft-invoked political relationship between Highland chiefs who had men and English governments who had money.

After Donald Dubh's death in 1545 internal division racked the Hebridean world. The Macdonalds of Islay and Kintyre were not always at one with their traditional West Highland allies and also had extensive interests in Ulster. In autumn 1558 an English fleet under the Earl of Sussex ravaged Kintyre. As the century wore on the Campbells and Macleans found themselves more in tune with Elizabeth of England; the Macdonalds and other Hebrideans with the chiefs of Gaelic Ireland who were trying to maintain their independence. One of Elizabeth's boats visited Duart in 1595 where Captain George Thornton discussed wage-rates with Maclean. But, as on so many other occasions the lack of political unity within the Highland and Hebridean world left it weakened and vulnerable.

Despite the long-term failure of such strategic alliances they left a record of themselves. The Tudor interest in Scotland was doubtless one of the reasons behind John Elder's missive. As he tells us in his letter Elder was careful to name the greatest chiefs on his map. He may have known that this would make it more useful to English civil servants. William Cecil also used to record the names of great magnates as he located regional centres of power. Doubtless this was also an incentive for Nowell who follows Elder in naming the greatest Gaelic chieftains. Cecil, who was Nowell's employer, wanted the best and most up-to-date information available in his pocket-book. Good-quality information was as valuable then as now. Politicians, diplomats, counsellors, soldiers and sailors were always on the look-out for cheap and accurate data. One of the ways in which Lindsay's rutter and its accompanying chart were transmitted is that they were acquired by an English admiral (Dudley), who lent them to a French military engineer (Nicolay), who made a copy.

After the Union of Crowns in 1603 the power of the monarchy was reinforced. Throughout the Civil Wars and the period of the Jacobite Risings the West Highlands and Islands were divided between different political and religious camps. They suffered occasional incursions but it was in the eighteenth century that the government really tried to assess the military and cultural composition of its Highland opponents. From the period of the Jacobite Risings (1689–1746) we have a number of reports assessing the military strengths of the Highland clans; we have the Wade roads and General Roy's maps; we have David Bruce's survey as well as material related to the garrisons at Fort George, Fort Augustus and Fort William. We also have the written evidence of military men such as Richard Franck from the Commonwealth period and Edmund Burt from the 1720s and 1730s.

Whether the stimulus was political or military the sixteenth century sees an explosion of factual information about the islands. Some of this is included in the work of historians such as Boece and Leslie, some of it is provided by reports specifically about the isles, such as Monro and the manuscript printed by Skene. We have little idea of the precise reasons for such reports. We can guess from their content that the three most important factors were political military and economic. Sometimes the information was gathered in person, as with Monro, in others it was more in the nature of a compendium drawn from other authors and travellers – as with historians like Major and Boece:

Between Scotland and Ireland are many more islands, and larger ones than the Orkneys, which likewise obey the Scottish king. The most southerly is Man, fifteen leagues in length, which we have ourselves caught sight of at Saint Ninian. In it is the episcopal see of Sodor, at the present day in the hands of the English. There is also the island of Argadia, belonging to the earl of Argadia, which we call Argyle, thirty leagues in length. There the people swear by the hand of Callum More, just as in old times the Egyptians used to swear by the health of Pharaoh. The greater Cumbrae is another island, rich and large. Another is the island of Arran, which gives the title of earl to the lord Hamilton. Then there is the island Awyna, in which is the cell of Saint Aidan. In it were formerly most excellent religious, and Bede says that it ought to belong to the Britons, but the Picts made grant thereof to Scottish religious. This island lies further to the north than Bute, and is but six miles from the coast of Ireland. There is further the island called Isola, or in the common tongue Yla [Islay], an exceeding beautiful island. Therein is wont to dwell the Lord Alexander of the Isles, whom men used to call the earl of the Isles. In this island he had two fair strongholds of large extent, and thirty or forty thousand men were at his beck . . . There is further the island of Bute or Rothesay, and the island of Lismore, which gives a title to the episcopal see of Argyle. Far to the north is the island of Skye, fifteen leagues in length. The island of Lewis has a length of thirty leagues. Besides these are many other islands, of which the least is greater than the largest of the Orkneys.

That great-souled Robert Bruce in his last testament gave this counsel to those who should come after him, that the kings of the Scots should never part themselves from these islands, inasmuch as they could thence have cattle in plenty, and stout warriors, while in the hands of others they would not readily yield allegiance to the king, whereas with the slender title of the Isles the king can hold them to the great advantage of the realm. (John Major (1521), in Hume Brown, *Scotland before 1700*)

Sen we ar now falling in commoning of the Ilis, we will discrive the same, in maner and forme as followis. Fornens Scotland, to the Ireland seis, lyis XLIII Ilis; of quhilkis sum ar XXX milis lang, utheris XII milis, utheris mair, and utheris les. Thir Ilis wer callit be sum auctouris, Ebonie; and be utheris ar callit Hebredes. The principall Ile is the Ile of Man, quhilk lyis fornens Galloway, and wes sum time the principall seit of the preistis namit Driades; as Cornelius Tacitus, Cesar in his Commentaries, and mony othir Romane auctouris testifyis. North fra the Ile of Man lyis Arrane, uthirwayis namit Botha. This secound name wes gevin to it be Sanct Brandane; for he biggit sum time ane hous in it, namit Both. Fra Arrane lyis Helaw, and Rothesay, namit fra the first Scot that brocht the Scottis out of Ireland in Albioun. Nocht far fra thir Ilis is Ailsay; quhair siclik plente of soland geis is, as we schew afore in the Bas. Fra Ailsay lyis mony uthir Ilis, devidit and severit be thair awin names, full of minis; sik as irne, tin, leid, and uthir metallis: Yit the maist notable Ile of Scotland is Ila, quhilk lyis, beyound the toung of Lorne, in the sicht of Lochquhabir; ane riche cuntre, xxx milis of lenth, richt plentuus of corne, and full of metallis, gif thair wer ony crafty and industrius peple to win the samin. Nocht far fra Ila lyis Cumbra, and Mula, als mekill as Ila, baith in lenth and breid. In this Ile of Mula is ane cleir fontane, two milis fra the see: fra this fontane discendis ane litil burne, or strip, rinnand ful of rounis to the seis. Thir rounis ar round and quhit, schinand like perle, full of thik humour; and, within two houris eftir that thay come to see, thay grow in gret cocles. Schort gait fra thir Ilis is Iona, othirwayis namit Colmekill; in quhilk is ane abbay, full of devot religius men. This abbay wes the commoun sepulture of all Scottis kingis, fra the time of King Fergus the Secound, to the time of King Malcolme Canmore, quhilk biggit the abbay of Dunfermling; quhair the maist part of our kingis lyis, sen the fundatioun thairof. Passand forthwart to the north-nor-west seis, fornens Ros, is ane Ile namit Lewis, LX milis of lenth. In this Ile is bot ane reveir. It is said, gif ony woman waid throw this watter at the spring of the yeir, thair sall na salmond be sene for that yeir in the said watter: otherwayis, it sall abound in gret plente. Beyound the Lewis lyis two Ilis, namit Sky and Rona. In this last Ile is incredible noumer of selch, pellok, and meirswine, na thing astonist for the sicht of men. The last and outmaist Ile is namit Hirtha; quhare the elevatioun of the pole is LXIII greis. And, sen the elevatioun of the pole abone the Ile of Man is LVII greis, ilk gre extending to LXII milis and ane half in distance, as Ptolome and uthir astronomeris nowmeris, I conclude, that fra the Ile of Man, the first Ile of Albion, to Hirtha, the last Ile thairof, ar CCCLXXVII milis. This last Ile is namit Hirtha, quhilk, in Irsche, is callit ane scheip; for in this Ile is gret nowmer of scheip, ilk ane gretar than ony gait buk, with hornis lang and thikkar than ony horne of ane bewgill, and hes lang talis hingand down to the erd. This Ile is circulit on every side with roche craggis; and na baitis may land at it bot allanerly at ane place, in quhilk is ane strait and narow entres. Sum time thair micht na pepill pas to this Ile but extreme dangeir of thair livis; and yit thair is na passage to it bot quhen the seis ar cawme but ony tempest . . . In the Ile of Lewis ar two kirkis; ane dedicat to Sanct Peter, and the tother dedicat to Sanct Clement. The fame is, als sone as the fire gangis furth in this Ile, the man that is haldin of maist clene and innocent life layis ane wosp of stra on the alter; and, when the pepill are gevin maist devotly to thair praers, the wosp kindellis in ane bleis. Beyound thir Ilis is yit ane uthir Ile, bot it is not inhabit with ony pepill. In it ar certane beistis, nocht far different fra the figure of scheip, sa wild that thay can nocht be tane but girnis: the hair of thaim is lang and tattie, nothir like the woll of scheip nor gait. (Hector Boece (1527), in Hume Brown, *Scotland before 1700*)

(Since we are now fallen in conversing of the Isles, we will describe the same, in manner and form as follows. Opposite Scotland, to the Ireland seas, lie 43 Isles; of which some are 30 miles long, others 12 miles, others more, and others less. These Isles were called by some authors, Ebonie; and by others are called Hebrides. The principal Isle is the Isle of Man, which lies facing Galloway, and was some time the principal seat of the priests named Druids; as Cornelius Tacitus, Caesar in his Commentaries, and many other Roman authors testify. North from the Isle of Man lies Arran, otherwise named Botha [Bute]. This second name was given to it by Saint Brendan; for he built some time a house in it, named Both. From Arran lies Helaw [Lamlash], and Rothesay, named from the first Scot that brought the Scots out of Ireland into Albion. Not far from these Isles is Ailsa Craig; where suchlike plenty of solan geese [gannets] is, as we showed before in the Bass. From Ailsa lie many other Isles, divided and separated by their own names, full of mines; such as iron, tin, lead, and other metals: Yet the most notable Isle of Scotland is Islay, which lies, beyond the tongue of Lorn, in the sight of Lochaber; a rich country, 30 miles of length, right plentiful of corn, and full of metals, if there were any crafty and industrious people to win the same. Not far from Islay lies Cumbrae, and Mull, as great as Islay, both in length and breadth. In this isle of Mull is a clear fountain, two miles from the sea: from this fountain descends a little burn, or rivulet, running full of roe to the seas. These roes are round and white, shining like pearl, full of thick matter; and, within two hours after that they come to [the] sea, they grow into great cockles. [A] short way from these Isles is Iona, otherwise named Colmkill; in which is an abbey, full of devout religious men. This abbey was the usual burial-place of all Scots kings, from the time of King Fergus the Second, to the time of King Malcolm Canmore, which built the abbey of Dunfermline; where the most part of our kings lie, since the foundation thereof. Passing forwards to the north-north-west seas, facing Ross, is an Isle named Lewis, 60 miles of length. In this Isle is only one river. It is said, if any woman wade through this water at the spring of the year, there shall no salmon be seen for that year in the said water: otherwise, it shall abound in great plenty. Beyond the Lewis lie two Isles, named Skye and Rona. In this last Isle is incredible number of seals, porpoises, and dolphins, not at all astonished by the sight of men. The last and outermost Isle is named Hirta [St Kilda]; where the elevation of the pole is 63 degrees. And, since the elevation of the pole above the Isle of Man is 57 degrees, each degree extending to 62 miles and a half in distance, as Ptolomy and other astronomers reckon, I conclude, that from the Isle of Man, the first Isle of Albion, to Hirta, the last Isle thereof, are 377 miles. This last Isle is named Hirta, which, in Irish [Gaelic], is called a sheep; for in this Isle is great number of sheep, each one greater than any goat buck, with horns long and thicker than any horn of a bugle, and have long tails hanging down to the earth. This Isle is circled on every side with rocky crags; and no boats may land at it

but only at one place, in which is a strait and narrow entrance. Sometimes there might no people pass to this Isle without extreme danger of
their lives; and yet there is no passage to it but when the seas are calm
without any tempest . . . In the Isle of Lewis are two kirks; one dedicated
to Saint Peter, and the other dedicated to Saint Clement. The rumour is,
as soon as the fire goes out in this Isle, the man that is held of most clean
and innocent life lays a wisp of straw on the altar; and, when the people
are given most devoutly to their prayers, the wisp kindles in a blaze.
Beyond these Isles is yet another Isle, but it is not inhabited with any
people. In it are certain beasts, not far different from the figure of sheep,
so wild that they cannot be taken without traps: the hair of them is long
and tatty, neither like the wool of sheep nor goat.)

All the sixteenth-century historians included sections on the Isles but by far
the most valuable single source is Donald Monro. Monro was Dean of the
Isles and, on the basis of his travels in 1549, wrote a description which lists
251 of them with varying amounts of detail. This list survives, in part or
whole, in three manuscripts and was also incorporated into Buchanan's
History, published in 1582. From these R.W. Munro has produced a modern
edition which I cannot recommend too highly.

   Dean Monro's *Description* has been published several times. For this reason,
and also because I have quoted from it elsewhere, I only give a few examples
here. Monro's descriptions usually give some idea of the island's physical
location in terms of the preceding islands, its Gaelic name, and, often, an
English translation of that name. If the isle has any economic importance then
this is detailed. The larger islands carry considerably more information.
Monro's account has the character of an official report. Although he was Dean
of the Isles, and although he notes information that was of interest to the
religious authorities, he does not seem to have had a spiritual motive. It is a
comprehensive list of all the islands, very probably produced for lay authorities.

   Of two isles off the coast of Lorn:
   *Narrest this lyis ane Iyle callit in the Erische Leid Ellan ard, callit in English
   the hich Ile.*
   (Nearest this lies an isle called in the Irish [Gaelic] tongue Eilean Ard,
   called in English the high isle.)

   *Narrest this lyis ane Iyle callit in the Erische Leid Ellan Iisall, callit in
   English the laich Ile.*
   (Nearest this lies an isle called in the Irish [Gaelic] tongue Eilean Iosal,
   called in English the low isle.)

   Of Ulva off Mull:

Be twa mile of sea fra this Ellan of Eorsay lyis ane Ile to the north-west callit Ulvay five mile lang, gude land with ane gude Raid for hieland galeis in it.
(By two miles of sea from this island of Eorsa lies an Isle to the north-west called Ulva five miles long, good land with a good road [anchorage] for Highland galleys in it).

Of Mingulay, south of Barra:

Beside the Ile of Berneray towards the north lyis ane Ile callit Megalay, twa mile lang, inhabite and manurit, verie gude for corn and fishing, perteining to the Bischop of the Iles.
(Beside the Isle of Berneray towards the north lies an Isle called Mingulay, two miles long, inhabited and manured, very good for corn and fishing, pertaining to the Bishop of the Isles).
(Italicised text from R. W. Munro, *Monro's Western Isles of Scotland*)

From the end of the sixteenth century we have another semi-official report which was published in 1880 as an appendix to volume 3 of Skene's *Celtic Scotland*. This also covers the isles comprehensively but contains a great deal more information about economic and military capacity. Apart from the descriptive text there is usually an assessment of the rental and the number of men who could be levied. These are related to an assessment unit known as the markland which was a measure of the productivity of the land. Skene reckoned the report was written between 1577 and 1595. It certainly reads as if it had been commissioned by government. Here follow the sections on Mull and Ulva:

Mule. This Ile is 24 mile of lenth and in sum pairtis 16 mile braid, and in uther pairtis thairof but 12 mile braid. It is all 300 merk land, and will raise 900 men to the weiris. McClane Doward, callit Great McClane, hes the maist pairt thairof, extending to aucht score merk land and ten, and will raise on it with the pairt he hes of the Bischop 600 men thairupon. McClane of Lochbuy hes thriescore merk land, and will raise 200 men thairon. The Bischop hes 30 merk land thair, but McClane Doward hes it in his possessioun occupiet be his kin. The Laird of McKynvin hes 20 merk land, and the uther 20 merk land pertenis to the Laird of Schellow (Coll) but thay will raise 100 thairon. Thair is mony woods and saltwater lochis in this Ile, and it is verie plentifull of all kind of fisches, speciallie hering and salmond. It is na less commodious for guides and store nor ony of the remanent Iles; but not sa gude for cornes. In everie pairt thairof are mony deiris, raes, and wild foullis. McClane of Doward hes twa castellis in this Ile, the ane named Doward, the uther callit Aross, quhilk sumtime perteinit to McConneill. McClane of Lochbuy hes ane castell thairintill callit the Castell of Lochinbuy. Ilk merkland in this Ile payis yeirlie 5 bollis beir, 8 bollis meill, 20 stanes of

cheese, 4 stanes of buttir, 4 mairtis, 8 wedderis, twa merk of silver, and twa
dozen of pultrie, by Cuddiche, quhanevir thair master cummis to thame.
(Skene, *Celtic Scotland*)

(Mull. This Isle is 24 miles of length and in some parts 16 miles broad, and in other parts thereof only 12 miles broad. It is all 300 markland, and will raise 900 men to the wars. MacLean [of] Duart, called [the] Great MacLean, has the most part thereof, extending to eight score markland and ten [170], and will raise on it, with the part he has of the Bishop, 600 men thereupon. MacLean of Lochbuy has threescore [60] markland, and will raise 200 men thereon. The Bishop has 30 markland there, but MacLean [of] Duart has it in his possession occupied by his kin. The Laird of Mackinnon has 20 markland, and the other 20 markland pertains to the Laird of Coll but they will raise 100 thereon. There are many woods and saltwater lochs in this Isle, and it is very plentiful of all kind of fishes, specially herring and salmon. It is no less commodious for livestock and cattle than any of the remaining Isles; but not so good for corn. In every part thereof are many deer, roe, and wildfowl. MacLean of Duart has two castles in this Isle, the one named Duart, the other called Aros, which once belonged to MacDonald. MacLean of Lochbuy has a castle there called the Castle of Lochbuy. Each markland in this Isle pays yearly 5 bolls barley, 8 bolls oatmeal, 20 stones of cheese, 4 stones of butter, 4 marts [cattle for beef], 8 wethers, two marks of silver, and two dozen of poultry, apart from free lodging, whenever their master comes to them.)

Ulloway is ane Ile twa mile lang, ane mile braid. It is twelf merk land
pertaining to McCower. It is plane land but ony hillis or woodis, and will
raise thrie score men. Ilk merk land payis conform to the Ile of Mule.

(Ulva is an isle two miles long, one mile broad. It is twelve markland pertaining to MacQuarrie. It is flat land without any hills or woods, and will raise three score [60] men. Each markland pays as in the Isle of Mull.)

We also glimpse a class of men who physically maintained the contact between Lowland government and the Highlands and Islands. These people made their living as runners. Some were probably retained by the King or the great families for correspondence. In later times they accompanied and retrieved the horses hired by travellers. In the Accounts of the Lord High Treasurer we find the following payments made in May 1512:

Item, to ane Ersche rynnar to feche ane wricht out of Arrane to the King to
mak ane galay, xiiii s . . .

Item, to ane to pas to warne the Maister of Ergile to cum with his army to his fader in Air, xviii s . . .
Item, to Pate, falconar, to pas for halkis to the Ilis for his expensis . . . iiii li . . .
Item, the xxvii day of Maij, to ane rynnar at brocht lettrez fra the Erle of Ergile to the King, v s.
(Accounts of the Lord High Treasurer of Scotland, 1473–1566)

(Item, to an Irish [i.e. Gaelic-speaking] runner to fetch a [ship]wright out of Arran to the King to make a galley, 14 shillings . . .
Item, to one to pass to warn the Master of Argyll to come with his army to his father in Ayr, 18 shillings . . .
Item, to Pate, falconer, to pass for hawks to the Isles for his expenses . . . £4 . . .
Item, the 27th day of May, to a runner that brought letters from the Earl of Argyll to the King, 5 shillings.)

Nearly thirty years later the runner has become a 'Pursuivant'. On the 27 April 1540 we find:

Item that samyn daye gevin to ane pursyvand at the kingis graice command to pas in to the Ilys with writingis of his gracis, xliiii s . . .
Item gevin the ix daye of Maye to ane pursyvand to pas in to the Ilis with the kingis letteris to caus provisione be maid agane his gracis cumin, vi lib. xii s.
(Pursemaster's Accounts, SHS Miscellany X, Edinburgh, 1965)

(Item, that same day given to a Pursuivant at the King's Grace's command to pass into the Isles with writings of his Grace's, 44 shillings . . .
Item, given the 9th day of May to a Pursuivant to pass into the Isles with the King's letters to cause provision [to] be made against his Grace's coming, £6 – 12 shillings.)

Two centuries later Paul Sandby sketched such a runner in watercolour and entitled him 'A Gillee wet feit or Errand Runner'.

There was another class of men whose line of work involved continual travel around the Highlands and Islands – the harpists. Not all of these were in the permanent employ of a noble family and some made their living as itinerant musicians. Their status and craft brought them into contact with the greatest in the Gaelic world – a trust which they someimes abused. A famous instance was the murder of Angus Og Macdonald, son of John, Lord of the Isles, about 1490, by an Irish harper called Diarmaid O'Cairbre. Diarmaid was subsequently drawn to death by horses and is the subject of a contemporary Gaelic poem about the event. Whether because of this or not, harpists became almost a literary convention. According to Monipennie:

> *Ethodius primus . . . succeeded the year . . . of Christ 163 . . . was traiterously killed by a harper, (whom he trusted), the thirty-third year of his reign, and was buried in Dunstaffage. This harper was most cruelly executed . . .*
> *Fethelmachus . . . succeeded . . . in the year of Christ 354; . . . he was traiterously murthered in his owne chamber by two dissembling Picts and an harper, the third year of his reign, and was buried in Dunstaffage. The murtherers were apprehended and most cruelly tormented. (J. Monipennie, Scots Chronicles)*

In 1624, Cornelius Ward, one of the Irish Franciscan missionaries, wanted to see Campbell of Calder:

> *Calder was a man of great importance, but a heretic; it was very difficult to gain access to him; knowing, however, that Calder held poets in high regard, Ward, having composed a poem in praise of Calder, disguised himself as an Irish poet; then, accompanied by a singer, carrying a harp, he presented himself before Calder, and was graciously received. (C.Giblin, Irish Franciscan Mission to Scotland)*

Official view

From the end of the sixteenth and the beginning of the seventeenth century we have an increasing number of notices in the official records of Scotland. In particular we have the sturdy Jacobean prose of the Registers of the Privy Council. In the context of the Highlands and Islands their tone is usually strident but this is an indication of the prevailing attitude of the Lowland Scots government. Since the Battle of Harlaw in 1411 the relationship between the Highlands and the Scottish realm had been fraught and fractious. It remained troubled until after Culloden in 1746.

The Registers make splendid reading but at the time they were part of the vicious political spin intended to justify any form of Lowland Scots imperialism towards the Highlanders. The enterprise of the Fife Adventurers in Lewis may have proved something of a fiasco but some of the other examples of Stuart colonialism had, and in Ulster still have, unhappy consequences. Sometimes it worked well. Kintyre saw a sizeable immigration from Ayrshire and the Argyll family also took incomers to Inveraray. After generations of difference, and sometimes friction, these stories are an undoubted success. Here though it was the Gaelic nobility which forced through and fostered the change. When it was attempted from outside the Gaelic tradition it engendered strong opposition. Fort William required at least a century of military support before it began to look like embedding into the Highland world.

Here is part of the official record of the commission against Lewis, 18 July 1605:

Forsamekill as, the Kings Majestie and Lords of Secret Councill considering the barbarous and deteastable murthers, slaughters, and others insolencies comittit be the rebellious theives and lymmers, violent possessors and inhabitants of the Lewis, quha not only hes extendit thair beastlie crueltie every ane of thaim against uthers, without respect to quhatsumever condition of persons, young or auld, male or female, bot with that thai have committit cruell and barbarous murthers and slaughters upon grite numbers of his Majesties peacable and guid subjects quha, in thair lawfull trade or be contrarious winds, resortit amangst thaim, and in all thair actions, courses, and progress of thair proceidings thair only delyte is in blude, reift and oppression, they being altogither voyd of the knawledge and feir of God, and having na regaird of our Soveraine Lords authoritie, royall power and laws; and, besydes thair barbarous and lawles forme of living, they are avowed enemies to all lawfull trafficque and handling in these bounds, and the maist profitable and commodious trade of fishing, quhairby his Majesties subjects micht be maist richlie benefited, is be reasoun of thair barbaritie altogidder neglectit and oversein, to the grite hurt of the comonweill; and the Kings Majestie and the saids Lords finding that it can nawise stand with his Majesties honour and princlie dignitie that sic ane tyranous byke of rebellious and lawles lymmers shal be sufferit to have ony langer oversicht or impunitie: Thairfoir . . . (Register of the Privy Council, vol VII, pp 84–5)

(Forasmuch as, the King's Majesty and Lords of Secret Council considering the barbarous and detestable murders, slaughters, and others insolencies committed by the rebellious thieves and limmers [rogues], violent possessors and inhabitants of the Lewis, who not only have extended their beastly cruelty every one of them against others, without respect to whatsoever condition of persons, young or old, male or female, but with that they have committed cruel and barbarous murders and slaughters upon great numbers of his Majesty's peaceable and good subjects who, in their lawful trade or by contrary winds, resorted amongst them, and in all their actions, courses, and progress of their proceedings their only delight is in blood, reif [plunder] and oppression, they being altogether void of the knowledge and fear of God, and having no regard of our Sovereign Lord's authority, royal power and laws; and, besides their barbarous and lawless form of living, they are avowed enemies to all lawful traffic and handling in these bounds, and the most profitable and commodious trade of fishing, whereby his Majesty's subjects might be most richly benefited, is by reason of their barbarity altogether neglected and overlooked, to the great hurt of the common good; and the King's Majesty and the said Lords finding that it can no way stand with his Majesty's honour and princely dignity that such a tyrannous bike [swarm] of rebellious and lawless limmers shall be suffered to have any longer oversight or impunity: Therefore . . .)

It wasn't just Lewis. Similar views found their way into the sonorous preamble to a grant made to the Earl of Argyll in 1607 of huge estates in Kintyre and Jura:

wherefore the underwritten lands were, for many years past, possessed by wild and barbarous people, destitute of knowledge and fear of God and the king, and respect for the laws of the kingdom, who will neither foster civil society amongst themselves, nor allow other subjects of the kingdom to do business there without danger to their lives and goods . . . (Register of the Great Seal, vol VI, 1911)

A further passage of July 1610 refers more specifically to the hurt suffered by the fishing industry:

that now thair is no pairt of the Yllis rebellious and dissobedient bot the Lewis, whiche being possest and inhabite be a nomber of thevis, murtheraris, and ane infamous byke of lawles and insolent lymmaris, undir the chairge and commandiement of the traytour Neill McCleud, who hes usurpit upoun him the auctoritie and possessioun of the Lewis, and thay concurring altogidder in a rebellious societie do committ mony murthouris, slauchteris, reiffis and villanyis not onlie amangis thameselffis bot upoun his Majesteis peciable and good subjectis who resortis amang thame in thair trade of fischeing, and be thair barbarous and savage behaviour aganis his Majesteis good subjectis thay haif maid the trade of fischeing in the Lewis, whiche wes most proffitable for the haill cuntrey, to become alwyse unproffitable, to the grite hurte of the commounwele. (Register of the Privy Council, vol IX, p 13)

(that now there is no part of the Isles rebellious and disobedient but the Lewis, which being possessed and inhabited by a number of thieves, murderers, and an infamous bike of lawless and insolent limmers, under the charge and commandment of the traitor Neill MacLeod, who has usurped upon himself the authority and possession of the Lewis, and they concurring altogether in a rebellious society do commit many murders, slaughters, robberies and villainies not only among themselves but upon his Majesty's peaceable and good subjects who resort among them in their trade of fishing, and by their barbarous and savage

behaviour against his Majesty's good subjects they have made the trade
of fishing in the Lewis, which was most profitable for the whole country,
to become wholly unprofitable, to the great hurt of the common good.)

The Registers also contain an abstract, probably dated about 1613, which lists
the principal strengths in the area. There was plainly a continuing demand for
information about military strongholds:

Thair is of yles abone tuay hundreth, whairof thair is fiftie inhabited.
   Of stane houses in the Sky thair is fyve, to wit :- Duntilloun in Trouternes,
being ane pairt of the Sky possessed by Donald Gorme without richt;
Dunvaigen in the Sky, perteaning to Macloyde in Hairish; Dounakine,
perteaning to Makenon in the Sky; Dunruissil, perteaning also to Makinon;
Caymes in Slait, perteaning to Donald Gorme; Duniskaith in Slait,
perteaning to Donald Gorme.
   The house of Stornowa in the Lewis is fallin, albeit it had biddin the canon
be the Erle of Argyle of auld, and be the Gentilmen Ventourares of lait.
   Ane castell in Barra perteaning to Makneill of Barra, callit Caisillum,
and cannot be dung bot be sea.
   Strenthis in the West Isles. -
   In Ila ane house callit [Dunivaig], *perteaning to Makconeill; Lochgur-*
mont, perteaning also to him, situat within ane loch, and usurped be
Makcleane.
   In Mull, the castell of Dowart, perteaning to Makcleane; the castell of
Lochbowie, perteaning to Makcleane of Lochbowie; the castell of Aros,
perteaning to Makcleane of Dowart.
   Cole, ane castell perteaning to Makcleane of Cole.
(Register of the Privy Council, vol X, p 821)

(There are of isles above two hundred, whereof there are fifty inhabited.
   Of stone houses in Skye there are five, to wit :- Duntulm in
Trotternish, being a part of Skye possessed by Donald Gorm [Mac-
Donald] without right; Dunvegan in Skye, pertaining to MacLeod of
Harris; Dounakine [Caisteal Maol], pertaining to MacKinnon in Skye;
Dunruissil [Dun Ringill], pertaining also to MacKinnon; [Castle]
Camus in Sleat, pertaining to Donald Gorm; Dun Skaith [Scaich or
Sgathaich] in Sleat, pertaining to Donald Gorm.
   The house of Stornoway in the Lewis has fallen, albeit it had endured
the cannon of the Earl of Argyll in the old days, and by the Gentlemen
Adventurers of late.
   A castle in Barra pertaining to MacNeill of Barra, called Kishmul,
which cannot be overcome but by sea.
   Strengths in the Western Isles. -
   In Islay a house called [Dunivaig], pertaining to MacDonald; Loch

Gorm, pertaining also to him, situated within a loch, and usurped by MacLean.

In Mull, the castle of Duart, pertaining to MacLean; the castle of Loch Buie [Moy Castle], pertaining to MacLean of Lochbowie; the castle of Aros, pertaining to MacLean of Duart.

Coll, a castle pertaining to MacLean of Coll).

It is to only to be expected that central government would want to know the details of the island bolt-holes of the Hebridean chiefs. Bringing them to task was no easy matter: '*Alexander MacLeod dwelleth in ye isles where ye Officers of ye law dare not pass for hazard of their lives.*' (Macleod, *Island Clans of six centuries*, document of 1527).

Island chiefs were almost unassailable in their island fortresses. In 1549 Dean Monro writes of Pabbay in the mouth of Loch Roag: *Besides this lyis Pabay . . . quhairin also Mccloyd of Leozus uses to dwell, quhan he wald be quiet* (R.W. Munro, *Monro's Western Isles of Scotland*) (Beside this lies Pabay . . . wherein also MacLeod of Lewis used to dwell, when he would be quiet.)

We can feel some sympathy for George Lesly, sheriff clerk of Inverness, who petitioned the Privy Council in 1669 to be excused from attempting to collect taxes in Inverness-shire. He starts by stating that this is really the job of sheriffs and their deputies, not sheriff clerks:

> *the clerkes being but mean persons and not of capacity nor trust to act for them in such a busines, much lesse the petitioner, who is clerk of the dismembred shyre of Innernes, there being litle or nothing left of that shreffdome bot the Hielands and Isles, as Lochaber, Badzenoch, Knoydart, Moydart, Glengarie and other hieland parts, whose inhabitants are not legallie disposed nor willing to his Majesties dues, being infested with poverty and idlnes, a task upon which accompt the petitioner is not able to undergoe, seing disobedience hes bein given be them to the pairties of his Majesties forces of a considerable strenth.* (Register of the Privy Council, 3rd series, Vol III, p 8)

Fortunately for George, the Council viewed his dilemma sympathetically.

Nevertheless within a century of Lesly's complaint every corner of the Hebrides had to bend to central government. With the Union of Crowns the Stuarts now had the resources of the rest of Britain behind them. During the seventeenth century the consolidation of Great Britain was fractured by civil and religious dissension. Once a lasting political settlement was achieved the Highlands and Hebrides could no longer withstand the force of central authority. The signs were all there long before Culloden.

The rebels in Islay were crushed from 1614–16. Highlanders took part in numerous campaigns during the Civil Wars; the Commonwealth made itself felt as far as Stornoway. In 1647 the Covenanting army massacred the

Highland garrison at Dunaverty in Kintyre and in 1692 was the Massacre of Glencoe. From 1689–1746 there was the long period of the Jacobite Risings. Central government built roads and established fortress towns in the Highlands. Men like Tucker and Dymes were sent to Scotland on fact-finding missions. Soldiers like Franck and Burt, who had been stationed in the Highlands, wrote about their experiences. Naval Captains like Fergusson kept logs. There is far too much evidence here to do more than glance at but travel, particularly of a military nature, brought the Highlands face-to-face with the rest of Britain.

Martin Martin gives an uncannily prophetic story in his account of the second sight. Whether or not you have time for such fancies, his tale captures the sense of security which Hebrideans had enjoyed in the long centuries between the arrival of the Vikings and the Royal Navy.

> *One who had been accustomed to see the second-sight, in the isle of Egg . . . told his neighbours that he had frequently seen an apparition of a man in a red coat lined with blue, and having on his head a strange sort of blue cap, with a very high cock on the fore part of it, and that the man who there appeared was kissing a comely maid in the village where the seer dwelt; and therefore declared that a man in such a dress would certainly debauch or marry such a young woman. This unusual vision did much expose the seer, for all the inhabitants treated him as a fool, though he had on several other occasions foretold things that afterwards were accomplished; this they thought one of the most unlikely things to be accomplished, that could have entered into any man's head. This story was then discoursed of in the isle of Skye, and all that heard it, laughed at it; it being a rarity to see any foreigner in Egg, and the young woman had no thoughts of going anywhere else. This story was told me at Edinburgh, by Norman Macleod of Grabam, in September, 1688, he being just then come from the isle of Skye; and there were present, the Laird of Macleod, and Mr Alexander Macleod, advocate, and others.*
>
> *About a year and a half after the late revolution [i.e. summer 1690], Major Ferguson, now Colonel of one of Her Majesty's regiments of foot, was then sent by the Government with 600 men, and some frigates to reduce the islanders that had appeared for King James, and perhaps the small isle of Egg had never been regarded, though some of the inhabitants had been at the battle of Killiecrankie, but by a mere accident which determined Major Ferguson to go to the isle of Egg, which was this: a boat's crew of the isle of Egg happened to be in the isle of Skye, and killed one of Major Ferguson's soldiers there; upon notice of which, the Major directed his course to the isle of Egg, where he was sufficiently revenged of the natives: and at the same time, the maid above-mentioned being very handsome, was then forcibly carried on board one of the vessels by some of the soldiers, where she was kept above twenty-four hours, and ravished, and brutishly robbed at the same time of her*

*fine head of hair. She is since married in the isle, and in good reputation: her
misfortune being pitied, and not reckoned her crime.*

In retrospect we may judge that whether or no the seer was troubled by
second-sight he was certainly far-sighted. The security of the islands was now
threatened as it had not been since the Viking invasions. In 1746 much worse
was to strike Eigg in the guise of Captain Fergusson:

> *he bespeaks Captain MacDonald, the doctor, and earnestly desires him, for
> the poor people's own safety and good of the country, he shoud call them all
> and perswad them to come in, the whole inhabitants with their whole arms of
> all kinds, and that he would give them full protections for both their persons
> and effects that woud save them against any future danger : otherwise, and if
> they shoud not come in heartily, all of them come to the years of discretion and
> to the age of bearing arms, he woud immediately . . . cause his men burn all
> their houses, destroy all their cattle and carry the whole men away. Mr
> MacQueen advises Captain MacDonald to send for the men with the
> remainder of their arms in the terms spoken by Ferguson. He sends some
> dozen of lads for them. They were seen comeing in a body. Immediatly
> Ferguson ordered Captain MacDonald to be seizd upon and made prisoner
> of, brought into a house to be confin'd thereto for ane hour. The men laid
> down their arms, such of them as had any. The few old people that came
> among them were picked out and dismist home. Then Captain MacDonald
> was brought out of the house, was stript of all his cloaths to the skin, even of
> his shoes and stockins, brought aboard the Furnace, barisdall'd [held in iron
> stocks] in a dark dungeon. And to the poor people's additional misfortune,
> there was a devilish paper found about him, containing a list of all the Eigg
> folk that were in the Princes service. Then that catalogue was read by their
> patronimicks in the name of giving the promised protection, which ilk one
> answered cheerfully, and was drawn out into another rank, so that there were
> noe fewer than 38 snatched aboard the man of war, were brought to London,
> from thence transported to Jamaica, where the few that lives of them continue
> slaves as yet. Many of them dyed and starved ere they arrove at the Thames.
> The most of them were marryed men, leaving throng families behind them.
> They slaughtered all their cattle, pillaged all their houses ore [ere?] they left
> the isle, and ravished a girl or two. This relation I had from the bailie of
> Canna and the bailie of Eigg.* (Alexander Macdonald in *Lyon in Mourn-
> ing, Vol III*, p 84ff)

Alexander Macdonald, the poet, was prone to paint in bold colours but even
Captain Fergusson's log admits to sixteen prisoners. He had also been busy
elsewhere: '*I am now Cruizing off of the Isle of Rarza and has my Boats Manned and
Armed ashore, burning and destroying the Lairds Houses with some others that belong
to His Officers.*' (John Fergussone of the *Furnace*, off Raasay, 12 May 1746.)

After the punitive raids of 1746 and patrols through the subsequent years we hear no more of military expeditions to the Highlands. The key to this was naval control. It had never been properly exercised by the Scottish kings and even James VI & I was reluctant to risk expensive capital assets in dangerous waters. The Highlanders were protected by distance from land-based forces against whom they could always fight a guerrilla war or escape by boat. They could not, however, fight the navy.

In 1898 Andrew Lang published a manuscript in the British Library known as King's MS 104. He thought that the author was probably David Bruce, a government agent who toured extensively in the Highlands and Islands after Culloden. Bruce conducted judicial rentals in Arisaig and Moidart and entered into negotiations with Clanranald to lease some of his lands. Some of his correspondence survives amongst the Hardwicke Papers in the British Library. His manuscript was clearly an attempt to summarize the military threat still posed by the Highlands and Islands. From the very beginning he gives his rationale. It could just as well serve for any number of reports from earlier centuries:

> *The Highlands of Scotland Described . . . Also a Scheme for Civilizing the Disaffected Clans and improving their Country*
> *In a Letter from a Gentleman at Edinburgh to his Friend in London.*
>
> *Sir,*
> *I am favour'd with your Letter dated – in which, you represent how much you, and all true Lovers of their Country are affected, to find that this part of Great Britain should, instead of Contributing to the Common Interest of Religion and Liberty, so readily and openly Embrace every Occasion to Rebel, and join the Common Enemy, and endeavour to overturn our Happy Constitution and deprive us of Blessings dearer to us than our Lives. You regret that you have not yet been able to get a perfect and Satisfactory Description of the Highlands of Scotland, and the People who inhabit them, either from a Want of a proper Knowledge of the Country in those who have attempted it, or their attachment to the Rebel Clans; that others have describ'd some Parts of the Country from particular Views, without having Regard to the Good of the Whole. You therefore entreat me to send you an impartial and particular Account of my Travels through Scotland, especially the Disaffected Highlands.*

Bruce was a not unsympathetic observer but he had more time for the islanders than those on the mainland:

> *The People in these Islands are more given to Labour and Industry both at Sea and Land than their Neighbours on the Continent: they are generally of a small Size, being much enslaved by Chamberlains or Factors and other*

Gentlemen who live among them. They are from their being separated by a pretty large sea from the rest of the World a more Tractable and Honest People than one would expect.

Besides they could be more easily contained:

if Effectual Measures were to be laid down for Civilizing the Disaffected Highlands, the Continent should be the first Concern, as the Islanders are not quite so Barbarous as these are, nor have they such Easy Access to make Rebellious Concerts, and in the worst Event they may be Hem'd in by a few Sloops of War properly Stationed.

He was also sanguine about the loyalty that could be expected from the Macdonalds:

The MacDonalds pretend that their Attachment to the Stuart Family proceeds from a Principle of Loyalty and Duty but it is observable of several Highland Clans, particularly the McDonalds, that they have been mostly Loyal to some King or other who was not in Possession, but seldom to any King upon the Throne, and when they could not find a Pretender they never were at a Loss for a pretence of some Kind or other for Rapine and Plunder. Their Rebellions against the State and their Depredations on the Subject on these Occasions if enumerated would fill a Large Folio, and an Octavo would hardly Contain their Rebellions against the Stuart Family whilst on the Throne.

Bruce here touched on the heart of the problem. The Macdonalds were the heirs of an autonomous, Gaelic-speaking, culture which found political expression in the Lordship of the Isles. They could not easily accommodate to a new order, whether based in Edinburgh or London.

By way of a postscript there is an account in Faujas de Saint Fond's Travels of his meeting with a M. de Bombelles at Killin. De Bombelles was also French but Faujas, who was a geologist, gives the distinct impression that he was there for very particular reasons: '*From the career which M. de Bombelles followed, from numerous military and other charts which he had along with him, I judged that diplomacy and politics were more to his taste than the natural sciences and the arts, and that he probably had some particular mission, very foreign to the object of my studies.*' (Faujas de Saint Fond, *A journey through England and Scotland to the Hebrides in 1784.*)

It was less than forty years since Culloden and the French probably retained a political interest in Scotland.

Chapter 4

The pre-Reformation church and travel

T he Christian church was arguably the greatest institutional patron of travel to, from and within the Highlands and Hebrides. The Church's great empire was held together by a bureaucratic structure of office and procedure, by networks of diocesan and monastic clergy. There was a pan-European organisation of bishoprics, another of religious orders. There were elaborate ecclesiastical hierarchies; the monastic orders, the abbots and priors, their female counterparts, the archbishops and bishops, the deans and parish clergy, the cathedral chapters, archdeacons, deacons, canons and prebendaries. There were also regional variations in areas such as the Celtic west which accommodated more slowly to the Roman form and where the older monastic styles had deep roots. In the Highlands and Hebrides, Christianity had not eradicated all pagan belief and there were some curiously Celtic forms and practices that survived. Nevertheless, from the thirteenth century when we first hear in detail about this area from papal records, we can assume that the Roman church had permeated every aspect of Hebridean life. The Hebrides were recognized by, and felt themselves part of, the Western Christian tradition.

Much more information survives for clerical than lay travel simply because the church was the better record-keeper. Members of the church made up the educated elite and maintained official records, some of which were preserved in the Vatican archives. We have letters and supplications to do with the Hebrides from the thirteenth century onwards. After the Reformation this is much reduced in scope and efforts were rather directed at keeping the Catholic flame alive. Catholic historians have done much to publish those records that survive – with particular regard to the Franciscan mission in the early seventeenth century and the efforts of Catholic priests in the Highlands since then. I am not going to deal with this later material but those interested may consult the works of Blundell and Giblin, as well as the periodical 'The Innes Review' (see Bibliography). This chapter reviews some of what we know about the earlier Highlands and Hebrides through the eyes of the church. The context is always what is revealed by travel and the evidence appears within a chronological framework.

Even in the so-called Dark Ages we should recognise the force and reach of the Christian ideal. Irish monasticism was deeply imbued with the spirit of eremitism, the desire to become a hermit. To lead the life of a solitary was the final stage, the ideal state of western monasticism. For many years Irish monks were captivated by the notion of the 'peregrinatio', the travelling, where they set off in a fragile boat for an unknown shore, sometimes without aid of oar or sail, symbolic of the human plight. The whole cult has a huge body of literature devoted to it and I do not propose to discuss it here. For the pilgrims the shore visited was less important than the impulse for going. These were not missionaries in the mould of Livingston searching for their darkest Africa. They craved inner peace not large flocks or the outward marks of success. They were not searching out communities to convert or minds to cultivate, but desert places for retreat and retirement. It was not a concern for the benighted that drew them but a concern for their own salvation that impelled them. They were not called, they were driven. As a result we have no reports of the island communities they reached. We have no record of the customs and habits of the settlements they found, instead all we have is the idea of their own inner fire and fanaticism.

The urge to seek a desert in the sea was already powerful in the latter half of the sixth century as the following anecdote from Adomnan's *Life of Columba* makes clear. Columba was using diplomacy to ensure the safety of fellow missionaries when they ventured into Pictish waters:

> *At another time Cormac, a soldier of Christ . . . attempted for a second time to seek a desert in the ocean.*
>
> *And after [Cormac] had sailed away from land with full sails over the limitless ocean, about the same time St Columba, staying beyond the Ridge of Britain, commanded king Brude in presence of the kinglet of the Orkneys, saying, 'Some of us have recently sailed out, desiring to find a desert in the impassable sea; and in case they chance after long wanderings to come to the Orkney isles, command this chieftain earnestly, since his hostages are in thy hand, that no harm befal them within his territories'.*
>
> *The saint said this because he foreknew in spirit that after some months this Cormac would come to the Orkneys. This occurred afterwards, and because of the holy man's aforesaid commendation [Cormac] was saved from imminent death in the Orkneys.* (Anderson, Early Sources)

That they reached further still is evident from the exploits of Brendan and Dicuil. They have left carved stones in the Faeroes and the Norse noted their presence in Iceland. That they also travelled extensively within the Hebrides is apparent from their own records. Adomnan's *Life of Columba* gives us numerous examples of Columba's miracles in calming rough waters, procuring favourable winds and even in raising storms to overcome the wicked. Monks and abbots travelled widely on ecclesiastical business, as arbitrators on their own behalf and as diplomats employed by the secular power. Monasteries were also property owners, and their estates might consist of widely scattered parcels of land. These all had to be administered and their renders fetched home for the consumption of the monastic community. In the Irish annals there are numerous references to travel between the monasteries. This could be dangerous:

> Annals of Ulster, c. 642
> *The wreck of a boat of the community of Iona.* (Anderson p 165)
> Annals of Ulster, 691
> *A great gale drowned certain six men of the community of Iona.* (Anderson, Early Sources)
> An abbot of Applecross was drowned with his crew:
> Annals of Tigernach, 737
> *Failbe, Guaire's son, the successor of Maelrubai of Applecross, was drowned in the deep sea with his sailors, twenty-two in number.* (Anderson, Early Sources)
> And, a few years later, Iona was similarly struck:
> Annals of Tigernach, 749
> *Drowning of the [monastic] household of Iona.*
> (Anderson, Early Sources – also in Annals of Ulster)
> Relics were transported around the Christian communities:
> Annals of Ulster, 1034
> *Macc-nia Ua-Uchtain, lector of Kells, was drowned while he came [to Ireland] from Scotland; and Columcille's flabellum, and three of the relics of Patrick, [were lost with him]; along with thirty men.*
> (Anderson, Early Sources)

We should not underestimate the strength of these early monastic communities as economic enterprises. They have not left us an architectural legacy comparable to their mediaeval counterparts but they may have played an equally important economic role. Church authorities probably made lists of their properties from the earliest times. For the most part we do not know how and when Iona was endowed with its various lands but some of them may have been in the hands of the monastery for about a thousand years. They were extensive and valuable and our earliest list comes from a document dated 1203.

> *The churches of Insegal, Mule, Coluansei, Cheldubsenaig, Chelcenneg, Ile.*
> *The islands of Hy, Mule, Coluansei, Oruansei, Canei, Calue.*
> *The land of Magenburg, Mangecheles, Herilnean, Sotesdal.*
> *The lands of Abberade in Yle, Markarna, Camusnanesre.*
> (Reeves, *Life of St Columba*, Appendix V, No 1)

Not all of these names are certainly identifiable, and it is doubtful if Iona owned more of Mull than the Ross, but the list is important in establishing Iona's early possessions. It also suggests that Iona maintained contact with its estates and expected a return from them. That required personal supervision and probably a great deal of sea-travel between Islay in the south and Canna in the north.

A 1672 contract between Argyll and Clanranald, for the island of Canna, includes the clause: '*and for serving the Earl, when required, with a galley of sixteen oars, sufficiently appointed with men and necessaries for thirty days yearly between the isle of Canna and Icolmkill*' (Fourth Report of the Royal Commission on Historical Manuscripts, 1874)

Quite probably this reflects the much older obligations imposed on Canna by the fact that it was owned by Iona for many hundreds of years. It is more than likely that earlier tenants were expected to provide a boat to ferry the surplus produce from this fertile island for the use of the monastic community on Iona.

The lands of Lossit in Islay are recorded as church-lands as early as 1507. In 1617 we learn that the reddendo for Lossit included a fourteen–oared *cymba* or boat. It seems likely that the reason for this was to provide a means of conveying the rent, then predominantly in kind, to the landowner (possibly the monastery of Iona). In a contract between the Bishop of the Isles and Maclean of Duart dated 1580 there is reference to: '*Lauchlane M'Donald M'Conych and his galey of seruice* [galley of service] *of the saidis landis of Rosse.*' [The Ross of Mull, which was an ancient possession of Iona] (Collectanea de Rebus Albanicis, p 15).

These three traces of ancient obligations, along with Adomnan's evidence, suggest that in the seventh and eighth centuries Hebridean waters were busy with currachs plying back and forth.

Adomnan describes how Columba's influence secured propitious winds for them during Adomnan's own time on Iona. (He became Abbot in 679.)

Our faith in such miracles in the past, which we did not see, is indubitably confirmed by present-day miracles which we have seen ourselves. For we ourselves have thrice seen contrary winds turned to favourable ones.

The first time, when long hewn-out ships of pine and oak were being drawn over-land, and timbers for the great monastery (and for ships likewise) were being conveyed, we took counsel, and placed the holy man's vestments and books upon the altar, with psalms and fasting, and with invocation of his name, that he should obtain for us from the Lord favourable prosperity of winds. And, God so granting it to that holy man, it happened thus; for on the day upon which our sailors had prepared everything, and intended to tow the logs of the above-mentioned timber over the sea with skiffs and curachs, the winds, on the previous days contrary, became suddenly favourable. Thereupon the whole day, God being propitious, prosperous breezes served them through long and devious ways; and with full sails, without any delay, the whole expedition of ships reached the island of Iona successfully. (Anderson, Early Sources)

Adomnan then goes on to describe a similar miracle some years later when they were towing oak timbers from the mouth of the River Shiel in order to restore the monastery. He lets drop that the fleet consisted of twelve boats or currachs. The ability to organise and maintain so many vessels suggests power and wealth.

The Hebrides contain innumerable little islets with resources which might only be accessed or valuable for a few weeks of the year. They were still jealously guarded. A great deal of the internal travel round the Hebrides was to take advantage of these during the spring and summer. An anecdote in Adomnan's *Life of Columba* shows that even from the very earliest times the rights to use natural resources such as seals, birds and grazing were nicely apportioned – and that monasteries protected their assets quite as jealously as laymen.

> *The holy man's prophecy concerning the thief Erc Mocu-druide, who dwelt in the island of Colosus.* [Perhaps Coll, rather than Colonsay].
>
> *At another time, when the saint abode in the island of Iona, he called to him two men of the brethren, their names being Lugbe and Silnan. And he bade them, saying, 'Cross over at once to the island of Mull, and in the little plains near the sea look for the robber Erc; for he came secretly alone last night from the island of Colosus, and endeavours to hide during the day among the sand-dunes, under his boat, which he has covered with hay, intending to sail over by night to the small island where the seals belonging to our sealing rights breed and are bred, and to kill some of them violently, and after very greedily and predaciously filling his boat to return to his habitation'.*
>
> *Hearing this they obeyed and sailed over, and found the thief hidden in the place indicated beforehand by the saint; and they brought him to the saint, as he had instructed them.*
>
> Anderson, From *Adomnan's Life of Columba*, pp 65–6 – (AD 563–597)

From the earliest times church institutions were jealous of their lands, their privileges and dues. They had rights of jurisdiction and sanctuary. They could expect renders in kind. All of these had to be safeguarded from laymen, occasionally from other churchmen. It is even possible that some of these rights and obligations were pre-Christian. As Christianity took over ancient sacred sites and burial grounds so it may have inherited the dues and duties that went with them.

We know little about the internal network of contacts although we may suspect it was extensive and elaborate. A people who could produce the wonders of graphical art that are the Book of Kells and the Kildalton cross were certainly capable of maintaining an elaborate bureaucracy, attending church synods, travelling abroad for education and keeping navigational records. Over the years they must have built up an extensive body of sea-lore. Whether this was transmitted orally or in writing, none, unfortunately, has survived. Their main method of transport was probably by skin-built vessels called currachs but wooden boats are also suggested by Adomnan. These may have been dug-outs rather than plank-built.

Unfortunately the disruption of the Viking invasions means we partially lose sight of monastic activity on the West coast from about 800. We can only guess at how successful the monastic communities were at maintaining their links around the Hebrides. What we can say is that since Iona is still found with enormous estates *after* the Viking period then she was at least partly successful in maintaining them *within*.

There was probably a great deal of organised travel in the monastic world of the early Hebrides. Monks were regularly in touch with each other, particularly within the same monastic family, and skilled craftsmen like sculptors must have travelled round the islands carving stones for different patrons. Unfortunately we know nothing about the mechanics of this. It is the emergence of Papal records from the thirteenth century that gives us our first solid evidence. From now on more travel had a diocesan rather than a monastic imperative.

The Mediaeval church

The empire of the Roman church gradually eclipsed its Celtic cousin from the seventh century and the parish system evolved during the early mediaeval period. For Rome travel was routinely invoked on an institutional basis. Parochial and diocesan administration required it. The Highlands and Hebrides shared in this common tradition. The bishopric of Sodor or the Isles existed by about 1079 and the bishopric of Argyll or Lismore was founded by about 1193.

It is difficult for us to grasp what a central role the church played in everyday life in earlier centuries. Firstly, matters of the spirit and concerns for the afterlife played a more prominent role in everyone's daily routine. Life was short, death was close; as were sickness, suffering and sorrow. Pain and danger lurked as near as your enemy, loss and grief might lie no further than tomorrow. Faith and fear marched hand in hand. In addition to this the church was an economic powerhouse. Monasteries were islands of wealth in a sea of want. Bishops were men of great political as well spiritual importance. The church offered a clear career path for the ambitious, the clever and the thwarted; the bright, the greedy, and younger sons.

The church incorporated an educated elite. As an institution it fostered and encouraged learning. Outside the universities, a few burghs, and the families of the greatest nobles, it offered the only means of education. In the monastic scriptoria, amongst the educated clerks and scribes employed by the bishops and archbishops, or as parish priests, were to be found Scotland's literati and historians.

The Highlands and Hebrides did not have great numbers of religious houses or clergy but they certainly had some. Iona was by far and away the most important religious centre in the area. It owned very considerable property in land and enjoyed international prestige. But there were other foundations at Saddell in Kintyre, Ardchattan on Loch Etive, Oronsay, and the college of Kilmun in Cowal. These were all islands of education and culture. Very little evidence of this survives except in the form of monumental sculpture and the names of some of the monks and clergy who appear in mediaeval documents. We have Papal correspondence with clergymen in the area and their names also appear in official Scots documents. They might be appointed to a post, or appear as a witness, or be asked to act as an arbiter.

There was a system of parish priests just as in the rest of Britain. From the earliest Highland charters we learn of the rights of 'advowson', (i.e. presentation to a living), held by the landowners. They could present clergy to the parishes within their estates. Lands which had been appropriated to maintain priests in churches and chapels were jealously guarded and competed for. Some of these gifts of land may well have dated back to the early Christian centuries. As time went on, so more and more parishes were appropriated for other ecclesiastical uses; to support a distant monastery; to support the local bishop; or to supplement the income of a cleric who was not content with the revenues from one ecclesiastical source. The letters to and from the Papacy throughout the mediaeval period are full of such issues and disputes. The Highlands and Hebrides share fully in this although their remoteness meant they usually escaped the closest attentions of Mother Church.

We know a surprising amount about some of these church disputes because they were referred up the ecclesiastical tree, sometimes as far as Rome. This involved enormous expense of time and money. For someone to travel to Rome in the course of his dispute meant that the pickings had to be worth it. Generally it is more likely that they employed the services of a third party or agent. We find this correspondence in the transcripts published by the Scottish History Society and the volumes of Papal Letters concerning Great Britain and Ireland (see Bibliography).

Church officials were also used by the lay authorities as diplomats. Robert de Torigni says that in the year 1166:

> *Thither came to* [king Henry] *William, king of Scotland, and the bishop of the Isles of Man and other thirty-one, which are between Scotland and Ireland and England* . . .
>
> *The bishop aforesaid came to the English king as legate of this king of the Isles. For the aforesaid king is the cousin of the English king on the side of Matilda the empress, his mother.* (Anderson, *Scottish Annals from English Chroniclers*)

As an example of the importance of church records as sources we have a *Life of St Cuthbert* written in the late twelfth century by Reginald a monk of Durham. At the end of Chapter 112 we have a specific date, 1172, and in the same chapter there is a marginal note, by a contemporary hand, of various lands and islands, most of them round Scotland. After Greenland the list runs as follows:

Yuiste	(Ivist or Uist)
Leothus	(Lewis)
Barreiam	(Barra)
Cole	(Coll)
Tirieth	(Tiree)
Coluense	(Colonsay)
Achum	
Slete	
Bote	(Bute)
Schy	(Skye)
Hyle	(Islay)
Hii Colmekille	(Hi of Columba = Iona)
Mulih	(Mull)
insulas Orcadum	(Orkney Isles)
Scotiam	(Scotland)
(Raine, Reginaldi Monachi Dunelmensis)	

Of this list only Achum and Slete present problems. The latter suggests Sleat, the southern peninsula of Skye, but Skye is also mentioned separately. Arran and Jura are perhaps the two islands most obviously missing from the list.

Church business was one of the principal reasons for travelling in the Middle Ages. We can recognise and list the various religious imperatives:

1 The Church as administrator and landowner

The church was a great institution with a huge estate and so travel was built into its everyday life and work. This included travel round and between parishes by priests to minister, by bishops to administer, and by chancellors to gather dues. There was travel to cathedrals or synods for meetings on church business, the investiture of new priests, bishops and other ranks of clergy. There was travel to render or collect church dues, at a parish, episcopal or papal level. The following are examples of travel around the Highlands and Islands on official church business during the Middle Ages.

To cleanse polluted churches – but not in person:

Indult to the Bishop of Sodor to reconcile polluted churches by means of any suitable priest, 1397

> *On your behalf it was represented to us that churches and [cemeteries] of certain islands in your diocese are often violated by the effusion of blood or emission of semen or the burial of excommunicates; and, because you are not able in person conveniently to reconcile them by reason of the remoteness of the isles and the sea crossing, and the dangers of wars in those parts, you have humbly petitioned us to provide you with opportune remedy thereanent. We, therefore, by authority of these presents grant you faculty, so long as you remain Bishop of Sodor, to reconcile churches and cemeteries of these isles by some fit priest as often as shall be needful, the bodies of the excommunicate (if they can be distinguished from the other bodies) being first exhumed and cast far from ecclesiastical sepulture, and with water first blessed by you or other priest, as the custom is: without prejudice to the constitution prescribing this to be done only by bishops.* (Vatican Transcripts, Highland Papers, Vol IV (pp 152–3)

On the same day of 1397, Michael, Bishop of Sodor, was granted a faculty to visit the churches and monasteries of certain islands in his diocese by a fit person:

> *Since on your behalf it has been represented to us that on account of distance and remoteness and the dangers of the sea-crossing you are not able personally to visit the churches, monasteries and other ecclesiastical places of certain isles in your diocese, in which by right and by custom the office of visitation is incumbent upon you, We, acceding to your supplications in this part, grant you the faculty of exercising the said office of visitation by some other person or persons of your choice, deputed or to be deputed, and of taking up in ready money the procurations due by reason of said visitation from the said churches, monasteries, places and persons, notwithstanding whatsoever constitutions of Pope Innocent IV or Gregory X or any others of our predecessors to the contrary.* (Vatican Transcripts, Highland Papers, Vol IV (pp 153–4))

The church was also a great landholder. Estates had to be supervised and renders collected. I have given, above, the possessions of the monastery of Iona as listed in 1203. Bishops also required funds. There is a bull, purporting to be from Pope Gregory IX and dated 30 July 1231, which lists the islands whose churches owed dues to the bishop of Sodor. This only survives in a copy dated to about 1600 which is itself badly torn. B. Megaw argued that the original was actually a forgery which might be dated to about 1377. Even at that, it is of interest. The bull was printed by R. Lane Poole in Vol VIII of the *Scottish Historical Review*. He supplied missing letters in square brackets and the modern names of the islands in round brackets. I have slightly amended his list on the basis of suggestions made by Maitland Thomson and Lindsay.

de Bothe, (Bute)
de Aran, (Arran)
de Eya, (Gigha)
de Ile, (Islay)
de Iurye (Jura)
de Scarpey, (Scarba)
de Elath, (Elachnave, the southernmost Garvelach?)
de Col[vansey], (Colonsay)
de Muley, (Mull)
de Chorhye, (Tiree)
de Cole, (Coll)
de Ege, (Eigg)
de Skey, (Skye)
de Carrey, (Barra, or possibly Canna)
de R[. . .], (Rum?)
et de Howas, (Uist or Lewis?)
de insulis Alne,
de Swostersey (Wattersay?)

Boece gives an interesting report on the priest's annual visitation to St Kilda:

> *In the moneth of Juny, ane preist cumis out of the Lewis in ane bait to this Ile,*
> *and ministeris the sacrament of baptisme to all the barnis that hes bene borne*
> *in the yeir afore. Als sone as this preist hes done his office, with certane messis,*
> *he ressavis the tindis of all thair commoditeis, and returnis hame the same*
> *gait he come.* (Hector Boece (1527), in Hume Brown, *Scotland before*
> *1700.*)

> (In the month of June, a priest comes out of the Lewis in a boat to this
> Isle, and ministers the sacrament of baptism to all the bairns that have
> been born in the year before. As soon as this priest has done his office,
> with certain masses, he receives the tiends [tithes] of all their commod-
> ities, and returns home the same way he came.)

Dean Monro, who knew the steward of St Kilda, gives a slightly more exact
version:

> *The inhabitants thairof are simple creatures, scant learnit in ony Religion:*
> *but Mccloyd of Haray his Stewart, or quhom he deputtis in sic office, sayles*
> *anes in the zeir at midsymmer with sum chaiplane to baptize bairns thair;*
> *and gif they want ane chaiplane, thai baptize thair bairns thameselfis . . .*
> *The saids Stewartis ressaves thair maillis in maill and reistit muttonis, wild*
> *reistit foullis and selchis.* (R. W. Munro, *Monro's Western Isles,* 1549)

(The inhabitants thereof are simple creatures, scant learned in any Religion: but MacLeod of Harris's steward, or whoever he deputes in such office, sails once in the year at midsummer with some chaplain to baptize bairns there; and if they are missing a chaplain, they baptize their bairns themselves . . . The said steward receives their dues in meal and dried mutton, dried wildfowl and seals).

This story sufficiently impressed Laurence Nowell, the Elizabethan antiquarian, for him to copy it, in about 1565, onto the page following his map of Scotland.

2 Travels to and from Rome, for disputes

For many centuries the church was the greatest international or supranational institution in Western Europe. It had its own judicial process, its own procedures for resolving disputes. Arguments arose frequently over jobs but by no means all disputes reached Rome. Few Highland benefices (clerical livings) could justify the expense involved. Nevertheless, career opportunities in the Highlands and Islands were scarce and desirable. In the mediaeval period, if you were a younger son or illegitimate, if you did not inherit great wealth or could not fight for it, then the church was just about the only career path open to you. The problem, throughout Europe, was that this was a highly competitive market. Religion offered great rewards to those with intelligence and aptitude.

As a result, parishes and other benefices were fiercely fought for, sometimes in a wholly unchristian manner. Disputes would start at a local level and then be referred up the long ecclesiastical tree as both sides mustered their clerical and lay supporters. In practical terms the endorsement of the local landowner was critical. But if the office had regional or national significance then it might be worth debating in Rome. Nobody was going to run up great expense to fight for a parish in the Rough Bounds or the Outer Isles but Glassary and Lismore offered richer pickings and lay closer to the centre of national government. It is from areas such as these that we see most disputes in the Roman and Scottish records.

In the following pages I give some examples of issues which travelled to Rome from the two dioceses of Sodor and Lismore. Sodor comes from the old Norse term for the Southern Isles (Sudreyar) and here means the diocese of the Isles or Hebrides. Lismore was the see of the bishopric of Argyll which stretched from Kintyre to Glenelg. Certain themes crop up again and again in the Roman records – principally the poverty of the benefices and the need to provide hospitality for visitors. Litigants at Rome always painted in black and white so much of what we learn of these remote dioceses presents a pretty bleak picture. You could be forgiven for thinking that it was barely possible to lead a religious life at the ends of the habitable earth; that war, dissension and the oppressions of the nobility were crushing Holy Church underfoot. On the other hand if there were not some profit to be gained from these church offices it is difficult to see why they were worth fighting for.

First, though, it is worth looking at some of the threats the church faced and some of the opportunities it offered – in purely material terms. The church was often bullied by laymen because of its fabulous wealth. In Lowland Scotland it might enjoy the protection of the king which would limit the power of a local aggressor. In the Highlands and Islands the Lord of the Isles occupied a similar position and certainly good John of Islay (1330–1386) enjoyed a glowing reputation as a protector of the church. But, in the absence of such protection the church might sufffer badly at the hands of the lay authorities. The following two examples have a Lowland context but illustrate a dilemma common throughout Scotland.

Hume Brown quotes from a letter from Dr Magnus, the English agent in Scotland, to Cardinal Wolsey, 22 December 1524. In this case it is perfectly obvious the church was being taken advantage of:

The good Abbot of Pasley of late shewed unto me he was likely to susteyn gret hurt and damage both to hymself and his monastery by the saide twoe erles (Angus and Lennox), if remedy were not founden and at a tyme convanient, for as he shewed unto me the saide twoe erles intended to kepe thair Christemas in his saide hous, and to use everything there at thair libertye and pleasur, booth for hors and man to the numer of 200 persons. (Hume Brown, *Scotland before 1700*, p 6 footnote)

In contrast we have a passage in the Auchinleck Chronicle which refers to the death, on 29 June 1459, of Thomas Tarvas, an earlier Abbot of Paisley. This gives a good example of how a robust abbot could build up a monastery's wealth:

the quhilk was ane richt gud man, and helplyk to the place of ony that ever was. For he did mony notable thingis, and held ane noble hous, and was ay wele purvait. He fand the place all out of gud rewle, and destitut of leving, and all the kirkis in lordis handis, and the kirk unbiggit . . . He biggit and theckit it with sclait, and riggit it with stane, and biggit ane gret porcioun of the steple, and ane staitlie yethous, and brocht hame mony gud jowellis, and clathis of gold silver and silk, and mony gud bukis, and maid staitlie stallis, and glasynnit mekle of all the kirk, and brocht hame the staitliest tabernakle that was in all Scotland, and the mast costlie. And schortlie he brocht all the place to fredome, and fra nocht till ane mychti place, and left it out of all kynd of det, and at all fredome till dispone as thaim lykit, and left ane of the best myteris that was in Scotland, and chandillaris of silver, and ane lettren of bras, with mony uthir gud jowellis.

(The which was a right good man, and [most] helpful to the place of any that ever was. For he did many notable things, and held a noble house, and was always well purveyed. He found the place all out of good rule, and destitute of living, and all the kirks in lords' hands, and the kirk unbuilt. . . . He built and roofed it with slate, and rigged it with stone, and built a great portion of the steeple, and a stately gatehouse, and brought home many good jewels, and cloths of gold silver and silk, and many good books, and made stately stalls, and glazed much of all the kirk, and brought home the stateliest tabernacle that was in all Scotland, and the most costly. And shortly he brought all the place to freedom, and from nothing to a mighty place, and left it out of all kind of debt, and at all freedom to dispose as they liked, and left one of the best mitres that was in Scotland, and chandeliers of silver, and a lectern of brass, with many other good jewels.)

3 Sorning and hospitality

In the Highlands and Islands there was a particular problem known as 'sorning' which was when landlords took free quarters for themselves and their followers at their tenants' expense. At the end of the sixteenth century the responsibilities of tenants in Lewis are described as follows:

> It is 40 lb. land of auld extent and payis yeirlie 18 score chalders of victuall, 58 score of ky, 32 score of wedderis, and ane great quantitie of fisches, pultrie, and quhyte plaiding by thair Cuidichies, that is, feisting thair master quhen he pleases to cum in the cuntrie, ilk ane thair nicht or twa nichtis about, according to thair land and labouring. (Skene, Celtic Scotland, Description of the Isles dating to 1577–1595)

> (It is £40 land of Old Extent and pays yearly 360 chalders of victual, 1160 cattle, 640 wethers, and a great quantity of fish, poultry, and white cloth apart from their Cuddich, that is, feasting their master when he pleases to come in the country, each one their night or two nights about, according to their land and labouring).

But the description of Sleat (Skye) in the same document makes it clear that if the landowner had a large retinue this could be a heavy burden:

> Slait is occupiet for the maist pairt be gentlemen, thairfore it payis but the auld deuties, that is, of victuall, buttir, cheis, wyne, aill, and aquavite, samekle as thair maister may be able to spend being ane nicht (albeit he were 600 men in companie) on ilk merk land.

> (Sleat is occupied for the most part by gentlemen, therefore it pays only the old duties, that is, of victual, butter, cheese, wine, ale, and aquavitae,

so much as their master may be able to spend being one night (albeit he had 600 men in [his] company) on each markland).

Although this practice was hallowed by tradition in the west it aroused the jealous attention of the Scots Parliament which tried formal curtailment in the early seventeenth century. In July 1616, at Edinburgh, obligations were laid upon certain island chiefs (Macleod of Harris, Mackinnon, Maclean of Coll, Maclean of Lochbuy and Clanranald):

And that the saidis personis at Martymes nixt sall sett the rest of thair landis to tennentis for a certane constant and cleir dewytie, and that thay sall exact no forder frome thair tennentis bot the cleir dewytie contenit in thair tak and sett; especiallie that thay sall in all tyme comeing forbeare the taking of cowdighis frome thair tennentis, and sall content thame selffis with the constant and cleir dewytie for the quhilk thair landis ar sett. And that the saidis personis principallis nor nane of thame, according to thair severall oblismentis, sall haif or keepe ony ma birlingis of xvi or xviii airis bot everyone of thame ane; and that, quhen thay travell athorte the Ilis with thair birlingis and comes on land, that thay nor nane in companie with thame in thair birlingis sall not sorne upoun the cuntrey. (Register of the Privy Council, Vol X pp773–75)

(And that the said persons at Martinmas next shall set the rest of their lands to tenants for a certain constant and clear duty, and that they shall exact no further from their tenants but the clear duty contained in their tack and set [lease]; especially that they shall in all time coming forbear the taking of cowdighis [cuddichs] from their tenants, and shall content themselves with the constant and clear duty for the which their lands are set. And that the said persons principals nor none of them, according to their several obligations, shall have or keep any more birlinns of 16 or 18 oars but everyone of them one; and that, when they travel athorte [about] the Isles with their birlinns and come on land, that they nor none in company with them in their birlinns shall not sorn upon the country.)

Disregarding the hypocrisy of the Scots Parliament in imposing these restrictions we should recognise a very real problem. The Highland aristocracy were probably expert in taking advantage of their tenants and the church whenever opportunity offered. It was difficult to object to such exactions when they were carried out by representatives of the landlord. Martin Martin draws attention to the practice in St Kilda:

The steward's retinue consist of forty, fifty, or sixty persons, and among them, perhaps the most meagre in the parish are carried thither to be recruited with good chear; but this retinue is now retrenched, as also some of their ancient and unreasonable exactions.

The steward lives upon the charge of the inhabitants until the time that the solan geese are ready to fly, which the inhabitants think long enough; the daily allowance paid by them is very regularly exacted, with regard to their respective proportions of lands and rocks; there is not a parcel of men in the world more scrupulously nice and punctilious in maintaining their liberties and properties than these are, being most religiously fond of their ancient laws and statutes. (Martin Martin, *A Voyage to St Kilda*, 1698)

In the age-old struggle between landlord and tenant there were many skirmishes. It was difficult for a group of tenants to resist when the landlord had with him a retinue of lusty young galloglachs. They might eat him out of house and home. But if the laird came without followers, or if he sent an underling, then he might be resisted, cheated, or short-changed. Martin gives us an inkling of some of these squabbles in St Kilda but also pays tribute to the sturdy independence of the islanders.

They are reputed very cunning, and there is scarce any circumventing of them in traffick and bartering; the voice of one is the voice of all the rest, they being all of a piece, their common interest uniting them firmly together.

All of us walking together to the little village where there was a lodging prepared for us, furnished with beds of straw, and according to the ancient custom of the place, the officer, who presides over them (in the steward's absence) summoned the inhabitants, who by concert agreed upon a daily maintenance for us, as bread, butter, cheese, mutton, fowls, eggs, also fire, etc all which was to be given in at our lodging twice every day; this was done in the most regular manner, each family by turns paying their quota proportionably to their lands.

But it wasn't just landlords who claimed free board and lodging. Martin Martin states that in North Uist:

The great produce of barley draws many strangers to this island, with a design to procure as much of this grain as they can; which they get of the inhabitants gratis, only for asking, as they do horses, cows, sheep, wool, etc. I was told some months before my last arrival there, that there had been ten men in that place at one time to ask corn gratis, and every one of these had some one, some two, and others three attendants; and during their abode there, were all entertained gratis, no one returning empty.

This is a great, yet voluntary tax, which has continued for many ages; but the late general scarcity has given them an occasion to alter this custom, by making acts against liberality, except to poor natives and objects of charity.

(Martin Martin, A Description of the Western Islands of Scotland c. 1695)

This was written about the time of the Ill Years, at the very end of the seventeenth century, when the whole of Scotland suffered from dearth. Despite this, expectation, and render, were still alive during the eighteenth century:

> but great numbers of the Keppoch, Glengarry, and Clanronald Families, tho' not worth a Shilling, would be ashamed to be seen at any Kind of Labour tho' they think it no Shame to Steal or go through the Country asking assistance of their Neighbours (which they call thigging) or living upon free Quarters wherever they happen to be, and they Reckon it an Honour done to other people that they should be entertained by them. (Lang, The Highlands of Scotland in 1750)

Bruce thought this such an important issue that he included it in his recommendations: 'that Thigging (which is a Genteel way of Begging with a Threatning in Case of Refusal) and Sorning (by which is meant Living on Free Quarters) be suppressed by inflicting a Severe Penalty both on those who Either Ask or Give Thigging or Free Quarters to such Vagabonds. (Lang, The Highlands of Scotland in 1750)

The Reverend MacQueen gave a native perspective on an ancient and honoured tradition:

> Men of narrow principles are disposed to attribute the uncommon hospitality of the Highlanders not so much to generosity as to self-love, the absolute want of inns making it necessary to receive the stranger, in hopes of being repaid in their own persons, or in that of their friends. Hospitality was founded on immemorial custom, before the thoughts of men were contracted by the use of weights and measures, and reckoned so far a sacred obligation as to think themselves bound to entertain the man who from a principle of ill-will and resentment, sorned upon them with a numerous retinue, which went under the name of 'the Odious Visitor', Coinimh Dhuimigh. Of this there have been instances within a century back; which kind of hospitality could scarce be supposed self-interested. (Rev. Donald MacQueen, 1774, Appendix to Pennant)

This sort of begging was, according to the testimony of the Rev. John Lane Buchanan, still alive in Harris at the end of the eighteenth century:

> Thus fleeced by the extortions of their superiors, the poor people are moreover exposed to the importunate solicitations, and demands of their equals, from the neighbouring isles. Swarms of the wives tenants of Uist, and the small

isles, come in Summer to the hills of Harris to spunge on the poor inhabitants, to get presents of wool and clothing. Each of these begging females must have a servant to carry the bags of wool which she collects. A dozen of them is often quartered on a poor tenant in a night. One of the family, the next day, accompanies them to a neighbouring farm The strangers carry their distaffs and spindles along with them, and spin as they proceed, and when they sit down to rest. As they are engaged in their own work, and are fed by others, they make their circuit at their leisure. The expense of those visitors, added to the rapacity of the tacksmen, compels the poor tenants to be half naked, and half starved, even in the coldest weather, and when engaged at the hard labour before described.

    It will naturally occur to the reader, that the gifts of the mendicant females are voluntary, and consequently not grievous. In fact, though nominally voluntary, they are really compulsory. The mendicants, have easier access to their landlords and landladies, and frighten them with threats of complaints. They even come often reinforced by the recommendations of the tacksmen's wives, or ladies (as they style themselves) which the tenants dare not disregard. Here, indeed, as in all countries where arbitrary power prevails, oppressive as the supreme despot may be, a great part of the suffering of the subjects arises from subordinate tyranny. (Buchanan, *Travels in the Western Hebrides from 1782 to 1790*)

Travellers today can expect a network of hotels and boarding houses to provide food and shelter. However, this is a very recent phenomenon in the Highlands and Islands, little more than two hundred years old. In earlier centuries such hospitality was provided either by social custom or the church. In either case it could bear heavily on resources, especially when landlords, patrons or benefactors were unreasonable in their demands. We know little of lay grievances but the clergy carried their pleas and excuses to Rome:

17 November 1421
Dominicus Dominici, priest, monk professed of Iona . . . that the Pope would dispense him, notwithstanding defect of birth as the son of a priest, religious of the order of St Benedict, and of an unmarried woman, to hold an ecclesiastical benefice . . . considering that the timber work and walls of the choir, bell-tower and other surrounding buildings of the said monastery, where he is professed, are utterly fallen to the ground, and also that the great and better part of its lands and possessions are preyed upon and devastated by wicked and perverse nobles, so that the monks are not able to complete the fabric of the monastery and to live there suitably for they scarcely have bread, barley, or ale, on account of the continual hospitality there maintained.
(Calendar of Scottish Supplications to Rome 1418–22, pp 267–68)

A number of contemporary texts make clear Iona's problems:

3 December 1421
By reason of the continual wars raging among the Western Islands of the kingdom of Scotland, the monastery of Iona . . . is so collapsed and impoverished in its buildings and rents that it is sinking to irreparable ruin, unless the Pope in his clemency provide an opportune remedy, especially because the revenues of the monastery do not suffice for its reparation and the sustenance of the monks, and for the maintaining of hospitality, which according to the custom of the country they are bound, even unwillingly, to observe. (Calendar of Scottish Supplications to Rome 1418–22, pp 271–2)

The burden of hospitality is a recurrent theme:

Whereas in the Western Isles subject to the Kingdom of Scotland, by reason of the feuds there existing the ecclesiastical benefices are so meagre that their fruits can scarce support a single priest, especially in view of the continuous hospitality which by the custom of those parts it behoves him to afford to strangers: Therefore Donald of Islay, grandson of the late Robert King of Scots, Lord of the Isles aforesaid and of the Earldom of Ross, petitions on behalf of his beloved chaplain and familiar the presbyter Adam, son of Dominic, perpetual vicar of the parish church of St Eugenius in the Ross of Mull, of the diocese of Sodor, that along with the foresaid vicarage, of which the yearly value does not exceed three pounds of sterling money, the said Adam may be permitted to hold for his life such other benefice, even if incompatible, as he may succeed canonically in obtaining, with power of transference, and that notwithstanding of the defect of his birth as the son of a monk in priest's orders and an unmarried woman.
Granted 24 November 1421 (Highland Papers, vol IV, p 165 ff Abstract)

It seems from subsequent documents that Adam's wish was granted only in part:

Whereas it has been conceded to Adam the son of Dominic, presbyter and perpetual vicar of the parish church of St Eugenius, that he may hold another benefice therewith as craved in his original petition, and that for the space of two years, and whereas this licence will be of but little advantage to the said Adam in respect of the great expense involved in a journey from these parts to Rome, and of the small value of the benefices in the diocese of Sodor, Donald of Islay . . . therefore prays that the dispensation may be extended to the lifetime of the foresaid Adam.
Granted for a period of seven years, 17 December 1421. (Highland Papers, vol IV, p 173)

Plaintiffs generally did their best to make their appeals heart-rending – as in this submission on behalf of Dominic, son of Dominic, December 1421, a monk of Iona:

> *And seeing that the Western Isles and other parts at the very end of the habitable earth are devoid of Collegiate Churches, prebends, priories, and other ecclesiastical benefices saving the said monastery and certain mean and ill-remunerated offices therein and parish churches held by secular priests, and further that the said monastery is so poor in every way that the religious and others dwelling there have no suitable living and can scarce obtain barley bread and similar victuals because of the constant feuds that rage and of the cost of entertaining strangers, the said Dominic therefore prays that having come to Rome at great expense and with much risk and remained there long and practically spent all his money, some benefice even if it be a cure of souls and usually ruled by seculars may be conferred upon him, and that he may be allowed to retain the same even if he should be elected abbot, and that he may be dispensed from his defect of birth and the rules of the said order (Benedictine) and of his own profession.*
> *Granted – if this may be without scandal.* (Highland Papers, vol IV, p 174–5, Calendar of Scottish Supplications to Rome 1418–22, p 275–76)

This particular appeal achieved its objective. However the Roman Curia must have grown inured to such pleadings, probably through knowledge of the self-interest of the plaintiffs. If something were asked for life it might only be given for a few years. In this case the qualification was 'if without scandal'.

Rome had rules about the holding of more than one benefice. Some were classed as compatible, others as incompatible because they might both include the 'cure of souls'. These rules were often broken and the scandals of 'pluralism' or the holding of more than one church office provide part of the backdrop to the religious disruption of the sixteenth century. Supplicants from the Highlands and Isles came up with ingenious arguments to circumvent the rules, one being that the overall shortage of church offices in the area made such breaches unavoidable:

> *It is represented to the Pope that whereas Celestin son of Celestin surnamed MacGillemichael, Rector of the parish church of St Maelrubha of Melfort, had applied for leave to hold along therewith the perpetual vicarage of St Finan in Kerry (of Cowal) . . . and permission had been granted for the space of three years, and whereas that period was far too short; the aforesaid Celestin prays that in respect of the dangers which he underwent and the spoiling of goods which he suffered in the long journey to Rome and the small yearly value of the said Rectory of St Maelrubha, and the expense of the hospitality to strangers which the possession of that benefice entails, and*

further because in these parts there is practically no benefice compatible with the said Rectory, almost all involving cure of souls, the dispensation craved may be granted for the period of his life as asked in the original petition. Granted for three years, 6 March 1422–3 (Highland Papers, vol IV, p 178, Calendar of Scottish Supplications to Rome 1423–28, pp 7–8)

Celestin (or Archibald) Carmichael does not seem to have been deterred because he was back pleading for dispensation to hold incompatibles in 1428. His reasons were: '*in those parts of the kingdom of Scotland where Celestine is beneficed, benefices are known to be lean and also the beneficed are bound to hospitality*' (Calendar of Scottish Supplications to Rome 1423–8, pp 189–190).

Even holders of some of the richer parishes were not above pleading poverty:

February 1420
It is represented for the part of Gilbert Machperson, priest, rector of the parish church of St Columba in Glascoc [Glassary]*, Argyle diocese, B. Dec., that, according to the custom of Scotland, he is bound to give hospitality to all who come to the place of the said parish church, and freely to afford them the necessary food and drink. But since the fruits (£40 sterling) are scarcely sufficient to support these burdens, Gilbert supplicates that the Pope would incorporate, annex and unite the vicarage with cure of the said church.* (Calendar of Scottish Supplications to Rome 1418–22, p 173)

On 30 April 1431 we find a plea for David de Petyn concerning the rectory of St Moldulf, Argyll diocese (Kilmallie, Loch Eil):

But fruits of vicarage (£6 sterling) and of rectory, also of lay patronage (£8 sterling), are so scanty in these days on account of hardships or of wars that for three years they scarcely amounted to £8 sterling, and the vicar is bound to afford hospitality to all comers according to custom of country, to pay episcopal dues and support other burdens, so that from the remainder of fruits he cannot be suitably sustained. David who is in Curia and has sustained great labours and expenses, supplicates that Pope would give mandate to expedite letters with dispensation to hold vicarage and rectory together for life with clause of exchange. (Calendar of Scottish Supplications to Rome 1428–32, pp 181–2)

But Highland churches were not just under threat from the expectations of travellers or the exactions of local bullies. Highland resources, particularly when channelled through the church, also fell under the eye of the Scottish realm. There are two examples of very dubious conduct by James IV in a Highland ecclesiastical context. In about 1507 he wrote to the church authorities claiming that there had been no religious life at Saddell Abbey within living memory, that it was scarcely worth £9 sterling, and that it had fallen to the use of laymen. The first two of these claims are of doubtful veracity and it may simply be that James IV wanted to transfer Saddell's significant landed estate to the bishop of Argyll.

The second example is James's letter of April 1512 to Pope Julius II in which he refers to Lismore lying deserted and ruinous and wants to transfer the see of Argyll to Saddell. This, too, was demonstrably untrue as we shall learn below. Whether the real villain was James IV or David Hamilton, bishop of Argyll from 1497 to c. 1523, is unclear. Certainly Hamilton was an active agent for royal control in Kintyre during the early years of the sixteenth century. It was an indication of changing times that one of the handful of Highland monastic houses should be suppressed, and the interests of the ancient cathedral site of Argyll should be ignored, in furtherance of royal power in Kintyre. In 1507–8 James IV also gave the bishop the two Kintyre churches of Kilchousland and Kilmichael. It may be that Bishop Hamilton was an attentive shepherd to his Highland flock, or it may be that he was seen as the local regent of an almost-foreign power.

4 The issue of language

In addition to the material found in the Papal records we also have evidence from within Scotland of the experiences of those travelling on church business. The bishopric of Argyll was created out of the diocese of Dunkeld about 1193 and covered a huge area of ground in mainland Argyll. According to Bower one of the reasons for its creation was a recognition of linguistic difference:

> At that time the whole of Argyll was subject to the bishop of Dunkeld and his jurisdiction as it had been from long before. Argyll is an extensive and spacious region, and containing in many places many and various goods, but owned by a ferocious and savage people who were in fact untamed up to that time. Besides they knew only one mother tongue into which they had been born and brought up, that is Scottish or Irish Gaelic, and they understood no other except that. What therefore was the man of the Lord who did not know this language to do? Because it seemed to him dangerous to abandon his own sheep, whose care he had undertaken, without a shepherd, even less did he judge it safe for himself to answer to the Chief Shepherd at the Last Judgement on their reckonings, since one party did not reciprocally understand the language of the other; but in any account that was to be demanded or rendered the people thought the pastor savage, and the pastor the people. Considering the salvation of souls to be more profitable than the increase of possessions, the bishop sought as much as he could to relieve himself of a burden and give satisfaction to God and the people. In no way did he agree to

have charge of those to whom he had no hopes of being of assistance, since they were like savages to him. Therefore he sent his chaplain called Harold, a discreet and honourable man who was knowledgeable and skilful in both languages, with his letter to the apostolic see, humbly requesting the lord pope to divide the bishopric of Dunkeld into two sees, namely Argyll and Dunkeld, and to consecrate his chaplain Harold as bishop of Argyll, with the bishopric of Dunkeld retained for his own service. For he confidently claimed that each bishopric would have sufficient resources to match the support needed for its bishop and his staff at a suitably honourable and affluent level, and to provide abundantly for all their needs without any shortage, provided they were the kind of men who were not extravagant, nor destroyers of Christ's patrimony, and not too greedy, but following moderation and the middle way within due limits in all things. (Bower, Scotichronicon, vol 3, Book VI, chapter 39)

Potentially the revenues of the Argyll diocese were significant but in practice it always had a reputation for poverty. There were certain offices associated with the bishopric such as dean, precentor, treasurer and chancellor, in addition to the diocesan archdeacons. Instead of receiving a money payment it was the practice for each of these officers to hold a farm of equivalent value. From later land exchanges we know of some of these farms on the island of Lismore, seat of the bishopric of Argyll. The chancellor, (who was responsible for collecting the bishop's revenues), held Auchnacrosche. The treasurer held Teirfoure and Teirlagane while the precentor had Killen, Teirewin and Pennyfurt.

However, as with many other offices in the mediaeval Highland world, these associated lands were jealously guarded by their incumbents, who tried, if at all possible, to pass them on to their children. Over time they came to be regarded as the hereditary preserve of one particular family. Technically, you may have only been a tenant, but if you could show you were a 'kindly' tenant, in other words that this particular heritage had been in your family for generations, or 'beyond the memory of man', then you regarded yourself as unmoveable. Trouble occurred, of course, when somebody else was given the job. If this change was instigated by a local magnate such as the Lord of the Isles or the earl of Argyll then little could be done about it. Families did occasionally lose their privileges even within the Highland world. It was a different matter when the pressure for change came from abroad.

Pont(?) relates the following story about Lismore which he presumably heard from sources in the area:

There was of Ancient certaine Bishops of Lismor of the race and name of Clanvickgilliemichaell and eftir these Bishopes there was other Bishops admitted and there was ane of these last Bishopes that wold depose and deprive certaine of the name of Clanvickgilliemichael, which were friends to

the Bishope of that name, so called who had certaine Offices from their friend
and Cosigne: and were in possessione theroff long tyme efter his death, being
acceptit of sundrie bishopes that succeidit their Cosignes place and speciallie
they having some right or title therto, and being better acquainted in that
trade then others that were in the Countrie At last it fortuned that one
Bishope wes admitted Bishop of Lismor He envying by hatred these ancient
men or race of that Clane; or others being willing to succeid in that Office,
And to obtaine the Bishopes favour that they might obtaine that Office from
him and depose these ancient men which were in possession theroff for a long
space; out of their Office. These race and Clan of Clanwickgilliemichael
perceiving themselves to be so dealt with be the Bishopes evill will towards
them, they took ane displeasure against him, and being strong in the
countrey, was of Intentioun and mind to revenge the same with the Bishope
And finallie determined how to frequent the Bishope in giveing ane equall
satisfactioune according to his deserving Which they wold redound to the
Bishopes uttermost destruction and ruine. Thaire pretendit determinatione
being finished, on a day they did meet with the Bishope who looked not for
such salutatione as he receaved at their hands – and they did kill him And so
he did finish his lyff out of this world And since that tyme as yet there was
never a Bishope that did come to Lismore to dwell. Pont(?), Macfarlane's
Geographical Collections

The nub of the matter seems to have been that the Carmichaels (or Mac Gillemichaels) regarded certain of the church offices connected with the bishopric of Lismore as more or less their family right. Pont (writing probably in the 1590s) claimed that they had killed a bishop who had displayed an unwelcome independence and that since then no bishop had dwelt in Lismore. Can we find any basis for this story in the historical record? We do have a similar sounding event concerning Lismore which occurred in 1452. It appears in the Auchinleck Chronicle.

In 1452 Gilbert MacLachlan, chancellor, and Maurice MacFadyen, treasurer, were trying to depose Hercules Skrymgeour, parson of the important parish of Glassary. Hercules appealed to the Bishop, George Lawder, who summoned the parties before him in order to settle the dispute. The bishop travelled to the cathedral chuch at Kilmaluag, Lismore, in company with Hercules Skrymgeour, John MacArthur, Alexander – a brother of Hercules, a priest called Adam and various servants. When they were within a quarter of a mile of the church they were attacked by the chancellor and treasurer, aided by the Clan Lachlan, on the grounds that the bishop intended to deprive them of their benefices and give them instead to the parson of Glassary. Apparently they:

Spak till himself richt dispituoslie with felloun wordis and scorne, and for
dispyte halsit him in Errische, sayand bannachadee, and dispytfully reft fra
him the forsaid Master Hercules, and pullit him fra his hors, and brak the

lordis belt, and tuke the clerke ande his brother and harllit and led thaim
away rycht dispytfully, and band the gentillman and thocht to strik of his
hed. (Auchinleck Chronicle pp 50–1)

(Spoke to him right spitefully with harsh words and scorn, and for spite
hailed him in Irish (Gaelic), saying 'Beannachadh De' ['The Blessing of
God'], and spitefully tore from him the aforesaid Master Hercules, and
pulled him from his horse, and broke the lord's belt, and took the clerk
and his brother and dragged and led them away right spitefully, and
bound the gentleman and thought to strike off his head).

When the bishop tried to proceed on foot his assailants threatened to kill him
and all his company unless he absolved them of their crimes. On the advice of
his companions the bishop very sensibly complied. The attackers kept a
couple of hostages overnight and robbed them of everything '*that they had that*
was oucht worth viz gowns, cloaks, hoods, bonnets and other small gear'.

This must have been a very frightening incident for the Bishop and may
well lie behind Pont's story 150 years later, even if the MacLachlans had
been replaced by the Carmichaels. It also helps to explain why James IV
and Bishop Hamilton were keen to transfer the see from Lismore in the
early sixteenth century. Perhaps they couldn't count on local co-operation!
From our point of view what is important is the myth that this incident
created and which Pont reported in the 1590s. Anyone reading Pont's
account could be forgiven for concluding that Highlanders were savage and
unchristian. If that was how they treated clergymen then what might a
layman expect?

    There is, though, another perspective on this issue – that of the local
Gaelic-speaking population. In fact we have some official documents which
help us to see it from their point of view. During the fourteenth century
Agnes, daughter of Gilbert of Glassary, married Alexander Scrymgeour,
Constable of Dundee, and brought to that family much of her father's estate.
This windfall included not just the lands but also the church benefices that
went with them. The introduction of a Lowland family to this Gaelic-
speaking area resulted in certain tensions and anomalies. In 1421 James
Scrymgeour was looking for papal confirmation of his accession to Glassary
parish church on the death of Gilbert Macpherson. One impediment was:
'*that he is not learned in the language of the country of the said parish church; and*
may the Pope dispense him thereanent, considering that he has for a substitute a fit
perpetual vicar well skilled in the language of that country.' (Calendar of Scottish
Supplications to Rome 1418–22, pp 258–9)

    A James Scrymgeour also features in a complaint of 9 March 1423
concerning the rectory of the parish church of St Columba in Glassary: '*a*
certain James Skremegeour, deacon, Brechin diocese, not understanding the
language and idiom of the parishioners, detained it for more than one and a half

years, as he does at present, unlawfully occupied, to the prejudice of the parishioners and damage of their souls.' (Calendar of Scottish Supplications to Rome 1423–28, pp 10–11)

Many years before the incident with Bishop Lauder, the Scrymgeour family had been flying in the face of local sentiment by taking plum ecclesiastical jobs without being able to speak the same language as their parishioners. In 1450–1 the issue reached Rome in the form of a complaint by the vicar of Kilberry in Knapdale:

> *the pope having been informed by Geoffrey Goffredi, perpetual vicar of St Ferchinus's in the diocese of Argyll, that [H]erculus Sgyrmogeior, a canon of Argyll, has committed perjury and has dilapidated and uselessly consumed the possessions of his canonry of Argyll and the rectory of the [parish] church of St Columba in Glassradh [Glassary], in the said diocese, a prebend in the same [church of Argyll], of which canonry and prebend he has held possession for more than twelve years.* (Calendar of Papal Letters, vol X, p 470)

There were several matters at issue in the incident on Lismore – pride, privilege and language. Local families felt their positions threatened by outsiders and were not inclined to let their inherited privileges go without a fight. Although these issues came to a head in 1452 they had obviously been simmering for years. It is clear from the language employed in the Auchinleck Chronicle that the pride of these high-ranking churchmen was bruised, and this rankled. The word spite appears four times in five lines and encapsulates the outrage felt at this affront to the dignity of their persons and office. Finally there is the issue of language itself. The assailants spoke to them in Gaelic, not English. From the local point of view 'Why shouldn't they?' This was a Gaelic-speaking area. Language was the symptom of the problem. In Argyll an alien culture and language were intruding into a Gaelic heartland. One of the reasons the bishopric of Argyll had been founded in the first place was to allow for a difference in language. It was not just local sensitivities that were at issue. Livelihood and culture were under threat. Language was an instrument of power.

This was not a new issue and Glassary was not the only location. In fact the Roman church had already grappled with this problem and, theoretically at least, had come up with a solution that met local concerns. In June 1433 the papacy agreed to the removal of a non-Gaelic speaking priest from Kilcalmonell:

> *To the dean, archdeacon and chancellor of Argyll. Mandate to collate and assign to John [son] of Finlaius Macpilibh, priest, of the diocese of Argyll, who was lately dispensed by papal authority, as the son of a priest, professed of the Cistercian order, and an unmarried woman, to be promoted to all, even*

holy orders and hold a benefice even with cure, the perpetual vicarage of
Kilcalmonell in the said diocese, value not exceeding 10 marks sterling, so
long void by the death of Malcolm McDubailwigh that its collation lapsed to
the apostolic see, summoning and removing John Arons, priest, of the diocese
of St Andrews, who does not well understand nor intelligibly speak the
language of the parishioners, and has unduly detained possession for three
years. (Calendar of Papal Letters, vol VIII p 470)

The appointment of an English-speaking Lowlander to a church post within a
Gaelic-speaking area was an issue that would run for centuries. In 1441 we
learn of Andrew of Dunoon who seems to have spoken some Gaelic, but not
fluently:

To Andrew de Dunnovin, archdeacon of Sodor . . . Collation and provision
to him (who is an abbreviator of apostolic letters and cannot speak intelligibly
the language of the city and diocese of Sodor as regards preachings and other
public acts, although he speaks it somewhat, even intelligibly) of the arch-
deaconry of Sodor, a major dignity with cure, value not exceeding £20
sterling. (Calendar of Papal Letters, vol IX, p 152)

In June 1450 the vicar of Kilcalmonell was claimed to be an absentee as well as
a non-Gaelic speaker:

To the abbot of St Mary's, Sagudul (Saddell), the prior of St Mary's,
Airdkatan (Ardchattan), in the diocese of Argyll, and the dean of Argyll.
Mandate (the pope having been informed by Cornelius Cornelii, priest, of the
diocese of Argyll, that Patrick Cornton, perpetual vicar of Kilcalmonell in the
said diocese, has taken part in violence, associated himself with men-at-arms
and committed manslaughter, fighting along with them and killing a man in
battle, and is accused in those parts of divers other crimes, and who, as
Cornelius alleges, inasmuch as he is a foreigner, does not perfectly understand
the language commonly spoken in the place where the said church is, and does
not intelligibly speak it, and that he does not reside at the said church)
(Calendar of Papal Letters, vol X, p 493)

In 1454 we meet a petition of John Guardnar, priest, holder of the perpetual
vicarage of Kilfinan, Cowal. This tells us that the Papacy was breaking its own
rules by appointing him, since:

although he is a native of Scotland, he does not perfectly speak nor under-
stand the language of the place . . . The pope hereby specially dispenses him
to receive and retain it, notwithstanding his late constitution to the effect that
in the event of his making provision or ordering provision to be made of a
parish church to a person unable to understand or speak the language, such

provision or mandate should be null and void. (Calendar of Papal Letters, vol X, p 697)

In the Calendar of Papal Letters, Vol XII, there is a brief reference to a lost bull of Paul II dated 1465 or 1466 which concerned Colin Campbell of Argyll. Apparently its subject-matter was a ruling that nobody should obtain a parish unless they spoke the language of the area. This is further elaborated on 8 March 1496 with a mandate in favour of Alexander Monereiff, MA, cleric, diocese of St Andrews to whom the pope intended to give the precentorship of Lismore:

> *Notwithstanding . . . certain privileges and apostolic letters granted to the said church in which it is said to be expressly stipulated that no one may acquire a dignity or other benefice in the said church unless he understands the language, which the people of Lismore commonly speak and knows how to speak it intelligibly, the which privileges etc. the pope, specially and expressly, derogates for this once only; and [notwithstanding] that Alexander is by nation a Scot . . . and neither understands the language nor knows how to speak it.* (Calendar of Papal Letters, vol XVII, Part II, No 53 p 58)

His definition as a 'Scot' marks Alexander out as an English-speaking Lowlander. It appears that on the one hand the Papacy was endeavouring to protect the indigenous Gaelic culture of the area. On the other it was happy to undermine this principle when it needed to find a benefice for someone deserving.

In the context of the above examples it is little wonder that Highlanders were suspicious of outsiders coming to take advantage of their resources. They felt themselves threatened by rapacious Lowlanders who were generally more successful in gaining the ear of the Scottish king or a Roman pope. Highlanders were justly suspicious of Lowland aspirations for the Highlands on either an individual or an institutional basis. They felt that their church, their language and their culture were under assault. They were prepared to be robust in their own defence. This mutual distrust must have informed all intending travellers.

In case we let our sympathy for indigenous Highland communities run away with us, we must also look at the evidence provided by the records about Highland priests. In 1433 John MacFinlay had secured the vicarage of Kilcalmonell on the removal of John Arons, a non-Gaelic speaker from the diocese of St Andrews. In July 1436 John MacFinlay was himself the victim of an ecclesiastical hachet-job.

> *To the chancellor of the church of Lismore in the diocese of Argyll. Mandate – the Pope having been informed by John [son] of Dougal Macmaelmichell, clerk, of the diocese of Argyll, that John Finlaii, perpetual vicar of Kilcal-*

monell in the said diocese, has publicly kept for several years as a concubine a certain woman, by whom he has had offspring still alive and has dilapidated the goods of the said church, etc. – if the said John will accuse Finlaii before him, to summon Finlaii, and if he find the above or enough thereof to be true, to deprive Finlaii, and in that event to collate and assign the said vicarage, value not exceeding 10 marks sterling, to John. (Calendar of Papal Letters, vol VIII, p 597)

This was followed up in March 1437–8:

To the Bishop of Argyll. Mandate – the pope having been informed by John Bricii, clerk, of the diocese of Argyll, that John [son] of Fynlaius Prioris Macphilib, perpetual vicar of Kilcalmonell in Cnapdul [then in Knapdale, now in Kintyre], *in the said diocese, has dilapidated the vicarage, is a notorious fornicator, and has committed simony and other crimes and excesses – if the said John Bricii . . . will accuse the said John Fynlaii before him, to summon John Fynlaii, and, if he find the above or enough thereof to be true, to deprive him, and in that event to collate and assign the vicarage, value not exceeding £7 sterling, to John Bricii.* (Calendar of Papal Letters, vol VIII, p 625)

So although the motives of the Scrymgeours or the royal Stewarts may not have been with the best interests of local communities in mind, neither were those of some of the Highland claimants. But, since they were native and spoke Gaelic, they probably aroused less resentment. It certainly seems that the Scrymgeours faced continuing opposition from local Highlanders. In March 1501 there is a similar issue to Lismore at the foot of Loch Awe:

Statute and ordinance as below. A recent petition to the pope on the part of James Skeymgeour, rector, and John Skeymgeour, lay patron, of the parish church of Kylleneur, d[iocese of] Lismore, stated that the church is in a quite wooded place and near the sea-shore and on the edges of land open to the sea and near it and even within the limits of its parish live wild men who cannot be coerced or punished by secular judge or power and within the said limits and surrounding vicinity, especially at the side of the mountain of Latyrewern', at the castle of Fynchaers and the lake of Lochquho, at the ford of the rivulet of Anygray and also the places of Strovesk, Terroner, and at Lochclea, Soctocha, Brenowc and Glusner, d[iocese of] Lismore – habitually carry out many homicides, thefts, robberies, burnings, oppressions, vulgarly called lesornyng [sorning] *and other similar evils which it is impossible to prevent by judge or power; and that the said men, albeit wild and up to a point ungovernable, are, however, exceedingly afraid of censures promulgated by apostolic authority; and that if it were to be established and ordained that everyone there of both sexes committing such homicides, thefts, burnings, oppressions and other evils would incur sentence of excommunication, many homicides would be avoided and it would also be to the good of souls because from dread of the censures they would abstain from homicides etc. The pope – at this supplication – hereby establishes and ordains, in perpetuity, that each and every one, of both sexes and wherever they may be from, and of whatsoever condition, religion and quality, who, within the limits of the parish, church and surrounding vicinity shall – after the present letters have been published in the church and surrounding vicinity – commit, or command and cause to be committed, such robberies etc., or anyone of them, shall automatically incur sentence of excommunication from which they shall be denied absolution save by the local ordinary after satisfaction has been made.* (Calendar of Papal Letters, vol XVII, Part 1, No 493)

Not all these places are certainly identifiable but Fynchaers (Fincharn), Strovesk (Stronesker), Lochclea (Loch Leathan), Soctocha (Sococh), Brenowc (Brenchellies?) and Glusner (Glasvar) can all be found at or near the south-west end of Loch Awe. 'Sorning' refers to the Highland habit of expecting free board and lodgings, which we have examined above. Essentially the Scrymgeours wanted to take advantage of the superstitious and credulous nature of their Highland flock. They wished to use the power of the Church to achieve social control, the threat of excommunication as a way of bringing people into line. Others have agreed with their interpretation of Highland character. In 1689 Thomas Morer wrote of the Highlanders:

Their religion, as to outward profession, is for the most part after the establishment of the kingdom; yet too many not only retain the Irish language, but the Irish religion; and not a few profess no religion at all, but are next door to barbarity and heathenism. However, in the general, they have so great a veneration for ministers, or men in holy orders, that notwithstanding their natural roughness, and perhaps rudeness to other sort of travellers, these persons coats are a sufficient protection and passport to them throughout that part of Scotland. Which respect is grounded on a principle they have, that should they in the least injure such a man, they must not expect to prosper all the days of their life. 'Tis true, at the skirmish at Brechin, some of Colonel Barclay's Dragoons found in one of their sacks, among other things, a minister's gown; and 'twas a hot report at that time, while we were in sight of their camp, that they used a clergyman hard by very ill both as to goods and person. But then this is imputed to the villainy of the Irish join'd 'em a little before, and who are remarkable enemies to men of this profession. For I was well assured by an old divine at Perth, who had spent many years among 'em, that this was not the way of the Highlanders themselves who reverenced gown-men to a degree, not much short of superstition. (Thomas Morer in Hume Brown, *Early Travellers in Scotland*)

The established church in Scotland, based on the centres of power and wealth in the south and east of the country, had a problem speaking to its Gaelic congregation. Latin was the official language of the church throughout Europe but only a tiny minority of Scots would have been able to read Latin, fewer still to speak it. For everyday communications between pastor and flock either English or Gaelic must be employed. Most of the important church offices, most of the monasteries, colleges and convents, were based in parts of the country where English was increasing at the expense of Gaelic. No doubt part of the issue in Lismore was the intrusion of English-speaking churchmen into a Gaelic environment. There had always been significant numbers of Gaelic-speaking clergymen but from the fifteenth-century we become aware of instances where language became an issue vis-a-vis appointments to Highland churches. Disputes were referred to Rome. The fact that the new incumbent did not speak the language of the local people could be used as an argument against him.

Within Scotland the attitude of the king was probably more important than that of the pope. We have a document recording the installation of John Makcaw as archdeacon of Lismore on 30 July 1531. Sir Adam Sym, procurator for John Makcaw, who is described as 'clerk and familiar servitor of James the Fifth', presented a letter of provision to

> *Dermit Makhecardych, vicar or curate of the cathedral church of Lesmore, at the high altar thereof, the dean and other canons of the church not being then present . . . which Dermit received and gave to the notary to read, and then asked it back; and after, by delivery of a silver chalice, gilt missal book, key of the door, and ornaments of the high altar, gave investiture of the archdiaconate of the said cathedral church of Lesmore, with fruits, rents, etc., to the said Sir Adam Sym, priest, as procurator for the said John Makcaw, and assigned him a stall in the choir and place in the chapter, receiving the oath from the said Adam for obeying the statutes of the said church, etc. And thereafter the said vicar warned the parishioners assembled in time of divine service, in their mother tongue, the Irish speech, and all others having interest, to answer and obey the said John Makcaw in fruits, rents, etc.* (Extracts from the Records of the Burgh of Stirling, 1519–1666, p 267)

This is a very different view of the chapter-life of Lismore compared with that presented by James IV in 1512 when he wanted to transfer the see to Saddell. About eighty years have now elapsed since the incident with Bishop Lawder. The locals appear more obedient and it was undoubtedly helpful that the local vicar spoke Gaelic.

The issue of language troubled Highland religious communities even after the lapse of Latin. There were, for instance, two churches in Campbeltown – one for the old Gaelic-speaking inhabitants of Kintyre, another for the new English-speaking immigrants from Ayrshire. This problem has been replicated throughout the Highlands as English has advanced at the expense of Gaelic. To best minister to a Highland flock the pastors should really be bilingual. By no means all were. Even up to the present day Highland churchmen have been attempting to solve this problem according to local circumstances. Gaelic services might be offered at one time of day, English at another. There were a variety of local arrangements.

5 Danger and difficulty

The papacy was aware of the difficulties and dangers entailed by travel in some of the remoter parts of Christendom. Technically the Bishopric of Sodor or the Isles was subject to the Norwegian see of Nidaros or Trondheim. Travelling to Norway by sea was expensive and dangerous so in 1244 the archbishop of York was given the task of confirming and consecrating the bishop-elect of Man 'the voyage to Throndhjem being long and dangerous'. For 1241 the Chronicle of Melrose reports: '*William, the bishop of Argyle, was drowned in the sea.*' (Anderson, Early Sources, vol II, p 529) while in 1248 the Chronicles of Man record the drowning of: '*Laurence, Bishop-Elect of Man and the Isles.*'

In the spring of 1349 William Russell was at Avignon to be consecrated bishop of Sodor by Pope Clement VI. Travelling from Man was an enormous expense so in May of that year the pope granted William the 'faculty to contract a loan of 1200 florins to meet his expenses at the apostolic see'. On 14 June William wrote to the pope:

> *Whereas the . . . petitioner is subject to the archbishop of Trondhjem, and does not dare to face the dangers of the long sea voyage, which he would have to take in going to pay his obedience, he prays the pope that if the archbishop exacts his obedience, or summons him to come for the discharge of that or other duties beyond the limits of the diocese of Sodor, he should not be bound to go.*

In response the Pope agreed that: '*For this time he may pay his obedience by a proctor.*' (Calendar of Entries in the Papal Registers, Petitions to the Pope, Vol I, p 168.)

For others, travelling to Rome was out of the question. So in 1406 there is the following petition: '*Donald Moricii. For confirmation of his election, and benediction by the ordinary, last Christmas, to the priory of Orwansay, in the diocese of Sodor, in the isles of Scotland, value 100 florins, void by the death of the last prior; the petitioner being unable, by reason of poverty, and the danger of the sea, to come to the Roman court.* (Calendar of Entries in the Papal Registers, Petitions to the Pope, Vol I, p 632.)

The Papacy was also realistic enough to understand the dangers for lay people travelling to remote regions where there was no recourse to normal legal process. In 1445–46, Elizabeth, wife of Alexander of Islay, earl of Ross and Lord of the Isles, had appealed to the pope because of her husband's liaison with one Cristiana Maclaide. The pope sent a mandate to the bishop of St Andrews and the archdeacons of Ross and Brechin that since: *'on account of the said earl's power, Elizabeth has no hope of being able to cause them to be with safety cited and monished'*, the recipients were:

> *to monish the said earl and Cristiana, and by ecclesiastical censure etc. to compel him to send away Cristiana and receive Elizabeth, and compel her not to seek to hinder the earl and Elizabeth from living together. If they find that it is not convenient to reach the presence of the said earl and Cristiana for making the said monitions, the pope grants them faculty to make them by public edict posted in public places which shall be near the said parts and from which it is probable that they can come to the knowledge of those monished, the pope's will being that the said monitions shall bind those monished as if they had been served on them in person.* (Calendar of Papal Letters, vol IX, pp 545–46)

This was a candid recognition of the dangers of venturing to beard the lion! History repeated itself in the next generation because in 1463–64 we learn of the suit of Elizabeth Livingstone, countess of Ross, against John, Earl of Ross, her husband, (son of Alexander of Islay), who had put her away in preference for his mistress:

> *To the bishop of Lismore, the chancellor of Glasgow, and Thomas de Forsyth, a canon of the same . . . At the petition of the said Elizabeth, who alleges that processes in virtue of these presents cannot be published to him on account of his power, for the commission to upright men in those parts of the cause which she intends to bring against him, the pope hereby orders the above three to summon the said John and others concerned, and if they find the foregoing to be true, after first monishing him, to compel him by ecclesiastical censure, even extending to interdict against his lands and the churches and persons thereof, ecclesiastical and secular, without appeal, to put away the said adultress, receive Elizabeth his wife, and treat her with marital affection, invoking, if necessary, the aid of the secular arm; with faculty, if they find that the presence of the said John and others concerned is not safely accessible for the serving of monitions and citations, to make such monitions and citations by public edicts in public places near those parts, which monitions and citations shall be binding upon those monished and cited as if served upon them in person.* (Calendar of Papal Letters, vol XI, pp 671–72)

Elizabeth was not alone. In the summer of 1470, Malcolm, clerk, petitioned the pope concerning the deanery of Lismore (Argyll) which, Malcolm claimed, had been wrongly given to Robert Mwyr eight to ten years earlier. The pope granted the deanery to Malcolm and instructed the Bishop and archdeacon of the Isles, with the abbot of Iona, to effect the change since Malcolm *'cannot safely meet the said Robert in the city or diocese of Lismore; summoning and removing the said Robert and any other unlawful detainer.'*

In the winter of the same year Malcolm returned to the attack by trying to gain the rectory of St Columba's, Morvern. He claimed that: *'Robert F[o]wlar, rector of the parish . . . is an open fornicator, has committed simony, has dilapidated the immoveable goods of the said rectory, does not reside in person, and is much defamed in those parts of several other crimes and excesses, to the shame of the clerical order.* (Calendar of Papal Letters, vol XII)

This business of non-residence occurs again and again. Absentee clergymen were an issue in the Highlands centuries before absentee landlords. When we look at the perennial war of attrition against Gaelic culture there is plenty of evidence that, long before Culloden or the Clearances, Highland clergy and their language were coming under pressure from Lowland Scotland.

6 Travel on pilgrimage

Pilgrimage has a long, if relatively unknown history in the Highlands, stretching back at least as far as Early Christian times:

> Dublin Annals of Innisfallen, c. 763
> *Donald, Murchaid's son, was king in Tara for twenty years, and died in pilgrimage in Iona of Columcille.* (Anderson, Early Sources, p 245)

> Annals of Ulster, 782–83
> *Entrance into monastic life of Artgal, Cathal's son, king of Connaught; and his pilgrimage to Iona in the following year.* (Anderson, Early Sources, pp 253–54)

> Annals of Tigernach, 980
> *Olaf, Sigtrygg's son, sovereign of the Foreigners of Dublin, went to Iona in penitence and pilgrimage after the battle [of Tara, and] died.* (Anderson, Early Sources, p 487)

The Chronicles of Man – writing of the death of Godred Crovan, King of Man, c. 1095:

> *He left three sons, i.e. Lagman, Harald and Olaf. Lagman, the eldest, seized the kingdom and ruled seven years. However, Harald his brother rebelled against him for a good while. But at last he was captured by Lagman and deprived of his genitalia and eyes. After this Lagman regretted blinding his brother and abdicated his kingdom of his own accord. Marked with the sign*

of the Lord's cross he undertook a pilgrimage to Jerusalem, but died on the way. (Broderick, *Chronicles of the Kings of Man and the Isles*)

Rognvald Kali, earl of Orkney, who died in 1158, also went on pilgrimage to the Holy Land.

Earl Rognvald . . . travelled with his men to Jerusalem, visiting all the most sacred places in the Holy Land. They all went and bathed in the River Jordan and, with Sigmund Fish-Hook, Earl Rognvald swam across the river. (Orkneyinga Saga, pp 178–79)

Annals of Ulster under the year 1188
Olaf Ua-Daigri went to Iona on pilgrimage. And he died in Iona, after excellent repentance. (Anderson, Early Sources)

Reginald became King of Man in 1188. His younger brother Olaf had a better claim to the throne and, after a dispute about Olaf's share of the islands, Reginald had him imprisoned by King William of Scotland from about 1207. On William's death, in 1214, Olaf was released: '*Olaf thereupon was freed from his chains and, having recovered his liberty; he came to Man to his brother Reginald; and shortly after set out with a considerable retinue of nobles for the shrine of St James* [at Compostella]. (Broderick, *Chronicles of the Kings of Man and the Isles.*)

These are the journeys we know about. There must have been many other undocumented pilgrimages from the Highlands and Hebrides to Jerusalem, Compostella, and even Rome.

There also appears to have been a great deal of small-scale local pilgrimage *within* the Highlands and Islands. This might involve visiting a holy well or stone or church. Some of this may well have been pre-Christian in origin. In his *Life of St Columba* Adomnan suggests that visiting wells was a common practice in Pictish Scotland:

Of a poisonous Fountain of Water to which the blessed man gave his blessing in the country of the Picts.

Again, while the blessed man was stopping for some days in the province of the Picts, he heard that there was a fountain famous amongst this heathen people, which foolish men, having their senses blinded by the devil, worshipped as a god. For those who drank of this fountain, or purposely washed their hands or feet in it, were allowed by God to be struck by demoniacal art, and went home either leprous or purblind, or at least suffering from weakness or other kinds of infirmity. By all these things the Pagans were seduced, and paid divine honour to the fountain. Having ascertained this, the saint one day went up to the fountain fearlessly; and, on seeing this, the Druids, whom he had often sent away from him vanquished and confounded, were greatly rejoiced, thinking that he would suffer like others from the touch of that baneful water. But he, having first raised his holy hand and invoked the name of Christ, washed his hands and feet; and then with his companions, drank of the water which he had blessed. And from that day the demons departed from the fountain; and not only was it not allowed to injure any one, but even many diseases amongst the people were cured by this same fountain, after it had been blessed and washed in by the saint. (Adomnan, *Life of St Columba*, ed. W. Reeves)

About 1380 Fordun had obviously heard of Kilmory in Scarba. Such fame was an incentive to travel. Those who were sick and suffering would be only too willing to make a pilgrimage in search of cure or release. '*Scarba, fifteen miles long, where there is a chapel of the Blessed Virgin, at which many miracles are performed.*' (Fordun, *Chronicle of the Scottish Nation*)

   Many of the pilgrimage sites of the pre-Reformation church were still visited for many generations afterwards. In the 1590s Pont tells us of a popular site called Cladh Churulain on the north side of Loch Creran. It was associated with St Patrick:

In this Loghgreveren there is one high Mountaine on the northsyde therof. And on the mid parte of the Mountaine betwixt the sea and the top of the Mountaine there is a chappell called Craikquerrelane And in this high craig where the Chappell stands, there is verie manie fresh springs and fountaine waters. And sundrie and divers multitudes of men and woemen from all Countries doe convein and gather togidder to this Chappell in the springtyme one day before St. Patrickmess day and drinking everie one of them of this springand fresh water alleadges that it shall recover them to their healthes againe, of the sicknes or desease which they have before their comeing to that place and uses the same yearlie, once a time in the year certaine of them doth come for pilgrimadge, and certane others in respect of their sickness bygone, of which they have recovered their health and certaine of them for their sickness present, And so they are perswaded to be restored to their health by the help and assistance of that holie saint, and drinking of the Waters. This holie place hes sundrie spring founts and wells of fresh water for divers and sundrie kynds of deseases and sickness whereof they are assured to be true in respect of the tryall they have had in this water. (Pont(?), *Macfarlane's Geographical Collections*)

Cladh Churulain also features prominently in Blaeu's map of Lorn which was drawn from data supplied by Timothy Pont. Pont further describes a pilgrimage site in Glen Urquhart:

There is one litle Chappell at this Loghsyde in Wrquhattane which is call Kil Saint Ninian. and certaine hieland men and woemen doeth travell to this

*chappell at a certane tyme of the zeare expecting to recover there health
againe and doeth drink of certaine springand wells that is next to the
Chappell.* (Pont(?), Macfarlane's Geographical Collections)

Lhuyd and Pennant, two Welshmen, were both very interested in charms and
amulets. Rock crystals were highly favoured in this respect and Pennant
writes: '*Captain Archibald Campbell shewed me one, a spheroid set in silver,
which people came for the use of above a hundred miles, and brought the water it
was to be dipped in with them; for without that, in human cases, it was believed to
have no effect.*' (Pennant, *A Tour in Scotland 1769.*)

There is plenty of contemporary evidence of the level of popular religious
devotion in the Highlands. The sanctity of particular churches, wells or
islands is recorded by Captain Dymes, Martin Martin and the church's own
records. To an extent the Papacy encouraged pilgrimage by granting in-
dulgences to those who visited particular church sites and contributed
towards their upkeep. Essentially this was a device for effecting repairs.
For Kilchoman parish in Islay we find:

17 July 1382
*To all Christ's faithful. Indulgence of one year and forty days is granted to all
who visit the chapel of St Columba in the parish church of St Congan, Sodor
diocese, on certain feasts, and fifty days indulgence during their octaves and
the six days following Pentecost, and contribute towards the repair of the
chapel, which has fallen to the ground on account of its great antiquity.*
(Papal Letters to Scotland of Clement VII, p 79; Highland Papers, vol
IV, pp 140–42)

Both the chapel at Nereabolls and the chapel on Orsay seem to have been
dedicated to St Columba. There is a similar letter for the Ross of Mull on:

30 May 1393
*To all Christ's faithful. Indulgence of one year and forty days is granted to all
who visit the parish church of St John the Evangelist in Arduis de Mulle,
Sodor diocese, on the principal feasts of the year, the feast of St John the
Evangelist [27 Dec] and on the feast of the dedication of the church, and fifty
days indulgence during their octaves and the six days after Pentecost, and
contribute towards its upkeep.* (Papal Letters to Scotland of Clement VII,
p 188; Highland Papers, vol IV, pp 144–46)

Quite possibly such letters were aimed at the local gentry who were the only
ones in a position to undertake such tasks.

Hebrideans showed a great deal of devotion to their ancient saints.
Amongst these, travellers noted the particular status of St Columba: '*the
people of the Hebrides . . . have a great devotion to Saint Columba and venerate*

him as their patron and apostle. (Giblin, *Irish Franciscan Mission to Scotland 1619–1646*, p 48)

St Columba had been revered for many centuries. According to Eirspennill's Hakon Hakon's son's Saga, the Hebrideans claimed it was Columba who appeared to Alexander II in the prophetic dream he experienced just before his death at Kerrera in 1249. Columba was not alone. Dymes makes clear that 'St Mallonuy' was equally revered at Ness in Lewis whilst seventeenth-century presbytery records shows that St Maelrubha was accorded similar devotion in Applecross.

7 Education

The church was always prepared to divert resources for educational purposes. It was in the church's own interest to create and maintain a literate elite. In the Vatican records we find occasional details which tell us something about where Highland churchmen were educated and to what level:

1366 – Petition:
John Dugaldi, archdeacon of Argyle, value 20 marks, advanced in canon law, and formerly the Pope's scholar. For a canonry of Dunkeld, with expectation of a prebend.

Response:
Granted, and let him first be examined, and information given touching the matters contained in the following schedule:

Information:
The church of Argyle, in which is the said archdeaconry, is distant a day's journey from that of Dunkeld, and the dioceses are conterminous; the said John knows the language and idioms of both, and speaks them well; he is present in the Roman court, where he was the pope's scholar. (Calendar of Entries in the Papal Registers, Petitions to the Pope, Vol I, p 530)

5 May 1380
To John de Congallis, priest, rector of the parish church of Kinlochgoil, Argyll diocese. Dispensation to hold another benefice, even involving cure, together with his parish church for a period of three years; at the end of which time he is to exchange it, or his parish, for another benefice compatible with the one retained, or else resign his parish. John is said to have studied canon law at Paris for over three years. (Papal Letters to Scotland of Clement VII, p 45)

Petition, 1380 – Roll of Robert, Earl of Fife and Menteith, second son of the King of Scotland:–

On behalf of his chaplain and secretary, Dugal de Ergadia [Argyll], *priest,
who has studied canon and civil law for three years, for a canonry of
Dunblane, with expectation of a prebend, notwithstanding that he has a
canonry and prebend of the same, and the church of Kilmor, in the diocese of
Argyll.* (Calendar of Entries in the Papal Registers, Petitions to the Pope,
Vol I, p 554)

*Petition, 1388 – Benedict Johannis, of the diocese of Argyle, of noble birth,
student at Paris in canon law. For the deanery of Argyle* (Calendar of
Entries in the Papal Registers, Petitions to the Pope, Vol I, p 573)

In June 1426, John Macarthua, clerk, Argyll diocese is described as a: '*student
in Canon and Civil Law of Bologna and other universities.*' (Calendar of Scottish
Supplications to Rome 1423–28, p 140)

In December 1427, John Angutii, clerk, Argyll diocese, sought the parish of
Kilchoan in Knoydart. He is described as one: '*who has studied profitably in
Canon Law and Arts*' (Calendar of Scottish Supplications to Rome 1423–28,
p 180)

At other times a Highland benefice was expected to fund an education:

17 September 1395
*To John Dugalli, rector of the parish church of Kylmore, Argyll diocese.
Indult for John to receive the fruits from Kylmore and from any benefice he
might later obtain, without being bound to residency while studying canon
law at a university for three years.* (Papal Letters to Scotland of Benedict
XIII)

Since this education invariably took place a long way from the Highlands it
required a good deal of expense:

11 April 1508
*A letter of gift maid to Kanoch Willzamsoun enduring the kingis will, of all
and hale his landis of Terunga of Kilmartin and the half of Terunga of
Baronesmore in Trouternes, with thair pertinentis, extending zerely to sax
merkis of auld extent, liand in the lordschip of the Ilys, to hald the said
Kanoch at the skolis and for to lere and study the kingis lawis of Scotland,
and eftirwart to exers and use the sammyn within the bondis of the Ilis*
(Register of the Privy Seal I, No 1654)

(A letter of gift made to Kenneth Williamson during the king's will, of all
and whole his lands of [the] Tirung [ounceland] of Kilmartin and the
half of [the] Tirung of Baronesmore in Trotternish [Skye], with their
pertinents, extending yearly to six merks [i.e. 6 marklands] of old extent,
lying in the Lordship of the Isles, to hold [maintain] the said Kenneth at

the schools to learn and study the king's laws of Scotland, and afterwards to exercise and use the same within the bounds of the Isles)

Education has often required young people to leave the Highlands.

8 The last journey

Travel was also involved at burial. This was neither conscious nor willing, but bodies were certainly conveyed – particularly to Iona. In 1549 Monro describes the tombs of the Scottish, Irish and Norwegian kings which were then visible on Iona.

Within this Ile of Colmkill thair was ane Sanctuarie or Kirkzaird callit in Irish Religoran, quhilk is ane fair Kirkzaird, well biggit about with stane and lyme. Into this Sanctuarie thair is three Tombs of stanes formit like little chapellis with ane braid gray [marble or] quhin stane in the gavill of ilk ane of the Tombs. In the stane of the mid Tomb thair is writtin Tumulus Regum Scotiae, that is to say, the Tomb or the Grave of the Scottis Kings. Within this Tomb, according to our Scottis and Irish Chronicles, thair lyis 48 crownit Scottis Kings, throw the quhilk this Ile has bene richlie dotit be the Scottis Kings, as we have hard. The Tomb on the south side of this foirsaid Tomb hes the subscription, to wit, Tumulus Regum Hiberniae, that is to say, The Tomb of the Irland Kingis; for we have in our Irish Chronicles that thair wes four Irland Kingis eirdit into the said Tomb. Upon the north side of our Scottis Tomb the inscription beiris Tumulus Regum Norvegiae, that is, the Tomb of the Kingis of Norway. In the quhilk Tomb we find in our ancient Irish Chronicles their lyis aucht Kingis of Norway . . . Within this Sanctuarie also lyis for the maist [pairt of] the Lords of the Iles with thair linages, tuay Clane lane with thair linages, Mckinvin and Mcguare with thair linage, with sundrie uther inhabitants of the haill Iles, because this Sanctuarie wes wont to be the sepulture of the best men of all the Iles, and als of our Kingis, as we have said; because it wes the maist honorable and ancient place that wes in Scotland in those dayis, as we reid. (R.W. Munro, *Monro's Western Isles*)

(Within this Isle of Iona there was a Sanctuary or Kirkyard called in Irish Reilig Odhrain, which is a fair Kirkyard, well built about with stone and lime. In this Sanctuary there are three Tombs of stones formed like little chapels with a broad grey [marble or] whin stone in the gable of each one of the Tombs. In the stone of the middle Tomb there is written Tumulus Regum Scotiae, that is to say, the Tomb or the Grave of the Scottish Kings. Within this Tomb, according to our Scottish and Irish Chronicles, there lie 48 crowned Scottish Kings, through which this Isle has been richly endowed by the Scottish Kings, as we have heard. The

Tomb on the south side of this aforesaid Tomb has the inscription, to wit, Tumulus Regum Hiberniae, that is to say, The Tomb of the Irish Kings; for we have in our Irish Chronicles that there were four Irish Kings buried in the said Tomb. Upon the north side of our Scottish Tomb the inscription bears Tumulus Regum Norvegiae, that is, the Tomb of the Kings of Norway. In the which Tomb we find in our ancient Irish Chronicles there lie eight Kings of Norway . . . Within this Sanctuary also lie the most [part of] the Lords of the Isles with their lineage, two MacLean [branches] with their lineage, MacKinnon and MacQuarrie with their lineage, with sundry other inhabitants of the whole Isles, because this Sanctuary used to be the burial-place of the best men of all the Isles, and also of our Kings, as we have said; because it was the most honourable and ancient place that was in Scotland in those days, as we read.)

We have some records of who they were:

'*The same year [1187] Godred, King of the Isles, died on 10th November on St Patrick's Isle in Man. The following summer his body was conveyed to the island called Hy [Iona].*' (G. Broderick, *Chronicles of the Kings of Man and the Isles.*)

Chapter 5

The post-Reformation church

T here is a considerable change in the type of evidence we gain from religious sources in the Highlands and Islands after the Reformation. Once the Roman Catholic church lost primacy the records it maintained were of a different nature. We no longer meet with disputes between priests as to who is to secure what benefice; instead their concerns are those of a fugitive or missionary church trying to maintain or regain its flock. Church lands were lost and religious life came to an end at the monasteries of Iona, Saddell, Ardchattan and Oronsay. We do however have some valuable evidence from the Franciscan mission of the early seventeenth century. In the archives of the Catholic church are reports from other missions in the seventeenth and eighteenth centuries.

On the Protestant side we have the records of the various presbyteries and, particularly from the eighteenth century, a string of reports on the social and economic life of the Highlands and Hebrides. We do not know Timothy Pont's motives for his great geographical surveys at the end of the sixteenth century but they may have been connected with the zeal of a Reformed Kirk. John Walker was a minister who surveyed the Hebrides between 1762 and 1771 and produced a compendious report. Alexander Webster was a minister who conducted the first population survey of Scotland in 1755; while Sir John Sinclair utilised most of the ministers in Scotland for the compilation of his great Statistical Account in the 1790s. There is, then, no shortage of evidence from a religious background.

In this chapter I am going to concentrate on the seventeenth-century evidence collected by the Franciscans, not least because we know so little about this period from within the Highlands. This will then be supplemented by some extracts from the much more copious eighteenth-century accounts. Firstly we should consider the common ground between the Hebrides and Ireland.

Many aspects of religion were shared by the Gaels with their Irish cousins. Hebrideans operated as mercenaries in Ireland from at least the thirteenth until the mid seventeenth century. They had close contact with Irish culture, a contact strengthened by a shared language and by dynastic alliances cemented through intermarriage. They shared an affection for the old church and its sacred images and rites; practices which the reformed church regarded as superstitious and idolatrous. There is plenty of evidence to show how Highland culture was riven by these stresses.

Contact was in either direction. The Irish seem to have been foremost amongst the visitors to the Pigmies Isle in Lewis, whilst the Scots often passed to Ireland on pilgrimage. On 19 July 1593 Sir Richard Bingham wrote from Ireland to Lord Burghley: '*Scots about to pass by boat into Mayo to offer at Knockpatrick (a superstitious ceremony).*' (Calendar of State Papers, Ireland, vol V, p 129)

Despite attempts by the Franciscan missionaries to present the Hebrides as an area of total darkness as far as religion was concerned this is not wholly true. Firstly there is the internal evidence about how the Franciscans had to flee Protestant ministers in the Isles (eight on one occasion). Secondly we know that families like the Omeys in Kintyre, who were prominent as priests under the old church, were equally prominent as ministers of the new. There is also evidence of frequent contact with Ireland and its religious life from the southern isles and Kintyre. Many Gaels went across to the Catholic friary of Bonamargy where Father Hegarty, (formerly one of the missionaries to the Hebrides) was guardian in the 1630s.

One of the glories of West Highland culture was its school of monumental sculpture which had produced a spectacular series of stone crosses, particularly in Argyll. Most of these seem to have survived the Reformation intact but probably succumbed in the 1640s. Leslie's expedition to Kintyre in 1647, the massacre at Dunaverty and a litter of broken crosses across south Argyll are all aspects of the fanaticism of these years. To the Reformer the cults and saint-worship of the Catholic church were anathema.

Their objections may be summed up in a quotation which W. C. Mackenzie gives from an English report in Ireland where St Patrick was declared to be 'of better credit than Christ Jesus'. The Reformers similarly abhorred the idolatry they found in the Highlands. There was an image of St Choan much revered by Highlanders which was taken to Edinburgh in 1600 and publicly burned at the Town Cross. It was known as 'Glengarry's god'. It seems that during the first half of the seventeenth century there was a very real attempt to break the hold which older religious practices had on people in the Highlands and Islands.

In 1630 Captain Dymes writes of a Lewis religious tradition at last being broken:

> *In their religion they are very ignorant and have been given to the idolatrous worship of divers Saints as doth appear by their Chapels which are yet to be seen, but they are now most especially devoted to one of their Saints called St Mallonuy whose Chapel is seated in the north part of the Isle, whom they have in great veneration to this day and keep the Chapel in good repair. This Saint was for cure of all their wounds and sores and therefore those that were not able to come unto the Chapel in person they were wont [used] to cut out the proportion of their lame arms or legs in wood with the form of their sores and wounds thereof and send them to the Saint where I have seen them lying*

upon the Altar in the Chapel. Within the Chapel there is a Sanctum Sanctorum [Holy of Holies] *which is so holy in their estimation that not any of their women are suffered to enter therein. Any woman with child dareth not to enter within the doors of the Chapel, but there are certain places without where they go to their devotions. They had two general meetings in the year at this Chapel, the one at Candlemas* [Purification of the Virgin Mary], *and the other at Alhollautide* [All Saints' Day] *where their custom was to eat and drink until they were drunk. And then after much dancing and dalliance together they entered the chapel at night with lights in their hands where they continued till next morning in their devotions. The last time of their meeting was at Candlemas last. They were prevented of their Idolatrous worship by a gentleman who is a Minister in the Isle, who albeit the place was far from his abode and out of his Cure, he met them at their Assembly in the Chapel where he began first to reason with them, then to admonish them and afterwards to threaten them both with God His Judgements and the Laws of the Realm, in so much as divers of the better sort of them promised to forsake that wonted Idolatry of theirs.* From 'A Description Of Lewis By Captain Dymes', in W. C. Mackenzie, *History of the Outer Hebrides*, Appendix F, with modernised spellings.

In 1669 a report was given to the Catholic authorities about the state of Catholicism in Scotland. The Rev C. Giblin summarises this as follows:

The inhabitants of the Highlands and Isles could not, in general, be called either catholics or non-catholics. They disliked the new religion, but had, of necessity, to listen to the non-catholic ministers. The people there erred in matters of faith because there was a shortage of priests to instruct them. They had great reverence for the catholic priest, made the sign of the cross, invoked the saints, recited the litanies, used holywater, and observed the principal feasts. They frequented the ruins of their old churches, and took water from the wells near them, and invoking the name of the patron saint of the church, drank some of the water in the hope of curing their infirmities. They baptised their own children if the ministers refused to do so. There was no evidence of any of them having been given to heresy, and a tradition among them, of which they were proud, said that none of them took any part in the demolition of the churches or altars during the persecution. (Giblin, Innes Review Vol 5, No 1, 1954)

This reads like a balanced and sanguine view of the true state of religion in much of the Highlands and Islands. A conservative rural people will have viewed the Reformation very differently to the artisans and merchants of the towns of Lowland Scotland. They retained a reverence for the old saints, sacred wells and ancient religious sites. A degree of primitive, almost pagan superstition seems to have lingered for centuries. Writing about 1695, Martin

Martin frequently refers to his own attempts to weaken superstitious practices such as making a sunwise tour before setting off on a journey. He also shows that the worship of saints' images was by no means extinct. He writes of Barra:

The natives have St Barr's wooden image standing on the altar, covered with linen in form of a shirt; all their greatest asseverations are by this saint. I came very early in the morning with an intention to see this image, but was disappointed; for the natives prevented me by carrying it away, lest I might take occasion to ridicule their superstition, as some Protestants have done formerly; and when I was gone it was again exposed on the altar. They have several traditions concerning this great saint. There is a chapel (about half a mile on the south side of the hill near St Barr's Church) where I had occasion to get an account of a tradition concerning this saint, which was thus: 'The inhabitants having begun to build the church, which they dedicated to him, they laid this wooden image within it, but it was invisibly transported (as they say) to the place where the church now stands, and found there every morning'. This miraculous conveyance is the reason they give for desisting to work where they first began. I told my informer that this extraordinary motive was sufficient to determine the case, if true, but asked his pardon to dissent from him, for I had not faith enough to believe this miracle, at which he was surprised, telling me in the meantime that this tradition hath been faithfully conveyed by the priests and natives successively to this day.
(Martin Martin, *A Description of the Western Islands of Scotland*)

Some time before 1626 Cornelius Ward stayed in the village of Carinish in North Uist where there was: '*a wooden statue of the Holy Trinity which was held in veneration in the village church, and which, according to local tradition, had worked many miracles since the suppression of catholicism.*' (Giblin, *Irish Franciscan Mission to Scotland 1619–1646*, p 85)

Protestants were generally very unsympathetic to such sentiments. Rev. John Walker writes of the superstition of the people of Iona: '*Their un-limited Veneration for Antiquity, supplies the Place of Truth, in the most marvelous and frightfull Legends, and their Slender Acquaintance with Religion, is but the Parent of that Superstition, which can only be remedied, by a more perfect Knowledge of divine Things.*' (McKay, *Walker's Report on the Hebrides*, 1764 and 1771)

It may well be that Martin Martin had a historical or aesthetic interest in this image of St Barr and this was certainly the case with his contemporary Edward Lhuyd. Lhuyd travelled to a number of religious sites in the Highlands and Hebrides although his interest could best be described as antiquarian. He had the old carved stones sketched and copies of these sketches survive in the British Library. (See Plate 5a). They help us to chart his itinerary up the west coast and one of his stops was at the old graveyard at Kilmichael, Ballochroy, on the north-west coast of Kintyre. Highland graveyards are now a tourist attraction, repositories of an art and culture which has disappeared. In a way tourists are the modern pilgrims, if with antiquarian rather than religious objectives.

One of the problems with pilgrimage is that pilgrims like to take home a momento. Religious objects have always needed protection from the light-fingered or unscrupulous. In the past they have been secured by curses or legends to frighten off a would-be thief. There is a cautionary tale in the *Chronicles of Man* about what happened to one of Somerled's followers who violated the sanctuary of St Machutus. Similar forces were at work in the Highlands and Hebrides. In July 1624, Ward, O'Neill and Hegarty arrived in the isle of Sanda just off Kintyre:

> *where they found a chapel dedicated to St Ninian which had a small cemetery attached to it; according to tradition, this cemetery was the resting place of fourteen saints, and it was said that any man or beast entering the burial place of the saints would die a sudden death or be stricken with a severe illness; it was said, too, that anything taken from the burial place would be miraculously restored.* (Giblin, *Irish Franciscan Mission to Scotland 1619–1646*, p 50)

As we shall see later the bell on St Finnan's Isle, Loch Shiel, has similar restorative properties. They were necessary. In 1772 Pennant writes of the altar of Iona Cathedral: '*The altar was of white marble veined with grey . . . The demolition of this stone was owing to the belief of the superstitious; who were of opinion, that a piece of it conveyed to the possessor success in whatever he undertook. A very small portion is now left; and even that we contributed to diminish.*' (T. Pennant, *A Tour in Scotland and Voyage to the Hebrides*, p 244)

The Franciscans

The Irish Franciscan mission in the first half of the seventeenth century was not the first or only Catholic mission to the Highlands. It seems that missionaries were active in Sanda before the end of the sixteenth century. Given the shortness of the sea-crossing between Kintyre and Ulster, and the frequent contacts, (political, military and family), throughout this period, it is probable that South Argyll and islands like Islay and Jura never lost touch with the Catholic church in Ireland.

The work of the Franciscans has been summarised by Giblin in his book *The Irish Franciscan Mission to Scotland, 1619–1646*. This deals with the missionary activities of those who were sent to preserve Catholicism in the Highlands and Islands. The book includes the original reports sent home by the missionaries with English summaries by Giblin. It provides invaluable first-hand evidence of conditions in the Hebrides at a time when written evidence from within the islands is very scarce. There were plenty of official records dealing with the Hebrides – for instance those covering the troubles in Islay and Kintyre in 1614–16. Since these were written from the government point of view they can hardly be regarded as unbiased. Giblins's evidence gives us another perspective.

Of the four Franciscan missionaries, two in particular, Patrick Hegarty and Cornelius Ward, give us the most illuminating information.

> Brother Cornelius Ward, in 1624, the first year of his mission, travelled more than two hundred miles, back and forth, within Scotland. The names of the lands and islands through which he went are these: Sanda island, where there is a church to St Ninian, Cara island where is a church to St Columba; Oronsa [Oronsay] island where there is a ruined monastery of canons, Colbosa [Colonsay] island whose chief is a convert, Mula [Mull] island, of which the second house [Maclean of Loch Buidhe] has been converted; Ulba [Ulva] island; Iona the isle of Saint Columba; the country of Kinntire [Kintyre]; Mocarna [Muckairn], whose chief, the Baron of Calder, is a convert; Locheabar [Lochaber]; Gleanngabhar [Glengour]; Gleanngara [Glengarry]; Inernesse [Inverness]; Sutherland; Catnesse [Caithness], etc. In 1624, in the aforesaid islands and places, Brother Cornelius Ward converted 387 to the faith. They lie, therefore, who say that he did not meet with success in the kingdom of Scotland. In the year 1625 in Kynntiria [Kintyre], Arainn [Arran], Duira [Jura] island, Colbosa [Colonsay] island, Arasoid [Arisaig], the island of Ygg [Eigg], the island of Ruum [Rum], Cana [Canna] island, the isle of West Ibisdia [South Uist], East Ibisdia [North Uist], Barra island, Ude [Fuday?] island, Brother Cornelius Ward converted 1,122 to the faith and baptized 245. In the year 1626 in the abovewritten islands and places the same Brother Cornelius Ward converted 929 to the faith and baptized 80.
>
> In the year 1625, in the abovewritten islands and places, Brother Patrick Hegarty converted 1,410 to the faith, baptized 155, as well as 60 Scots and one heretic minister in Ireland. Brother Patrick Brady, in the places through which he travelled, converted 260 heretics. Brother Paul O'Neill, in the places through which he travelled, converted 390 to the faith. In 1630 and 1631, Brother Patrick Hegarty . . . converted 2,229 to the faith, baptized 1,222 and celebrated 117 marriages in the aforesaid islands and places.
>
> Total number of converts in the aforesaid places and islands 6,627, total of baptisms, 3,010
> The other two reports which we sent have been lost, I believe.
> (From Latin given by Giblin, Irish Franciscan Mission to Scotland 1619–1646)

The total number of those converted or baptised was 9,637, close to the claimed figure of 10,000 which was under dispute in Rome. We can assume that many of those baptised were young children.

Giblin gives in full a report on Patrick Hegarty's activities during 1630 and 1631. Much of this reads as a list of how many conversions, baptisms, marriages and last rites he performed. I give a few abbreviated extracts both to convey the flavour of the original and also to demonstrate how extensively these Irish missionaries travelled around the Hebrides and west coast.

13 July 1630 Brother Patrick crossed from Ireland to Rathlin . . .
16 July Arrived in Kintyre . . . 16 converted
17 July . . . crossing to Cara . . . converted another 5 . . .
18 July . . . Fled to Jura . . . converted 5
20 July Taken from there to Colonsay . . . converted 20, baptized 4 . . .
28 July . . . Sailed to Mull, converted 20, baptized 6
29 July Carried to Iona, converted 4
30 July Returned to Mull from Iona, 20 converted, 6 baptized . . .
10 August Crossed to the nearby island of Muck, converted 3, baptized 2 . . .
crossed to Eigg
12 and 13 August converted 100 in Eigg, baptized 12, heard the confessions
of many who were converted in previous years, performed 2 marriages.
14 August Coming from Eigg to Moidart, a promontory on the mainland of
Scotland, converted 6 . . .
22 August Returned to Eigg . . .
26 August . . . Taken to Canna . . .
28 August Carried to Uist . . .
1 October . . . taken to Barra . . .
7 October Converted 8, baptised 14, performed 5 marriages . . .
22 October Returning to Uist, converted 2, baptized 16 . . .
1 November Converted 14, administered last rites to 1

(He remained in the more southerly of the Western Isles until April 1631 when he returned to Canna, then Colonsay and Kintyre, eventually reaching Ireland in early May 1631. From Latin given by Giblin, Irish Franciscan Mission to Scotland 1619–1646.)

In the summer of 1624 Patrick Hegarty spent eight weeks in Kintyre and converted 206. For security reasons the missionaries did not always list their flock but in this instance Hegarty sent details to his superiors. Giblin prints the latinized list in full. This is an invaluable source because although we have lists of tenants in Kintyre dating back to 1505 this is the only early document which includes the names of ordinary men, women and children. Despite the Latin disguise many of the names are still recognisable in Kintyre today. A full analysis, coupled with other evidence of where particular families were located would reveal more of Hegarty's itinerary. Probably no area in the Highlands has as much evidence of its early inhabitants as Kintyre. This document adds to that body of data and conjures the possibility of a reasonably complete demographic database stretching from the present day back to 1500.

The names also tell us something of the historical roots of the people of Kintyre. Naming practices display extraordinary conservatism with specific Christian names passing down within a family for hundreds of years. Sometimes these names become heavily disguised by the slow process of anglicization. The famous mediaeval family of O'Brolchans seem to have become Brodies by the early nineteenth century. A woman called Finola (or similar) might be Florence two hundred years later. The old Norse name of Effric (or Oighrig) became Euphemia or Effie. As an indication of the value of this data I give the names of a handful of Hegarty's converts with their modern equivalents.

Nola Cneill	(Finola MacNeill)
Emerus Kay, nobilis	(Ivar MacKay, nobleman)
Daniel Kay, nobilis	(Donald MacKay, nobleman)
Aphrica Kay	(Effric MacKay)
Aphrica Cneill	(Effric MacNeill)
Aphrica Kyaragan	(Effric MacKerral)
Margareta Ragnaldi	(Margaret MacRanald or MacRuari)
Godfredus Alexandri	(Godfrey MacAlister)
Maria Claberty	(Mary MacLaverty)

(From Latin given by Giblin, *Irish Franciscan Mission to Scotland 1619–1646*)

At first glance such information can be quite unprepossessing. But if we reflect that names like Ivar, Effric, Ranald and Godfrey are all Norse in origin we see the continuance of a Viking tradition first established eight hundred years earlier and supposedly ended at least four hundred years earlier.

This data was provided by travellers who were there on the ground. They were not retailing stories from other people. They were in the islands; these were their experiences. The first question, as with any historical data, is how reliable is it? Of course the Franciscans were biased but we must not discount their evidence just because of that. For much mediaeval data we have only one source and we have to take it at face value. Fortunately for us the figures provided by the Franciscans were challenged at the time by sceptical rivals amongst the Scottish Catholic community in Rome.

The Roman court, like all political institutions, has always suffered from lobbying by different groups and jealous interests. The Franciscans came up against opposition from other priests working in Scotland while certain Scots at Rome, (including, perhaps, a certain George Conn), cast doubt on their figures of the number of conversions. As a result the Franciscans found their salaries withheld and over the next few years they had an uphill struggle to get paid for their labours. They had to provide all sorts of supporting evidence and testimonials which, taken together, give us even more confidence in their accounts. Much of the correspondence contained in Giblin is effectively a vindication of their efforts.

Eventually they seem to have triumphed morally, if not financially. The dissenting voices in Rome certainly tested their enthusiasm for continuing a mission that seemed so unappreciated. We have no reason, therefore, to doubt the evidence of where they visited and who they converted. However there are other aspects of this mission we should be more cautious about. Perfectly understandably for any group fighting their corner they perhaps overestimated their own achievements in the long term. Under Campbell control most of Argyll became firmly Protestant. There is also no doubt, not least from internal evidence provided by the Franciscans, that the Reformed church had a stronger and more active presence in the Highlands and Islands than the missionaries gave them credit for. Despite their claims to the contrary, there undoubtedly were some Gaelic-speaking clergymen. Inconveniently for the Franciscans, they were Protestants.

According to a Catholic report quoted by Giblin, the Protestant bishop of the Isles wrote to King James VI warning him of the danger of the Franciscan missionaries converting the people of Kintyre to Catholicism. An attendant read the letter to the king who dissolved in gales of laughter and said 'So, at last my Kintyre folk are to become Christian! Anybody', he said, 'who converts a people as savage, fierce and godless as they deserves our gratitude'. The chamberlain, from whom the writer of the report had heard the story, was astonished by the king's reply and did not dare to pursue the matter any further.

Through the missionaries we also learn something of how the Highlands and Hebrides appeared to the outside world.

> the mission territory is not only a very difficult place to live in, but is well-nigh inaccessible; the inhabitants have a greater taste for military exploits than for food and are content with fare which would be scarcely sufficient for other people when fasting . . . this inaccessibility is responsible for the fact that there are today to be found in the Highlands and the Isles as many uneducated people as there were anchorites there in olden times
> (Giblin, Irish Franciscan Mission to Scotland 1619–1646, p 48)

Not only was the territory difficult and demanding but the population was so miserably poor that they could do little to provide comfort for the Franciscans. In 1637 Ward discusses the situation of Ranald Macdonald, the former Protestant minister they had converted into a Catholic priest. He tells how Macdonald had to till the land, fish and gather shellfish in order to survive: 'the islanders are so poor that they cannot support MacDonald as well as the non-Catholic minister, to whom they are compelled to pay tithes; besides, the people of the islands are so ignorant that they think the priests and all true servants of Christ *should work without any recompense'* (Giblin, *Irish Franciscan Mission to Scotland 1619–1646*, pp 174–75)

The Franciscans provide more evidence of the cultural and linguistic chasm between Highlander and Lowlander:

> *there is not one priest to be had who is a native of the Highlands and the Isles, and there are no priests there from outside except the four Irish Franciscan missionaries . . . besides, there is a lasting and mutual enmity between the Anglo-Scots and the Gaelic-speaking Scots; furthermore, the Anglo-Scots do not know Gaelic, and there is only one priest among them who has a knowledge of that language; there is as much difference in mode of life and in outlook between the Anglo-Scots and the Gaelic-speaking Scots as there is between the Scots and the Greeks, and, indeed, the Anglo-Scots would be about as useful as the Greeks in helping the people in the Highlands and the Isles.* (Giblin, *Irish Franciscan Mission to Scotland 1619–1646*, p 90)

The picture of poverty and ignorance is repeated endlessly: '*there is no school in the Highlands and the Isles, nor is there a schoolmaster, nor anybody who teaches the simple alphabet.* (From Latin in Giblin, *Irish Franciscan Mission to Scotland 1619–1646*, p 90)

Ward claimed that in Kintyre: '*there were no scribes or public notaries or other priests to be had*' (Giblin, *Irish Franciscan Mission to Scotland 1619–1646*, p 120) and that: '*in the whole of the mission territory there is no city or town, nor is there a notary, or a catholic priest, nor anybody who can write Latin, except the four missionaries*' (Giblin, *Irish Franciscan Mission to Scotland 1619–1646*, pp 126, 128). Moreover: '*In the foresaid Highlands and Islands of Scotland there is no city, no town, no school, no polity; none can read except the few who were educated in far off places.*' (From Giblin, *Irish Franciscan Mission to Scotland 1619–1646*, p 173).

However we must take this evidence with a pinch of salt. There were Gaelic-speaking Protestant ministers and there were also some Highlanders who were literate. Indeed one of the documents given by Giblin is a copy of a testimonial letter signed, in March 1629, by four Gaels who bore witness to the conversions made by the missionaries in the Highlands and Islands.

The reports also contain some delightful human touches, two in particular from the Small Isles. Ward visited the roofless church on Eigg in August 1625: '*At that time I reconciled a certain 80–year-old lady, who remembered mass being celebrated many years before on Eigg and the surrounding isles.*' (From Giblin, *Irish Franciscan Mission to Scotland 1619–1646*, p 66)

In October, Ward went to Canna where he stayed for nearly a fortnight. His report states that he preached to the people but found that although: *the truths preached by Ward pleased the people . . . having to put them into practice did not, for, children of the earth as they were, they were intent on the crops, not their salvation, and, as it was autumn, they paid more attention to the harvest than to their souls.'* (Giblin, *Irish Franciscan Mission to Scotland 1619–1646*, p 68)

The Protestant minister John Lane Buchanan said much the same in the Outer Isles nearly two centuries later:

> *With regard to the great mass of the people, so much of their time is taken up in temporal avocations, in ploughing or digging their arable spots of land, rearing cattle, making kelp, cutting peats, driving cattle for their masters, and other services, that it is not in their power to assemble regularly together, in a fit frame for public worship: not to mention that it is chiefly on the Sundays, after the labour of the preceding week is over, that their masters chuse to send them on errands to distant countries and islands.* (Buchanan, *Travels in the Western Hebrides from 1782 to 1790*)

Ward was not the only visiting cleric to have a struggle. Rural agrarian societies are very practical and very conservative. Ward may have experienced the former trait in Canna, Martin Martin gives a nice example of the latter in Barra:

> *All the inhabitants observe the anniversary of St Barr, being the 27th of September; it is performed riding on horseback, and the solemnity is concluded by three turns round St Barr's church. This brings into my mind a story which was told me concerning a foreign priest and the entertainment he met with after his arrival there some years ago, as follows:- This priest happened to land here upon the very day, and at the particular hour of this solemnity, which was the more acceptable to the inhabitants, who then desired him to preach a commemoration sermon to the honour of their patron St Barr, according to the ancient custom of the place. At this the priest was surprised, he never having heard of St Barr before that day; and therefore knowing nothing of his virtues, could say nothing concerning him: but told them, that if a sermon to the honour of St Paul or St Peter could please them, they might have it instantly. This answer of his was so disagreeable to them, that they plainly told him he could be no true priest, if he had not heard of St Barr, for the Pope himself had heard of him; but this would not persuade the priest, so that they parted much dissatisfied with one another.*

Safe travel for the sake of religion was checked by the struggles of seventeenth century. While much of Argyll became Protestant there were parts of western Inverness-shire, such as Clanranald's estate, which remained faithful to Catholicism. The Franciscan missionaries from Ireland faced harassment and pursuit in their journeys round the Isles. But it also worked the other way. Ministers were made to feel unwelcome on Catholic estates during the seventeenth and eighteenth centuries.

There was always an element of risk in travelling in the strife-torn Highlands and Islands. On 17 March 1575–6, James Macdonald of Castle Camus in Skye

byndis and oblisses me, in manir abone written, to causs my sone Jhone Oig satisfie the said reuerend fader of all skayth sustenit be him throw the breking of the said reuerend faderis blak boitt, committed by the said Jhone Oig vpoun the coist of Kyntyir, in the moneth of Merche, the yeir of God, (1574), throw the taking of hir cabillis and ankris fra hir. (Collectanea de Rebus Albanicis, p 11)

(binds and obliges me, in manner above written, to cause my son John Og satisfy the said reverend father of all skaith [damage] sustained by him through the breaking of the said reverend father's black boat, committed by the said John Og upon the coast of Kintyre, in the month of March, the year of God, (1574), through the taking of her cables and anchors from her.)

In this case the 'said reverend father' was the bishop of the Isles! What was at issue here was probably a question of money – the bishop's dues. The church was not only weakened by division, it also had a difficulty collecting its rents. Amongst the business conducted by the Privy Council, probably in July 1623, there is a section concerning the Island Chiefs where it is stated that: '*The Lords would be pleased to injoyne them that the bishop, his officials, factors, deputs, and officers, may have at al occasions safe and secure passage through the Isles.*' (Register of the Privy Council of Scotland, Vol XIII (1622–1625))

That this was not always the case on the mainland appears in February 1624 when a complaint was made by the Bishop of Argyll and Mr Donald Omey, minister of Ardnamurchan. The latter was preaching in church one Sunday when:

'*thair come a young man in to the kirk in the middis of the preatching armed with a sword, a targe, and a hagbuitt, and verrie rudlie with ane awfull and feirce countenance addrest him selff directlie to the minister*', giving to him a letter from John McDonald . . . Captain of the Clanronald . . . that the minister '*sould, with all convenient diligence, reteir him selff frome these boundis and have him hame, utherwayes it sould coast him his lyffe*'. (Register of the Privy Council of Scotland, Vol XIII (1622–1625))

Donald Omey was from a long-established, Gaelic-speaking, family of clerics in Kintyre. He was a Protestant but wisely decided, in this instance, that flight was more attractive than martyrdom. Clanranald was not going to suffer any religious interference in what he regarded as his sphere of influence. The attempt by the Bishop of Argyll to extend the Reformation north and west would suffer a temporary setback.

There are a number of clerical reports on the Highlands and Islands in the eighteenth century. These have appeared in books by Blundell, Craven and more recent historians as well as issues of the *Innes Review*. They are invaluable for all sorts of information, including population figures, but I omit them here on grounds of space and because they are relatively straight-forward to access. Instead I finish with two quotations, the first to remind ourselves that language was always an issue in the Highland church, the second to show that ministers became a critical part of the social and intellectual framework of the Highlands and Islands.

The Rev. John Lane Buchanan was scathing about Protestant ministers in the Western Isles in the late eighteenth century. He implies that to some visiting missionaries it was little more than a holiday job:

> *It has sometimes happened, as I have been told, that the managers, in their choice of a visitant, have been more attentive to the wishes and importunities of certain bustling, restless and intriguing spirits, who wanted to have a post, and a Summer excursion, free of expence, than to the qualities of his mind.*
>
> *I have heard of a visitant who had no other motive for soliciting the appointment, than that he wished to have respite for some months, from being hen-pecked by his wife. That appointment the clergyman alluded to certainly received, although, what will appear incredible, he was ignorant of the Galic tongue.* (Buchanan, *Travels in the Western Hebrides from 1782 to 1790*)

Buchanan's evidence was usually one-sided, and certainly many visitors were complimentary about Highland ministers, but it is interesting to see language still an unresolved issue in church appointments.

In Appendices III and IV of Pennant's 1769 Tour are printed two questionnaires addressed to the clergy and gentlemen of North Britain: '*Queries, addressed to the Gentlemen and Clergy of North Britain, respecting the antiquities and natural history of their respective parishes, with a view of exciting them to favour the world with a fuller and more satisfactory account of their country, than it is in the power of a stranger and transient visitant to give.*' (Pennant, *A Tour in Scotland 1769*)

Between them the questionnaires asked seventy-two questions, many of them very open-ended. Not everybody approved of Pennant's appeal to local authorities – Boswell for one. However we can recognise the beginnings of a more quantitative, scientific approach. Pennant was not content to be a literary dilettante. He saw the restrictions of time and circumstance, he knew how finite were his own powers, how insufficient the anecdotal reports of most travellers. He was not the first to adopt this line. Seventy years earlier Edward Lhuyd had sent out his own questionnaire. A generation later Pennant's approach was copied by Sir John Sinclair in his appeal to all the parish ministers in Scotland which resulted in the great compendium that is the (Old) Statistical Account. The point about all of these is that it was to the ministers that they addressed their queries. The ministers were educated, literate men. When travellers wanted information it was the representatives of the church they turned to. In mediaeval times they were expected to offer hospitality. Now they were expected to supply statistics.

Chapter 6

Commerce and industry

W e have virtually no documentary evidence for trade to or within the Highlands and Islands for the Dark Age and early mediaeval periods. Trade there certainly was, but we know little about it. Since there was no road network, inland trade would have been confined to livestock or what could be carried on horseback. Bulky items had to travel by water. Logs could be floated down a loch or river; cargoes could be carried by birlinn or galley. There was likely a good deal of coastal trade between the islands and the west coast mainland, and from both to Northern Ireland. There were probably old and well-established land-routes across Scotland, from Skye via Glenelg to Inverness, and from Loch Linnhe through the Great Glen. The following quotations give some idea of the evidence available for the earlier period.

> *Alexander* [III] *King of Scots to the King* [Edward I]. *Informs him that he has learned that certain men of a Baron of his, Alexander of Argyll, touching at the King's port of Bristol, were arrested there with their vessel and goods on suspicion of piracy. But that the King may see they are the writer's liegemen, he sends the names of some – first Master Alan, the 'gubernator'* [helmsman and skipper?] *of the vessel; another is Gilfolan Kerd* [=Gaelic 'ceard' for a smith or metal-worker?], *and their comrades, names unknown at this date. Begs the King to cause the bailiffs of Bristol to permit the men freely to depart for Scotland with their goods. 15 August 1275.* (Calendar of Documents relating to Scotland, vol II, pp 12–13)

Edward subsequently authorised the release of this vessel whose goods were valued at 160 merks (£106–13s-4d). On 11 July 1292 Edward granted safe-conduct to Alexander of Argyll who, apparently, frequently dispatched merchants and goods to buy and sell in Ireland. Similar letters were issued to Angus Macdonald of Islay and his son Alexander.

On 16 July 1310 (Edward II):
Protection for merchants going with supplies to the men of the Isle of Argyll who have conducted themselves loyally to the King.
(Calendar of Documents relating to Scotland, vol III, p 29)

On 20 September 1337 (Edward III):
The King commands Robert de Rotyngdone his bailiff of Coupeland, to

release the galley, crew, and goods of John of the Isles, which had been arrested on suspicion that they were the enemy's, whereas he has always been the King's liege.
(Calendar of Documents relating to Scotland, vol III, p 227)
Presumably 'Coupeland' refers to Copeland Island off Belfast and the term 'goods' implies that John's men were trading with Ireland. Copeland could also be written 'Copman', probably from the Norse *kaupman* or merchant.

On 24 May 1338 (Edward III):
Protection and safe conduct till All Saints' day for William Herbert of Droghda, William Hybert of Portrosse, and Douenald Vinor, merchants, whom John of the Isles is sending to England and Ireland to buy victuals for himself. (Calendar of Documents relating to Scotland, Vol III, No 1273)

On 1 August 1357 (Edward III):
Safe conduct at the request of John of the Isles, for John Longus of Portrous, John son of Stephen, Doncan of the 'Dormitory', William of Ulster, Henry of Abyndon, and Adam le Taillour, merchants of the said isles, to trade in England and Ireland and the King's dominions, with their vessel and six mariners, making oath to ship nothing for the King's enemies in Scotland, and to produce in Chancery the certificate of John of the Isles that their goods were discharged in the isles, within three months thereafter. (Calendar of Documents relating to Scotland, Vol III, No 1639)

On 18 July 1489 (Henry VII):
Safe conduct and protection for two years from date, at the instance of Thomas Grafton of London, merchant, for 'Archebald Makelar of Argile, Scottyshman,' to come on horseback or foot by sea or land into the King's dominions, with 'almaner goodis and merchaundises,' and trade within the realms of Scotland and France, and elsewhere beyond seas, also in Flanders and other parts of the Duke of Burgundy's dominions – all so long as there shall be truce with these countries.
(Bain, Calendar of Documents relating to Scotland, IV, p 316)

20 April 1546 (Henry VIII):
John Eldar, the King's servant. Licence to export 200 dickers of tanned leather, hides or backs.
(Letters and Papers of the Reign of Henry VIII, vol XXI, Pt I, p 481)

This last was a licence to John Elder, author of a letter and 'plotte' or map of Scotland to Henry VIII in 1543–4. Elder wrote that he had been:

educatt, and brought vp, not onely in the West yles of the same plotte, namede
Sky and the Lewis, wher I haue bene often tymes with my friendis, in ther
longe galleis, arrywing to dyvers and syndrie places in Scotland, wher they
had a do.
(Collectanea de Rebus Albanicis)

(educated, and brought up, not only in the West Isles of the same plotte,
named Skye and the Lewis, where I have been oftentimes with my
friends, in their long galleys, arriving to various and sundry places in
Scotland, where they had a do).

Elder seems to have spent some time in exile in England and he may have
turned his hand to a little commercial enterprise. A 'dicker' is a unit of ten so
he was exporting no less than 2000 hides. Hides were one of the principal
products of the Highlands and Islands in earlier times and I like to think Elder
had kept contact with his friends in Skye and Lewis and was acting as some
sort of agent!

Later sources

The economic resources of an area, any area, have always interested outsiders; indeed this has been one of the key triggers for colonial expansion. It
might be a mineral resource such as gold, silver or lead; it might be land for a
growing population; it might be people if there was a requirement for slaves.
The motive for such expansion was usually some rumour or report of the
area's supposed wealth. Since rumours were not always accurate it was
common for the rich or powerful to commission an investigation to research
the matter more fully. In early days this might be undertaken by a merchant,
mariner, or military detachment. Today it is done by a consultant. The
problem then, as now, is that if the reporter had a financial interest in the
outcome then his report might be biased. We have good examples of this in
the late sixteenth and early seventeenth centuries when some of the projected
plantations, for instance in Lewis and Ulster, were swept along by the greed
and ambition of their promoters.

Accordingly, an area's natural resources are often mentioned in early maps.
Nowell's manuscript map of Scotland shows mountains of marble and
alabaster. These were not just wonders, they were potential riches. Pont
marks woodland in a precise manner, iron production in Sutherland, lead in
Islay. In the 1640s Gordon comments on the rich fishing in Loch Nevis.
Moll's eighteenth-century maps of the Hebrides give much ancillary detail
about the fisheries of the area.

This is even more obvious in the written reports. Undoubtedly, part of the
purpose of Dean Monro's account was to list the economic resources of the

isles. Most economic activity was agricultural, but there were also resources of fish, birds and marine mammals that had to be detailed. If he drew attention to an island having a falcon's nest then this was not for the ornithological interest – but simply because this was a potential source of wealth. To enable comparisons to be made between the different reports here follow some reviews of the small island of Muck.

Monro writes of Muck in 1549: '*ane Ile of twa mile lang, callit in Irish Ellan na muk, and in Inglish the Swines Ile, ane verie fertile frutfull Ile of cornis and girsing for all store, verie gude for fische, inhabite and manurit, with ane gude falcon nest, perteining to the Bischop of the Iles; with ane gude hieland heavin* [haven] *in it, the entrie at the west cheek of it.* (R. W. Munro, *Monro's Western Isles*)

In the 1590s Pont gives a similar summary but includes Muck's land-assessment valuation in marklands

> *there is ane Illand called Illand Muck that is to say the hoggisilland and . . . it is verie profitabill and fertill of corne and abundance of milk and fish in this Illand and there is a strenght in it on a rock or craig builded be the Master and Superior of the Illand in tyme of warrs which was betwixt him and certaine enemies. This Illand appertaines to the Bishop of the Illes of the highlands of Scotland being but sex merkland* (Pont(?) in Macfarlane's Geographical Collections.)

The anonymous report printed by Skene is more concerned to quantify the island's economic output and military capacity. It shows that Muck was temporarily under the sway of Maciain of Ardnamurchan and the land-assessment given is not correct:

> *Ellan na Muk is but ane little Ile of ane mile lang and half mile braid. It perteins also to the foirsaid Bischop, and is possesst be the Laird of Ardinmwrthe callit Maken. It is four merk land, and payis to the said Laird and his factors aucht score bollis victuall, quhairof four score to the Bischop and four score to the Laird. It will raise to the weiris 16 able men.* (Skene, Celtic Scotland 1577–1595)

In 1630 Captain Dymes makes his brief abundantly clear:

> *A breife Description of the Isle of the Leweis beinge one of the Islands of ye Hebrides subiect to his Ma(jes)te Kingdome of Scotland wherein is contained the nature of the soyle, ye manners of ye people the severall fishings and theire seasons alsoe the places most comodious for a free towne or Mart for traffique, accordinge as it was ordered to bee done by certaine of the Lords of his Ma(jes)ts most hono(ra)ble privie Councell and performed in Anno 1630 by Captaine John Dymes.* (W. C Mackenzie, *History of the Outer Hebrides*, Appendix F)

As does the Rev. John Walker in his *Report on the Hebrides* written on the basis of visits from 1762–1771:

> *To His Majesties Commissioners at the Board of Annexed Estates*
> *My Lords and Gentlemen*
> *The following History of the western Islands, undertaken at your Desire and executed under your patronage, I have endeavoured as much as possible to render subservient to your excellent and Patriotic Designs, for the Improvement of these wild and remote Parts of the Kingdom.*
> *It consists for the most part of a Narration of Facts designed to serve as so many Data, from which, every intelligent Person, though he has never seen these Countries, may form a proper Idea of their Oeconomy and Improvement. And, in this View, it is hoped, they may be of Use to those who have the Police of these distant parts of Scotland, under their immediate Inspection.*
> *They were collected with the utmost Care, during the Course of above Seven Months, in a Journey by Land and Water of upwards of 3,000 Miles, through the Islands North of Cantire [Kintyre] and the adjacent parts of the Highlands.*
> (M. McKay, *Walker's Report on the Hebrides, 1764 and 1771*)

And facts he certainly gave! With Walker's Report, surveys of the Highlands and Islands are established on a scientific basis. Anecdote gives way to quantity, rumour to fact.

It is not just John Walker's survey that we owe to the Commssioners of the Annexed or Forfeited Estates. They also sponsored reports and surveys by men like Mungo Campbell, Archibald Menzies and William Morison on the estates of Barrisdale (Knoydart) and Lochiel. Such men were not local, they travelled about the area, noting what could be improved and what, occasionally, they admired. In 1768 Archibald Menzies wrote of the skilled stock management he witnessed in Knoydart. Such local knowledge is slowly learned and quickly lost:

> *They are good managers of cattle, which are esteemed of a quality equal to any of the West Highlands . . . Their grass, where best managed, is divided into summer, harvest, winter and spring grasses, which is laid out in some parts in districts . . . They have the grass for each season divided into as many divisions as it will admit of, as they look upon it [as] of consequence to change their grass often . . . It is remarkable the skill they show in chusing their pasturages for the different seasons. It is not the local situation but the quality of the grasses they study. Every farmer is so far a botanist as to distinguish the particular season each grass is in perfection. I have seen some of their wintering ground very high and exposed and at a very great distance from the sea, when at the same time they had grasing close by the sea and where no snow lay in winter. Yet the quality of the grass as winter grass determined them to chuse the high, stormy country. . . .*

From what I have said above it will appear that the tenents in that part of the country are very attentive to the management of their cattle, which is the principal thing worthy of attention there, as their climate and soil are against agriculture. (V. Wills, *Reports on the Annexed Estates* p 100)

Managing natural resources

There has been trade within and between Highland and Hebridean communities since the first settlers came here. Commodities like flint and bloodstone are only found in certain districts and these became early items of commerce since they were essential to make tools and weapons in a hunter-gatherer economy. Groups had to to travel to take advantage of different resources in different seasons. Seabirds, fish and marine mammals congregated in different areas at different times. Men travelled in pursuit of them and then travelled again to sell the products; eggs, feathers, meat, hair, hides and oil. Trade has been built into the fabric of the Highland economy from the very earliest times. It is a marginal area where an island or locality might be poor in land or timber but rich in seabirds or fish. Hebridean communities have always depended upon exchange to compensate for their deficiences.

The example of Ailsa Craig may illustrate this. Ailsa Craig, off the Ayrshire coast, is to all intents and purposes a barren rock which happens to support a huge seabird colony. Yet it was formerly thought important enough to be included in a charter of Robert Bruce to John of Menteith in 1323 where he is given the lands of Glen Breackerie in South Kintyre and Aulesai or Ailsa. Why would anybody bother to specify it? The answer lies in its economic value. We may not have as much documentary evidence for Ailsa Craig as we do for the precisely analogous Bass Rock in the Firth of Forth but both places were prized for their seabird resources and were noted by travellers through the centuries.

Gannets or solan geese make spectacular vertical descents when diving for fish and I wonder if this lies behind a sentence in the Irish Nennius concerning the wonders of the Island of Britain: '*There are also innumerable birds there on a certain rock, and they dive under the sea as if into the air.*' (Todd, *The Irish Version of the Historia Britonum of Nennius*). The gannets on either the Bass Rock or Ailsa Craig could easily match this description. In 1549 Dean Monro writes of Ailsa Craig: '*Ellsay an Isle of ane mile lang, quhairin is ane great heich hill round and roche, and als abundant of Solan-geese*' (R. W. Munro, *Monro's Western Isles*). He also writes of the annual cull of young solan geese on Sula Sgeir (Norse for 'solan goose skerry') off the Butt of Lewis:

This Ile is full of wild fowls, and quhan the fowls hes thair birds ripe, men out of the parochin of Niss in Leozus uses to saill thair and tarry thair 7 or 8 dayis and to fetche with thame hame thair boatfull of dry wild fowls with wild fowl fedderis.(R. W. Munro, *Monro's Western Isles*)

(This isle is full of wild fowl, and when the fowl have their young ready, men out of the parish of Ness in Lewis are accustomed to sail there, and stay there seven or eight days, and to fetch home with them their boat full of dry wild fowl, with wild fowl feathers).

Nearly five hundred years later this annual expedition still continues although now threatened by animal rights activists.

In an age before the battery-farmed chicken, wild fowl were an important food source. In St Kilda, gannets were preserved for up to a year and were an essential component of the island economy. But they were accounted a delicacy in other parts of Scotland as well. In 1618, John Taylor enjoyed solan goose from the Bass Rock:

Amongst our viands that wee had there, I must not forget the Soleand Goose, a most delicate Fowle, which breedes in great aboundance in a little Rocke called the Basse, which stands two miles into the Sea. It is very good flesh, but it is eaten in the forme as wee eate Oysters, standing at a side-board, a little before dinner, unsanctified without grace; and after it is eaten, it must be well liquored with two or three good rowses of Sherrie or Canarie sacke. The Lord or Owner of the Basse doth profite at the least two hundred pound yearely by those Geese. (John Taylor, *The Pennyles Pilgrimage*, 1618)

In 1636 Sir William Brereton writes of Ailsa Craig:

In this isle of Ellsey . . . there breed abundance of solemne [solan] *geese, which are longer necked and bodied than ours, and so extreme fat are the young, as that when they eat them, they are placed in the middle of the room, so as all may have access about it; their arms stripped up and linen cloaths placed before their clothes, to secure them from being defiled with the fat thereof, which doth besprinkle and besmear all that near unto it.* (Hume Brown, *Early Travellers in Scotland*)

About 1662 John Ray wrote of the solan greese on the Bass Rock in the Firth of Forth: '*The young ones are esteemed a choice dish in Scotland, and sold very dear (1s 8d plucked) . . . The laird of this island makes a great profit yearly of the soland geese taken; as I remember, they told us £130 sterling.*' (Hume Brown, *Early Travellers in Scotland*). While Pennant says of Ailsa Craig: '*This rock is the property of the Earl of Cassils, who rents it for £33 per annum to people who come here to take the young gannets for the table; and the other birds for the sake of their feathers.*' (T. Pennant, *A Tour in Scotland and Voyage to the Hebrides*, 1772) Tastes, and needs, change – so the gannet is no longer a dietary or economic necessity. Today we have drawn some rather arbitrary distinctions between various types of animal. Some are kept to be eaten, others may be pursued legitimately, others still may not be hunted at all. As a result the populations of some of our wildlife species fluctuate erratically. It is ironic that if we read Martin Martin's account of St Kilda, written three hundred years ago, it is clear that the St Kildans carefully managed their seabird resources in terms of the numbers of eggs, young and adult birds they took. They were practical conservationists to the extent that they almost farmed their seabird colonies. They certainly regulated both the time and the degree of their culls. They wanted all they could have – but it was not in their interests to take too many. They may have struck a better balance than we.

Of course it was not just gannets. Hebrideans culled a great many types of seabird. They also took geese, otters, seals and whales. Today this has almost all gone. We would far rather eat the eggs and flesh of battery-reared birds whose wings and beaks are clipped, who are kept caged indoors but of whose lives and welfare we know little and wish to know less. In today's climate this is more morally acceptable than culling a proportion of those wild creatures reared on the open sea.

This dilemma as to whether we should eat wild creatures or befriend them has always been with us. Vegetarianism may have a higher profile today but objections to killing wild animals are very ancient. Sometimes these taboos were specific to particular animals and we can only guess at the original reasons. Taboos about pork and some fish are often to do with health or hygiene. Shellfish in certain seasons may make you sickly, certain meats go off very quickly in heat. Sometimes these rules are to do with the condition of the animal itself. A kelt (salmon that has spawned and is on its way back to the sea) is not as good eating as a grilse (salmon on its first journey upriver). Other taboos may be quite local and there has been speculation that these are linked to the tribal totems of some of the most ancient peoples of Britain. The inhabitants of what is now Caithness may once have been associated with the cat, those of Kintyre with the horse. Some parts of the Highlands seem to have been less keen on pork than others.

Today of course the restrictions are imposed by legislation and monitored by the various animal rights and conservation organisations. The farcical results are illustrated by the issue of geese in Islay. For centuries the rents of farms in Islay included a number of geese as a render. Some quantities are given at the end of the sixteenth century:

Ilk merk land in this Ile payis yeirlie three mairtis and ane half, 14 wedderis, 28 geis, 4 dozen and 8 pultrie, 5 bollis malt with ane peck to ilk boll, 6 bollis meill, 20 stane of cheis, and twa merk of silver . . . Ilk town in this Ile is twa merk land and ane half, and payis yeirlie of Gersum at Beltane four ky with calf, four zowis with lamb, 4 geis, nine hennis, and 10s. of silver. (Skene, Celtic Scotland 1577–1595)

On this basis the total number of geese rendered in Islay was 10,656 per year, disregarding any that locals may have taken for the pot. For various reasons I think this figure is too high but the point is that the sustainable local cull was significant. It would be impossible to argue that it threatened the survival of the population else they would not be with us today. The local cull has now disappeared. Instead local farmers are paid to allow their crops to be devoured by geese. Once the population over-expands then others are paid to shoot the geese the farmer is paid to indulge.

Ancient Highland trading entrepot?

One of the reasons for the weakness of Highland culture relative to Lowland was the complete absence of any towns in the north-west. The lack of either a mercantile or manufacturing class left Highland society poorer and weaker. However we do have suggestions that they may once have existed in the area. Certainly there is plenty of saga evidence of how important merchants were in Scandinavian society. Paradoxically, in Highland folk-tradition the Danes and Norse were held responsible for destroying both Highland trade and Highland forests:

> *In the mouth of Lochtie wes ane riche toun namit Inverlochtie, quhair sum time wes gret change, be repair of uncouth marchandis; quhill at last it wes sa uterlie destroyit be weris of Danis, that it come nevir to the honour and magnificence as it had afore: and quhiddir the samin procedis be sleuth of our pepill, or be invy of limmers, quhilkis may suffir na wallit tounis in this cuntre, it is uncertane.* (Boece in Hume Brown, *Scotland before 1700*)

> (In the mouth of [the River] Lochy was a rich town named Inver-lochy, where some time was great exchange, by repair of foreign merchants; until at last it was so utterly destroyed by wars of Danes, that it came never to the honour and magnificence that it had before: and whether the same proceeds by sloth of our people, or by envy of rogues, which may suffer no walled towns in this country, it is uncertain.)

Leslie elaborates this slightly with details of the foreign merchants:

> *At the entry of Louth was afor tyme a citie maist welthie to name Inverlouth, to quhilke the frenche men and Spanizeards oft becuase of thair treffik sailed ouir; bot this eftirward be thame of Denmark and Norway was ouirthrawin, and nevir agane restored be us, quilke [is a disgrace to us].* (Dalrymple's translation in E. Cody (ed.), *Leslie's History of Scotland*, 1578)

(At the entry of the Lochy was beforetime a city most wealthy called Inverlochy, to which Frenchmen and Spaniards often sailed over because of their trade; but this afterwards by them of Denmark and Norway was overthrown, and never again restored by us, which [is a disgrace to us]).

In 1582 it almost sounds as if Buchanan had seen the site of Inverlochy:

At the mouth of the river a magnificent city is said to have flourished formerly, called Innerlochtee, and indeed, whether we consider the nature of the soil in the neighbourhood, or its convenience for navigation and sea carriage, the place appears admirably adapted for a commercial station. Induced by these advantages, for several ages, our ancient kings inhabited there the Castle of Evonia, which some now imagine was the same as Dunstaffnage, although the vestiges and rubbish of that castle are still shown in Lorn. (G Buchanan, *Rerum Scoticarum Historia*, translated by J. Aikman.)

This theme is repeated in Pont who gives an implausible place-name derivation involving the Latin word *navis* (a ship):

This water of Neves the ancient men and woemen did hear it of divers others, Ancient men in tymes by gone that war in Loquaber reported that Neves is deryvin from Naves because certane shipps wer wont to come with certane Kings, that used to haunt and dwell in Inverlochie, did lye at the mouth of the water of Neves. And so the water is called Neves and the Countrie Glenneves and the Mountain Beanneves efter the name of the water so called . . .
This Innerloghie is ane ancient toune, and a palace builded be ancient King which was King Ewin the . . . of that name, which is written in the Scots Chronicles, and sundrie Kings were wont to dwell therein. (Pont (?) in Macfarlane's Geographical Collections, vol II)

And just a little further up the Great Glen:

There is one litle toune where there was a chappell builded of ancient, not two mylls from Kilmanevag and ancient men and women did say that they did sie in this chappell called Achanahannat, manie Inhabitants and houses of that toune selling and buying wyne, ale, aquavitae & sundrie drinks and merchandise. And these ancient men do testifie that the Scotts quart of wyne, which is asmuch as four English quarts was sold for Scotts eighteen pennies which is but thrie English halfpence And one quart of nutts for and ane Scots quart of Ale good and strong for a shill. and a quart of oatmeall for thrie Scots pennies. And that this chappell was a sanctuarie and holie place keipit amongst the Countreymen in the said antient tyme. And that they did report

ot long nor manie years since the same hes bein, and that this
toun is without anie Inhabitants but waste and desolate. (Pont (?) in
Macfarlane's Geographical Collections, vol II)*

It is difficult to know what to make of these anecdotes. They may just
represent another hare started by Boece. If Pont had Boece in mind when he
made enquiries in Lochaber it may be that his request was father to the local
report. On the other hand Inverlochy is precisely where you would expect to
find a trading centre. It lies at the north end of Loch Linnhe whose shores
open up access to a huge section of the West Highlands. North from
Inverlochy runs the Great Glen, the quickest and easiest access route to
the East coast.

Highland resources

In 1786 John Knox summarised the economic assets of the Highlands:

*Thus we find that the Highlands, besides supplying home demands, exports
fish, black cattle, horses, sheep, timber, bark, lead, slate, and kelp; to which
may be added sundry articles of less importance, as skins, feathers, oil.*
  *The aggregate amount of these exports is surely sufficient to procure the
necessary articles of grain, and various utensils in iron, steel, timber, etc.
wherewith to improve their lands, extend their fisheries, furnish themselves
with decked vessels, and erect more comfortable dwellings.* (Knox, *The
Highlands and Hebrides in 1786*)

This book is not an economic history of the Highlands and Hebrides so I shall
bypass most of these resources in order to give travellers' accounts of two of
them – fish and timber. In early times these were not necessarily the most
important. Fish could not be preserved and carriage costs prevented the
export of timber. In the mediaeval period, hides, feathers and hair may have
been just as valuable. The Rev. Walker says of Rum:

*There is a great Number of Goats kept upon the Island, and here I found an
Article of Oeconomy generally unknown in other Places. The People of Rum
carefully collect the Hair of their Goats, and after sorting it, send it to
Glasgow where it is sold from 1sh. to 2sh. and 6d. p. pound according to its
Fineness, and there it is manufactured into Wigs, which are sent to America.*
(M. McKay, *Walker's Report on the Hebrides, 1764 and 1771*)

Hides were always of use. Cattle hides were readily available but seals were
also pursued:

To the north-west of the Keantuach of Vyist lyis ane Ile be 12 mile of sea callit Haifsker, quhairin infinite slauchter of selchis is maid at certane times in the zeir. (R. W. Munro, *Monro's Western Isles*, 1549)

(To the north-west of the North Head of Uist lies an Isle off 12 miles of sea called Haskeir, wherein infinite slaughter of seals is made at certain times in the year).

Hides were given an extra lease of life by trophy-hunters in the nineteenth century:

The Bay of Arisaig is a favourite resort of seals. The Highlanders still attribute the common habit of these animals of following boats, to their love of music . . . But we had no music for the entertainment of our pursuers but that of a rifle, which was successful in one instance. The animal shot sunk, and floated afterwards ashore . . . The price of the skin varies from twelve to twenty-four shillings. The public-house, at the head of the bay, contains a large assortment, for sale, of the skins of seals, wild-cats, pole-cats, and otters. (Lord Teignmouth, *Sketches of the Coasts and Islands of Scotland*, 1836)

Nevertheless Knox concluded that: '*the great varieties of fish which are found in the lakes, channels, and seas of the Highlands, may be considered as the grand natural staple of that country, exceeding in value all the other resources united* (Knox, *The Highlands and Hebrides in 1786*).

Fish

Scotland was proverbially 'fishy'. In 1498 the Spanish ambassador writes: '*It is impossible to describe the immense quantity of fish. The old proverb says already 'piscinata Scotia'.* (Don Pedro de Ayala, in Hume Brown, *Early Travellers in Scotland*.)

This was almost regarded as part of the divine order: '*But whose ordination, if not that of the Divine Wisdom, was this – that the northern people, far from the sun, should be blessed with deep waters, and, in consequence, with waters that abound more in fish; since wherever, in sea or river, there is greater depth, there, other things being equal, is greater store of fish.*' (John Major in Hume Brown, *Scotland before 1700*)

The Norse certainly fished in the Highlands and Hebrides and although they passed on their boat-building skills to the natives it has always been something of a mystery why they did not pass on their fishing and trading expertise. We have little beyond place-names such as Fiscavaig (Skye), Fishnish (Mull) and odd saga references.

Fish-traps, or yairs, probably represent one of the oldest methods of catching fish in the area. They are widespread and quite probably only a fraction of those that once existed are now recognisable. Some, such as Kinloch in Rum, are probably prehistoric. Others, such as at Castle Coeffin in Lismore, are probably coeval with the first fortifications. Monro writes of a type of fish-trap in Uist:

> *In this ile there are infinite number of fresh water loches; but ther is ane maine loche callit Lochebi, three myle lang, and a arme of the sea has worne the earth, that was at the a(n)e end of this loche, quhilk the sea has gotten enteries to this fresche water loche, and in that narrow entries that the sea has gotten to the loche, the countreymen has bigit upe ane thicke dyke of rough staines, and penney stanes caste lange narrest, notwithstanding the flowing streams of the sea enters throughe the said dyke of stanes in the said fresche water loche, and so ther is continually getting stiking amange the rough stains of the dyke foresaid, fluikes, podloches, skatts, and herings.* (Monro, *A Description of the Western Isles of Scotland*, (Birlinn edition, 1994))

(In this isle there are infinite number of fresh water lochs; but there is one main loch called Lochebi, three miles long, and an arm of the sea has worn the earth, that was at the one end of this loch, (by) which the sea has gotten entrance to this freshwater loch, and in that narrow entry that the sea has gotten to the loch, the countrymen have built up a thick dyke of rough stones, and penny stones cast long nearest (set length-ways), notwithstanding the flowing streams of the sea enter through the said dyke of stones in the said freshwater loch, and so there is con-tinually getting stuck among the rough stones of the dyke aforesaid, fluke, pollack, skate, and herring.)

Monro gives plenty of other evidence about fishing in 1549. Of Rona, north of Lewis:

> *In this ile they use to take maney quhaills and uther grate fisches.*
> (In this isle they are accustomed to take many whales and other great fishes).

> *Raarsay . . . It is excellent for fishing . . .*
> *On the eist shore of Watternesse lyes ane ile callit Ellan Askerin . . . guid for fishing and slaughter of selchies.*
> (On the east shore of Waternish lies an isle called Eilean Askerin . . . good for fishing and slaughter of seals).

Monro also makes it clear that boats travelled to fish:

> *Wattersay . . . ane excellent raid for shippes that comes ther to fische*
> (Wattersay . . . an excellent road (anchorage) for ships that come there to fish)

Hettesay . . . excellent for all sorte of quhyte fish taking.
(Hettesay . . . excellent for all sort of white fish taking).
(Monro, *A Description of the Western Isles of Scotland*, (Birlinn edition, 1994))

A generation later Leslie made the following comments about Lochaber:

Loquhabre is thairfor nychtbour to Lorne, in pastoral, in wodis, and in yrne abundant, in corne nocht sa plentiful. Thair, twa riueris, amang the rest, of alde ar not a litle famous, the name of the ane Louthe, the name of the vther Hispan, quhilkes ar esteimed to excel mony vthirs riueris baith in Salmonde, and in abundance of vthiris fishes. Bot the truth of the mater is nocht publised, because the rude peple, quha ar inhabitouris, strukne throuch a vane feir, that throuch the abundance of thair fishe thay cum nocht sum tyme to skaithe, and that of strangers, thay admitt na man thair with thame to the fisheng willinglie excepte thair awne nychtbouris and cuntrey men. Nathir ony maner of way gif thay labour to fishing bot sa mekle as serues to thair awne vse for the tyme, nocht kairing as it war for the morne.
(Dalrymple's translation in E. Cody (ed.), *Leslie's History of Scotland*, 1578)

(Lochaber . . . is therefore neighbour to Lorn, in pastoral [grazing], in woods, and in iron abundant, in corn not so plentiful. There, two rivers, among the rest, of old are not a little famous, the name of the one Lochy, the name of the other Spean, which are esteemed to excel many other rivers both in Salmon, and in abundance of other fishes. But the truth of the matter is not published, because the rude people, who are inhabitants, stricken through a vain fear, that through the abundance of their fish they come not sometime to skaith (harm), and that of (by) strangers, they admit no man there with them to the fishing willingly except their own neighbours and countrymen. Neither any manner of way if they labour to fishing but so much as serves to their own use for the time, not caring as it were for the morn.)

And concerning Loch Broom, which was now fished by Scots, French, Flemings and English:

Afor xx zeirs was neuir seine, that fisheris uset to frequent Loch brune: [But from that time I know not if in any part of the world, in so small a place, more (herrings) have been taken than here in certain years].
(Dalrymple's translation in E Cody (ed.), *Leslie's History of Scotland*, 1578)

(Before 20 years (ago it) was never seen, that fishers used to frequent Loch Broom: [But from that time I know not if in any part of the world, in so small a place, more (herrings) have been taken than here in certain years].)

And of the Firth of Clyde and Loch Fyne:

in the Westir Seyes, in that bosum of Clide, in thir bosumis neirhand, quhilkes Loches thay cal, the hail haruest and beginning of Winter is a gret schule of herring, bot in no place sa fatt, and of sa pleisand a taste as in that loch mair Westirlie, quhilke afor we expremed vndir the name of Fine.
(Dalrymple's translation in E Cody (ed.), *Leslie's History of Scotland*, 1578)

(in the Western Seas, in that bosom of Clyde, in those bosoms near-hand, which Lochs they call, the whole (of) harvest(time) and beginning of Winter is a great shoal of herring, but in no place so fat, and of so pleasant a taste as in that loch more Westerly, which before we expressed under the name of (Loch) Fyne).

And as if that wasn't enough:

As tueching vthiris fishes, I can nocht tell, gif in ony place of the warlde, athir be mair varietie or mair abundance, of sum kyndes, baith freshe and salt water fishe, of Turbat, ffluik, and plase fluik, of ostiris, Buckies, and vthiris schal fishe, wilkes, and vthiris fishes amang the craigis and stanes. Also makrel, the codfishe, and perches maist fine . . . finalie of the Sea calfes, and gret monstruous quhales, of quhilkes in our Sey is a gret number (Dalrymple's translation in E Cody (ed.), *Leslie's History of Scotland*, 1578)

(Touching other fish, I cannot tell, if in any place in the world, (there be) either more variety or more abundance, of some kinds, both fresh and saltwater fish, of Turbot, flounders, and plaice, of oysters, Buckies [whelks], and other shellfish, whelks, and other fish among the rocks and stones. Also mackerel, codfish, and perch most fine . . . finally of the seals, and great monstrous whales, of which in our sea is a great number.)

Traps could also be set:

Neir this is a famous furde in the Riuer of Forn called the Stocfurde of the Rosse, and this is another maner of fishing mekle esier qlke in vthiris places amaist ouer al lykwyse may be seine, for nocht sa mekle fishe thay with nettis, as with skepis, or long kreilis win with wickeris in the forme of a hose sa round wouen, thir quhen thay lay in the furdes and waterdames that fast thay stik in the sand, than wt al facilitie thay fishe; for quhen the Sey flowis

and cumis in at thir places, the fishe esilie cumis in ouer the damis and furdes,
and enteris in the creilis: Bot now the Sey ebbis, and the fishe bydes in the
creilis dry without water, and sa with litle trauel of the fisher ar takne.
(Dalrymple's translation in E Cody (ed.), *Leslie's History of Scotland,*
1578)

(Near this is a famous ford in the River of Forn called the Stockford of
Ross, and this is another manner of fishing much easier which in other
places almost over all likewise may be seen, for not so much fish they
with nets, as with skeps (baskets), or long creels made with wickers in
the form of a hose (stocking) so round woven, these when they lay in the
fords and waterdames that fast they stick in the sand, then with all
facility they fish; for when the sea flows and comes in at these places, the
fish easily come in over the dams and fords, and enter in the creels: But
now the sea ebbs, and the fish bide in the creels dry without water, and
so with little travail of the fisher are taken.)

Leslie was bishop of Ross so may well have been speaking from personal
knowledge.

In the 1590s Pont regularly noted the importance of fish as a resource: '*here*
is a logh on the West syde of Loghfyne fyfteen myles from Inveraray called
Lochgair. And there is abundance of fish slaine in this loch and specially herrings.
There is another Logh called Loghgailbe [Loch Gilp] being out fyve mylls from
Loghgur [Lochgair], there is abundance of herrings in this Logh.' (Pont(?) in
Macfarlane's Geographical Collections, vol II)

Pont also noticed when locals could not take advantage of this resource.
However it may have been because they lacked the capital for boats and
nets rather than the skill: '*Eig. [Eigg] this Illand is profitable and fertill of corne*
and milk and abundance of fish in the sea about that Illand but they have no skill
to slay the said fish. (Pont(?) in Macfarlane's Geographical Collections, vol
II.)

And a bumper harvest of salmon was as remarkable then as now:

In the parish of Wuicg [Uig] there is a Logh which is called Loghdua. And
there is a river runneing in that Logh where there is abundance of fish slaine
in one round water at the mouth of that river, And when the sea doeth flow
there will come abundance of fish in that pairt of the river therein. And efter
the sea ebbs abundance and Innumerable fisch will be slaine in that place.
There is on the Northwest en(d) of Lewis ane Logh which is called Logh-
bervais [Loch Barvas] and the fresh water river which doth runne out of this
Logh is but halff a myll in length. there was thrie thousand bigg salmond
slayne in this river in anno 1585. (Pont(?) in Macfarlane's Geographical
Collections, vol II)

Quite apart from the fishermen from Highlands and Lowlands there were doubtless Irish, English and Continental boats. Sir Thomas Phillips projected a plantation in Ulster in 1611. He paints a very optimistic picture of the economic justification. Apparently Portrush already drew a quantity of French fishermen each season who caught dogfish and rays. Moreover: *'Portrushe is but a cut over into the Isles of Scotland where there are great fishings, and yield great store of other commodities as cattle, hides, wool, etc.* (Carew Manuscripts p 148 ff)

As the documentary evidence builds up in the seventeenth century it is apparent that the biggest commercial fishers in Highland and Hebridean waters were not native but outsiders. For Rockall to appear on Waghenaer's map of Europe in 1583 there must have been Continental fishermen operating in the area. The fact that his, and other, pilot-guides soon included maps and text of the Hebrides suggests a demand from sea-captains. The most likely reason they wished to come here was for fish.

As in other areas the Highlanders must have felt jealous and protective of their resources. Were these, like so many clerical benefices, to fall prey to Lowland acquisitiveness? In the records of the Privy Council of Scotland we can follow disputes between Highlanders and Lowland fishermen:

> *Petition by William Strang, skipper of Anstruther, complaining that in December last, while petitioner was in his 'bark' fishing in his Majesty's waters, the Captain of Clanranald and his servants hindered the fishing and damaged the 'laidning' to the extent of 'thrie last of hering'. He and his men further violently entered the petitioner's ship and compelled him to give them victuals, so that he was obliged to furnish new provision at great expense. Also, when the petitioner had only 'tua last of herring' in his ship, the Captain and his men took boat, nets, and herring, and compelled the petitioner to buy them back again. They also took four nets from him, and restored only one, at the same time striking and wounding his men. He craves redress, estimating his loss at three last of herring at £120 per last, and £40 each for his three nets, and £20 for redelivery of the boat, or £420 in all.* (Register of the Privy Council, vol XIII, p 741, probably about 27 July 1622)

Strang was supported by Thomas Smytht, an Edinburgh burgess whose skipper, Alexander Small, had suffered at Clanranald's hands at the same time.

> *In December last, while he was fishing in the King's waters within the bounds of the Captain of Clanronald, the said Captain, with 300 men, impeded the fishing and 'damnifiet' the complainer to the extent of 'fyftein lastis of hering, pryce of ilk last sex scoir pundis', and also took his nets from him, 'tuelff doubill nettis, ilk nett being of valour tuentie merkis, and forder tuik away*

withe the saidis nettis the ankeris, stringis, and bearupis, bowis and bow towis, of the valour of fourtie pundis'. In proof, it is stated that the said Captain *'causit delyver tua of the saidis nettis bak agane'* to Alexander Small, the complainer's skipper, in presence of William Strang, skipper; *'quhilk he can not deny, upoun his conscience'.* The Captain's men also at that time boarded the complainer's ship, struck his skipper, and remained in the vessel till they destroyed his victuals, the damage being estimated at 3000 merks; and the complainer was forced to come home with his bark not one third laden. He therefore craves that the Captain of Clanronald be compelled to satisfy him in the sum of 300 merks. (Register of the Privy Council, vol XIII, p 742, 1 August 1622)

and as if that wasn't enough:

Petition by George Hay of Kirkland. – He had 'outreikit ane schip of xxxvi last, and tua fischeing barkis frome the west coist, of the birth of four or fyve last the peice, with men, nettis, furneissing, and uthir provisioun sufficient for laidning of the said schip and barkis' at great cost and expense: and, while the ship was 'lying in Loch Skipport and the saidis barkis in Loch Hynard, and the barkis being enterit in the tak of hering, and having slane tuentie last of hering or thairby, and having payit the haill land deuties according to the Capitane of Clanrannald his desyre,' the said Captain, being at the loch side with his men, 'haillit' the nets set by the complainer's servants, spoiled the same, struck the servants, took from them 'ane anker and tow,' thus violently debarring them from fishing in his Majesty's free waters, and damaging the complainer to the extent of twelve last of herring, the whole loss valued at £1200. Petitioner prays the Lords to take order with the said Captain. (Register of the Privy Council, vol XIII, p 742–3, 1 August 1622)

(Petition by George Hay of Kirkland. – He had 'outrigged a ship of 36 last, and two fishing barks (boats) from the west coast, of the berth of four or five last each, with men, nets, furnishing, and other provision sufficient for laidning (victualling) of the said ship and barks' at great cost and expense: and, while the ship was 'lying in Loch Skipport and the said barks in Loch Hynard, and the barks being engaged in the catching of herring, and having slain twenty last of herring or thereabouts, and having paid the whole land duties according to the Capitan of Clanranald his desire,' the said Captain, being at the loch side with his men, 'hauled' the nets set by the complainer's servants, spoiled the same, struck the servants, took from them 'an anchor and tow,' thus violently debarring them from fishing in his Majesty's free waters, and damaging the complainer to the extent of twelve last of herring, the whole loss valued at £1200. Petitioner prays the Lords to take order with the said Captain).

Now it may be that what was at issue was whether the Lowland boats had paid a sufficient sweetener to their Highland hosts. The money raised thereby would be of great assistance to an impoverished Highland laird. In 1755–56 Mungo Campbell reported from Knoydart: '*that Coll McDonald late of Barrasdale was in use of exacting from the proprietors of each vessel or boat employed in the fisherie a day's product each week of whatever fish they caught, in consideration of shore dues and fireing etc, which turned out to considerable account.* (V. Wills, *Reports on the Annexed Estates*, p 51)

We can contrast this evidence from the Hebrides with evidence for Shetland where there seems to have been a mutually beneficial annual trade between the Dutch and the natives. On Blaeu's map of Orkney and Shetland there is a Latin comment by the Shetland map to the effect that the Dutch fish there yearly for herring and distribute the catch throughout Europe. The cartouche gives this a delightful symbolic representation with bunches of herring hanging like fruit therefrom. No such feature appears on the Blaeu map of Uist! In fact it is another century before we find analogous comments on Moll's map of the Hebrides.

Not only was there jealousy between Highlander and Lowlander over fish stocks, there was also a Lowland desire to prevent any erosion of their privileges. The Hebrides might have enjoyed a similarly beneficial relationship with the Dutch had it not been for the envy of the Scottish burghs. The Dutch established a colony in Stornoway early in the seventeenth century, evidently with the approval of the earl of Seaforth. This aroused jealous interests elsewhere who brought the matter before the Privy Council of Scotland. Here we learn of a dispute between the royal burghs and the earl of Seaforth concerning the latter's introduction of strangers (i.e. Dutch) to Stornoway. After hearing arguments on both sides:

> the Lords of Secreit Counsell commands and ordains the said Erle of Seafort that he on no wayes imbring to the Lewes nor suffer anie moe strangers then the twelffe persouns presentlie resident there to be brought in and planted in these bounds till his Majesteis forder pleasure be signified thereanent.
> (Register of the Privy Council, Second Series, vol III, p 428 ff, 1630)

> (the Lords of Privy Council command and ordain the said Earl of Seaforth that he in no way brings in to the Lewis, nor suffers any more strangers than the twelve persons presently resident there, to be brought in and planted in these bounds, till his Majesty's further pleasure be signified about this.)

These complaints should be seen in the context of commercial competition between Lowlanders and Hebrideans. This rancour and hostility would have conveyed itself to any traveller. It would also have affected the way in which the area was seen by the outside world – particularly if they received their information via Lowland channels. Until about the 1770s the Highlands suffered from an almost universally bad press. Martin tried to put the Highland case; sympathisers like Lhuyd, Burt and Bruce gave relatively balanced judgements, but the image presented by others was not endearing.

Fortunately we have further information on the role of the Dutch in Lewis from Captain John Dymes in 1630. He described the various fisheries and tried to quantify the profits which the Dutch made:

But the great and rich comoditie w[hi]ch might bee made of this land is the Fishinge whereof the inhabitants doe make but small benefitt besides theire owne food, there beinge in the Island not above a dozen boates w[hi]ch doe kill anie fish for sale. But the Dutch w[hi]ch have fished there theis two last yeares past have found that great and extraordinary gaine thereof, whoe onely wth 4er Busses wth 16 men and 25 netts in a Busse have within the space of three monethes killd three hundred last of Herrings w[hi]ch Herrings by theire factors and owne confession vnto mee was sold the last year at Danske for 400 gilders p[er] last w[hi]ch is about some 38 li [£] sterlinge at w[hi]ch rate the 300 last did come to 11400 li of w[hi]ch if there be rebated one third part for all chardges (w[hi]ch is as much as needs to bee) it will plainely appeare that those 4er Busses in lesse then three monethes space did make 7500 li cleare gaine. The Master of one of those Busses w[hi]ch transported me from the Island into the mayne continent did protest vnto mee that the fish was in such great abundance yt they were sometymes constrained to cast it into the sea againe they haveing more in halfe theire netts then they were able to save, and he was of opinion that if there had bene a thouzand Busses more there was fish enough for them all. As for the Cod and Ling the Dutch doth kill none of it themselves, but buyeth it at easie rates of the Inhabitants; w[hi]ch are alsoe so farr from haveinge the true industry of killinge that fish, that one boate with our Newfoundland men will kill more in a daie then they doe with one of theire boates in a yeare.

The Dutch have also made provision of fornaces and other necessaries for the Whale fish, but they have not yett made any vse thereof, they beinge as yet scarce settled in theire busines, there beinge noe more of them besides Seamen yett then sixe servants and a Factor w[hi]ch are always resident in Stornway where they have built a pretty dwellinge house and a Magazine where they lay vpp theire salt and caske and all other necessaries for theire fishinge.

The severall seasons for the fishings doe alter accordinge vnto the seasons of the yeares. The first season for Herrings doth beginne about the beginninge of June, and lasteth vntill the latter end of August. The second fishinge for Herrings is from August vntill Mich[ael]mas, and then the Herrings will bee shotten and come neare the shoare. And the last season for Herrings is from Mich[ael]mas vntill Christmas, and then they come in to the Loughes. The two later seazons the Dutch cannott as yett make any vse of with their great

Busses, because the nights be longe, and there is not scope enough for them to drive within the Bayes and Loughes.

Cod and Ling are taken all the yeare longe vpon the Coast, but the chiefest season for it is from Christmas vntil Easter, soe that it doth appeare that if there were vessells fitt for ye purpose the fishinge might bee continued all the yeare longe either about the Island or in the Loughes over agt it in the Continent or else vpon a certaine Banke w[hi]ch stretcheth on the west side of the Island from one end thereof to the other about some 5 leagues of from the shoare where there is abundance of Cod and Ling, and as I have bene certified by the Inhabitants of the Island that one fish taken there is as bigge as twoe taken elsewhere, but this side of the Land is very little frequented espetially by straingers by reason of the manie Rocks w[hi]ch are vpon that Coast, and of the fowle seas w[hi]ch are brought in by the Westerne Ocean.

This last yeare there came in great stoare of young Whales into one of theire Loughes w[hi]ch the inhabitants inclosed wth boates, and killd more then one hundred of them wth their swords and their bowes and arrowes, for want of better engines, and made meat of them all, and for want of salt to save it they tooke the sea Oare (ware) and burned it and then powderd it with the ashes thereof, w[hi]ch afterwards beinge dryed in the smoake they eate it like Bacon.

They have alsoe a yearely fishinge vpon a small Ile called Causmoun where they kill great store of Seales w[hi]ch fishinge may rather bee called an huntinge then a fishinge, for the inhabitants repaire thither once in the yeare manie of them togeather well arm'd both for offence and defence where they find theis fish vpon the Rocks, the weapons wherewith they kill them, are great batts and swords, and to defend themselves ag[ains]t the teeth of theis fish (whose nature is not to lett goe theire hold till they feele the bones bruise betweene theare teeth) they lyne theire Trooses wth Charcoales, soe that when those fish chance to bite anie of them, when they feele the coals crash within their teeth they give over theire hold and are the sooner overcome, this fish alsoe they make meate of as they doe by theire Whales. The great abundance both of ravenous fishes and fowles w[hi]ch that Coast doth affoord is an infallable argumt of that abundance of other fish whereupon they prey. (W. C. Mackenzie: *History of the Outer Hebrides*, 1903, Appendix F)

When I read this story I could not understand the significance of coals in their trousers until I heard a Mallaig fisherman describe a catfish he had recently taken in his creels. He told me that catfish were more common on the east coast of Scotland and the fishermen there used to put 'cinders' in their boots to prevent bites. It appears that the sound or sensation of clinker or charcoal crunching between their teeth was enough to make the catfish, or seals, slacken their hold for long enough for the man to escape.

Martin Martin credits the Dutch with a beneficial influence on Stornoway: '*the small idea of fishing they had from the Dutch has had so much effect as to make*

the people of the little village of Stornvay to excel all those of the neighbouring isles
and continent in the fishing trade ever since that time.'

But by the end of the seventeenth century the Highlanders were still not
reaping the benefits of their fishing resources: '*If the Dutch in their public edicts*
call their fishery a golden mine, and at the same time affirm that it yields them more
profit than the Indies do to Spain, we have very great reason to begin to work upon
those rich mines, not only in the isles, but on all our coast in general. (Martin
Martin, *A Description of the Western Isles of Scotland.*)

Fishing is full of taboos and superstitions, some of which are very old.
Boece, Leslie and Martin recount a widespread belief that the herring would
desert a place where blood had been shed:

> *In the mouth of Nes standis the toun of Innernes; quhare sum time wes gret*
> *plente and tak of herying, howbeit thay be now evanist, for offence that is*
> *maid aganis sum Sanct. Treuth is, quhen ony avaricius and unhappy men*
> *fechtis for the fische that God sendis, be his infinit gudnes, to the sustenta-*
> *tioun of the peple, and diffoulis the see be thair blude; mony yeris eftir, na*
> *fische swomis in that place.* (Boece, in Hume Brown, *Scotland before*
> *1700*)

> (In the mouth of [the River] Ness stands the town of Inverness;
> where some time was great plenty and take of herring, howbeit they
> be now vanished, for offence that is made against some Saint. Truth
> is, when any avaricious and unhappy men fight for the fish that God
> sends, by his infinite goodness, to the sustenance of the people, and
> befouls the sea by their blood; many years after, no fish swim in that
> place.)

> *ffor gif in ony place quhair a tak of herring is, as thair, be ony slauchtir, or*
> *ony scheding of manis blude aryse, for a certain [number] of zeiris following,*
> *throuch verie instinctione of nature, thay ar said to abhor frome that place*
> *and to abunde in vthir places* (Dalrymple's translation in E Cody (ed.),
> *Leslie's History of Scotland*, 1578)

> (for if in any place where a catch of herring is, as there, be any slaughter,
> or any shedding of man's blood arise, for a certain [number] of years
> following, through very instinct of nature, they are said to abhor from
> that place and to abound in other places)

> *It is a general observation all Scotland over, that if a quarrel happen on the*
> *coast where herring is caught, and that blood be drawn violently, then the*
> *herring go away from the coast, without returning during that season.*
> (Martin Martin, *A Description of the Western Isles of Scotland*)

But bloodshed could also be responsible in another way:

> *Several barques come yearly from Orkney to the Western Isles, to fish for cod and ling: and many from Anstruther in the shire of Fife, came formerly to Barray and other isles to fish, before the battle of Kilsyth, where most of them being cut off, that trade was afterwards neglected.* (Martin Martin, *A Description of the Western Isles of Scotland*)

It was not just whales that were stranded. Writing of Loch Eport, Martin Martin says: '*In the month of July the spring tides carry in a great quantity of mackerel, and at the return of the water they are found many times lying on the rocks. The vulgar natives make use of the ashes of burnt sea-ware, which preserves them for some time instead of salt.*' (Martin Martin, *A Description of the Western Isles of Scotland*)

Writing of Loch Maddy, Martin Martin makes it clear that, even at the end of the seventeenth century, the locals were not exploiting the herring fishery:

> *This loch hath been famous for the great quantity of herrings yearly taken in it within these fifty years last past. The natives told me, that in the memory of some yet alive, there had been 400 sail loaded in it with herrings at one season; but it is not now frequented for fishing, though the herrings do still abound in it . . . yet it is strange that in all this island there is not one herring net to be had; but if the natives saw any encouragement, they could soon provide them.* (Martin Martin, *A Description of the Western Isles of Scotland circa 1695*)

This was still true half a century later:

> *Loch Broom*
> *To the North of Gairloch is the Country of Loch Broom the property of Several small Heritors of the McKenzie Clan. The Arm of the Sea called Loch Broom comes in about 14 Miles within the Land. At this place 100 Sail of Ships have been often Loaded with Herrings in a Season, but when the Herrings do not Come within the Mouth of the Loch, the Country People have neither Ability or Skill to fit out proper Vessels to Catch them, and the Gentlemen do not Concern themselves with it. Herrings come often into all the Lochs on this Coast; but Loch Broom is the most Remarkable place, besides that 200 Sail of Ships may Anchor safely, whatever Way the Wind blows, either at Loggy Bay, or Island Martin.* (A. Lang, *The Highlands of Scotland in 1750*)

In a separate report David Bruce provides further evidence that the fishing industry was largely undertaken by outsiders:

Eriskay is a Small Island lying between South Uist and Bara, about two miles in length, and one in breadth It is mountaneous and Rocky, and only fit for pasture of Cattle; On the East side of which there is a fine Commodious Harbour for fishing; and for these Several years bygone Eleven or twelve Wherreys have come from Ireland, and two from Argyleshire, in the Month of April In order to fish for Cod & Ling. This being Esteem'd the most Commodious place in the Highlands for that fishing There was Caught there last year about 27000. The People of this and the Neighbouring Islands begine now to Employ themselves at the fishing, they Caught about 6000 last year, which they sold to the Irish at six pence a piece before being Cured.
(David Bruce, *Hardwicke Papers, Vol 99,* c. 1750)

There is little doubt that lack of capital was a prime cause for the neglect of fishing in the Hebrides. Walker writes of Skye: '*There are great Numbers of open Boats, but not a decked Vessel of any kind in all the Island.*' (McKay, *Walker's Report on the Hebrides, 1764 and 1771*)

That the herring really did visit the west coast in stupendous quantities is not in doubt. Nevertheless, memory is fallible and some of the details became confused over the years. Different travellers retail slightly different versions of what is presumably the same story about an immense shoal of herring that arrived in Loch Hourn sometime between 1753 and 1819. Otherwise it is just Highland hokum!

Archibald Menzies in 1768:

In the year 1753 a shoal of herring was left by the tide in the inner Loch Urin [Hourn] *above the Skiarries. They were computed at half a mile square from three to five feet deep. All the way down to the Sound of Sky the herring were so thick that, a boat going on the loch, the oars made the herrings fly out of the water like flying fish.* (V. Wills, *Reports on the Annexed Estates,* p 99)

Thomas Pennant in 1772:

A little farther the loch suddenly turns due South, and has a very narrow inlet to a third reach: this strait is so shallow as to be fordable at the ebb of spring-tides; yet has within, the depth of ten and seventeen fathom: the length is about a mile; the breadth a quarter. About seven years ago [1765] *it was so filled with herrings, that had crowded in, that the boats could not force their way, and thousands lay dead on the ebb.* (T. Pennant, *A Tour in Scotland and Voyage to the Hebrides 1772*)

James Anderson in 1785:

At Loch-Urn, in 1767 or 1768, they came in in such quantity, that, from the narrows to the very head it was quite full: such a quantity ran on shore, that the

beach, for four miles round the head, was covered with them from 6–18″
deep . . . I am also of opinion that the strongest fish being without, in forcing
their way into the inner bay, drove the lightest and weakest on shore. So thick
were these last, that they carried before them every other kind of fish they met, –
even ground-fish, skate, flounders etc. and perished together. They continued at
that time several weeks, but not so thick after they had run on shore. (James
Anderson, *An account of the present state of the Hebrides*, 1785)

William Daniell in 1819

In the fishing season it presents a busy and animated appearance, the ground
being frequently so well stocked as to afford occupation to three hundred
vessels. Two or three years ago a singular occurrence took place, which is
mentioned as an instance of the amazing quantity of fish that annually resort
hither. A large shoal of herrings were steering boldly up the loch; and as they
held their course, though the tide was rapidly falling, they took ground at the
head and stranded. The numbers thus left ashore were estimated at the
enormous amount of six thousand barrels. For some days the putrid effluvia
from such an aggregation of animal substances were intolerably potent, but
there were very few inhabitants to be incommoded with this nuisance.
(William Daniell, *A Voyage round Great Britain*)

This story highlights the difficulties we have in accepting travellers' tales as
evidence. I have no doubt all these worthies relayed the information as it was
told them. The problem is – how reliable were their informants?

The problems between Highlanders and Lowlanders continued at least
until the end of the eighteenth century. In 1786 John Knox wanted to visit
Loch Hourn:

to learn, upon the spot, if all the complaints that I had heard, were well
grounded. Besides personal information from the proprietors of herring
busses, in the ports of the Clyde, I had received sundry papers, stating, that
the herring fisheries in the Highlands were greatly obstructed by the natives,
who, in the night time, cut the nets, and stole or cut the buoys which belonged
to the busses; that to these, and other irregularities, were owing, in some
measure, the bad success of the fisheries of late years; that the evil was
increasing daily, and unless a remedy should be devised, many industrious
persons would be driven out of the trade. (J. Knox, *A Tour through the*
Highlands of Scotland)

At the mouth of Loch Hourn he anchored near a deserted village:

but in our return to the vessel, we were informed by a transient traveller, that
the people of the village had just gone to the shielings. By him also we learned,

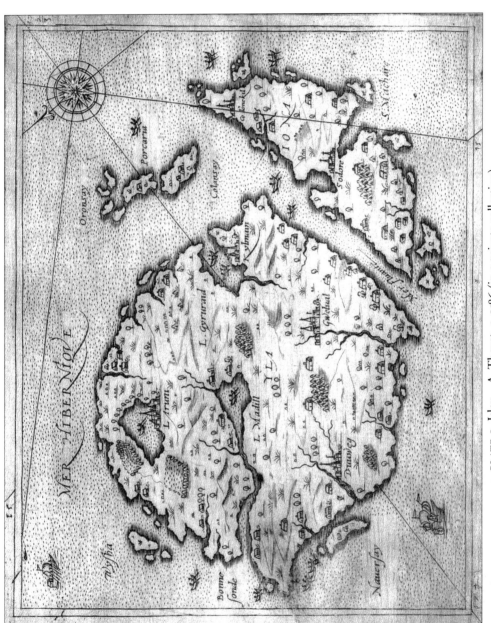

PLATE 1. Islay – A. Thevet, c. 1586 (in a private collection)

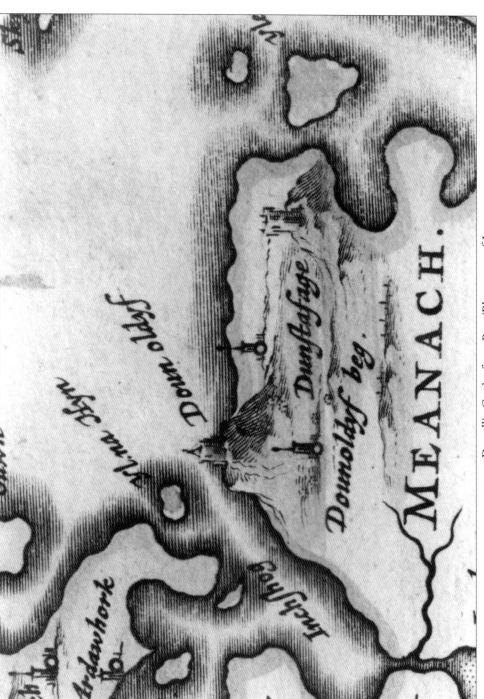

PLATE 2. Dunollie Castle, from Pont/Blaeu map of Lorn

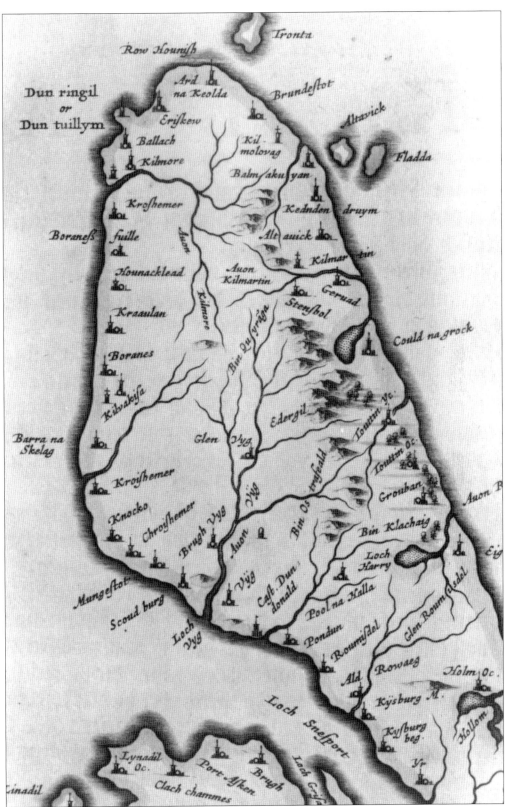

PLATE 3. Trotternish, from Pont/Blaeu map of Skye

PLATE 4. Lewis and Harris (National Library of Ireland)

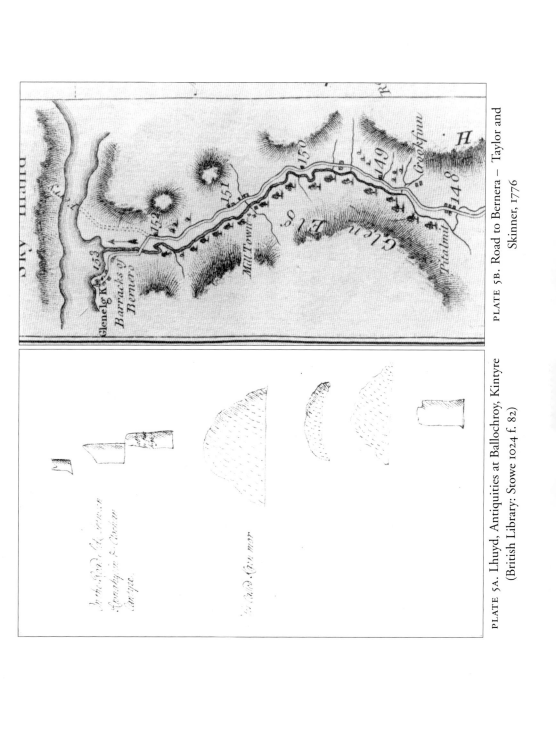

PLATE 5A. Lhuyd, Antiquities at Ballochroy, Kintyre
(British Library: Stowe 1024 f. 82)

PLATE 5B. Road to Bernera – Taylor and
Skinner, 1776

PLATE 6. Angling off Staffa – J. Clevely, 1772 (British Library: Add 15510 f. 21)

PLATE 7. Kilarrow, Islay – J. Clevely, 1772 (British Library: Add 15509 f. 11)

PLATE 8A. Stepping Stones – Lochan Stole, North Morar

PLATE 8B. A road in the trees – The Loch na Gaul road today

*that there had been a good take of herrings, and great disturbances between
the buss-men and the Highlandmen, which, he said, had driven the herrings
out of the loch. . . .*

*The shore was covered with little hovels, or tents, which serve as temporary
lodgings to the natives, who flock to these fisheries, and who, in their turn,
were full of complaints against the buss-men. This year Mr Macdonald
junior, of Barrisdale, a gentleman of great bodily strength, and who is both
loved and feared in this loch, attempted in vain to preserve peace and good
order.* (J. Knox, *A Tour through the Highlands of Scotland, 1786*)

Timber

Like fish, Caledonia was early famed for its woodland. Nevertheless, travellers' accounts in earlier centuries were almost unanimous in commenting on
the scarcity of timber in the Lowlands so the question of woods and forests
applies more particularly to the Highlands. The term 'forest' can also cause
confusion when used in the context of an estate dedicated to deer-hunting.
Such a forest, especially in an area like Lewis, might not have any trees in it at
all.

It is difficult to write in general terms about trees in the Highlands and
Islands. The region is so big and so diverse that the quantity and type of
woodland varied from one district to another. Parts of the Outer Isles are bare
and treeless. On the mainland you might find a wood of oak on the northern
shore of a loch, facing a wood of pine on the southern. Nevertheless areas
within the Highlands had an ancient reputation for trees. Lochaber's woods
gave rise to the Gaelic proverb *B'e sin fiodh a chur do Loch Abar* ('That were
sending wood to Lochaber'), which has a similar meaning to the English
saying about sending coals to Newcastle. Two of the mid thirteenth-century
maps associated with Matthew Paris use the phrase 'A mountainous and
wooded region' to describe the Highlands. Woods also extended to some of
the Islands: '*There is many woods in all parts of Skye, specially birkis (birch) and
orne (oak) but the most wood is in Slait and Trotternish. There is ane wood in Slait
8 miles long.* (Skene, *Celtic Scotland, 1577–1595*)

Perhaps the best proof of the importance of trees in the Highlands are the
various attempts at commercial exploitation. In this context we have evidence
from the notes made by Timothy Pont in the period 1585–1610. He was
obviously considering the feasibility of commercial exploitation because he
raises the issue of freight costs.

Att the head of Lochzeld [Lochiel] *there is ane litle river called the water of
Keanloghyeld . . . And there is one glen which goeth up northward, And there is
verie manie firr trees in that glen but verie great difficultie to be transported anie of
the saids wayes to the sea. There is great number of Oaktrees, and one bigg wood of
Oak on the Northsyde of Loghyeld at the head of the said Logh which is verie*

pleasant and profitable. And they wont to build shipps of the said Oakin wood And the same wood pertaines to the Laird of Loghyeld being the Chieff and Principall house of the Clancameron. (Pont(?) in Macfarlane's Geographical Collections, vol II)

Of Glen Cona in Ardgour: '*and there is a great number of firr trees in this glen . . . and there is a water in the glen which doeth transport great trees of firr and masts to the seasyde.*' And of Glen Scaddle just to the south: '*There is a great number of fir trees in this glen, and easlie to be transported to the seasyde. There uses manie shipps to come to that Countrie of Ardgoure, and to be loadned with firr Jests Masts and Cutts.*' And of Glen Moriston off the Great Glen: '*This next Countrey next Abirtarff is Glenmoriestoune and it is a verie profitable and fertill litle glen, or countrie both plenteous of corne and abundance of butter cheese and milk and great and long woods of firr trees doeth grow in that countrey. and the river doeth transport big Jests and Cutts of timber to the fresh water Loghnes.*' (Pont(?) in Macfarlane's Geographical Collections, vol II)

Pont also draws attention to woods on his maps. Pont 13 is a very attractive map of Mamore and on the south side of Loch Leven is written: '*Many Fyrre Woods heir alongs*'.

And in his notes on Ross he writes of Loch Ewe: '*it is compasd about with many fair and tall woods as any in all the west of Scotland, in sum parts with hollyne, in sum places with fair and beautifull fyrrs of 60, 70, 80 foot of good and serviceable timmer for masts and raes, in other places ar great plentie of excellent great oakes, whair may be sawin out planks of 4 sumtyms 5 foot broad.* (Macfarlane's Geographical Collections, vol II, p 540)

I have earlier quoted Sir Thomas Phillips' projected plantation in Ulster. As far as the availability of timber was concerned: '*For masts, I hear there are very fair ones to be had out of the Isle[s?] of Scotland.*' (Carew Manuscripts, p 148 ff, 1611)

But the distribution of woodland among the islands was always patchy. Dymes writes of Lewis: '*for this place is soe destitute of wood that there is not one tree growinge in the whole Island.*' (Dymes, 1630, in Mackenzie, *History of the Outer Hebrides*, Appendix F)

Freight was always a crucial factor in mediaeval economic enterprises. Early galley-building accounts in England show how big an item carriage was. This is as true now as then. The distance between the point of production and the point of sale (and the cost of carriage between them) is still a critical factor in any economic equation.

Taylor, after describing the hunting in the Braes of Mar, tells of the native forests and the reason they are not yet exploited:

and after supper a fire of firre wood as high as an indifferent May-pole: for I assure you, that the Earle of Marre will give any man that is his friend, for thankes, as many Firre trees (that are as good as any shippes mastes in

England) as are worth (if they were in any place neere the Thames, or any
other portable River) the best Earledome in England or Scotland either: For I
dare affirme hee hath as many growing there, as would serve for mastes (from
this time to the end of the world) for all the Shippes, Carackes, Hoyes,
Galleyes, Boates, Drumlers, Barkes, and Water-craftes, that are now, or can
bee in the world these fourtie yeares.

  This sounds like a lie to an unbeleever; but I and many thousands doe
knowe that I speake within the compasse of truth: for indeede (the more is the
pitie) they doe growe so farre from any passage of water, and withall in such
rockie Mountaines, that no way to convey them is possible to bee passable
either with Boate, Horse, or Cart. (John Taylor, *The Pennyles Pilgrimage,*
1618)

Burt was firmly of the belief that timber extraction in the Highlands would
prove uneconomic:

There are, indeed, some mountains that have woods of fir, or small oaks on
their declivity, where the root of one tree is almost upon a line with the top of
another: these are rarely seen in a journey; what there may be behind, out of
all common ways, I do not know; but none of them will pay for felling and
removing over rocks, bogs, precipices, and conveyance by rocky rivers, except
such as are near the sea coast, and hardly those. (Edmund Burt, *Letters*
from a Gentleman in the North of Scotland, late 1720s)

One of the reasons iron furnaces were established in the Highlands was the
local availability of some or all of the essential raw materials. In Blaeu's map
of Strathnaver, Pont has marked extensive woodland, the hill where iron ore
was found and the nearby glen where it was made into iron. In an addition to
the materials in Macfarlane's Geographical Collections it is noted that there
is: '*a saw mill upon the river of Argaig* [Arkaig], *where it comes out of the Loch*
and he is making ane Iron Mill, there is much Iron Ore over all the highland,
with which they furnished themself formerly. there be great woods on each side of
Lochargaig the woods of Oake.' (Macfarlane's Geographical Collections,
vol II)

  It was the availability of cheap timber that brought the Scots and English
ironworking companies to Loch Ewe, Invergarry, Furnace and Bonawe in the
seventeenth and eighteenth centuries. Sometimes it was just the trees that
were sold off – as on the Clanranald estates. Naturally, exploitation brought
about some tension with locals. Kirk tells a story which shows how Highlanders were suspicious of those they feared came simply to steal their
resources. It also helps explain the proverbial curiosity of the Highlander.
If you knew a visitor's business then you knew whether or not he was a
potential threat.

Friday the 6th, went from Dorno[ch] up the river Tane [Tain], above sixteen miles, to see a fir-wood. Sir Robert Gordon having ordered a countryman to convey us, we passed by Lough Magidale [Migdale], and we saw the hill on which Montrose was defeated. Within five miles of the wood we took another guide, and near the wood we got another, all three being few enough to guard us, for several people near the edges of the woods would have stopped us if we had not had these men, their acquaintance, along with us; they all spoke Erst (the Highlanders' language), and blamed these men for bringing us thither, supposing that the King had sent us with orders to cut down the wood; others said, that before the late wars some English gentlemen travelled those parts, and none knew their business, and they looked on our coming as a bad prognostic. One old man amongst them was prevailed with to show us the wood, which was called—; but there were many woods together, extending many miles, wherein are many larger trees than any we saw, though those we did see were very high and straight, but of no great substance, about a man's fathom. (T. Kirk, Tour in Scotland 1677)

What is at issue here is the jealous protection by one culture of its resources against the acquisitive embrace of another culture that has often proved hostile. In the event there were many different types of accommodation. Sometimes, as with Clanranald at the beginning of the seventeenth century, there was outright hostility. At other times a deal appeared to have been struck with the local chief only for him to renege on the terms, (or be accused of reneging), once the project was underway. Clanranald's quarrels with the economic undertakings of incomers were repeated by Glengarry and Lochiel in later years. Even today these mutual suspicions between locals and outsiders are not wholly dead. Who stands to gain most from whatever planning application is at issue? Will it benefit locals, or outsiders, or both?

Just to prove there is little new under the sun I finish with Martin Martin's notion that strangers in reduced circumstances should move to the Highlands because of the lower cost of living. This has a strangely modern ring to it. In the last century there has probably been more demographic change in the area than since the Norse invasions 1200 years ago. Not everybody has the motives Martin Martin suggested but he is proving uncannily prophetic. Whether fleeing the rat-race, searching for the good life or just wanting to find themselves, incomers are challenging and transforming Highland communities. The old tensions have new forms:

If any man be disposed to lead a solitary, retired life, and to withdraw from the noise of the world, he may have a place of retreat there in a small island, or in the corner of a large one, where he may enjoy himself, and live at a very cheap rate.

If any family, reduced to low circumstances, had a mind to retire to any of these isles, there is no part of the known world where they may have the products of sea and land cheaper, live more securely, or among a more tractable and mild people. (Martin Martin, *A Description of the Western Isles of Scotland circa 1695)*

Chapter 7

Maps and charts

'I had with me a map of Scotland . . . Mr M'Aulay and I laid the map of
Scotland before us; and he pointed out a rout(e) for us from Inverness, by Fort
Augustus, to Glenelg, Sky, Mull, Icolmkill, Lorn, and Inveraray, which I wrote
down. (Boswell, The Journal of a Tour to the Hebrides, 1773)*

One of the first requirements of any traveller, in any age, is a map. He, or
she, wants a paper representation of the ground they will cover, the physical
realities they will experience. Where are the rivers, mountains, coasts and
settlements? What distances separate them? What hazards face them by land
or sea? Which routes are the most direct? How long, in distance and time, will
the journey be?

Through the centuries maps and charts have provided information about
spatial relationships, revealed some or all of these factors. Cartography itself,
both land and marine, has evolved its own styles, classes, genres. Knowledge
has increased, skills have developed and the methods of symbolising and
displaying knowledge have been refined. Printing and engraving techniques
have transformed the dissemination of geographical information. Moreover
this knowledge has then been subjected to practical verification. Maps and
charts are tested in the field. Errors are soon discovered; one person's
projection is challenged in the light of another's experience.

> *Loch Screban, in Mull, soon opens to our view. After passing a cape, placed
> in our maps far too projectingly, see Loch-in-a-Gaal; a deep bay, with the
> isles of Ulva and Gometra in its mouth.*
>
> *On the west appears the beautiful group of the Treashunish Isles. (These
> are most erroneously placed in the maps, a very considerable distance too far
> to the north). (T. Pennant, A Tour in Scotland and Voyage to the Hebrides,
> 1772)*

Cartographic conventions have developed, particularly with regard to a
formalized representation of objects. Common features such as settlements,
roads, rivers, forests, castles and churches invite symbolic expression. Cartography has developed its own library of symbols which we imbibe subcon-
sciously from the first maps we look at. Many such images were tried before
cartographers settled on those conventions with which we are now familiar
through habit and experience. Not all have withstood the passage of time.
When looking at old maps some of these conventions may appear strange and

incongruous. Some were discarded for good reason, others we are the poorer for losing. A critical feature in many early accounts of the Hebrides is the whirlpool at Corryvreckan between Jura and Scarba. Mercator symbolised this on his map of 1564 by a little flailing wheel. As a cartographic symbol I don't think this can be improved upon.

When the author of the Gough map wanted to represent the wildlife and sporting customs of the Highlands he drew a little picture of a wolf and another of a stag. We may smile at these for being quaint or outlandish but we immediately grasp what he is trying to convey. The coastline on some of our earliest maps is often shown as a series of semi-circular or half-moon embayments. This is a common convention in Mediterranean *isolarii* but they also appear in our earliest map of the Orkneys (dating to about 1500). It was a stylised representation of a coastline the cartographer did not know intimately.

Instead of contour lines there may be a little picture of a particular hill or mountain. Timothy Pont's sketch of Ben Nevis in his map of Mamore (Pont 13) makes it perfectly clear that this is the highest mountain in the area. Murdo Mackenzie, the late eighteenth-century chart-maker, included a very emphatic drawing of the Cuillins of Skye. They were, and are, of paramount importance to the mariner. On his chart of Lewis and north-west Scotland, Van Keulen drew a dense forest east of Loch Broom, presumably because he thought this feature would be a helpful landmark to his clients. Pont's sketch of Dunollie Castle by Oban has not survived except in the Blaeu map for Lorn. However it is characteristic of his work and draws attention to the citadel's defensive strength as well as the track leading up to it. (See Plate 2). Rivers on mediaeval maps, and in Lawrence Nowell's manuscript maps of Scotland, are often shown as starting in lakes or lochs – whether they did or not. Van Keulen's charts of the Hebrides have north at the foot of the page, a perspective that would have appealed to the Viking mind.

And so the styles and conventions of cartography have developed. The science has an art and a history. Its progress has not always been onwards and upwards. Mistakes have been made. Symbols, projections, conventions have been tried, rejected and forgotten. Blind alleys, such as the false eastward orientation of Scotland based on Ptolemy, were pursued for decades. It is only through the process of time, practical experience and criticism that the conventions we are familiar with today have become established. This chapter is not going to catalogue every hiccup or celebrate every burst of progress. It merely gives an overview of what became available, through the years, to the Hebridean traveller.

Travellers also wanted more information than could be conveniently or symbolically portrayed in what was essentially a picture. The first maps were hand-drawn for the rich and powerful. Whether on skin or paper they were expensive and laborious to produce. With the development of printing and engraving techniques from the latter half of the sixteenth century they would become accessible to a much wider audience of merchants and lesser nobles. On the reverse of an engraved map could be put some printed text, a practice which soon became conventional.

The quality of the text, as of the maps, varied greatly. Sometimes it was simply borrowed or plagiarised from earlier sources. Errors were repeated, lies and distortions magnified. Since the accompanying text often repeated the more colourful or fabulous accounts, some of these ran for centuries. Hoary old chestnuts about barnacle geese, or cockles in Barra, or the floating island of Loch Lomond, became ever hoarier. The maps, then, are not to be seen in isolation. They accompany the contemporary texts. Pont's maps of the west coast should be read in conjunction with his matching texts in Macfarlane's Geographical Collections.

A critical difference between the new printed maps and the earlier manuscript versions on paper and vellum is the fact that the former helped to disseminate knowledge. Before printing people could, and did, copy and borrow maps, but the numbers in circulation were always restricted by the fact that they were time-consuming and laborious to produce. By the same token this also meant that they were treasured and preserved. The Gough Map of Britain may have originated in a map drawn for Edward I and therefore enjoyed a degree of state security. Nowell's manuscript maps of Scotland were drawn for William Cecil, principal counsellor to Elizabeth I. Knowledge of these maps was restricted to a wealthy and educated elite but at least this elite audience conserved their manuscripts, or some of them. It would be wonderful to have John Elder's map of Scotland drawn for Henry VIII c. 1543, but at least we have Lawrence Nowell's version of it.

Printing, however, transformed the situation. The dissemination of geographical knowledge in the late sixteenth century, through the work of Mercator, Ortelius and Nicolay, opened up a visual dimension of the Highlands and Hebrides that had not been previously available. Other maps by Lily (1546) and Leslie (1578) look muddled in comparison. The island names are there, but relative size and position are completely awry.

The importance of printing is even more apparent with Timothy Pont. Pont's surveys were the foundation for Blaeu's maps of Scotland, but if it hadn't been for Blaeu much of Pont's work might well have died with him. Some of his manuscript maps survive but many others don't – particularly of the west coast and Hebrides. We no longer have any of his island maps except for Uist, and yet Pont's pioneering survey work is enshrined in Blaeu's maps, no less than ten of which deal specifically with islands in the Hebrides and Clyde. By the same token when such work was not printed then the knowledge remained hidden from a wider audience. We have a detailed manuscript map of Cowal by Timothy Pont. For some reason this was never engraved by Blaeu, and so the benefit of Pont's survey of this district was lost.

Expert knowledge that was only expressed in manuscript was always in danger. On 31 July 1593 the Lord Deputy wrote to Burghley from Ireland that he: '*Is sorry that Burghley has mislaid the plot of Ulster, as there is never a man that can make another.*' (Calendar of State Papers, Ireland, vol V, p 132)

The other point about the diffusion of such knowledge is that not only did more people learn of the Highlands and Islands through Mercator, Ortelius, Nicolay and Blaeu, but their maps were subjected to critical scrutiny. An observer who compared either Mercator or Nicolay's printed maps of Scotland with Nowell's manuscript maps would have noticed that Jura was wrongly labelled in the two former. Travellers who visited Islay would soon have established that the names for the islets of Texa and Orsay had been transposed by both Nowell and Mercator. Those who knew Loch Linnhe and the coast of the Rough Bounds (Knoydart to Moidart) would have been aware of the shortcomings of the outline produced by Mercator, Ortelius and Leslie. In fact by 1595 the Mercator firm had abandoned their own outline of this area in favour of the more accurate version found in maps by Nowell and in *The Booke of the Sea Carte* (British Library Add MSS 37024). Those who knew Gaelic would have realised that the two settlements marked *Cheulis* and *Luingach* on the island of Shuna off Craignish did not exist. Blaeu's Dutch engravers had simply misplaced two Gaelic words which signified the kyle or straits between Shuna and the neighbouring island of Luing.

Progress was not always onwards and upwards. There was more copying than original survey work. In fact it was not until Roy's military survey of the mid-eighteenth century that anybody matched Pont's conscientious and comprehensive labours. Blaeu's representation of Ardnamurchan and Morvern was cruelly distorted – but was continued by Jansson through the latter half of the seventeenth century. At the end of the eighteenth century, von Reilly, a major Austrian cartographer, was still using Blaeu's representation of islands like Skye, in turn based on Pont's work at the end of the sixteenth century.

The early cartography of the Highlands and Hebrides provides important evidence of what travellers might know of this area. There is such a scarcity of documentary evidence that maps are even more important here than elsewhere. By its very nature such evidence is largely graphic and there is a limit to how many illustrations this book can include. This chapter will briefly look at some pre-nineteenth century maps and their creators, following through with examples of the evidence they provide. Its theme is the historical cartography of the Highlands and Islands, the mapping of this area over time. However, we are not dealing with some monolithic, abstract body of knowledge – as can sometimes appear today. Instead we have the partial survival of lots of different, sometimes conflicting, representations, made by different people, at different times, for different purposes.

Nowadays, once a map, book or article is published in paper or electronic form, it becomes accessible to a worldwide audience of readers. Some are scholars, others are expert, but they all scrutinise the representation and criticise it according to its merit, their own agenda, prejudice or institutional bias. The advantage of such a system is that we like to think that, this way, truth and knowledge are better served. It is the process of argument, criticism and amendment that establishes better knowledge. Of course this is not foolproof. Errors can still become well-established but because scrutiny calls all in doubt so we should, theoretically, be able to come closer to truth. One of the crucial differences between the early and the modern period as far as the Highlands and Islands is concerned is in the diffusion and dissemination of knowledge. This takes a huge leap forward in the sixteenth century.

With reference to the earliest geography of the Highlands and Hebrides we must think of things differently. There was knowledge, but owned by different people who did not necessarily communicate with other groups at all. Who were these people? Principally the inhabitants, and the seamen and merchants who traded with them. After the period of Scandinavian domination this latter group became very small, in fact even the knowledge possessed by Lowland Scots was abysmal.

Outsiders were always interested, but since their knowledge was seldom tested or challenged in the crucible of experience so it became repeated uncritically generation after generation. This so-called 'knowledge' even percolated back to inform the inhabitants of the Highlands and Islands. This is how we find firm local belief in a freshwater origin for cockles, mystery islands in the Atlantic, barnacle geese and pigmies. When we look at early representations of the Highlands we should be aware of the agendas of those responsible for them.

The earliest representation on a map of islands which may include the Hebrides is British Library MS Cotton Tiberius B V f.56v (Figure 1). Around the north of Scotland are a number of islands. These carry the label Orcades but it is quite possible some of those to the northwest actually represent the Hebrides. Certainly at the time the map was composed the Anglo-Saxon authorities in England were aware of the Hebrides. Florence of Worcester tells us King Edgar was rowed up the River Dee in 973 by eight under-kings, one of whom was 'king of very many islands'. This theme resurfaces many years later in a chart by Grenville Collins of the area round the mouth of the Dee. He includes a little picture of King Edgar being rowed.

Our earliest certain indication of Hebridean islands is on British Library MS map Cotton Claudius D VI f.12v, which is often attributed to Matthew Paris. Whether actually drawn by Matthew Paris or not it seems entirely reasonable to credit him with the geographical knowledge that lay behind it. Despite being a monk of St Albans, (just north of London), Matthew probably met Ewen Macdougall of Lorn in Bergen, Norway, in 1248. Matthew was on an ecclesiastical business trip trying to sort out the financial affairs of a Norwegian monastery. Ewen was on a political mission trying to persuade King Hakon of Norway to make him sub-king over the Northern Hebrides. A meeting between them is the most likely reason for an otherwise incongruous passage in Matthew's *Cronica Majora* where he discusses, with considerable sympathy, the political problems then being faced by Ewen.

Ewen Macdougall was the head of one of the three great branches of Somerled's family. He held extensive possessions in mainland North Argyll and in the neighbouring Hebrides. The Macdonalds of Islay were his competitors immediately to the south, the Macruaris of Garmoran to the North. The Macdougalls were probably then the most powerful of the three branches They certainly were 50 years later when, according to the Macvurich chroniclers: '*all the garrisons from Dingwall in Ross to the Mull of Kintyre were in the possession of MacDugald during that time, while the tribe of Ranald were under the yoke of their enemies.*' (Book of Clanranald in *Reliquiae Celticae*, Vol II, p 157)

In 1248 Ewen was coming under considerable pressure from King Alexander II of Scotland who was trying to extend the power of the Scottish realm to the west. This process had been going on for at least fifty years with the ultimate aim of expelling the Norse who controlled the Hebrides and, through their Hebridean subjects, a large part of the west coast of Argyll and Inverness-shire. Ewen was in something of a dilemma since he held his island possessions of King Hakon of Norway but his mainland possessions of King Alexander of Scotland. Matthew Paris describes Alexander's machinations:

As he planned to disinherit him, he accused him of treachery because in the previous year he had done homage to the king of Norway for the tenure of a certain island which Owen's [Ewen's] father had held from the same king and had peaceably possessed for many years in return for homage. The island is situated between Scotland and the Orkneys. Owen, fearing the threats of his lord the king of Scotland, let him know that he would fully render the service he owed, both to the king of the Scots and the king of the Norwegians. But when the king of the Scots retorted that 'No man can serve two masters', he received the reply from Owen that it was easy to serve two lords well, provided they were not hostile to each other. The king raised an army and advanced against Owen, who, unwilling to offend his lord the king of Scotland, entreated him to grant him a truce so that he could resign to the king of Norway both his homage and the aforesaid island. When the king of the Scots denied him this, his hatred became apparent, and so he offended both God and St Columba, who is buried and honoured in those parts, and many of the nobles. The king defied this Owen and pursued him by sea as far as Argyll . . . But the king, on disembarking from his ship, before he could mount his horse, as if by divine vengeance, was struck down by a sudden and deadly attack of illness. Thus he abruptly expired in the arms of his nobles while trying to disinherit an innocent man. (Vaughan, *The Illustrated Chronicles of Matthew Paris*).

There are three strikingly similar maps of Britain dating to the mid-thirteenth century which are attributed to Matthew Paris and the monks of St Albans. (Two are in the British Library, one in Corpus Christi College, Cambridge.) Even so, Matthew's written information about Ewen is a lot clearer than his cartographical representation of the area from which Ewen hailed. The most detailed of the three maps is B.L. Cotton Claudius D VI f.12v (Figure 2) and it shows the far north-west almost as an island detached from the rest of Scotland by a strip of water. We should probably interpret this as a representation of the Great Glen. This geological fault stretches from Loch Linnhe to the Moray Firth and is largely made up of water (Loch Linnhe, which is salt, and Lochs Lochy, Oich and Ness which are all fresh). This remarkable natural feature nearly divides Scotland in two and its significance was not lost on early geographers. The accompanying text gives us some idea of what the monks were trying to convey:

North-west of the Great Glen:
A country marshy and impassable, fit for cattle and shepherds.

In the central Highlands
A mountainous and woody region, producing a people rude and pastoral, by reason of marshes and fens.

In the sea off the north-west coast of Scotland:
A boundless and trackless sea.

In the margin opposite north-west Scotland:
This part, from north to south, looks only towards a sea where there is nought but the abode of monsters. However, an island exists there.
(Translations from the Latin by Hume Brown, *Early Travellers in Scotland*).

Similar themes appear in B.L. Cotton Julius D VII f. 50v-53r where the sea in the far north-western corner bears the caption:
The sea facing the desolation to the west and north. There are islands to be found therein which islands . . .
(Translation from the Latin by S.M. Campbell)

The Orkney Isles appear in B.L. Cotton Claudius D VI f.12v and Corpus Christi College, Cambridge, MS 16, f.Vv although they are positioned to the east rather than the north of Scotland. However in Cotton Claudius D VI the words *I(n)sula colu(m)killi* and *tyren i(nsul)a* appear in black ink in the sea to the west and south-west of the Firth of Clyde. The former is definitely Iona and the latter has always been assumed to be Tiree. There are some problems with this in that the islands are located too far south and their relationship is wrong (Tiree is actually north of Iona). However we should probably not worry too much about this. Erasure marks in the original suggest that the monastic cartographer was uncertain of some of the spatial relationships in western Scotland.

Insula Columkilli means 'the island of Columcille' or 'the island of the church of St Columba'. Columba, the most venerated of Celtic saints in Scotland, was also the saint whom Matthew refers to in the passage given above and about whom he is likely to have learned from Ewen Macdougall. What is intriguing is why do the islands of Iona and Tiree, and only these two, occur? Other islands on the same map, (the Orkneys, Anglesey, Man, Lundy, Wight etc.), are all given distinct shapes, each of which is surrounded by a green wash of sea. The names of Iona and Tiree are given no island shapes and are written directly onto the sea in black ink. This suggests they may have been added as something of an afterthought, perhaps as a consequence of Matthew's trip to Bergen in 1248. If the map itself was largely finished before 1248 then perhaps Matthew picked up this further information when meeting Ewen in Norway and wished to include it. It was too late to make new islands – the sea had already been filled in; but the names could be superimposed.

The inclusion of the tiny island of Iona (off Mull) should not surprise us. Matthew was a Benedictine monk and the St Albans' maps show a predisposition to locate other Benedictine houses. Iona was one of the most famous ecclesiastical sites in Scotland and had become a Benedictine community about 1200. Why though Tiree? Tiree did have ancient religious connections, but not as strong as Iona. In 1248 it may well have been possessed by the Macdougalls. One possible reason for its inclusion was its economic value. Despite its relatively small size Tiree was always regarded as one of the most valuable of the Hebrides. The Norse had a unique method of land-assessment in terms of ouncelands and pennylands and if we compare islands using this system of land-valuation then we get an idea of their relative economic importance to contemporaries. Tiree was worth twenty ouncelands, twenty times as important, for instance, as the island of Rum. Tiree was always regarded as the granary of the isles and perhaps this helped project it onto the map.

Another possibility is that this was where Ewen Macdougall resided and is the disputed island which Matthew Paris refers to in his text. The three great branches of the Macsorleys used their island homes as much as their mainland ones. The Macdonalds were based in Islay whilst the Macruaris (and later the Clanranalds) often resided in Uist rather than at Castle Tioram in Moidart. Quite possibly Ewen Macdougall favoured Tiree as much as Dunstaffnage or Dunollie where we would otherwise expect him to base himself. There is some precedent for this in Viking times. From the saga evidence it appears that Coll and Tiree made up a sort of regional centre within the Hebrides. In Njal's saga there is reference to an Earl Gilli in Coll before the end of the tenth century. In Orkneyinga saga, Svein Asleifarson had links with Holdbodi Hundason of Tiree who is described as 'a great chieftain' in about 1136.

A third possibility is that *tyren i(nsul)a* refers to Eilean Tioram, site of Castle Tioram in Moidart, ancestral home of the Macdonalds of Clanranald and, before them, the Macruaris. At some stage in the first half of the thirteenth century the Macruaris seem to have relocated from Kintyre to the Rough Bounds. The reasons and timing are unclear although it may have been to do with Alexander II's campaign(s) in Argyll in the 1220s. Although Eilean Tioram subsequently became their base it may not have been theirs in 1248. The Macruaris may, as the above Macvurich quotation implies, have been subordinate to the Macdougalls in mainland Scotland.

Tioram means 'dry' in the sense of 'dries out at low tide'. The Castle is built on a small tidal island by the mouth of the River Shiel. It became one of the most important mediaeval castles in the West Highlands and may already have been such in 1248. The fact that it was tidal, and was home to an important fortress, may mean that it was the island that Alexander II was being so difficult about. He may have argued that, being dry at low tide, it was technically part of mainland Scotland.

In case this seems a little far-fetched we should remind ourselves how legalistic some mediaeval disputes could become. At heart was the definition of an island. At the beginning of Orkneyinga Saga there is a mythical division of Norway between the two brothers Nor and Gor: '*Nor was to have all the mainland and Gor the islands, wherever a ship with a fixed rudder could be sailed between them and the mainland.* (H. Palsson and P. Edwards, *Orkneyinga Saga*.)

Using precisely such a definition Magnus Bareleg claimed Kintyre from Scotland in 1098 by having a boat drawn across the isthmus at Tarbert with the rudder set and himself at the helm. This was such a propaganda coup that, according to Barbour's poem, Robert Bruce repeated it in reverse in 1315 or 1316. Eilean Tioram is not the only tidal island on the west coast mainland. But perhaps it was the only one with a powerful fortress whose ownership really mattered.

That the monks of St Albans could keep up-to-date with Scottish events and acquire fresh information about Scotland is shown by Matthew's comments some years later. He is writing of the year 1259 in his *Cronica Majora*:

> *And in the same year about the* [1st of March] *master William de Horton, monk and treasurer of the church of St Albans, returned from the remotest parts of Scotland. He had long before undertaken the laborious journey thither . . . by command of the lord king and by provision of his counsellors, moreover also by the benevolence of his abbot. For difficult but secret affairs had been intrusted to him on behalf of the king and queen and magnates of England, to announce to the king and queen and magnates of Scotland.*
> (Anderson, *Scottish Annals from English Chroniclers*)

Subsequent to this embassy the king and queen of Scotland visited England. Each in turn stayed at St Albans where King Alexander made the gift of a pall. The monks of St Albans travelled when they acted as diplomats and in turn acted as hosts to others who travelled. This dual role fitted them well for cartography.

Gough map

The next map which represents the Hebrides in any detail is the Gough Map (dated to c. 1360 and named after a later owner) which is now in the Bodleian Library, Oxford (Figure 3). Although this has faded with the passage of time the representation of north-west Scotland shows a major improvement on the Matthew Paris maps. Nine islands are shown off the west coast of Scotland. One of these is named *Insula de Bote* (Bute) and in another appear the words *Les outisles*. Pelham has made the entirely plausible suggestion that this map, if not drawn at the time, then at least derives from knowledge accumulated during Edward I's reign.

Edward I was a belligerent king and conducted many campaigns in Wales and Scotland. Military campaigns, then as now, involved the construction of careful maps. These were particularly important from a logistical point of view. An army always marches on its stomach, (except Highland ones), so careful planning of supply lines was an essential prerequisite for any campaign. To do this properly, Edward's military planners needed the best available cartographic knowledge. The Gough Map is impressive for its correct north-south orientation of Scotland, particularly when it is remembered how many later maps laboured under the Ptolemaic inaccuracy of distorting Scotland towards the east.

In the early stages of the Wars of Independence there must have been a good deal of correspondence between Edward I's officials and his Macdonald allies in the Hebrides. After his death this continued between Edward II and the Macdougalls of Lorn. Some of these letters survive. Names that occur include Ross, Lochaber, Argyll, Glassary, Kintyre, Bute, Islay, Skye and Lewis, so it is reasonable to assume that Edward had some idea where these districts and islands lay. The phrase *Les outisles* is itself intriguing. It is a French rendering of an English expression denoting islands amongst whom Norse speech was then dying out in favour of Gaelic. The 'Out isles' is a phrase we come across in other English documents and here it has just been given a French gloss. (French was commonly used in official correspondence at the time.)

There are some further details about this map which have particular reference to the outsider's view of the Highlands. Cartographers have always struggled to fill the blank spaces of large and remote regions, information about which was hard to come by. Oceans might be filled with imaginary marine monsters whilst the device of 'Here there be tygers' has become notorious. The Gough Map gives us a couple of Highland variations on the same theme. There are two delightful sketches in the north-west which suggest that the cartographer was aware of some of the travellers' tales about the area and seized on them as a way of filling a blank space. West of the caption *Comitatus de Sotherland* (earldom of Sutherland) is a sketch of a wolf with the text *hic habundant lupi* (here live wolves). Scotland had wolves until the eighteenth century and certainly in the sixteenth century they were common in the far north-west of Sutherland. In Pont 3, which is a map of Eddrachillis and North-West Sutherland, Timothy Pont comments that there are '*Many Woolfs*' in the area c. 1600.

South of Badenoch and north-east of a caption reading *Plaga que dicit(ur) Loren* (District called Lorn) is a picture of a stag and beside it the caption *Colgarth hic maxima venacio* (Colgarth – here is great hunting). Gough and Parsons suggested that this was the area between Badenoch and Atholl now known as Gaick Forest. The precise location is perhaps less significant than the fact that the cartographer had heard of the great huntings to be had in the Highlands.

This was certainly true in the Dark and Middle Ages. Hunting was an important social and cultural undertaking which was conducted on an epic scale in the Highlands until well into the seventeenth century. Huge drives of deer were channelled into traps known as elerigs and there slaughtered. This was a particularly Highland phenomenon and the kings and nobility of Scotland travelled into the Highlands to take part. It seems entirely possible that the unknown cartographer behind the Gough Map had heard of these events.

Finally there is the following caption beside Loch Tay: '*In this lake are three marvels: a floating island, fish without fins, wave without wind.*' These reports were commonly made of Loch Lomond and I think their occurrence here is a simple misplacement. Geographical lore like this was already centuries old.

The Gough map used outline and symbol to tell contemporaries, and us, something new of the Highlands and Islands.

John Elder

It must not be thought that there were no maps of Scotland between the Gough map and those of Mercator and Nowell. John Hardyng produced maps of Scotland, but, as far as the Highlands and Islands are concerned they are the visual equivalent of his poem quoted earlier. The Highlanders were 'wild Scots' and their abode was represented in marginal, almost diagrammatic fashion.

However, the mid-sixteenth century saw a transformation in the outside world's comprehension of the Hebrides. Not only do we have the first documentary survey of the islands, written by Dean Monro in 1549, but there were huge strides in cartographic skills and knowledge. This owes much to John Elder, a shadowy figure whose map of Scotland has not survived. We learn of it in a long letter to Henry VIII, dated probably to 1543, in which Elder describes his map. What he says gives us a clue as to the source of some of the material used by Nowell, Mercator and Dudley.

I can no les do, then offer this plotte of the realme of Scotland vnto your excellent Maiestie, wherein your Highnes shall perceaue and se, not onely the descripcion of all the notable townes, castels, and abbeis ther set fourthe, and situat in ther propir places, as they stand in euery countie and schyre, with the situacion of all the principall yles, marched with the same, callid Orknay and Schetlande, and of the Out-ysles, commonly namede the Sky and the Lewys: but also your noble Grace shall se the cost of the same, the dangers lying therby, with euery port, ryver, loigh, creke, and haven there, so truely drawyn and set fourthe as my poore witt and lernynge can vtter and discerne. Which plotte, I haue not made by relacion of others; but in so moche (and pleas your Highnes) that I was borne in Caitnes, which is the northe part of the saide plotte, marched with the East yles of the same, callid Orknay; educatt, and brought vp, not onely in the West yles of the same plotte, namede Sky and the Lewis, wher I haue bene often tymes with my friendis, in ther longe galleis, arrywing to dyvers and syndrie places in Scotland, wher they had a do: but also, beinge a scholer and a student in the southe partis of it, callid Sanctandrois, Abirdene, and Glasgw, for the space of XIIth yeares, wher I haue travailde, aswell by see as by the land, dyuers tymes; by reason whereof, knowinge all the notable places ther euery wher, with ther lordis and masters names, and from thens vnto the said countreth wher I was borne, I am the bolder (pardon cravide) to offer the saide plotte vnto your excellent Maiestie; wherein I haue written the principal erlis and lordis names in Scotlande, annext to ther common habitacion and duellinge place in the same; with a brief declaracion of all the ryvers, loighis, and havens ther also, to the intent your noble Maiestie may perceaue, se, and reide the same ther, without any farther investigacion. And fforsomoche, and pleas your Grace, that I haue written the names of all the Yrische lordes of Scotland, commonly callit the Reddshanckes, and by historiographouris, Pictis; joynede also to ther cuntreth and duellinge places.

and again:

Therfor I have written the said Yrische Lordes names of Scotlande in the said plotte, as Your Grace may perceaue and se. (John Elder, *Collectanea de rebus Albanicis*)

(I can do no less, than offer this plot [map] of the realm of Scotland unto your excellent Majesty, wherein your Highness shall perceive and see, not only the description of all the notable towns, castles, and abbeys there set forth, and situated in their proper places, as they stand in every county and shire, with the situation of all the principal isles, marched [bordering] with the same, called Orkney and Shetland, and of the Out-isles, commonly named the Skye and the Lewis: but also your noble Grace shall see the coast of the same, the dangers lying thereby, with every port, river, loch, creek, and haven there, so truly drawn and set forth as my poor wit and learning can utter and discern. Which plot, I have not made by relation of others; but in so much (and may it please your Highness) that I was born in Caithness, which is the north part of the said plot, marched with the East isles of the same, called Orkney; educated, and brought up, not only in the West isles of the same plot, named Skye and the Lewis, where I have been often times with my friends, in their long galleys, arriving to various and sundry places in Scotland, where they had a do: but also, being a scholar and a student in the south parts of it, called Saint Andrews, Aberdeen, and Glasgow, for the space of 12 years, where I have travelled, as well by sea as by the land, divers [various] times; by reason whereof, knowing all the notable places there everywhere, with their lord's and master's names, and from thence unto the said country where I was born, I am the bolder ([your] pardon craved) to offer the said plot unto your excellent Majesty; wherein I have written the principal earls and lords names in Scotland, annexed to their common habitation and dwelling place in the same; with a brief declaration of all the rivers, lochs, and havens there also, to the intent your noble Majesty may perceive, see, and read the same there, without any further investigation. And for so much [i.e. accord-ingly], and [may it] please your Grace, that I have written the names of all the Irish [Gaelic] lords of Scotland, commonly called the 'Red-shanks', and by historiographers, Picts; joined also to their country and dwelling places.

Therefore I have written the said Irish [Gaelic] Lords' names of Scotland in the said plot [map], as Your Grace may perceive and see).

Elder's map is lost but we can trace his influence in the work of Nowell and Mercator. About 1565 Laurence Nowell, an antiquary working for Cecil, Elizabeth I's principal counsellor, produced a beautiful coloured manuscript map of Scotland and another in black ink at a larger scale. Elder gave the names of ten Irish (i.e. Gaelic) lords on his map and lists them in his letter. Eight of these are also marked by Nowell. In 1564 Mercator produced his famous Atlas with the best map yet printed of the Hebrides. Mercator acknowleges a debt for some of his information to an unknown friend in Britain. Most of Elder's Gaelic lords have now gone but the telling phrase

Lord of the Redshanks appears twice, once by Islay, base of the son of John of the Battles, who is also named by Nowell. It seems likely that both Nowell and Mercator derived a significant amount of their Scottish material from John Elder and that Nowell's maps may have been slightly closer to the original.

Loch Linnhe and the waters connected to it are more accurately represented in Nowell than Mercator. The same could be said of the number, order and position of the west coast sea-lochs between Loch Duich and Loch Sunart. Nevertheless both these maps represent a huge advance in knowledge of the islands and their relative positions. Nowell's, which was never printed, did not inform the public domain. Mercator's assuredly did, through his own work and that of Ortelius (1573). However we should also credit John Elder and the Gaelic background of the islands. A peculiarity of all these maps of Mercator (1564), Nowell (1565), and Nicolay (1583), is that they include parish names from Uist. John Elder must have tapped into Gaelic sources on the west coast and we should acknowledge their silent contribution.

The significance of this input can best be assessed by looking at maps which did not draw on these sources. Lily (1546), Leslie (1578), and those who copied them, produced maps of the Hebrides that are a dreadful muddle by comparison. They knew of the islands, they knew some of their names, but their size and relative position is pure guesswork. Figures 1–5 reproduce the outlines of various early maps which include the Hebrides. The advance represented by those derived from John Elder is dramatic.

From the end of the sixteenth century we have our first individual island maps. The earliest of these belong to the Frenchman, André Thevet, and were made for his *Grand Insulaire* c. 1586. This encyclopaedia of islands was never actually published but some of the engravings were made and prints produced. Collections of these prints survive in the Bibliotheque nationale in Paris, in the British Library in London, in the Huntington Library in California and in private collections. Maps were planned for several Hebridean islands of which, as yet, I only know of two – Mull and Islay (see Plate 1). Although the maps are fascinating it is difficult to know just how much of Thevet's material was based on his own research, and how much was borrowed from elsewhere. This is a large and important issue which I hope to deal with more fully at some future date.

Timothy Pont

With Timothy Pont we are on safer ground. A number of his manuscript maps survive in the National Library of Scotland and have been reproduced by Jeffrey Stone in his book *The Pont Manuscript Maps of Scotland*. They are also available via the National Library of Scotland's website. Pont's work in the Highlands and Islands is of the greatest importance. He was the first cartographer to survey the individual islands in any detail. He has left us a huge body of place-names, some of which we would not otherwise be able to locate. He left copious notes, many of which have been printed in Macfarlane's Geographical Collections.

Pont's work was uneven. He does not seem to have been able to collect good quality data for much of the mainland west coast between Glenelg and Morvern. This may not have been his fault. Travel around the Highlands in the period 1584–1596 was neither easy nor altogether safe. In most areas Pont must have been dependent on support from the local magnate and, where this was not forthcoming, he may have decided that discretion was the better part of valour. The results are sometimes patchy. In his map of Skye, (in Blaeu), the Macdonald and Mackinnon estates are covered in far more detail than that of Macleod. Does this reflect differing levels of support from the respective lairds? It would also be unfair to blame Pont for the fact that so much of his work was left unimproved for so long after his death. The longevity of Pont's maps reflect the difficulty of survey work in the Highlands and Islands and the thoroughness with which he carried out his task.

In order to give a taste of Pont's work in the Hebrides I include some text from Macfarlane's Geographical Collections which is directly attributed to him. The reader may then compare this with the district of Trotternish which is taken from the Blaeu map of Skye and reproduced in Plate 3.

NOATES AND MEMOIRS drawn furth of Mr TIMOTHEY PONT his papers.

The ISLE of SKIANA commonlie called the SKIE.

Item betwix Bracadil and Tronternesse is the water of Snisort. Item twa waters betwix Keylburg and Snisort towit Glenhaltin within a myle to Kysburg. the uther water of Glen Rumbisdaill or Rumbisdaill water. Glentillisdaill water mouth some myles be north Kysebourg. Item nixt the water of Glenvig five myles be south west Duntuyllin, called otherways Dunringill. it is 8 myles betwix Dundonald and Duntuyllin. Duntuyllin is within a myl to the poynt of Trouterness. Betwix Duntuyllin and the poynt midway the seat of Eriskew.

The port of Trouternesse is five myle broad, betwix Duntuyllin and Ghervad. Item Kilmartin a myle neerer then Ghervad. Within a myle thence Stensboll nix Ghervad beyond the water of Kilmartin. Nixt Ghervad 2 myls Could na grock, 2 myls nixt Touttin Icra. a myl thence Touttin Ocre. half a myle thence Grouban. hard besyde Growban is Avon Roik or Ryce, with Eik and the fresche Loch Harry a myl thence Bordmeanach, Item nixt Hollom Ocra and Ycra. with Loch Hollom. Above thise is Bonstoure thence thrie myles Fairnan. thence a myle Port Ry with Evon Portry . . .

Item in Trouterness countrey, Kisburg moir and Beg, thence a myle Polldun, thence a myle Poolnahalla. Heir is Dundonald Castell, thence a myle Ouig, thence twa myle Edirgill moir and Beg, thence a myle upon the water of Vig, Bruchvig, thence a myle Scoudbruch, thence a myle Mungistot, hard by Chroshemer, thence 1 myle Knocko 1 myl Barranasketaig a myl thence Kroshemer, 1 myl Kilvakisa, a quarter thence Kraaulan thence a myle Borraness and Borraness-fuille, 1 myl Hownacklead 1 myl Chroshemer thence a quarter Kilmore with Avo Kilmore, a half myl thence Ballach a half thence Duntvyllim it is a myl hence to Rowhoumish. Ardnakeldan a quarter myl from the poynt. from the poynt eastward a myl Brundestot, hard by Kilmo-Lowag. thence half a myle Balmakuyan, a burne betwix it and the former a myl thence Keandendruym. a myl thence Altavick seat and Isle (Macfarlane's Geographical Collections)

(Notes and memoirs drawn from Mr Timothy Pont's papers.

The Isle of Skiana commonly called Skye.

Item, between Bracadale and Trotternish is the water of Snizort. Also two rivers between Kingsburgh and Snizort, to wit Glen Haultin within a mile of Kingsburgh; the other is the river of Glen Romesdal or Romesdal Water. The mouth of River Hinnisdal is some miles north of Kingsburgh. Next is the water of Glen Uig, five miles south-west of Duntulm – otherwise called Dun Ringill. It is eight miles between Dundonald and Duntulm. Duntulm is within a mile of the point of Trotternish. Halfway between Duntulm and the point is the settlement of Erisco.

Trotternish is five miles wide between Duntulm and Garafad. Kilmartin is a mile nearer than Garafad. Within a mile is Stenscholl, next is Garafad beyond the Kilmartin River. Two miles after Garafad is Culnaknock, two miles further is Lower Tote, another mile to Upper Tote, half a mile from there to *Grouban*. Just beside *Grouban* is Rigg Burn, with *Eik* and the freshwater Loch *Harry*; a mile from there to *Bordmeanach*. Next are Holm Upper and Lower with Loch Holm (Loch Leathan?). Above these is Beinn Storr (The Storr); from there three miles to Fiurnean. Then a mile to Portree with River Portree (Varragill River?) . . .

In Trotternish are Kingsburgh Mor and Beg, then a mile to Am Bagh-dhuin, and another to Poll na-h-Ealaidh. Here is Dundonald Castle (Castle Uisdean); then a mile to Uig, from there two miles to Idrigill Mor and Beg, then a mile up the River Uig (Conon?) is *Broch Uig*. From there a mile to Skudiburgh, then a mile to Monkstadt, and just by is

Chroshemer. Then a mile to Knockhoe, a mile to Bornesketaig, a mile from there *Kroshemer*, a mile to Kilvaxter, a quarter-mile from there to Greaulin, then a mile to *Borraness* and *Borraness-fuille* (Feall?), a mile to Hungladder, a mile to *Chroshemer*, and then a quarter-mile to Kilmuir with River Kilmuir. A half mile from there to Bealach, another half-mile to Duntulm. It is then a mile to Rubha Hunish. *Ardnakeldan* is a quarter mile from the point. A mile east of the point lies *Brundestot*, just by it is Kilmaluag, then half a mile to Balmaqueen. There is a burn between Balmaqueen and Kilmaluag. A mile further is Kendram, another mile to the settlement of *Altavick* (Flodigarry) and Isle . . . (Eilean Flodigarry)) I have italicised names where identification is not straightforward.

Elsewhere, Pont clearly identifies himself as the source for this survey note:

it is a myl betwix Kilchrist which I did see and Killurid.
(It is a mile between Kilchrist, which I saw, and Kilbride.) (Macfarlane's Geographical Collections, Vol II)

Pont's work was enormously influential. He provided information for Gordon, Blaeu and Jansson and all their later copyists. But, by the same token, his weaknesses became their weaknesses. Parts of the West Highlands remained without proper maps until the eighteenth century.

The precise reasons for Pont's great survey are still uncertain. In Ireland, maps sometimes accompanied ambitious new development schemes. They added weight to an investment prospectus. Something similar may lie behind a map of Lewis and Harris which is now in the National Library of Ireland (Plate 4). This may be connected with the survey of Captain John Dymes in 1630, along with a plan of Stornoway which does not survive.

And thus haveinge made a breife survey of the whole Island, I have taken a more perticuler viewe of that place therein wch is most convenient for the seatinge of a Burrough towne wch I hould to bee in the Lough of Sternway.

First of al for the comodity of shippinge, this Lough hath a very faire cominge in to it cleare of all dangers, haveinge within it safe rideinge for shipps with all windes wth places most convenient from whence both Roade an harboure may bee comaunded for the securinge both of towne and shippinge from the danger of an Enimy as it doth more plainely appeare by a draught wch I have made thereof . . .

There are alsoe divers places about the Island very necessary for ye buildinge of Magazines and Stoarhouses for the layinge vpp of salt, packinge of fish, and all other necessaryes belonginge vnto the fishings wch will always shift from place to place, accordinge vnto the seuall seasons of the yeare, wch places wth theire proprietyes because they cannott bee soe well vnderstood and conceived of by words I have made a platt of the Island whereby I hope to give your honors the better satisfaccon both of what I have heere related, and many other things concerninge the same.

Since Dymes's report was much concerned with the economics of fishing in the Outer Isles we can assume a map was necessitated by his instructions.

Blaeu's maps became available in 1654 – perhaps fifty to sixty years after Pont's survey. But, as far as the Highlands and Islands were concerned, the mapping of the land probably did not advance so much in the seventeenth century as the mapping of the sea. However the eighteenth century saw further huge strides. If we confine our attention specifically to the Highlands and Islands there are two particular areas of development. Firstly there were an increasing number of estate maps. Alexander Bruce produced a map of Ardnamurchan and Sunart in 1733, Stephen Macdougall produced maps of Islay, Gigha and Taynish (Knapdale) around 1747. Stobie produced enormous coloured maps of the Macdonald estates in Skye in the 1760s. Morison produced maps of the farms on the forfeited estates such as Barrisdale and Lochiel in the 1770s. By 1810 Langlands had produced detailed maps of Argyllshire and Bald some fine estate maps of the Clanranald properties in western Inverness-shire.

Secondly, if we look at the overall picture, General Roy's military survey (1747–55) was the first comprehensive re-mapping since Timothy Pont. It survives in two forms – the rough draft or 'Protracted Copy' and the more polished 'Fair Copy'. These show settlement sites and areas of cultivation so we can trace where the surveyors travelled. They also had a military bias and particular attention was paid to features like river estuaries where boats might be landed and troops taken ashore. The estuary at Morar is shown in great detail with the river channel clearly marked. Just as with Pont, this survey became the basis for other maps thereafter. By the end of the eighteenth century we have books of Scottish road maps which include at least some Highland destinations. In 1776 you could buy a book of road maps by Taylor and Skinner which included routes to Glenelg, Bonawe, Inveraray, and Campbeltown. (Plate 5b) There is not room in this book to do justice to all these maps but we only have to compare them with the first efforts of Matthew Paris 500 years earlier to see how much more information was available for the traveller. But it is with the work of Elder and Pont that we move from the mediaeval to the modern world.

Charts

In the same way that land-travel required land-maps so sea-travel required sea-charts. The ocean wastes themselves must remain chartless but the coastlines, harbours and hazards could be mapped and nautical charts developed their own styles and conventional symbols. Instead of heights above sea level, mariners were more interested in depths below. Instead of rivers and forests, such charts could display reefs and whirlpools, sands and shallows, harbours and havens. Anchorages were marked, currents and tides were noticed, and how the land looked from the sea.

Similar documents evolved over the centuries in many sea-faring countries. There are a number of foreign terms which denote the various types of marine document and the information they include. One is *portolan*, a hand-drawn sea-chart, often on vellum. In early times these were typically of the Mediterranean but were gradually extended to include the Atlantic coastline. Many of these took notice of Scotland and Scottish waters but a lot of the data was very corrupt by the time it reached the chart-maker. So we have charts of Diego Homem in the British Library (1570) and the Bibliotheque nationale in Paris (1583) which show the place-names Mul (Mull) and Cumbrae (Great Cumbrae by Largs) marked on the mainland of Scotland. The names of these two islands had travelled correctly even if their context hadn't. For this chapter I am going to sidestep discussion of portolans to concentrate on documents that provide more original data.

Another class of document were the *isolarii*. These were catalogues of islands; 'islandries' we might call them. Initially they were in manuscript form and accompanied by highly decorative pictures of the islands themselves. The archetype is Christopher Buondelmonti's Mediterranean Isolario done in the 1440s. The Orkneys appear in one such isolario completed about 1500 and now in the British Library. The author, (probably Italian), may have heard of the Orkneys and wished, for the sake of completeness, to include them but it is plain that he knew little about them. Apart from some enigmatic compass points and a short caption explaining that there were thirty of them there is not a single place-name on the map. We see this 'scientific' approach in a number of early maps of the Hebrides. The Scottish islands represented an unknown quantity and the most obvious ways to quantify them were to count them up, measure them, or give their latitude and longitude. Sixteenth-century maps and documents include lots of this type of data.

These isolarii eventually began to appear in book form. An example by Porcacchi called *L'isole piu famoso del mondo* was published in Venice in 1571 and enjoyed many subsequent editions. This includes two maps, one of Scotland, and one more specifically of the Orkneys and Hebrides. Unfortunately this is less accurate than Mercator's map, seven years earlier.

A third term is *rutter*, coming from the French *routier*, which means a marine travel guide or book of sailing directions. We are very fortunate that an early Scottish rutter dating to about 1540 has survived. Of course there may well have been rutters for centuries previously. The Norse in particular must have passed on some of their accumulated knowledge about the North Atlantic in written form. Elsewhere we shall look at some of the advice contained in the *King's Mirror*, dating to the 1240s, which condenses their practical common sense. No doubt there were other written sources of information. It is unlikely that everything was passed on orally. We have a table of tide-times at London Bridge dating to the mid thirteenth century which may have been compiled by the monks of St Albans. These are surviving fragments of what must once have been a vast body of marine lore.

As an example of this maritime knowledge base we can instance Sgeir na Caillich (The rock of the old woman) between Kyle of Lochalsh and Kylerhea off the island of Skye. The rock was already known by this name when Hakon's great fleet arrived on its way south to Largs in 1263: '*They sailed to Rona, and thence into the Sound of Skye, and lay there at a place called Carlinestone [Kerlingar-steinn].* (Dasent, Saga of Hakon)

The word *kerling* passed from Norse into English and survives in Scots usage as 'carline' meaning an 'old woman'. The Norse Kerlingar-steinn is the same as Sgeir na Caillich which begs the question whether it was first *kerling* or *cailleach*. Did the Norse borrow from the Gaels or vice-versa?

Around 1695 Martin Martin tells us why the rock was so noteworthy. It marked a turning point in the flow of currents between Skye and the mainland. Today we can look up this information. In earlier times such knowledge was critical. What appears at first sight to be an insignificant skerry must be marked and remembered.

The tide of ebb here runs southerly, and the tide of flood northerly, where no head lands or promontories are in the way to interpose; for in such cases the tides are observed to hold a course quite contrary to the ordinary motion in these isles and the opposite mainland. This is observed between the east side of Skye and the opposite continent, where the tide of ebb runs northerly, and the tide of flood southerly, as far as Killach-stone, on the south-east of Skye, both tides running directly contrary to what is to be seen in all the western isles and opposite continent. The natives at Kylakin told me that they had seen three different ebbings successively on that part of Skye. (Martin Martin, A Description of the Western Islands of Scotland)

We have a Scottish rutter which has been attributed to Alexander Lindsay, pilot to James V on his voyage to the Hebrides in 1540. It is very unlikely that it was composed purely for this. Instead it probably represents the best of the currently available data for conditions round the Scottish coasts. This rutter passed into the hands of the French cosmographer-royal Nicolas de Nicolay, along with a sea-chart 'rather roughly made'. He eventually published both the sailing directions and a map in France in 1583. The document was republished in English in 1710, 1819, and edited in National Maritime Museum Monograph (No 44) in 1980.

Lindsay's editors reckon his rutter both accurate and useful. They conclude that although the north-west section from Cape Wrath to the Crowlins is the least satisfactory there was no part of the coastline for which he was badly short of information. The following quotations relevant to the west coast between Kylerhea and Kintyre give an idea of its flavour. Where the names are difficult I have inserted the modern version in square brackets. A 'road' is an anchorage.

Courses of tydis from Dungisbe [Duncansby] Head in Caitnes to the Mulle of Cantyer [Kintyre] . . .

From Kylra [Kylerhea] to Ardmurth [Ardnamurchan] by the Iles of Ege, Rum, Muk and Canay it floweth est and west.

From Ardmurth to Comkill [Iona] and on the cost of Mull, Wlway [Ulva], Cardburghe [Cairnburgh, Treshnish Islands], Coll and Terrey [Tiree] it floweth est by north and west by south.

From Logh Quhaber [Lochaber] alongis the cost and throw the Iles of Carueray [Kerrera], Lowing [Luing], Ceyll [Seil], Scarbay, Dura [Jura], (O)ronsay and Collansa [Colonsay] it floweth est northest and west south-west.

In the Sound of Ila [Islay] it floweth south and north, a great stream . . .

Floodes and ebbes from Dungisbe Head to the Mull of Cantyir . . .

From Ardmurth alongue the costis of Mull, Coll and Terrey the moone south to wast, full sea.

From Mull alongue the costis of Lorne and the ylles of Carway, Lowng, Cewill and Skarbay the moone southwest to south, full sea.

In the Sound of Ila the moone southwest, full sea.

From Ila alongue the cost of Knapdell and Cantyir unto the Mull of Cantyir the moone southest, full sea.

Courses and Keningis frome Dungisbe Head to the Mull of Cantyir . . .

From Kilra to Ardmurth south southwest, xxxiii myle.

From Ardmurth to Lesmoir [Lismore] in the mought of Lough Abir south to est, xxii myle.

From Lismoir to Lough Spelle [Spelve] south southwest, x myle.

From Lough Spell to Colansa south southwest to west, [one] kenning and xii myle.

From Collansa to the Sound of Ila south to est, x myle.

From the Sound of Ila to the Mule of Cantyre south southest to south, ii kenningis and vi myle.

Hauins [havens], sounds and dangers from Dungisbe Head to the Mulle of Cantyir both on the Mayneland and throw the Iles . . .

This Kyilra is a streat [narrow] passage and a dangerous stream.

If ye ly in the Sound of Mule at the castell Arroys [Aros] ye sall have good ryd. at x or xiiii fadomes.

Iff ye lye at the castell of Dewar [Duart] ye sall find xxviii fadomes.

There is a good rode for all wyndis in the Calyow [Calve Island] of the

Mull, in the Sound of Wllway, and in the Lough Spelle, also amongst the ylles of Caruera, Cewill, Lowyng and Swinnay [Shuna].

The whirlpool at Corryvreckan receives a special mention:

Betuixt Scarba and Dura is the most dangerous stream knowing in all Europe, for manie of the seas which flowethe betuixt the Mulle of Cantyir and Yla passeth throwe this narrow channell and in the passyng they fall with such a great violence upon the cost of Scarba that they retourne to the cost of Dura with a great noys, making in thair returning a depe horlepoole quhairin if schippis do enter thair is no refuge but death onlie. Notwithstanding the best tyme that may be had of it is the tyme of full sea and low watter. This passage is callit Correbreykin.
    Item the Tarbat of Dura is a good road for shippis, and also is the Sound of Ylla, except it is a stronge dangerous stream.
(National Maritime Museum, Monograph (44))

This body of information also became mediated through other hands. A late sixteenth-century English copy of Lindsay's rutter survives in *The Booke of the Sea Carte* (British Library Add MSS 37024) where a kenning, in the Scottish section, is reckoned as fourteen miles. Attached to this is an attractive outline map of Scotland.

Local knowledge, however, was of paramount importance. In his account of Tiree, Walker writes of the above rutter: '*It is remarked by D'Arfeville in his Account of the Voyage of King James the 5th through the Hebrides that along the Coasts of Coll and Tirey, it is high Water, when the Moon is at S. one fourth S.E. But by the Information of the Inhabitants, eastern and western Moons make full Sea at Tirey.*' (McKay, *Walker's Report on the Hebrides*, 1764 and 1771)

A great deal of this local knowledge was orally transmitted. We glimpse it through the pages of Martin Martin: '*A s.e. moon causeth high tide; the spring-tides are always at the full and new moon, the two days following they are higher, and from that time decrease until the increase of the moon again, with which it rises gradually till the second after the full moon. This observation the seamen find to hold true betwixt the Mule of Kantyre, and the Farrow Head* [Cape Wrath] *in Strathnaver.*' (Martin Martin, *A voyage to St Kilda*, 1698)

Corryvreckan

At the end of the twelfth century Gerald of Wales had written: '*Not far to the north . . . is a certain wonderful whirlpool in the sea. All the waves of the sea from all parts, even those remote, flow and strike together here as if by agreement . . . If a ship happens to touch it, it is caught and pulled with such violence of the waves that the force of the pull downwards immediately swallows it up for ever.* (J. O'Meara, *Gerald of Wales – The History and Topography of Ireland,* p 67 and note 28.)

It is not absolutely clear which whirlpool Gerald is writing about. His translator John O'Meara thought he was writing about the maelstrom off Norway. He could well have been referring to Corryvreckan which was a lot nearer to hand. Corryvreckan received many other reports over the centuries. Monro writes in 1549:

> *Betwixt thir twa iyles ther runnes ane streame, above the power of all sailing and rowing, with infinit dangers, callit Corybrekan. This stream is aught myle lang, quhilk may not be hantit bot be certain tyds.* (Monro, *A Description of the Western Isles of Scotland,* Birlinn, 1994)

> (Betwixt these two isles [Jura and Scarba] there runs a stream, above the power of all sailing and rowing, with infinite dangers, called Corybrekan. This stream is eight miles long, which may not be hantit [tried?] but be [at?] certain tides.)

Bishop Leslie compares the navigational hazards in the Isles:

> *Amang thir Iles . . . ar mony quick sandes, scharp rockis, and gret goufes ful of perrellous and deip dangeris, bot the worst, cruellest, and maist suspecte amang thame al, thay cal Corbreche; because within the space of a myle, it swallyis vp hail schipis, and throuch the violence, and vehement force of contrare working of the wais of the sey, quhen ilke streme stryues with vthir, drounes thame in the deip. Quha sailis frome thir Iles is verie radie to incur sik danger* (Dalrymple's translation in E. Cody (ed.), *Leslie's History of Scotland,* 1578)

> (Among these Isles . . . are many quicksands, sharp rocks, and great gulfs full of perilous and deep dangers, but the worst, cruellest, and most suspect among them all, they call Corryvreckan; because within the space of a mile, it swallows up whole ships, and through the violence, and vehement force of contrary working of the ways of the sea, when each stream strives with [each] other, drowns them in the deep. Who[ever] sails from these Isles is very ready to incur such danger)

Leslie also refers to the dangerous currents off the Mull of Kintyre:

> *The ground heir is maist plane, baith in pastoral and in cornes abundant. The boundes heirfra till Irland is only xvi. myles: bot lykwyse for the concurring of ye troublous ebbing and flowing of the Sey, surges, and wais with vthiris, is verie perilous to the seymen and marinelies.*

(The ground here is mostly flat, both in grazing and in corns abundant. The passage herefrom to Ireland is only 16 miles: but likewise for the concurring of the troubled ebbing and flowing of the Sea, surges, and waves [contending] with [each] other, is very perilous to the seamen and mariners.)

Pont(?) also describes Corryvreckan:

Betwixt it and Jura runns the most dangerous gulff called Coirrabreaggan. there can neither shipps gallies nor boatts goe nor saill between these two Ilands except it be in ane quarter of ane hour in respect of the strong streame of this gulff, Nor goe throw the samen unless it be ebbing or full sea. (Pont (?) in Macfarlane's Geographical Collections)

The name Corryvreckan is supposed to derive from the *coire* or cauldron of Brecan. We are more used to the word *coire* in the sense of a bowl-shaped depression in the hills or 'corrie'. Nevertheless it is used elsewhere on the west coast to describe dangerous pieces of water. There is Loch Corry at Kingairloch and in the Blaeu map of Islay we find the narrow stretch of water separating Orsay from the Rhinns is labelled Kory. Monro writes of Orsay:

It hath ane paroch kirke, and is verey guid for fishing, inhabit and manurit, with ane right dangerous kyle and stream callit Corey Garrache; na man dare enter in it bot at ane certain tyme of the tyde, or ellis he will perish. (Monro, *A Description of the Western Isles of Scotland*, Birlinn, 1994)

(It has a parish kirk, and is very good for fishing, inhabited and manured, with a right dangerous kyle (strait) and stream called Corey Garrache; no man dare enter in it but at a certain time of the tide, or else he will perish.)

The idea of a cauldron goes well with the image of a boiling sea. Martin Martin conjures this:

Between the north end of Jura, and the isle Scarba, lies the famous and dangerous gulf, called Cory Vrekan, about a mile in breadth; it yields an impetuous current, not to be matched anywhere about the isle of Britain. The sea begins to boil and ferment with the tide of flood, and resembles the boiling of a pot; and then increases gradually, until it appears in many whirlpools, which form themselves in sort of pyramids, and immediately after spout up as high as the mast of a little vessel, and at the same time make a loud report. These white waves run two leagues with the wind before they break; the sea continues to repeat these various motions from the beginning of the tide of flood, until it is more than half-flood, and then it decreases gradually until it hath ebbed about half an hour, and continues to boil till it is within an hour of low water. This boiling of the sea is not above a pistol-shot distant from the coast of Scarba Isle, where the white waves meet and spout up: they call it the Kaillach, i.e., an old hag; and they say that when she puts on her kerchief, i.e., the whitest waves, it is then reckoned fatal to approach her. Notwithstanding this great ferment of the sea, which brings up the least shell from the ground, the smallest fisher-boat may venture to cross this gulf at the last hour of the tide of flood, and at the last hour of the tide of ebb. (Martin Martin, *A Description of the Western Islands of Scotland*)

Corryvreckan was so well known that its reputation sometimes did more damage than the reality. Herbert Campbell quotes an advocate's opinion for the Duke of Argyll in 1713: '*on a ship cast as a wrack upon the lands of Duntroon wherein was found nothing but a cat, yet the men were not lost, but, foreseeing the hazard of a rough sea and being near the Gulf of Corriebreckan like to swallow them up, they escaped in the boat to the island of Jura and came thereafter to the ship hearing she was safe.* (H. Campbell, *The Genealogist* Vol 36, 1920)

The Rev. John Walker ends his long description of Corryvreckan by stating: '*The Inhabitants [say] that when the Whirlpool is in its Fury its Attraction extends to a great Distance, which renders it dangerous for any Vessel to enter the Sound. But for above an Hour at High and Low Water, any Boat may pass near it, and even over it, with Safety.*' (In McKay, *Walker's Report on the Hebrides*, 1764 and 1771)

We also have an interesting comment by Lhuyd which raises the possibility of changing sea levels in the Firth of Lorn: '*Dwvsker (i.e. Black Rock) halfway betwixt Cloch[an] Swyl and Myl was scarce visible 60 years since, but is now seen much more frequent & a bigger bulk & so there are diverse other Rocks.* (J.L. Campbell & D. Thomson, *Edward Lhuyd in the Scottish Highlands*)

Campbell thought this was Dubhsgeir north of Eilean nan Caorach off Seil Island. We can assume Lhuyd had his attention drawn to it as something rather remarkable and certainly a lowering of sea-level that was visible over just 60 years would be of great significance. Lhuyd was writing at the end of the seventeenth century during the 'seven ill years' when Scotland suffered appalling weather. Were some climatic changes taking place? Unfortunately, with one piece of evidence we can do no more than speculate but I have often wondered about the possibility of changing sea-levels along the west coast. This need not be because of a general change in mean sea-level; it could be caused by changing tidal patterns which create a greater or lesser tidal range, shift or deposit sand. In this context we can also note those islands with the name Oronsay or similar. This comes from the Norse word for a dry or tidal island which leads on to the question of why Orsay, off Islay, once earned this name. The passage by Monro which is quoted above could be interpreted as implying access by foot at certain times.

Certainly western waters had a reputation for being stormy. Government was always wary of the expense of losing a capital ship. On 27 October 1615 James VI wrote members of the Privy Council of Scotland to the effect that now that the rebellion in the Isles was over his ship should be returned:

> *oure shippe can have no worthie imployment in those seas this tyme of the*
> *yeare (being unfitt to chace small boitis), and utherwyse may be subject to*
> *manifest dainger in those tempestuous, narrow, shallow, and rockie*
> *wateris . . . Bot, gif ye think thair remayneth as yit sufficient employment*
> *for some vessell of ware, we ar contented that ye reteyne our pinnace, which*
> *amangis those Iles will now be the fitter of the two.* (Register of the Privy
> Council, vol X, p 756)

Waggoners

Towards the end of the sixteenth century Lucas Waghenaer published the first of a succession of pilot-guides that became so successful that the word *waggoner* passed into the English language as an everyday term to describe such a book. The first edition includes a general map of Europe, dated 1583, which marks Rockall to the west of the Outer Hebrides. By this time Dutch and other seamen must have had more than a nodding acquaintance with western Scottish waters. Further editions rapidly followed and although the first edition contained nothing for the west coast of Scotland later editions included both text and chart for the Hebrides.

W. J. Blaeu produced an English-language version called *The Light of Navigation* (Amsterdam, 1612) which was closely modelled on the above. This included maps, views and sailing directions for the Western Isles, Orkney and Shetland. As the publisher recognised, knowledge of these furthermost corners of Europe was by no means complete: '*Whosoever travileth into these parts may help himself with that description which we have heere made, till such time as we can gette further and fuller knowledge of them.*' And what there was sounded daunting: '*He that falleth upon anie of these Ilands must looke well to him self, for the most part of them are inhabited by wilde and cruell men.*'

The guide includes sketches of some of the islands as they appeared to a boat at sea. These *look* worse than useless but to an anxious mariner, desperate for information about an unknown area with a poor reputation, they must have been greeted like manna from heaven. The map of the Hebrides is even worse – showing Uist both north **and** south of Lewis! In fact it is less accurate than those of Mercator, Ortelius or Nicolay – all of which had been available for years. But then, as now, material about a strange area could quickly find its way into print if no one else knew enough to contradict it. The text was just as bad. After a garbled and inaccurate list of the Hebrides we read the following:

Upon the east side of S. Kilda there is a good rode for a west, and northwest winde: this Iland lyeth by the other Ilands, whereof two are not verie great, on that which lyeth west you may see some houses standing, and those small Ilands lye eleven leagues distant west from the great Iland of Leeus. Upon the coast of Leeus there lye two faire great rockes, as if they were Ilands, they lye south and north and somewhat easterlyer and westerlyer from each other, about seven or eight leagues.

The southerlyest lye by three Ilands, but the northerlyest lye by eight small Ilands or rockes. You must understand that the Iland of Leeus is divided into manie peeces, through the which you may sayle to manie places. Leeus with his Ilands reacheth southsouthwest and south and by west about 29 leagues . . .

Iona, Ila, Mulla and Bragedul, are four of the greatest Ilands that lye on the west coast of Scotland, they lye close by the firme land, but there are manie havens and rivers, so that you may sayle in and round about them all. (W. J. Blaeu, *The Light of Navigation*, 1612)

It is apparent from both text and map that Dutch knowledge was neither complete nor wholly accurate. Obvious mistakes have been made. The name of the island of Skye has somehow been lost and replaced by that of one of its principal lochs – Bracadale. There are two extra islands to the north of Lewis which are presumably supposed to be a misplaced Uist. The elevations or 'landfalls' of the coastline as viewed from the sea are pretty rough and ready and it is doubtful that they would have been much use to a weatherbeaten mariner in difficult conditions. No matter; it was something, and in an unknown situation, or in stormy waters, we will all grasp at the spars of someone else's information, however inadequate.

In the Dartmouth collection of the National Maritime Museum, Greenwich, there is a map of north-east Ireland executed by an unknown author about 1602. This is of interest because one of the principal features of the map is the depiction of fleets of West Highland galleys raiding the coasts of Ireland. The text builds on the same theme:

The Description of the Scottishe coastes and out Isles of Scotland affronting the Irishe; and of the fleetes of Shippes and Gallies, or rather Skulles of open boates, and woodden Barges, is onlie to shewe the frequent and usualle navigations of those wilde beggers the Redshankes alonge the Irish coastes to robbe and spoile . . .

The usualle parada of the fleetes of the Redshankes of Cantyre and those out Iles of Scotland when they meane with 2 or 3000 uppon a suddeine to fall uppon Ulster by west of the Banne is the Raughlines . . . The usualle Parada of the Redshankes fleetes when they designe to fall uppon the Clandeboyes is the Mulle of Gallowaye or the Isles of Arranne . . . (National Maritime Museum, Dartmouth Collection, p 49, Map 25)

The Spanish word *parada* seems to have here the meaning of a rendezvous or meeting-point. If the Highlanders intended to raid west of the River Bann then they assembled at Rathlin. If they intended travelling down the east coast to Clandeboyes then they met at the Mull of Galloway or Arran.

The Hebrides do register in other seventeenth-century charts, if not always with the detail or originality we might like. They appear in two charts of Robert Dudley whose famous sea atlas, *Dell'Arcano del Mare*, was first published in 1646 and reissued in 1661. Dudley was particularly fortunate in his choice of engraver Lucini, whose elegant and simple line helped him produce charts that were clear and visually attractive.

One shows the east coast of Britain and the north-west coast of Scotland from Ardnamurchan to Cape Wrath. The other shows Ireland and the Argyllshire coastline south of Ardnamurchan. This latter map gives a clue to the cartographic line of descent since it includes the caption *I(sole) Hebrides nominata in Inghilese Redshankes* (Hebridean islands, called in English 'red-shanks'). Despite the ambiguities caused by translation from a Scottish context to an Italian publication we can recognise here the shades of John Elder.

Grenville Collins, a famous English chart-maker of the late seventeenth century, did produce a general map of Scotland but none specifically for the north-west coast. However the fact that the area was no longer regarded as impossibly remote is suggested by the work of continental chartmakers. The Frenchman, Bellin, produced beautiful coloured charts of the islands, including Rockall. The Dutchman, Van Keulen, presented the Hebrides in a novel way, with south at the top of the page. In the 1770s, Murdo Mackenzie, an Orcadian, produced the first really detailed sea-charts of the west coast of Scotland. On these he marked depths and safe anchorages and with his work we move into the modern age. Marine charts, like maps, were working documents. What makes some of the old weather-beaten copies so intriguing, in contrast to the crisp library versions, is that they may include notes and additions by former owners. They almost become manuscripts.

As an example of the sort of extra detail which some manuscript maps may offer we have Stobie's map of Trotternish in Skye dated to 1764. By Lachasay, in the north of the peninsula there is the following note: '*At A. Tytallm the Ruins of a Large House below ground Inhabited of old in times of War.*' This site is also referred to by Martin Martin: '*There are several little stone houses, built underground, called earth-houses, which served to hide a few people and their goods in time of war. The entry to them was on the sea or river side. There is one of them in the village Lachsay.*' (Martin Martin, *A Description of the Western Islands of Scotland*)

Forbes explains Stobie's name for the site in his book, *Place-Names of Skye*, where he refers to such a house as *tigh-fo-thalamh* or 'house underground'. It is fully described in the RCAHMS Inventory for the Outer Isles (No 556) where it is called Tigh Talamhain.

Such earth-houses or souterrains are relatively common in the islands. Monro describes something similar in Uist in 1549: '*Into this north heid of Ywst ther is sundrie covis and holes in the earth, coverit with heddir above, quhilk fosters maney rebellis in the countrey of the north heid of Ywst.*' (Monro, A Description of the Western Isles of Scotland, Birlinn, 1994) (In this north head of Uist there is sundry caves and holes in the earth, covered with heather above, which fosters many rebels in the country of the north head of Uist.)

And Pennant writes of Islay:

> *In various parts of this neighbourhood are scattered small holes, formed in the ground, large enough to hold a single man in a sitting posture: the top is covered with a broad stone, and that with earth: into these unhappy fugitives took shelter after a defeat, and drawing together sods, found a temporary concealment from enemies* (T. Pennant, *A Tour in Scotland and Voyage to the Hebrides*, 1772)

Monro, Martin, Stobie and Pennant offer an extended use, and history, for what otherwise might be regarded simply as a prehistoric monument.

Unknown islands

The seas harbour many islands, real and imagined. The North Atlantic has its fair share of mystery islands and they surface periodically in the literature of travel. There is a story in Macfarlane's Geographical Collections of Macneill of Barra looking for one. When he failed to find it he took a spoil from Ireland and returned home.

> *The Inhabitants theroff are verie antient Inhabitants and the Superior or Laird of Barray is called Rorie McNeill. he is sex or sevin score of years as himself did say. This ancient man in tyme of his youth being a valiant and stout man of warr and hearing from skippers that oftymes were wont to travell to ane Illand which the Inhabitants of the Illand alledged this McNeill and his predecessors should be their Superiors. which Illand is sein oftymes from the tope of the mountaines of Barray.*
>
> *This Rorie hearing oftymes the same newes reported to him and to his predecessors, he fraughted a shipe but nowayes could find the Illand, at last was driven to Ireland on the West syd theroff. And took up a Spreath, and returned home therefter.* (Macfarlane's Geographical Collections)

Martin Martin tells us that: '*The natives of Islay, Colonsay, and Jura say that there is an island lying to the south-west of these isles, about the distance of a day's sailing, for which they have only a bare tradition.*' (Martin Martin, *A Description of the Western Islands of Scotland.*)

He then goes on to give an account of this mysterious island, supposedly from the master of an English vessel who had landed on it.

It is easy to imagine how distant sightings of Rockall in earlier centuries might give rise to legends like this. Rockall first appears in Waghenaer's map dated 1583. It may have been known to the inhabitants of St Kilda long before this. Martin refers to: '*Rokol, a small rock sixty leagues to the westward of St Kilda; the inhabitants of this place call it Rokabarra.*'

Apparently:

a company of French and Spaniards . . . lost their ship at Rokol in the year 1686, and came in, in a pinnace to St Kilda, where they were plentifully supplied with barly-bread, butter, cheese, solan geese, eggs, etc. Both seamen and inhabitants were barbarians one to another, the inhabitants speaking only the Irish tongue, to which the French and the Spaniards were altogether strangers; upon their landing they pointed to the west, naming Rokol to the inhabitants, and after that, they pointed downward with their finger, signifying the sinking and perishing of their vessel; they showed them Rokol in the sea map, far west off St Kilda. (Martin Martin, *A Voyage to St Kilda*, 1698)

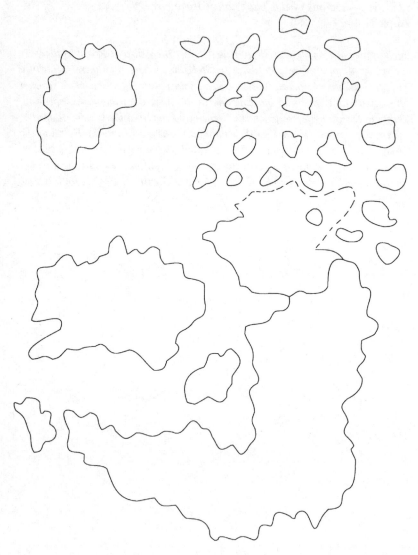

Fig. 1. The British Isles c. AD 1000 from British Library:
Cotton Tiberius B. V. f. 56v

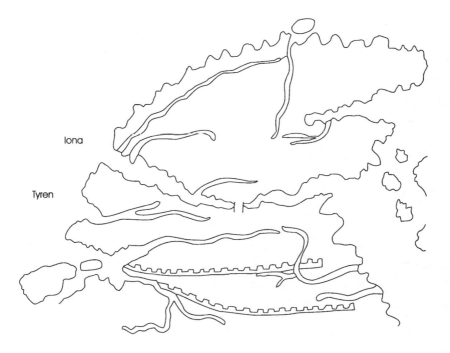

Iona

Tyren

Fig. 2. Scotland c. AD 1250 from British Library:
Cotton Claudius D. VI. f. 12v

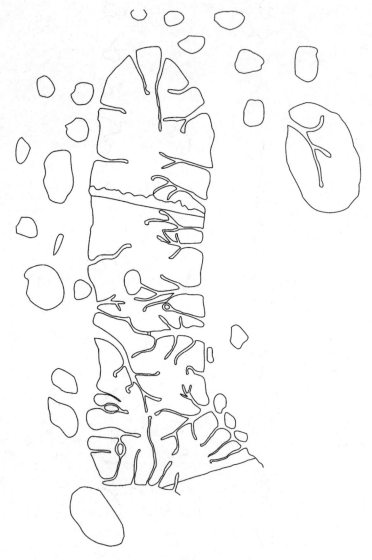

Fig. 3. Scotland c. AD 1360 from Bodleian Library
MS Gough Gen. Top. 16

Fig. 4. Scotland by Lily, AD 1546

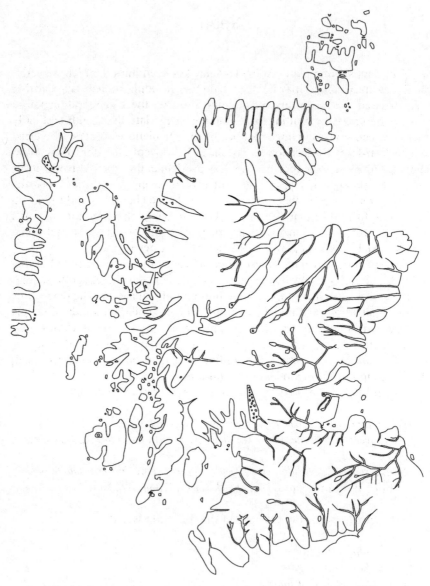

Fig. 5. Scotland by Nowell, c. AD 1565 from British Library:
Cotton Domitian A XVIII

Chapter 8

Sport

Hunting, shooting and fishing have always been important leisure activities in Britain. It may be that we no longer indulge in the slaughter that characterised our ancestors but angling remains the biggest participatory sport. The craze for hunting and shooting in the late nineteenth and early twentieth centuries saw huge swathes of the Highland landscape converted from sheep-farm to deer-forest. As sheep had swept all before them from about 1770 so now, as they became less profitable, they were driven out for deer. The process of change falls outside the scope of this book but the context is relevant. People have been coming to the Highlands and Islands to hunt and fish for many centuries. Unfortunately the accounts of such travellers are more often about the prey than the area but we still come across valuable evidence, which is what this chapter reviews.

We have a great deal of sculptural evidence for the importance of hunting in Dark Age and mediaeval times. Prey included birds, fish, seals, otters, boar, deer and wolves. Some of these were hunted individually but the deer-hunts in particular were great social gatherings where literally hundreds of people participated. The deer were driven into deer-traps known as elerigs – an element which survives in several place-names. I have dealt with deer-drives in *The Small Isles* so here I will confine myself to other quotations which demonstrate the various methods of hunting.

Fordun implies that certain islands were reserved for hunting:

Little Cumbrae, renowned for sport, but thinly inhabited . . .
Dura, twenty-four miles long, with few inhabitants, but affording very good sport . . .
Rum, a wooded and hilly island, with excellent sport, but few inhabitants.
(John of Fordun, *Chronicle of the Scottish Nation*, c. 1380)

In 1549 Monro speaks of hunting in the following islands:

Soay – *hunting games*
Skye – *fair hunting games*
Islay – *faire games of hunting*
Mull – *verey fair hunting games*
Scalpay – *ane faire hunting forrest*
Arran – *good for hunting*

– as well as describing the *timchioll* or deer-drive in Rum and Jura. The latter island may have been favoured by the kings of Scotland.

Upone the westsyde above the sea there is a number of great Coves that is within the same alse whyte as if they wer fylled and laid with Lyme, and are lyk vaults of Stone and lyme. And the King and all his howshold wold come therintill, they wold gett lodgeing and chambers therin. And in tyme of stormie weather and in tyme of great tempest of snow the deir doth lodge in these Coves. The McDonalds and the Mcleans in ancient tyme, when they wer wont to come to Jura to hunt, they did lodge in these Coves with their companies. Pont (?) in Macfarlane's Geographical Collections

Otters were prized for their skins. Dean Monro writes of Harris:

In this countrey of Harrey, northwart betwixt it and the Lewis, are maney forrests, quherein are aboundance deir, bot not grate quantitie, verey faire hunting games without any woodes, with infinite slaughter of otters and macttickes. This ile has neather wolfes, taides, nor edders in it. (D. Monro, *A Description of the Western Isles of Scotland*, Birlinn, 1994)

(In this country of Harris, northwards betwixt it and the Lewis, are many forests, wherein are abundance [of] deer, but not [of] great quantity (size), very fair hunting games without any woods, with infinite slaughter of otters and martins. This isle has neither wolves, toads, nor adders in it.)

And of Ellan Hurte or Iffurt which RW Munro identifies with Eilean Iubhard at the mouth of Loch Sealg:

Ellan Hurte, with manurit land, guid to pasture and schielling of store, with faire hunting of ottars out of thair bouries. (D. Monro, *A Description of the Western Isles of Scotland*, Birlinn, 1994)

(Eilean Hurte, with manured land, good to pasture and shieling of store (cattle), with fair hunting of otters out of their burrows.)

Bishop Leslie illustrates the draw of hunting as a social gathering:

Ouer all with ws in the hichest mountanis Gret hartis are sa frequent, that commounlie in a solemne hunting . . . now fyue hundir, now viii. hundir, sum tyme 1000 at ane tyme ar slayne: for than throuch the cry of men and the barking of litle dogs round about, the space, sum tyme of x., sum tymes of xx. myles and mair, [they are driven] within the narrow boundes of a certane valley, quhair the Lordes and noble men (take up their seats). Out of that place the hundes being hunted, arrowis schott, jaiuelinis castne, and hounting cloubs: and with al kynde of armour they sett vpon the hartis, not without gret danger baith of men and dogs. (Dalrymple's translation in E Cody (ed.), *Leslie's History of Scotland,* 1578)

(Overall with us in the highest mountains great harts are so frequent, that commonly in a solemn hunting . . . now five hundred, now eight hundred, sometimes 1000 at a time are slain: for then through the cry of men and the barking of little dogs round about, the space, sometimes of 10, sometimes of 20 miles and more, [they are driven] within the narrow bounds of a certain valley, where the Lords and noblemen (take up their seats). Out of that place the hounds being hunted, arrows shot, javelins cast, and hunting clubs: and with all kinds of armour they set upon the harts, not without great danger both of men and dogs.)

The Latin uses the word 'sedes' for the positions of the huntsmen. This is literally 'seats' and the word is appropriate because that is what they were known as in old hunting parlance. Leslie was speaking from personal experience:

Bot this is worthie of Rememberance, quhilke our selfes sawe, quhen we war present, of thir summe ar quhais fatt is funde ten inches thick, of quhilke sorte principallie ar in Argyle. (Dalrymple's translation in E. Cody (ed.), *Leslie's History of Scotland,* 1578)

(But this is worthy of remembrance, which ourselves saw, when we were present, of these some are whose fat is found ten inches thick, of which sort principally are in Argyll.)

Of the hunting dogs are sindrie kyndes, and sindrie natures, of quhilkes the first kynde is gretter than ane tuelfmoneth alde calfe; and this sort commonlie huntis the gretter beistes, as ze sall sie, athir the harte or the wolfe. (Dalrymple's translation in E Cody (ed.), *Leslie's History of Scotland,* 1578)

(Of the hunting dogs are sundry kinds, and sundry natures, of which the first kind is greater than a twelvemonth old calf; and this sort commonly hunts the greater beasts, as ye shall see, either the hart [stag] or the wolf.)

In 1769 Pennant writes of Castle Gordon, seat of the Duke of Gordon:

I saw also here a true Highland greyhound, which is now become very scarce: it was of a very large size, strong, deep chested, and covered with very long and rough hair. This kind was in great vogue in former days, and used in vast numbers at the magnificent stag chases, by the powerful chieftains. (T. Pennant, *A Tour in Scotland,* 1769)

The greater lords of the Highlands and Islands had to preserve their deer for hunting by creating reserves and retaining foresters to protect them: '*one of the Mcleods principals forrests which is called Oysserfaill in Irish and in English Oysserfeild on the southsyde of the parish of Loghes, wherein there are bigg mountaines with Innumerable Deir.*' (Pont(?) in Macfarlane's Geographical Collections, vol II)

If they did not then human competition soon drove them out. In Kintyre this seems to have happened before the end of the sixteenth century: '*There was abundance of deir in this mountaine of ancient tyme but now there is none to be sein nether in this Mountaine nor in the rest of the mountaines and lands of Kintyre but foxes and Raes whereoff there is abundance in this countrie* (Pont(?) in Macfarlane's Geographical Collections, vol II).

Pennant gives credit for this to the Duke of Argyll: '*The duke also shows much humanity in . . . permitting his tenants, in the places of his estates where stags inhabit, to destroy them with impunity; resigning that part of the ancient chieftains magnificence, rather than beasts of chase should waste the bread of the poor.* (T. Pennant, *A Tour in Scotland and Voyage to the Hebrides,* 1772)

But in reality he may just have inherited a situation he could not reverse. Population pressure was always going to be heavy in a fertile area like Kintyre.

Taylor, the poet, writes in great detail on hunting in the east central Highlands in the early seventeenth century. Firstly he describes the dress code:

For once in the yeere, which is the whole moneth of August, and sometimes part of September, many of the nobility and gentry of the kingdome (for their pleasure) doe come into these highland countries to hunt, where they doe conforme themselves to the habite of the Highland-men, who for the most part, speake nothing but Irish; and in former time were those people which were called the Red-shankes. Their habite is shooes with but one sole apiece; stockings (which they call short hose) made of a warm stuffe of divers colours, which they call Tartane: as for breeches, many of them, nor their forefathers, never wore any, but a jerkin of the same stuffe that their hose is of, their garters being bands or wreathes of hay or straw, with a plead about their shoulders, which is a mantle of divers colours, much finer and lighter stuffe then their hose, with blue flat caps on their heads, a handkerchiefe knit with two knots about their necke; and thus are they attyred. Now their weapons are long bowes and forked arrowes, swords and targets, harquebusses, muskets, durks, and Loquhabor-axes. With these armes I found many of them armed for the hunting. As for their attire, any man of what degree soever that comes amongst them, must not disdaine to weare it: for if they doe, then they will disdaine to hunt, or willingly to bring in their dogges: but if men be kind unto them, and be in their habit; then are they conquered with kindnesse, and the sport will be plentifull. This was the reason that I found so many noblemen and gentlemen in those shapes.

Taylor himself must have worn Highland dress because he speaks of Lord Mar 'having put me into that shape'. The convention of adopting Highland dress was universally maintained because Taylor specifically comments: '*all and every man in generall in one habit, as if Licurgus had beene there, and made lawes of equality.* (John Taylor, *The Pennyles Pilgrimage*, 1618)

The adoption of Highland clothing has a long history. Our most famous early example is the Norwegian king, Magnus Bareleg, who annexed the Hebrides and Kintyre in 1098:

So men say, that when king Magnus came from western piracy, he had much those fashions and manner of dress that were usual in the western lands; and so had many of his men. They went bare-legged in the street, and had short tunics, and also [short] over-cloaks. Then men called him Magnus Bareleg or Barethigh. (Heimskringla, Magnus Bareleg's Saga, in Anderson, *Early Sources*, II, p 118)

We can only speculate as to Magnus's reasons for adopting Highland habit. Was it military utility, comfort, sympathy or political expediency? The evidence from later commentators suggests that it was the sort of policy that would have gone down well with the locals – and perhaps eased the process of conquest.

The desire to appear as one with the Highlanders may lie behind the purchase of the following items for King James V in the Lord High Treasurer's accounts for August 1538. In the twin cultures of Scotland, clothing could have political and cultural significance:

Item, in the first, for ii elnis ane quarter elne of variant cullorit velvet to be the Kingis grace ane schort heland coit . . .
Item, for iii elnis of heland tertane to be hois to the Kingis grace . . .
Item, for xv elnis of holland claith to be syde heland sarkis to the Kingis grace
(Accounts of the Lord High Treasurer of Scotland, Vol VI, p 436)

(Item, firstly, for 2 ells [a measure of length] (and) a quarter ell of varicoloured velvet to be (for) the King's Grace a short Highland coat . . .
Item, for 3 ells of Highland tartan to be hose [either stockings or trousers] for the King's Grace . . .
Item, for 15 ells of Dutch cloth to be long Highland shirts for the King's Grace.)

The Highlanders themselves, although they might have to adapt to Lowland customs when they went to court, were quick to resume the Highland habit on their return:

> gif thair Princes, or of thair Nobilitie, visit the kingis court, thay aray thame selfes of a courtlie maner, elegantlie, quhen thay returne to thayr cuntrey, casteng aff al courtlie decore, in al haist, thay cleith thame selfes of thair cuntrey maner, excepte thay wil incur al manis danger and hauie offence. (Dalrymple's translation in E Cody (ed.), *Leslie's History of Scotland*, 1578)

> (If their Princes, or their Nobility, visit the king's court, they array themselves in a courtly manner, elegantly. When they return to their country, casting off all courtly habit, in all haste, they clothe themselves in their country manner, otherwise they will incur all men's danger and heavy offence.)

Edmund Burt, ever down-to-earth and sympathetic, viewed the Highlanders' attachment to their ancient dress as founded in practicality. Whereas most outsiders simply criticised those Highland customs they did not favour, Burt took the trouble to understand the reasons for them. Nevertheless, he could also see that Highland obstinacy was sometimes due to prejudice as much as practicality:

> The whole people are fond and tenacious of the Highland clothing, as you may believe by what is here to follow.
> Being, in a wet season, upon one of my peregrinations, accompanied by a Highland gentleman, who was one of the clan through which I was passing, I observed the woman to be in great anger with him about something that I did not understand: at length, I asked him wherein he had offended them? Upon this question he laughed, and told me his great-coat was the cause of their wrath; and that their reproach was, that he could not be contented with the garb of his ancestors, but was degenerated into a Lowlander, and condescended to follow their unmanly fashions. (Edmund Burt, *Letters from a Gentleman in the North of Scotland*, late 1720s)

Faujas de Saint Fond gives another instance of this fidelity to costume:

> Mr Macdonald, who accompanied me from Oban with the intention of visiting the isle of Staffa, had no sooner reached Aros than he changed his dress. He had been in English regimentals, but upon arriving here he opened his portmanteau, and to my great surprise, in about an hour after, appeared in the complete habiliment of the inhabitants of the isles; plaid, jacket, kilt, feathered bonnet, buskin-hose, dirk in the waist-belt; nothing was forgotten. I

could scarcely recognise him in this costume. He told me, that it was the garb of his fathers, that he never appeared in any other when in these islands, and that the wearing of it was a mark of attachment to his fellow-countrymen, with which they were much pleased. (Faujas de Saint Fond, *A journey through England and Scotland to the Hebrides in 1784*)

He also tells what an effect this had on their two Hebridean guides:

They were delighted and proud to see a man of distinction dressed like themselves; and showed their satisfaction by coming up to Mr Macdonald, and, with a smile on their faces, telling him in their expressive language, that they would follow him to the world's end. (Faujas de Saint Fond, *A journey through England and Scotland to the Hebrides in 1784*)

After describing the costume Taylor then describes the hunt:

The manner of the hunting is this. Five or six hundred men doe rise early in the morning, and they doe disperse themselves divers wayes, and 7, 8, or 10 miles compasse they doe bring or chase in the Deere in many heards, (two, three, or foure hundred in a heard) to such or such a place as the Noblemen shall appoint them; then when day is come, the Lords and Gentlemen of their Companies, doe ride or goe to the said places, sometimes wading up to the middles through bournes and rivers: and then they being come to the place, doe lye downe on the ground, till those foresaid Scouts which are called the Tinckhell do bring downe the Deere: But as the Proverbe sayes of a bad Cooke, so these Tinkhell men doe lick their owne fingers; for besides their bowes and arrowes which they carry with them, wee can heare now and then a harguebuse or a musquet goe off, which they doe seldome discharge in vaine: Then after wee had stayed three houres or thereabouts, wee might perceive the Deere appeare on the hills round about us, (their heads making a shew like a wood) which being followed close by the Tinkhell, are chased downe into the valley where wee lay; then all the valley on each side being way-laid with a hundred couple of strong Irish Grey-hounds, they are let loose as occasion serves upon the heard of Deere, that with Dogges, Gunnes, Arrowes, Durks and Daggers, in the space of two houres fourescore fat Deere were slaine, which after are disposed of some one way and some another, twenty or thirty miles, and more then enough left for us to make merry withall at our Rendevouze. (John Taylor, *The Pennyles Pilgrimage*, 1618)

Hunting therefore required travel; of the participants to the forest, of the royals, the aristocrats, their guests and servants, the beaters and bearers, the dogs and their handlers. And after it was all over the quarry had to be cut up and dispersed to those regarded worthy of receipt. Some quotations from the

Pursemaster's accounts for 1540 will establish how game and other luxury goods travelled as gifts from the Highlands to the Lowlands:

> *Item gevin the samyn daye* [26 March] *to tua servandis of the lard of Glenurquhartis that brocht venasone and aquavite to the kingis graice, x s . . .*
> *Item the samyn daye gevin to ane servand of James Campbellis that brocht venasoun to the kingis graice, x s.*
> *Item gevin the xxvii daye of Marche to ane servand of my lord of Ergalys that brocht venasoun and aquavite to the kingis graice, xiiii s . . .*
> *Item gevin the samyn daye* [28 March] *to ane servand of the lard of Lawmontis that brocht aquavite to the kingis graice, xxii s . . .*
> *Item gevin the samyn daye* [3 May] *to ane servand of the lard of Glenurquhartis that brocht aquavite to the kingis graice, xxii s.*

> (Item, given the same day to two servants of the Laird of Glenurquhart's who brought venison and aquavite [spirits, probably whisky] to the King's Grace, 10 shillings . . .
> Item, the same day given to a servant of James Campbell's who brought venison to the King's Grace, 10 shillings.
> Item, given the 27th day of March to a servant of my Lord of Argyll's who brought venison and aquavite to the King's Grace, 14 shillings . . .
> Item, given the same day to a servant of the Laird of Lamont's who brought aquavite to the King's Grace, 22 shillings . . .
> Item, given the same day to a servant of the Laird of Glenurquhart's that brought aquavite to the King's Grace, 22 shillings).
> (Pursemaster's Accounts, Scottish History Society, Miscellany X,)

It seems likely that shortly before the arrival of these delicacies there had been a great deer hunt in Argyll and that the leading men of Clan Campbell, and other familes such as the Lamonts of Cowal, were sending diplomatic gifts to the king. March was a difficult time of year as far as food stocks were concerned. Most of last season's crops had been consumed. Domestic animals were weak and thin after the winter. Wild game would have been a welcome addition to any diet and the pursemaster's accounts for this period are full of references to fish (both fresh and saltwater), shellfish, eels, lampreys, wildfowl (partridges, swans and particularly geese), birds' eggs and 'wild mete' which probably included a variety of smaller game. It seems that at this time of year the king's highways were relatively busy with the great and the good sending food parcels to court. Diplomatic exchanges took place within as well as between countries and in a world of scarce resources food would always be welcome. The Highlands played their part in this. Almost stereotypically their contribution was venison and whisky.

Sport made a much greater economic contribution to mediaeval life than it does today. The Highlands and Islands contained a huge area of land with a

great many birds and wild animals. In the past these were an important
resource and the pursuit of them played a large part in rural social life. We see
the legacy in sculpture, poetry, place-names and travellers' accounts.

Great deer hunts still took place as late as the mid-seventeenth century – as
the following quotation from the *Wardlaw Manuscript* makes clear. The year
is 1655 and Scotland is under the jurisdiction of the Commonwealth which
maintained a military garrison in Inverness. The earl of Seaforth was
technically a prisoner in the citadel but had obtained leave, under bail, from
Governor Miles Man. The author of the manuscript, Mr James Fraser, was
apparently one of the hunting party:

> *Seaforth . . . went to visit his friends the length of Kintail; and resolving to
> keep a hunting be ther way in the Forrest of Monnair, he prevaild with the
> Master and Tutor of Lovat to goe along with him, Captain Thomas Fraser
> his brother, Hugh Fraser of Struy . . . and with them the flower of all the
> youth in our country, with a 100 pretty fellowes more. We traveled through
> Strathglaish and Glenstrafarrar to Loch Monnair. The Tutor pitcht his tent
> upon the north bank of the river, and Struy his tent upon the south. Next day
> we got sight of 6 or 700 deere, and sportt off hunting fitter for kings than
> country gentlemen. The 4 days we tarried there, what is it that could cheere
> and recreat mens spirits but was gone about, jumping, arching, shooting,
> throwing the barr, the stone, and all manner of manly exercise imaginable,
> and every day new sport; and for entertainment our baggage was well
> furnished of beefe, mutton, foule, fishes, fat venison, a very princly camp, and
> all manner of liquors. The 5 day we convoyed Seaforth over the mountain in
> sight of Kintail, and so returned home, with the Master of Lovat, a very
> pretty train of gallant gentlemen, that Mr Hill and Man, two Englishmen
> who were in company, declared that in all their travels they never had such
> brave divertisment, and if they should relate it in England it would be
> concluded meer rants and incredible. (Chronicles of the Frasers, *Wardlaw
> Manuscript*, Scottish History Society)

Great deer-hunts seem to have died out, for reasons that have not yet been
explored. A number of factors may have been involved including the Union of
Crowns and the fact that the Scottish royal family moved south to London.
Pennant offered his own explanation: '*But hunting, meetings, among the great
men, were often the preludes to rebellion; for under that pretence they collected great
bodies of men without suspicion, which at length occasioned an Act of Parliament
prohibiting such dangerous assemblies.*' (Pennant, *A Tour in Scotland 1769*)

It is unlikely to have been simply a decline in blood-lust. The Scottish
aristocracy retained their game reserves, but hunting became more individual.

With these hunts there was a whole paraphernalia of customs. We can still
see some of the huntsman's equipment on mediaeval carved stones in the
Highlands and Islands. There are good examples on the Macmillan cross at

Kilmory, Knapdale, and on a panel of the Macleod wall-tomb at Rodel in Harris, dated to 1528. Martin Martin describes the right of the forester to the hunting costume of a new chief: '*The chieftain is usually attended with a numerous retinue when he goes a hunting the deer, this being his first specimen of manly exercise. All his clothes, arms, and hunting equipage are, upon his return from the hills, given to the forester, according to custom.*' (Martin Martin, *A Description of the Western Islands of Scotland*)

He also writes specifically of Harris:

> *There are abundance of deer in the hills and mountains here, commonly called the forest; which is 18 miles in length from east to west: the number of deer computed to be in this place is at least 2000; and there is none permitted to hunt there without a licence from the steward to the forester. There is a particular mountain, and above a mile of ground surrounding it, to which no man hath access to hunt, this place being reserved for Macleod himself, who when he is disposed to hunt, is sure to find game enough there.* (Martin Martin, *A Description of the Western Islands of Scotland*)

The Macleod family claimed Norse descent and had been the principal clan in Lewis, Harris and much of Skye for hundreds of years. Their practices, and this reserve, may be very ancient. Old hunting customs are very tenacious.

Deer-hunts on the grand scale may have become extinct but hunting continued on an individual basis as the normal sporting activity of those who could afford a gun. Pennant gives rather a tall story about using bagpipes to lull stags into a false sense of security: '*I have been assured that they are greatly delighted with the sound of music, and that they will be tempted to remain in the deepest attention: that they are frequently shot, allured to their destruction by the melody of the pipe.*' (Pennant, *A Tour in Scotland 1769*)

Faujas de Saint Fond describes climbing Ben More with the son of Maclean of Torloisk:

> *This young man, who was dressed in the Hebridian costume, immediately presented us with fowling-pieces, saying, that he had excellent dogs, and that we should certainly find some black-cocks; for he could not imagine that we should wish to climb so rugged a mountain, for any other purpose than the pleasures of the chase, which he passionately loved himself.* (Faujas de Saint Fond, *A journey through England and Scotland to the Hebrides in 1784*)

Seals, seabirds and wildfowl were also pursued for their skins, oil and meat. Since guns were expensive to buy and maintain the natives devised all sorts of traps and snares. Martin Martin wrote of Harris: '*The amphibia here are otters and seals; the latter are ate by the meaner sort of people, who say they are very nourishing. The natives take them with nets, whose ends are tied by a rope to the strong alga, or sea-ware, growing on the rocks.'* (Martin Martin, *A Description of the Western Islands of Scotland*)

The same two animals were still important a century later: '*Otters and Seals are swarming over the whole coast, and their skins and oil bring the merchants considerable profits at market.'* (Buchanan, *Travels in the Western Hebrides from 1782 to 1790*)

Heiskir was always famous for its seal catch:

> *There is a narrow channel between the island of Heiskir and one of the lesser islands, in which the natives formerly killed many seals in this manner: They twisted together several small ropes of horse-hair in form of a net, contracted at one end like a purse; and so by opening and shutting this hair net, these seals were caught in the narrow channel.* (Martin Martin, *A Description of the Western Islands of Scotland*)

On the western coast of Heiskir is the rock Eousmil:

> *it is still famous for the yearly fishing of seals there, in the end of October . . . I was told also that 320 seals, young and old, have been killed at one time in this place . . . The natives salt the seals with the ashes of burnt sea-ware, and say they are good food.* (Martin Martin, *A Description of the Western Islands of Scotland*)

By Loch Gruinord in Islay dogs were trained to help:

> *quherin runs the water of Gyinord, with high sandey bankes, upon the quhilk bankes upon the sea lyes infinit selccheis, whilkis are slain with doges lernt to the same effect.*

> (wherein runs the water of Gruinord, with high sandy banks, upon the which banks upon the sea lie infinite seals, which are slain with dogs learned [taught] to the same effect.)
> (Monro, *A Description of the Western Isles of Scotland*, Birlinn, 1994)

As they were for puffins in St Kilda: '*The puffins hatch under ground, and are easily found out by a hole dug by their beaks. They have dogs trained up for this purpose: these are a species of terrier or spaniel. The women are much exercised in fowling; and the dogs find them out, and bring the birds of their own accord to the tops of the rocks.'* (Buchanan, *Travels in the Western Hebrides from 1782 to 1790*)

Even the wild sheep of the Flannan Isles were hunted:

> *infinit wyld sheipe therein . . . bot M'Cloyd of the Lewis, at certaine tymes in the zeir, sendis men in, and huntis and slayis maney of thir sheipe.*

(infinite wild sheep therein . . . but McLeod of the Lewis, at certain times in the year, sends men in, and hunts and slays many of these sheep.) (Monro, *A Description of the Western Isles of Scotland*, Birlinn, 1994)

Angling

The art of angling is very ancient and there is every reason to suppose that it is also ancient in the Highlands and Islands. What is difficult, is to distinguish between angling as a leisure activity and angling for necessity. The Highland economy was so marginal that extra protein was always welcome, whatever the catcher's precise intention. However it is perfectly possible that this was a leisure activity as well – even many centuries ago.

Monro writes of Lewis in 1549:

Ther is ane cove in this countrey quherein the sea fallis, and is twa fadome deepe at the ebb sea, and four faddom and maire at the full sea. Within this cove ther uses whytteins to be slain with huikes, verey maney haddocks, and men with their wands sitting upon the craiges of that cove, and lades and women also.

(There is a cave in this country wherein the sea falls, and is two fathom deep at the ebb sea, and four fathom and more at the full sea. Within this cave there uses whitings to be slain with hooks, very many haddocks, and men with their wands (rods) sitting upon the crags of that cave, and lads and women also.) (Monro, *A Description of the Western Isles of Scotland*, Birlinn, 1994)

Eels are commonly found in the lochs along the west coast and Pont(?) writes of Loch Etive:

And there is abundance of salmon fish slaine yearlie in this Logh and lykwayes ther is abundance of Eells, in that Lochediff which the men of the Countrey alleadges and perswade others that the saids Eells are alse bigg as ane horse with ane certane Incredible length, which I think not to be reported of, alwayes it is liklie to be true in respect none of the Countreymen dare hazard themselves in a boatt to slay the ells with lynes. They were wont to sie them slaine by ane ancient man, who had great practize and arte of the said trade; Ancient men of Mucarne and Beanderlogh the countreys which are on the South and Northsyde of that Logh reportit that this Ancient fisher of the Eells his lyne wherewith he did slay these bigg and exceeding long Eells were alse bigg in greatness as a mans finger, and that his hook was exceding bigg, and the Lyne whereon the hook did hang, was knitt all with feathers to hold

and keep itself uncutt from the eells to the length of twall inches or thereby And
so these Marvelous bigg eels were tane be the said Ancient fisher, and
thereafter he did slay them with another device made for the purpose.
And so the countreymen will not devyse anie Instruments to take these Eels
in respect of their bigness. Bot certane men of the countrey do take and slay
small Eels alse bigg as a mans thigh or thereby with a lyne als big as ones
finger. And there hook is very bigg. And when Eell is tane on the hook to the
land, they have a bigg crook of Iron or pikes made for that purpose. (Pont(?)
in Macfarlane's Geographical Collections, vol II)

Martin Martin writes of Loch Bruist, Bernera: '*There is likewise plenty of eels*
in this lake, which are easiest caught in September; and then the natives carry lights
with them in the nighttime to the rivulet running from the lake, in which the eels fall
down to the sea in heaps together. (Martin Martin, *A Description of the Western*
Islands of Scotland)
Nevertheless there is not a great deal of evidence that eels were much used
as a source of food. Pennant writes of Loch Tay: '*Of these species, the*
Highlanders abhor eels, and also lampries, fancying, from the form, that they
are too nearly related to serpents.' (Pennant, *A Tour in Scotland 1769*)
Salmon were always immensely important. As a result they were jealously
guarded by the landowner. If the landowner was new, or not in sympathy with
his local tenants, then they might band together to thwart him. Pont(?) writes
of the River Nant on the south side of Loch Etive: '*It is verie profitable and a*
pleasant river in tyme of harvest for its abundance of salmond at which tyme the
tennents and superiours of the Countrie, when the Laird of Calder is not in the
Countrie, will conveen and gather themselves togidder by night oftentimes, and slay
abundance and innumerable salmond fishes. And in the daytime also they doe slay
abundance of fish in all pairts of the Water.'
And of the nearby River Awe which was supposed to be as valuable as one
hundred marklands: '*It is alleadgit that this river is in rentall for ane hundreth*
merk lands of Lorne but it is not to be comparit to the lands in anie wayes, but
alwayes it is verie profitable and they use to slay abundance of salmond in this river
of Aw. (Pont(?) in Macfarlane's Geographical Collections, vol II)
Pont seems to have acquired a great deal of information about local
conditions on his travels. Writing of the River Shiel in Moidart he says:
'*And there is abundance of salmond fish slaine in this river yearlie when there is no*
great speats nor raine in the yeare but fair weather.' (Pont(?) in Macfarlane's
Geographical Collections, vol II)
Such information must have been acquired locally. If there was a lot of rain
then the salmon went swiftly upriver and were more difficult to take in any
quantity. If however the weather was good, (i.e. dry), the river would be
lower. The salmon would then congregate at the mouth of the river (or in
pools higher up) and be more easily caught – at least by net.
Writing of the country round Glen Urquhart on the west side of Loch Ness:

'*In the midle of this Countrey there is a fresh water Logh and abundance of fish are slaine with lynes in all tymes of the zeare.*' (Pont(?) in Macfarlane's Geographical Collections, vol II.) And of the eastern part of Islay: '*There is other manie fresh water Loghes in Ila full of great and bigg trowts and fresh water eels. There is one Logh in a mountaine in a Countrie called Beanlargi which is called Loghnabreak which is by interpretatione the trowt Logh. There is verie manie trouts in that Logh and neither spring water running nor sein goeing into that Logh, nor comeing out of it.*' (Pont(?) in Macfarlane's Geographical Collections, vol II)

The last sentence is about the puzzling absence of any streams in which the fish may spawn.

Richard Franck, a Cromwellian soldier stationed in the north about 1656–57, was a fanatical angler. Unfortunately, his book, *Northern Memoirs*, makes heavy reading. Unless he is writing specifically about catching fish his prose becomes florid and wearisome. Here is what he has to say about Machany Water in the parishes of Muthill and Blackford, Perthshire, where he obviously spent some pleasant hours with rod and line:

> *And here we cross the moor to Mockeny, whose limpid streams are pleasant beyond report, and her fords generally furnished with trout, as if nature had there designed to entertain the contemplative angler, in those liberal streams, where the artist in a storm may shelter himself under shady trees, elevated upon lofty mountains, over the melting amorous smiling banks; as if the boughs were barnicles, and ready to drop into the silent glittering streams, that glide softly along a delightful meadow; excepting here and there some small cataracts of water that tumble down a precipice of rocks, that encircles and surrounds great stones in the sandy foundation of this mystical Mockeny, whose glittering sholes are gently moved by the soft breathings of Zephyrus, that dash the smaller waves ashore, and discover to the angler the intricate angles of Mockeny, so that here we assume a poetick liberty, in some sort, to call Scotland Arcadia.*

Franck was almost writing an angling guide to Scotland. His dedication shows that he had been impressed by the country, or at least its angling potential:

> *But I'll do what I can in these northern tracts, to bring you a discovery of some of her rarities, whose solitary shades strike a damp to my pen, because to behold there such unexpected landskips, meanders and labyrinths (which I frequently met with) as exposed my resolution to a farther progress, whereby to discover all her northern gaieties that shin'd so splendidly in every fir-wood, as also in her lofty domineering hills, that over-top'd the submissive shady dales, and over-look'd the rapid torrents of rivers, and pretty purling gliding rivulets; where the polish'd rocks, and imbellish'd fortifications beyond belief, so surpriz'd my genius, that it puzzles me to report these remote curiosities.*

For you are to consider, sir, that the whole tract of Scotland is but one single series of admirable delights, notwithstanding the prejudicate reports of some men that represent it otherwise. For if eye-sight be argument convincing enough to confirm a truth, it enervates my pen to describe Scotland's curiosities, which properly ought to fall under a more elegant stile to range them in order for a better discovery. For Scotland is not Europe's umbra, as fictitiously imagined by some extravagant wits: No, it's rather a legible fair draught of the beautiful creation, drest up with polish'd rocks, pleasant savanas, flourishing dales, deep and torpid lakes, with shady fir-woods, immerg'd with rivers and gliding rivulets; where every fountain o'reflows a valley, and every ford superabounds with fish. Where also the swelling mountains are covered with sheep, and the marish grounds strewed with cattle, whilst every field is fill'd with corn, and every swamp swarms with fowl. This, in my opinion, proclaims a plenty, and presents Scotland, a kingdom of prodigies and products too, to allure foreigners, and entertain travellers. (R Franck, *Northern Memoirs*, 1656/7)

That he had succeeded, as least as far as his friends were concerned is suggested by part of a eulogistic poem by John Slator. He says of ladies who read Captain Franck's work:

> *They now may tread*
> *On Scotish ground with pleasure; for that place*
> *Looks brisk and fair, since you have wash'd its face.*
> *'Twill please them when they do behold the state*
> *Of this new structure bravely situate:*
> *And then immediately they'l fall in love*
> *With that alluring and delightful grove;*
> *And those harmonious birds that sit and sing,*
> *Whilst ev'ry pretty purling pleasant spring*
> *Doth murmur as it glides.*
> (R. Franck, *Northern Memoirs*, 1656/7)

I'm not sure that I would describe a Highland burn in spate with words like *glide, purl* or *murmur,* but no matter. Franck, in his Scottish travels, had presented his friends with a vision of an angling paradise. But Franck, like the Commonwealth, was ahead of his time. It was to be another 150 years before people were taking fishing holidays in the Highlands. Nevertheless he expressed a desire for solitude and the opportunities for peaceful contemplation that have been bringing people ever since. In his case it was to escape the political and military turmoil of the Civil War. Our turmoils may be more personal, but the responses are similar. Franck had a love of solitude, as a place to think. He too was seeking his desert, only not with the fervour of the Irish monks, nor in the tempestuous sea, but rather by a peaceful river:

I advise, therefore, the lovers of a solitary life, to study sobriety, temperance, patience, and chastity; for these divine blessings are the gift of God. So is contemplation, which never shines so clearly as when retired from the world and worldly incumbrances. Woods, rocks, grottas, groves, rivers, and rivulets, are places pick'd out for contemplation; where you may consider creational work, and melt with the warbling notes of Philomel, and the innocent harmony of musical birds, that deliciate the air, and delight the attention. Or you may proportion your meditations with the pulse of the ocean, or the soft and murmuring complaints of purling streams, that imprint their passions as they pass along, when melting the smiling florid banks. (R. Franck, *Northern Memoirs*, 1656/7)

or, more simply:

Now for a book and a brook, to contemplate and recreate. (R. Franck, *Northern Memoirs*, 1656/7)

Nature, for him, and countless others since, put the rest of life into perspective:

Study patience, practise humility, and let repentance be our daily exercise . . . these, and such like divine impressions, we ought to imprint on our immortal minds, when with impatiency we pursue our exercise, either to the river, or solitary lough. For the taper burns, and the thread of life (because lap'd up in this fine tiffany web of mortality) like a meteor terminates sometimes in a blaze: Too late then to confer with reason, or think of religion. (R. Franck, *Northern Memoirs*, 1656/7)

But scattered through the moral soliloquies are some nice local details such as this description of porpoises pursuing salmon off the River Ness:

Here the salmon relinquish the salts, because by the porposses pursued up the freshes . . . as I my self and others have often observed the porposses pursue them in the frothy foming waves of the Ness, for it may be some two or three miles together.

He further claimed that being in a boat nearby:

the vessel that conveyed us was in danger to overset, by reason the porposses vented so vehemently at the stem of our boat, insomuch that one of them had almost invented his passage amongst us; which if he had, there was no way but one.

Whilst here is his view of a chilly Loch Ness:

And this is that famous and renowned Lough Ness . . . whose streams are strewed with eel and trout, whilst her deeps are saluted with the race of salmon; whose fertil banks and shining sands are hourly moistned by this small Mediterrane: which I fancy is besieged with rocks and mountains; whilst her polite shores are frozen in the winter, by the frigid lungs of blustring Boreas, that perplexes her banks and masquerades her rocks with a cristalline hue of polished ice. Where the Tritons and Sea-nymphs sport themselves on the slippery waves, sounding an invasion to her moveable inmate; supposed by some, the floating island. (R. Franck, *Northern Memoirs,* 1656/7)

(By the last sentence Franck meant the mythical floating island which others usually associated with Loch Lomond).

Franck's work is not just interesting for local references but also for what he tells us about the contemporary angling knowledge base. When he brought his angling skills to bear in Scotland we can assume some interchange of lore and practice. Franck was very much a fly-fisherman and displays an impressive knowledge and expertise. He gave advice on the necessary equipment:

if salmon or trout be your recreation, remember always to carry your dubbing-bag about you; wherein there ought to be silks of all sorts, threads, thrums, moccado-ends, and cruels of all sizes, and variety of colours; diversified and stained wool, with dogs and bears hair; besides twisted fine threads of gold and silver: with feathers from the capon, partridg, peacock, pheasant, mallard, smith, teal, snite, parrot, herronshaw, paraketta, bittern, hobby, phlimingo, or Indian-flush; but the mockaw, without exception, gives flames of life to the hackle. Thus arm'd at all points, with rods rush-grown, hooks well temper'd, and lines well tapered, you may practise where you please in any river in Scotland, provided always the season be sutable. And forget not be sure to purdue your distance, always taking the head of a stream, and leisurely fish downwards, lest your game discover you, and flie before you. (R. Franck, *Northern Memoirs,* 1656/7)

And on choosing the right fly:

For the brighter the day is, the obscurer your fly; but the more promiscuous the season is, by so much the more ought your fly to be bright and shining. I also advise you to prepare the ground and body of your fly with bear's-hair, as at other times from the obscurities of wool; but then let the head be obscure and dark, since generally most flies their heads are blackish. The wing also you may strip from the pinion of a teal, which above measure allures the trout to destruction . . . But presupposing the day be gloomy, as frequently it happens from melancholy clouds . . . You must then consult a brighter fly.
(R. Franck, Northern Memoirs, 1656/7)

Or again:

> let me advise you, that the ground of your fly be for the most part obscure, of a
> gloomy, dark and dusky complexion; fashioned with tofts of bears-hair,
> blackish or brownish discolour'd wool, interwoven sometimes with peacocks
> feathers, at otherwhiles lap'd about with grey, red, yellow, green, or blewish
> silk, simple colours, or colours sometimes intermingled. For instance, black
> and yellow represent the wasp or hornet; and a promiscuous brown the flesh
> fly . . . The next thing necessary is the shape of your rod, which ought in all
> respects to represent the rush in its growth; for that end we call it rush-grown:
> and be sure it be streight and plient. Your line also that must be accurate and
> exactly taper'd; your hook well compassed, well pointed, and well barbed:
> and be mindful that your shank exceed not in length; I mean not so long as
> when you drag with the ground-bait. Nor is it proper for the artist to court a
> stream, except he be always provided of his dubbing bag, wherein are
> contained all sorts of thrums, threads, silks, moccado-ends, silver and gold
> twist; which are of excellent use to adorn your fly . . .

whilst for those who preferred hackled to winged flies:

> And among the variety of your fly-adventurers, remember the hackle, or the
> fly-substitute, form'd without wings, and drest up with the feather of a capon,
> pheasant, partridg, moccaw, phlimingo, paraketa, or the like, and the body
> nothing differing in shape from the fly, save only in ruffness and indigency of
> wings. Another necessary observation, is the wing of your fly, which ought to
> proceed from the teal, heron, malard, or faulcon. The pinion and wing thereof
> ought to lie close, and so snug as to carry the point exactly downward. But the
> last thing material is, the moderate stroak [strike], which always proves
> mortal, and best succeeds if used without violence; the line also, keep that
> streight as occasion requires, so that nothing be remiss, nor any thing
> wanting; (R. Franck, Northern Memoirs, 1656/7)

Franck was a fly-fisherman and often used natural flies. However he was not
above bait fishing and recommends a wide variety of baits for different types
of fish. These include worms, small fish, live frogs (for pike), a variety of
scents and pastes, toasted cheese, green cheese and clotted blood. He even
addresses the moral issues raised by angling. But for his language he could be
writing for any fishing journal today.

Then, as now, there were differences about the relative merits of different
types of fishing. To the natives it is likely that all that really mattered was
success – whatever method that invoked. Martin Martin says of Lewis:

> There are a great many fresh-water lakes in this island, which abound with
> trouts and eels. The common bait used for catching them is earthworms, but a

handful of parboiled mussels thrown into the water attracts the trouts and eels
to the place; the fittest time for catching them is when the wind blows from the
south-west. (Martin Martin, *A Description of the Western Islands of*
Scotland)

And of St Kilda:

there are also laiths, podloes, herring, and many more; most of these are
fished by the inhabitants upon the rock, for they have neither nets nor long
lines. Their common bait is the lympets or patellae, being parboil'd; they use
likewise the fowl called by them bowger, its flesh raw, which the fish near the
lesser isles catch greedily; sometimes they use the bowger's flesh, and the
lympets patellae at the same time upon one hook, and this proves successful
also. (Martin Martin, *A Voyage to St Kilda*, 1698)

And Harris:

The best time for angling for salmon and trout, is when a warm south-west
wind blows. They use earth-worms commonly for bait, but cockles attract the
salmon better than any other. (Martin Martin, *A Description of the Western*
Islands of Scotland)

Of Skye:

There are many fresh-water lakes in Skye, and generally well-stocked with
trout and eels. The common fly and the earth worms are ordinarily used for
angling trout. The best season for it is a calm, or a south-west wind. (Martin
Martin, *A Description of the Western Islands of Scotland*)

And Loch Maddy in Uist:

and on this coast every summer and harvest, the natives sit angling on the
rocks, and as they pull up their hooks do many times bring up herrings.
(Martin Martin, *A Description of the Western Islands of Scotland*)

There was always a competitive element in angling. He writes of Raasay:

There is a law observed by the natives that all their fishing lines must be of
equal length, for the longest is always supposed to have best access to the fish,
which would prove a disadvantage to such as might have shorter ones.
(Martin Martin, *A Description of the Western Islands of Scotland*)

And of St Kilda:

They are very exact in their properties, and divide both the fishing, as well as fowling rocks with as great niceness as they do their corn and grass. One will not allow his neighbour to sit and fish on his seat, for this being a part of his possession, he will take care that no encroachment be made upon the least part of it; and this with a particular regard to their successors, that they may lose no privilege depending upon any parcel of their farm. (Martin Martin, *A Description of the Western Islands of Scotland*)

There was similar jealousy in Rona (north of Lewis):

they are very precise in the matter of property among themselves; for none of them will by any means allow his neighbour to fish within his property. (Martin Martin, *A Description of the Western Islands of Scotland*)

In a world of scarce resources, those we currently enjoy must be jealously protected against all-comers, strangers or locals. Highlanders have shown a remarkable tenacity in protecting their ancient rights and privileges – a trait that has often drawn criticism from travellers. This was precisely what was at issue in connection with church offices, or sea fisheries, which were discussed in earlier chapters. This continues today. Highlanders have been victims for so long that once they secured legal protection through crofting legislation they have hung onto it despite internal abuse or external challenge.

In St Kilda the fishing-rods were multi-purpose tools:

they catch their fowls with gins made of horse-hair, these are tied to the end of their fishing-rods. (Martin Martin, *A Description of the Western Islands of Scotland*)

E.D. Clarke noticed the same a hundred years later: '*Ailsa cocks* [puffins], *which they took in great numbers by means of a slender pole like a fishing-rod, at the end of which was affixed a noose of cow hair, stiffened at one end with the feather of a Solan goose.* (E.D. Clarke, *Journal,* 1797)

Martin Martin also describes a situation where the natives used their fishing rods as weapons to deter a party sent by the steward to exact what the St Kildans felt was an unreasonable taxation.

Martin Martin tells of meeting an old lay Capuchin in Benbecula. This man was known as a 'poor brother', which was literally true since he had nothing but what was given him, and led a life of great simplicity. His days however were not wholly without pleasure: '*This poor man frequently diverts himself with angling of trouts.*'

It seems that there was already a well-established body of angling lore in the Highlands and Islands:

*The best time of taking fish with an angle is in warm weather, which disposes
them to come near the surface of the water; whereas in cold weather, or rain,
they go to the bottom. The best bait for cod and ling is a piece of herring,
whiting, thornback, haddock, or eel. The grey-lord* [fully grown coal-fish] *,
alias black-mouth, a fish of the size and shape of a salmon, takes the limpet
for bait. There is another way of angling for this fish, by fastening a short
white down of a goose behind the hook; and the boat being continually rowed,
the fish run greedily after the down, and are easily caught. The grey-lord
swims in the surface of the water, and then is caught with a spear; a rope
being tied to the further end of it, and secured in the fisherman's hand.*
(Martin Martin, *A Description of the Western Islands of Scotland*)

The lack of fishing boats and gear made it even more important to catch fish
from the shore:

*Though the Isle of Mull is almost every year visited by the Hering Shoals,
and though there is plenty of Cod and Ling upon many parts of its Coast,
there is not a Net or Long Line in all the Island. None of the Inhabitants are
acquainted with any kind of Fishing, but with the Rod, and in this way, they
procure the most part of their Subsistance in Summer, by catching great
Plenty and variety of Fish from the Sea Rocks.* (McKay, *Walker's Report
on the Hebrides*, 1764 and 1771)

*Their daily implements of fishing are the rod, and the taubh, or net. This last
is a pock-net, bound round a large circular ring of wands or hoops, and that
tied to the end of a long pole of eight feet in length. By throwing a little boiled
wilks, chewed out of their mouths, over the top of it, when sunk below the
surface, the cuddies will get in after the meat, and when they are on the
bottom, the upper part is elevated above the sea, and some hundreds are
catched, at times, at each dipping.* (Buchanan, *Travels in the Western
Hebrides from 1782 to 1790*)

The absence of trade and industry could cause temporary shortages. One
specific problem was obtaining fish-hooks. Pennant writes of Canna:

*fish and milk was their whole subsistence at this time: the first was a
precarious relief, for, besides the uncertainty of success, to add to their
distress, their stock of fish-hooks was almost exhausted: and to ours, that
it was not in our power to supply them. The rubbans, and other trifles I had
brought would have been insults to people in distress. I lamented that my
money had been so uselessly laid out; for a few dozens of fish-hooks, or a few
pecks of meal, would have made them happy.* (Thomas Pennant, *A Tour in
Scotland and Voyage to the Hebrides*, 1772)

Locally produced hooks must have been distinctive in shape and style. Martin Martin writes of the nests of gannets on St Kilda: '*English hooks . . . are found sticking to the fish bones in their nests, for the natives have no such hooks among them.*' (Martin Martin, *A Description of the Western Islands of Scotland*)

Another method of fishing which was practised in some parts of Scotland was spear-fishing. This may have been what Pont(?) had in mind when describing the night-fishing on the R. Nant. It was certainly practised on the Solway: '*in which they were wont after a delightful manner on horseback, with spears to hunt salmons, of which there are in these parts a very great abundance.*' (James Brome, (1669) in Hume Brown, *Early Travellers in Scotland*)

The traditional three-pointed salmon-spear was known as a leister. Both the name and the practice may derive from the Norse colonists on the west coast. Martin Martin implies that it was once the norm in Islay: '*I was told by the natives that the Brion of Islay, a famous judge, is according to his own desire, buried standing on the brink of the river Laggan, having in his right hand a spear, such as they use to dart at the salmon.*' (Martin Martin, *A Description of the Western Islands of Scotland*)

Visitors might wonder whether trout might not have played a bigger role in the Highland economy but, although there is plenty of evidence for the importance of salmon, shellfish and sea-fish, trout are conspicuous by their absence. Burt reflects on this:

> *It is true, there are small trouts, or something like them, in some of the little rivers, which continue in holes among the rocks, which are always full of water, when the stream has quite ceased for want of rain, these might be a help to them in this starving season* [spring]*; but I have had so little notion in all my journeys that they made those fish a part of their diet, that I never once thought of them as such till this moment. It is likely they cannot catch them for want of proper tackle, but I am sure they cannot be without them for want of leisure.* (Edmund Burt, *Letters from a Gentleman in the North of Scotland,* late 1720s)

Samuel Johnson also found this neglect puzzling. He writes of Coll: '*Col has many lochs, some of which have trouts and eels, and others have never yet been stocked; another proof of the negligence of the islanders, who might take fish in the inland waters, when they cannot go to sea.*' (Johnson, *A Journey to the Western Islands of Scotland,* 1773)

Burt may have done some angling of his own because he remarks of the green plover or peewit: '*What kind of food this bird is I do not know, for, although I have shot many of them here, I never made any other use of them than to pluck off the crown or crest to busk my flies for fishing*' (Edmund Burt, *Letters from a Gentleman in the North of Scotland,* late 1720s)

It was not unknown for other methods to be used for catching fish: '*Otters are frequently tamed in the Western Islands, and taught to fish for their masters.*

Mr. Maclean, of Col, had one of these animals. They will resort to the sea, catch young salmon, and bring them home entire.' (E.D. Clarke, Journal, 1797)

Every year now, a great many people travel to the Highlands and Islands to enjoy a holiday in which game or sea angling play an significant part. This has been important since the early nineteenth century although we associate its heyday with the latter part of that century. People were coming to Arisaig for shooting and fishing holidays at least as early as 1828. Catherine Sinclair writes of the inn there:

> *the landlady . . . ushered us into the kitchen, apologising that her parlour and three best bed-rooms had been constantly occupied during the last twelve summers by a trio of gentlemen from Oxford, who come there to enjoy fishing and shooting during the whole season . . . Late in the evening, we were at length shown into a sitting-room, resembling an armoury of guns, varied by fishing rods, and adorned with a . . . variety of flies.* (C. Sinclair, *Scotland and the Scotch*)

So when did people start travelling here for sporting purposes alone? In general terms, after the 1770's when a new era of travel to the Highlands and Islands opened up. Prior to this there were exceptional visits. Taylor, Franck, Burt, and other members of the English garrisons in the North, all enjoyed the sporting facilities of the area, but for most of them it was under exceptional circumstances. Angling was probably incidental for most early visitors. It gradually became a reason in itself as the opportunities were grasped. Since so much travel had to be by sea it was almost inevitable that visitors would while away a calm with some angling. Pennant writes of fishing in Little Loch Broom: '*For two hours amuse ourselves with taking with hand-lines abundance of cod, some dogfish, and a curious ray.*' (T. Pennant, *A Tour in Scotland and Voyage to the Hebrides*, 1772.) While Samuel Johnson writes of Ulinish in Skye: '*In our return, we found a little boy upon the point of a rock, catching with his angle, a supper for the family. We rowed up to him, and borrowed his rod, with which Mr Boswell caught a cuddy.*' (Johnson, *A Journey to the Western Islands of Scotland*, 1773)

And even when the normal method of fishing was by net, alternatives were sometimes employed. Pennant writes of young sea-trout off Fort William: '*Phinocs* [finnock] *are taken here in great numbers, 1500 having been taken at a draught. They are about a foot long, their colour grey spotted with black, their flesh red; rise eagerly to a fly. The fishermen suppose them to be the young of what they call a great trout.*' (Pennant, *A Tour in Scotland* 1769). And of herring: '*as soon as they become foul or poor, they will greedily rise to the fly, and be taken like the whiting pollack.*' (T. Pennant, *A Tour in Scotland and Voyage to the Hebrides*, 1772)

J. Clevely, one of the artists who accompanied Banks's expedition which passed through the Hebrides in 1772, drew a sketch of some anglers off Staffa (see Plate 6). Unfortunately the boat disappears in the finished picture but the scene was probably typical of a fine day in summer.

Games

James Fraser's quote from the Wardlaw Manuscript makes it clear that hunting events could also involve a variety of other games and sports. I am not going to pursue the origins of today's Highland Games but will draw attention to a few examples of native sporting tradition. The first is horse-riding which was very popular in the western isles and certainly drew the attention of early travellers. Martin Martin discusses cavalcades in Harris, North Uist, South Uist, Barra, St Kilda, Skye and Tiree. These were associated with Michaelmas, one of the most important dates in the Christian calendar. On North Uist:

> The natives . . . observe an anniversary cavalcade on Michaelmas Day, and then all ranks of both sexes appear on horseback. The place for this rendezvous is a large piece of firm sandy ground on the sea-shore, and there they have horse-racing for small prizes, for which they contend eagerly. There is an ancient custom, by which it is lawful for any of the inhabitants to steal his neighbour's horse the night before the race, and ride him all next day, provided he deliver him safe and sound to the owner after the race. The manner of running is by a few young men, who use neither saddles nor bridles, except two small ropes made of bent instead of a bridle, nor any sort of spurs, but their bare heels: and when they begin the race, they throw these ropes on their horses' necks, and drive them on vigorously with a piece of long seaware in each hand instead of a whip; and this is dried in the sun several months before for that purpose. This is a happy opportunity for the vulgar, who have few occasions for meeting, except on Sundays: the men have their sweethearts behind them on horseback, and give and receive mutual presents; the men present the women with knives and purses, the women present the men with a pair of fine garters of divers colours, they give them likewise a quantity of wild carrots. (Martin Martin, A Description of the Western Islands of Scotland)

And Barra:

> They have likewise a general cavalcade on St Michael's day, in Kilbar village, and do then also take a turn round their church. Every family, as soon as the solemnity is ended, is accustomed to bake St Michael's cake . . . and all strangers, together with those of the family, must eat the bread that night. (Martin Martin, A Description of the Western Islands of Scotland)

And St Kilda:

> *The inhabitants ride their horses (which were but eighteen in all) at the anniversary cavalcade of All-Saints.* (Martin Martin, *A Description of the Western Islands of Scotland*)

Samuel Johnson describes something similar in Coll while Pennant tells us the situation in Canna:

> *. . . horses in abundance. The chief use of them in this little district is to form an annual cavalcade at Michaelmas. Every man on the island mounts his horse unfurnished with saddle, and takes behind him either some young girl, or his neighbor's wife, and then rides backwards and forwards from the village to a certain cross, without being able to give any reason for the origin of this custom. After the procession is over, they alight at some public house, where, strange to say, the females treat the companions of their ride. When they retire to their houses an entertainment is prepared with primaeval simplicity: the chief part consists of a great oatcake, called Struan-Micheil, or St Michael's cake, composed of two pecks of meal, and formed like the quadrant of a circle: it is daubed over with milk and eggs, and then placed to harden before the fire.* (T. Pennant, *A Tour in Scotland and Voyage to the Hebrides*, 1772)

Another example of a native sport is shinty. A game involving a ball and a curved stick was once common throughout the British Isles. We have mediaeval illustrations from England and descendants of this game may include shinty (Scotland), hurley (Ireland) and hockey. In a Hebridean context we have some details from an early seventeenth-century description of Sanda (off Southend in Kintyre) and twentieth-century recordings made on Eigg.

> *There is an isle Sanda in the Scottish Sea on the west a mile from the mainland of Kintire. It is one large mile in circumference. Its soil is genial, and, if cultivated, would be fertile in fruit and grain. In it is a small church sacred to Saint Ninian, to whose monastery in Galloway the whole island belongs. Adjoining the church is the sepulchre of the fourteen sons of a most holy man Senchanius an Irishman, renowned for their sanctity, surrounded by a low stone wall and including seven large polished stones covering those sacred bodies, in the midst of which (as at this moment occurs to my recollection) was an obelisk higher than a man's usual stature. None can enter that enclosure with impunity. The oldest of the islanders, and the father of nearly all the rest, related to me the prodigy which I here add. Angus Macdonell lord of Kintire and the island of Ilay, whom I myself have seen, once entered the island accompanied by a numerous band, among whom were*

the chief of the youth of Kintire. The lord and his nobles, after treating of more serious matters, exercised themselves, as they were wont, with the game of shinty, [literally a game of ball and sticks]. *The ball bounded into the cemetery, and a lad who dared to fetch it died of a swelled foot. In this island was found an arm of Saint Ultan, which enclosed in a silver shrine was religiously kept before this war by a gentleman of the illustrious family of the Macdonells. Not far from the chapel is a perennial spring, noted for miracles, as the islanders and many on the continent informed me. Indeed it was frequented in my own time by the neighbours all around, chiefly by those in whose minds any remains of the ancient religion dwelt.* (MS in the Burgundian Library at Brussels, circa 1600, entitled *Insulae Sandae seu Auoniae Hibernice Abhuinn Brevis Descriptio*, by friar Edmund M'Cana, in Origines Parochiales Scotiae.)

In *Tocher* 36–7 (The Journal of the School of Scottish Studies) there is a transcript of an interview by DA Macdonald with Hugh Mackinnon of Eigg in 1965. The subject was the shinty that was played on Laig beach until about 1925. From the description, I doubt it had changed at all since 1600:

HM: it was Christmas Day and New Year's Day and the Day of the Three Kings [Epiphany], these were the three days I remember when people used to go down to play. But the generation before me, and other generations before that, they started on All Saints' Day. They would have All Saints' Day, St Andrew's Day, and Christmas Day and New Year's Day and Epiphany. They had the five days and since Epiphany was the last day they had of the shinty, if the tide allowed them, they would stay there till night had fallen and the stars were in the sky before they came home and they would be so tired that they couldn't sup milk from a spoon by the time they came home.
DAM: And what sort of ball did they have?
HM: It was a lump of hazel root . . .
DAM: And how did they shape it?
HM: Oh, they'd whittle at it with a knife first of all and then they'd rub at it and make it smooth with a rasp or a file. And . . . to make it tougher so that it wouldn't split apart with the blows . . . they would boil it in a pot of water over the fire . . .
DAM: And now the camans [sticks]?
HM: Oh, the camans: they used to cut them in the woods. They could be hazel or elm or oak or willow or birch, or any kind of wood that would make a caman. Birch made a fine light caman but it was very easily broken . . . And undoubtedly, oak, certainly it was the hardest and strongest and most durable caman of them all, but very often it had a sting in it.

Both activities feature in this account of St Kilda:

For divertisment, the inhabitants ride their horses at the anniversary Caval-
cade of Michaelmas; this they never fail to observe. They begin at the shore, and
ride as far as the houses; they use no saddles of any kind, nor bridle, but a rope of
straw, which manages the horse's head; and when they have all taken the horses
by turns, the show is over for that time. These superstitious days they observe
very punctually, they being at certain set times, and they call them holy days;
but can give no reason for this observation, other than practical antiquity; on
which they will also be very jovial in singing, dancing, and feasting.

Their diversions are short clubs and balls of wood: the sand is a fair field
for this sport and exercise; in which they take great pleasure, and are very
nimble at it; they play for some eggs, fowls, hooks, or tobacco; and so eager are
they for victory, that they strip themselves to their shirt to obtain it. They use
swimming and diving, and are very expert in both. (Rev A Buchan, *A*
Description of St Kilda, 1773)

In 1699 Edward Lhuyd wrote to James Fraser, minister of Kirkhill in
Inverness-shire, enclosing a questionnaire under various headings, one of
which was 'peculiar Games and customes'. Fraser's reply included the
following: '*in the generall they were litigious, ready to take arms upon a small*
occasion, very preydatory, much given to tables, carding, and diceing; there games
was military exercise, and such as rendered them fittest for warr, as arching,
running, jumping, with and without race, swimeing, continuall hunting and
fouling [fowling], *feasting specially upon their holydays'* (Campbell and Thomson, *Edward Lhuyd in the Scottish Highlands*, p 31.)
Pennant discusses the loss of traditional Highland sports:

Most of the ancient sports of the Highlanders, such as archery, hunting,
fowling and fishing, are now disused: those retained are, throwing the
putting-stone, or stone of strength, as they call it, which occasions an
emulation who can throw a weighty one the farthest. Throwing the pen-
ny-stone, which answers to our coits. The shinty, or the striking a ball of
wood or of hair: this game is played between two parties in a large plain, and
furnished with clubs; whichever side strikes it first to their own goal wins the
match. (Pennant, *A Tour in Scotland 1769*)

Shinty has survived and is particularly strong in the Spey valley. The
Michaelmas cavalcades have gone but Highland games go from strength
to strength, particularly in North America. Fox-hunting was widespread
when sheep swept over Highland hillsides but is not practised in the Highlands as a social activity. Deer-hunting has been reduced to stalking. Angling
is, if anything, even more important now than it was in the past although few
can afford the pursuit of wild salmon. Game angling and sea angling are
valuable leisure activities for locals and visitors alike. Many now come here to
pay homage much as Richard Franck did some 350 years ago.

Chapter 9

Marvels, miracles and other curiosities

One reason why visitors travel to an area – any area, at any time – is because of some marvel, miracle or curiosity associated with it. Sometimes this is religious: such-and-such a local saint is responsible for something deemed miraculous. Sometimes it is medicinal: to drink from a well, bathe in a spa, or breathe in sea air. Occasionally it is a natural phenomenon: some rock or bird or creature has a curious property. It can be antiquarian: here lies an ancient monument. Or it can be ghoulish: here lived giants, pigmies, or monsters.

Today we endeavour to find a rational explanation for Nature's curiosities. We demystify them. Once we have done so they become less magical and less fascinating. However, to see the power of magic and mystery we only have to acknowledge the enduring fame of the Loch Ness monster. She is not alone of course. There are other monsters in Scottish waters. These include Morag in Loch Morar and various kelpies or water-horses. None, though, have matched Nessie for power and longevity. Moreover she is worth a great deal of money.

This aspect of the miraculous should not be overlooked. Miracles have always been money-spinners, a fact not lost on those who propagate or promote them. The pilgrimage industry was big business in the Middle Ages and there is no reason to suppose the Highlands and Islands were any different to the rest of Europe.

For these reasons it is perhaps sensible to approach the marvels of the Highlands in the same way as the folklore historian might. Perhaps what we are looking at when we meet a miraculous tale is not some unique revelation peculiar to a people or place or time, but instead the local manifestation of a universal phenomenon. It may be disguised in Highland trappings; it may appear specific and idiosyncratic, but there could be close parallels elsewhere.

For instance, the story of Barnacle geese appears time and again in early accounts of Scotland and yet we also read it in Gerald of Wales' *History and Topography of Ireland* dated to c. 1185. Here too we find a story of drowned landscapes that reads very like Pont's(?) note on Uist found in *Macfarlane's Geographical Collections*. Gerald also refers to a mysterious island to the west of Ireland. This idea occupied travellers and map-makers for centuries – the trackless wastes of the Atlantic were the ideal place for undiscovered islands. This geographical red herring has a whole history and literature of its own so I will do no more than point out that this belief was still active in the seventeenth century. Robert Dudley included imaginary Atlantic islands in his great sea-atlas *Dell'Arcano del Mare* in 1646 while Pont(?) reported that Macneill of Barra went in search of one.

In Gerald of Wales again we find the story of wood turning to stone in a certain well in Ireland. This is also reported in the Irish version of Nennius' *History of the Britons* and in the thirteenth-century Norse text *The King's Mirror*. Something rather similar appears in Pont's(?) note about Arnisdale (Glenelg) in *Macfarlane's Geographical Collections*. Loch Lomond had enormous importance to early geographers. It is referred to in Nennius (from the early ninth century), and, in an even more fabulous manner, in Geoffrey of Monmouth's *History of the Kings of Britain* (early twelfth century). Apart from the number of its islands it had three marvels – a floating island, waves without wind, and fish without fins – which are also referred to in the fourteenth-century Gough Map of Britain, albeit beside Loch Tay.

Highland and Hebridean marvels have a context therefore, and should not be seen in isolation. They have a pan-European background and a period of many centuries when fabulous occurrences in far-off places were part of the stock-in-trade of travellers' tales. Experience, scepticism, and reason, have gradually whittled them down leaving the Loch Ness monster as almost the sole vestigial remnant. Amongst the quotations that follow I have given some parallels from Ireland, the country with the closest cultural links to the Gaelic world of the Highlands and Islands.

Cockles in Barra

Amongst islands of scarce resource, natural bounty was ever remarkable. The plentiful cockles of Barra always drew comment and there was long speculation as to their origin:

In the north end of this ile of Barray ther is ane round heigh know, mayne grasse and greine round about it to the heid, on the top of quhilk ther is ane spring and fresh water well. This well treuly springs up certaine little round quhyte things, less nor the quantity of confeit corne, lykest to the shape and figure of a little cokill, as it appearit to me. Out of this well runs ther ane little strype downwith to the sea, and quher it enters into the sea ther is ane myle braid of sands, quhilk ebbs ane myle, callit the Trayrmore of Killbaray, that is, the Grate sandes of Barray. This sand is all full of grate cokills, and alledgit be the ancient countrymen, that the cokills come doun out of the forsaid hill throughe the said strype in the first small forme that we have spoken off, and after ther coming to the sandis growis grate cokills alwayses. Ther is na fairer and more profitable sands for cokills in all the warld. (D. Monro, *A Description of the Western Isles of Scotland*, Birlinn, 1994)

(In the north end of this isle of Barra there is a round high knowe, much grass and green round about it to the head, on the top of which there is a spring and freshwater well. This well truly springs up certain little round white things, less than the quantity of sweet(?) corn, most like to the shape and figure of a little cockle, as it appeared to me. Out of this well runs there a little stream down to the sea, and where it enters into the sea there is a mile broad of sands, which ebbs one mile, called the Traigh more of Killbaray, that is, the great sands of Barra. This sand is all full of great cockles, and (it is) alleged by the ancient countrymen, that the cockles come down out of the aforesaid hill through the said stream in the first small form that we have spoken of, and after their coming to the sands grow great cockles always. There is no fairer and more profitable sands for cockles in all the world.)

In the Sibbald manuscript of Monro, (see RW Munro's edition), the writer appeals to Hector Boece for confirmation of his story about Barra. Whether or not this is Dean Monro's own comment, or a later interpolation, it is wrong since both Boece and Leslie actually tell the story of Mull rather than Barra. Given the strength of tradition concerning Barra I think we can disregard Mull, although Boece's evidence is important for the supposed origin of cockles:

> *In this Ile of Mula is ane cleir fontane, two milis fra the see: fra this fontane discendis ane litil burne, or strip, rinnand ful of rounis to the seis. Thir rounis ar round and quhit, schinand like perle, full of thik humour; and, within two houris eftir that thay come to see, thay grow in gret cocles.* (Boece, in Hume Brown *Scotland before 1700*).

(In this Isle of Mull is a clear fountain, two miles from the sea: from this fountain descends a little burn, or stream, running full of roes to the seas. These roes are round and white, shining like pearl, full of thick humour [matter]; and, within two hours after that they come to [the] sea, they grow in[to] great cockles.)

Pont(?) gives the same story in the 1590s:

> *There is one litle springand fresh water running out of ane grein hill above the Church, which doeth flow into the sea, And there is springand there certane litill Cockles shells which they alleadge that the samen doth flow into the sea out of the Well and doeth grow in another place next the Church not the tenth part of ane myll from the Church of Barray called Kilbarray. And there is abundance of choice litle cockle shells found. The wholl countreymen and tennants doe conveen togidder to this place when the sea doeth ebb and bring with them certaine number of horses and gather in this place abundance of*

Cockles. The length of this sandie place is ane myll and ane half or therby. and no less broad. Certaine of these Inhabitants will come fyve mylls with ther horses. and bring home asmuch with them as their horses will beare of these cockles. And if ten thousand cold come, they should have als many as there horses were able to carrie everie day gotten and gathered in this place. And it is gotten below the sand, And when you doe come and stand on that sand with your horses you will think the place verie dry, but when you doe put zour hands below into the sand you shall see abundance of the saids cockles comeing above the sand, and als much of the sea Water as will wash them from the sand. (Macfarlane's Geographical Collections, Vol II)

Martin Martin is strangely, or diplomatically, circumspect: *'And they say that the Well of Kilbarr throws up embryoes of cockles, but I could not discern any in the rivulet, the air being at that time foggy.'*

The shellfish were an important economic resource for centuries. About 1794 the Rev Edward Macqueen wrote for the first Statistical Account:

Shell-fish abound here . . . but what is singularly beneficial to the inhabitants, is the shell fish called cockle. It is found upon the great sand on the N end of Barray, in such quantities, that in times of great scarcity all the families upon the island (about 200) resort to it for their daily subsistence. It has been computed, that the two last summers, which were peculiarly distressing on account of the great scarcity, no less than from 100 to 200 horse-loads of cockles were taken off the sands at low-water every day of the spring-tides during the months of May, June, July, and August. (Old Statistical Account, Barra, pp 336–37)

However as Mr Macqueen makes clear in a footnote the strange belief about the origin of cockles was still prevalent locally at the end of the eighteenth century. He is referring to George Buchanan who incorporated Donald Monro's account into his own *History of Scotland* in 1582:

Buchanan is undoubtedly mistaken, when he asserts, that the cockle originated from small animalculi coming down along with the water of a spring in the top of a green hill above the sand. It is true, there is such a hill, with a spring on the summit of it; but any water running from it does not come to the sea, being absorbed by the intervening ground, which is sandy; besides, that it is allowed by all naturalists, that every animal procreates its own species. But this vulgar notion prevails among the inhabitants to this day. (Old Statistical Account, Barra)

We shall probably never know whether locals believed this *because* of what they were told by travellers – or vice-versa. At any rate the story was very ancient and must predate Boece whose work was first published in 1527.

A clue to the reason for the fame of these cockles may lie in the account given by the Rev. Alexander Nicolson, in January 1840, for the New Statistical Account. Like his predecessor for the Old Statistical Account he denigrates the idea of a freshwater origin but he also says:

> Cockles are to be found in the sands of Barray in such immense quantities, that scores of horse loads may be taken up during a single tide, and the people consider them the most nourishing shell-fish on their shores . . . They commence the use of them in times of scarcity in April, and continue the use of them till the beginning of August. The people allege that the quantity of this fish found on the shores is much greater in scarce seasons than at any other time . . . In very scarce years, such as 1836 and 1837, they subsist, in a great measure, upon cockles and other shell-fish, with very little bread and milk.

Nicolson may have hit upon the true reason for the fame of cockles. They were a great natural larder which prevented mass starvation in Barra every year the harvest failed. In times of scarcity, islanders always turned to shellfish. Few Hebridean islands offered comparable bounty. It is no coincidence that two of the best known wonders of the Scottish islands – barnacles and cockles – should both have concerned food supply.

Barnacle geese

The story of barnacle geese became a perennial chestnut in travellers' tales about Scotland but is also found in Gerald of Wales's *History and Topography of Ireland* written c. 1185. Although there are general references to their presence in the western islands they are more specifically associated with Orkney. Hume Brown quotes Aeneas Sylvius (later Pope Pius II), writing in the reign of James I:

> I had previously heard that there was a tree in Scotland, that growing on the banks of rivers produced fruits in the form of geese, which, as they approached ripeness dropped off of their own accord, some on the ground and some into the water; that those which fell on the ground rotted, but that those submerged in the water immediately assumed life, and swam about under the water, and flew into the air with feathers and wings. When I made enquiries regarding this story, I learned that the miracle was always referred to some place further off, and that this famous tree was to be found not in Scotland but in the Orkney Islands, though the miracle had been represented to me as taking place among the Scots. (Aeneas Sylvius (c. 1431–37?) in Hume Brown, *Early Travellers in Scotland*)

The Orkneys were not then in Scotland but Aeneas makes the nice crack that such miracles always lay a little further off!

Geese, like cockles, were an important economic resource in mediaeval Scotland and Bishop Leslie used this as his justification in 1578:

I thocht gude, heir of the geis to speik a few wordes, for thair meruellous multitude in our cuntries, cheiflie in the west yles (Dalrymple's translation in E Cody (ed.), *Leslie's History of Scotland,* 1578)

(I thought good, here of the geese to speak a few words, for their marvellous multitude in our countries, chiefly in the west isles.)

Leslie quotes Hector Boece on the controversy over whether the Claik (or Barnacle) goose is bred from fir trees, or the worms that thrive in rotting tree-trunks in the Western Isles. According to Leslie, Boece did not believe these geese came from Hebridean trees but rather from the sea and sea shells:

And to the intent, he mycht preiue, that to thir stockis and tries, that grows in thir Iles, this vertue sulde nocht be attributed, he says farther, that him selfe present, he saw bred of a sey tangle, mussilis, and quhen thay were apned, throuch desyre to knawe quhat was in thame was fund inclosed nocht fishe, bot foules, euerie foul conueining to the gretnes of the schel, quhairof is euident and cleir, his opinione is, that this generatione of Geis proceids not of ane rotne stock, or of the frutes of thir tries that grow in the Iles, bot rathir of the maine Sey. (Dalrymple's translation in E. Cody (ed.), *Leslie's History of Scotland,* 1578)

(And to the intent, he might prove, that to these stocks [trunks] and trees, that grow in these Isles, this virtue should not be attributed, he says farther, that himself present, he saw bred of a sea tangle [i.e. seaweed], mussels, and when they were opened, through desire to know what was in them, was found enclosed not fish, but fowls, every fowl convening [matching] to the greatness of the shell, whereof [it] is evident and clear, his opinion is, that this generation of Geese proceeds not of a rotten stock [trunk], or of the fruits of these trees that grow in the Isles, but rather of the main Sea.)

Leslie goes on to support this argument with an account of his own experience viewing a Portuguese ship in 1562. A century later Richard Franck also summoned personal experience in support of Barnacle geese in the Caithness area:

Now that barnicles (which are a certain sort of wooden geese) breed here-abouts, it's past dispute; and that they fall off from the limbs and members of the fir-tree, is questionless; and those so fortunate to espouse the ocean (or any other river, or humitactive soil) by virtue of solar heat are destinated to live, but to all others so unfortunate to fall upon dry land, are denied their nativity.

When Theophilus, (his rhetorical sparring-partner), challenges this proposition:

But if eye-sight be evidence against contradiction, and the sense of feeling argument good enough to refute fiction, then let me bring these two convincing arguments to maintain my assertion; for I have held a barnicle in my own hand, when as yet unfledg'd, and hanging by the beak, which as I then supposed of the fir-tree; for it grew from thence, as an excrescence grows on the members of an animal: and as all things have periods, and in time drop off, so does the barnicle by a natural progress separate it self from the member it's conjoin'd to.

Franck goes on to describe the birth of the barnacle in more detail and repeats the story that only those that fall on water are destined to live. But further dangers await these:

And though some of them are commissioned to live, yet how difficult is it to preserve life, when hourly sought after by the luxurious devourer? (Franck, *Northern Memoirs*, 1656/7)

As far as the Western Isles were concerned Sir Robert Moray claimed to have seen them in embryo in Uist c. 1677–8:

In the Western Islands of Scotland much of the Timber, wherewith the Common people build their Houses, is such as the West-Ocean throws upon their Shores. The most ordinary Trees are Firr and Ash. They are usually very large, and without branches; which seem rather to have been broken or worn off than cut; and are so Weather-beaten, that there is no Bark left upon them, especially the Firrs. Being in the island of East [Uist], I saw lying upon the shore a cut of a large Firr-tree of about 2.5 foot diameter, and 9 or 10 foot long; which had lain so long out of the water that it was very dry: And most of the Shells, that had formerly cover'd it, were worn or rubb'd off. Only on the parts that lay next the ground, there still hung multitudes of little Shells; having within them little Birds, perfectly shap'd supposed to be Barnacles . . .
This Bird in every Shell that I opened, as well the least as the biggest, I found so curiously and compleatly formed, that there appeared nothing wanting, as to the internal parts, for making up a perfect Seafowl: every little part appearing so distinctly, that the whole looked like a large Bird seen through a concave or diminishing Glass, colour and feature being every where so clear and neat . . . All being dead and dry, I did not look after the Internal

parts of them . . . Nor did I ever see any of the little Birds alive, nor met with any body that did. Only some credible persons have assured me they have seen some as big as their fist. (Robert Moray, 1677–78, in Max Muller)

Thomas Kirk, like other travellers, was intrigued but sceptical of the tales of barnacle geese. When in Orkney in 1677 he asked the Provost of Kirkwall:

We inquired of him and the rest of the company with him, and of all others we thought fit to answer us, concerning the Barnacles, of which we had various accounts; but I could not understand that they proceed in any kind from a tree, though some of the inhabitants have faith enough to believe it upon this ground, that some shaken timber is found in these parts, which is brought thither by the sea, having laid some time there, whereon they find several shells sticking, wherein they find some small creatures, which some of them fancy to bear the shape of birds, and others of worms; and because these fowls are never seen to breed in this country, therefore they conclude they proceed from these shells; but it is but absurd ground for it, and some of these fowls have been shot, and eggs found in their bellies; they come but here about August, and stay most part of the winter. (Kirk in Hume Brown, *Tours in Scotland*)

Martin Martin is similarly dubious in his section on Orkney:

There is also the cleck-goose; the shells in which this fowl is said to be produced are found in several isles sticking to trees by the bill; of this kind I have seen many: the fowl was covered by a shell, and the head stuck to the tree by the bill, but I never saw any of them with life in them upon the tree; but the natives told me that they had observed them to move with the heat of the sun. (Martin Martin, *A Description of the Western Islands of Scotland*).

The whole issue of barnacle geese was researched by Max Muller in *Lectures on the Science of Language*, vol II, Lecture XII, in 1880. He traces the story back through British, Jewish and Continental sources as far as the twelfth century. He quotes the claim that Pope Innocent III (1198–1216) prohibited the eating of barnacle geese during Lent and shows that parts of the barnacle shell could be construed to look like the rudiments of a bird. Here we have the basis for a rationalisation; that it was acceptable to eat barnacle geese because they were fish rather than fowl.

The legends survived longest in remote parts of north-western Europe where locals were reluctant to forego essential foodstuffs during Lent. Giving up geese was one thing in the valleys of the Po, the Rhone or the Seine. It was quite another in the Orkneys or Western Isles where seabirds were a critical component of people's diet.

It is possible that solan geese (gannets) were viewed in the same way.

Richard Franck writes of the solan geese on the Bass Rock in the Firth of Forth: '*Is this the place where the solon geese breed, that are flesh in hand, but fish in the mouth? a mystery I fancy not inferiour to the barnicle.*' (R. Franck, *Northern Memoirs*, 1656/7)

The geese that overwintered in Colonsay must have seemed like manna from Heaven: '*Barnacles appear in vast flocks in September, and retire the latter end of April or beginning of May.*' (T. Pennant, *A Tour in Scotland and Voyage to the Hebrides*, 1772)

Some islanders ate seals for the same reason. Martin Martin states:

> *The Popish vulgar, in the islands southward from this* [i.e. Benbecula, S. Uist and Barra], *eat these seals in Lent instead of fish. This occasioned a debate between a Protestant gentleman and a Papist of my acquaintance: the former alleged that the other had transgressed the rules of his church, by eating flesh in Lent: the latter answered that he did not; for, says he, I have eat a sea-creature, which only lives and feeds upon fish. The Protestant replied, that this creature is amphibious, lies, creeps, eats, sleeps, and so spends much of its time on land, which no fish can do and live. It hath also another faculty that no fish has, that is, it breaks wind backward so loudly, that one may hear it at a great distance. But the Papist still maintained that he must believe it to be fish, till such time as the Pope and his priests decide the question.* (Martin Martin, *A Description of the Western Islands of Scotland*, c. 1695)

Giants, pigmies and bones

People have always been fascinated by tales of giants and pigmies. There was once an inhabitant of Petty in Moray whose enormous size gave him the nickname of Little John and whose fame earned him a caption on Mercator's map of 1564. John is also mentioned on the page following Nowell's monochrome map of Northern Scotland in British Library Manuscript Cotton Domitian A XVIII: '*In Pette of Murray lie the bones of litle Jhon 14 foote in length.*'

Both cartographers seem to have drawn their information from Boece who claimed to have seen Little John's haunch bone in 1521:

> *In Murray land is the Kirk of Pette, quhare the banis of Litill Johne remanis, in gret admiratioun of pepill. He has bene fourtene fut of hicht, with square membris effering thairto. VI yeris afore the cuming of this werk to licht, we saw his hanche bane, als mekill as the haill bane of ane man; for we schot our arme in the mouth thairof: be quhilk apperis how strang and square pepill grew in our regioun, afore thay wer effeminat with lust and intemperance of mouth.* (Boece in Hume Brown, *Scotland before 1700*)

(In Moray land is the Kirk of Petty, where the bones of Little John remain, in great admiration of people. He has been fourteen foot of height, with square members offering [matching] thereto. 6 years before the coming of this work to light, we saw his haunch bone, as much as the whole bone [skeleton] of a man; for we shot our arm in the mouth thereof: by which appears how strong and square people grew in our region, before they were effeminate with lust and intemperance of mouth.)

Bishop Leslie attempted to date Little John to the thirteenth century:

In Moray land in the kirk of a certane village or clachan named Petty ar keipit the banes of a certane persone quhome thay cal litle Johne, departed bot the space of thrie hundir zeirs, as the commone brute amang thame is . . . quhais Wydnes of his banes and gretnes teiches that he was xiiii. fute lang. (Dalrymple's translation in E. Cody (ed.), *Leslie's History of Scotland*, 1578)

(In Moray land in the kirk of a certain village or clachan named Petty are kept the bones of a certain person whom they call little John, departed but the space of three hundred years, as the common bruit [rumour] among them is . . . whose wideness of his bones and greatness teaches that he was 14 foot long.)

We find something similar on the west coast with the interest in both giants and pigmies – or, more usually, their bones. *Additional MSS 15509–15512* in the British Library include the sketches made to illustrate Sir Joseph Banks' voyage to the Hebrides, Orkney and Iceland during 1772. His party included the artists Miller and Clevely who drew people, landscapes, houses and churchyards as they visited some of the islands in the Southern Hebrides. When they came to the priory at Oronsay in August they examined the various bones and skulls they found in the graveyard. One item they drew, which appears rather ghoulish to modern taste, was an enormous thigh bone. On the back of the anonymous sketch it says: *The Thigh bone of the man from out of the Second grave measured 1' 6".*

Their attitude to skeletal remains was perhaps more Shakespearean than ours but we should recognise this rather morbid interest in human relics as a motive for visiting churchyards and battlegrounds. (See Plate 7). Highlanders had no aversion to old bones either. Boswell writes of the chapel on Raasay:

We here saw some human bones of an uncommon size. There was a heel-bone, in particular, which Dr Macleod said was such, that if the foot was in proportion, it must have been twenty-seven inches long. Dr Johnson would not look at the bones. He started back from them with a striking appearance

of horrour. Mr M'Queen told us, it was formerly much the custom, in these
isles, to have human bones lying above ground, especially in the windows of
churches. (Boswell, *The Journal of a Tour to the Hebrides*, 1773)

Worse, for Johnson, was to come in Col Maclean's house at Breacacha Bay on
Coll: '*In the charter-room there was a remarkable large shin-bone; which was said*
to have been a bone of John Garve, one of the lairds.' (Boswell, *The Journal of a*
Tour to the Hebrides, 1773)

Edward Daniel Clarke recorded something similar on his visit to the graves
on Culloden battlefield in 1797: '*Our guide with his spade gently raised the turf*
from some of these rude tumuli as we passed. We found them filled with the bones
and skulls of bodies, which seemed to have been hastily covered without much
attention to order or disposition. In some of them were shoes and rotten pieces of
wood.'

Clarke's interest was antiquarian rather than morbid. He persuaded the
Laird of Coll to open a cairn on that island, much to the distress of an old
islander who protested that it was unlucky to disturb the bones of the dead. At
that time, though, the feelings of old, but poor, islanders seem to have counted
for little in the face of treasure-hunting by wealthy southerners or local lairds.
Clarke records stories of other finds of human bones at the Bay of Martyrs on
Iona and in a cave by Oban. Of the former he writes:

> *In returning from the quarry we passed the Bay of Martyrs. Whenever the*
> *natives dig in or near this bay, they find human bones two feet below the*
> *surface. Six years ago the Marquis of Bute, to ascertain the truth of this,*
> *ordered search to be made, and at two feet the bones were found in abundance.*
> *There is no account whatever of these bones on record, nor have the natives*
> *any tradition relating to them.* (E.D. Clarke, *Journal*, 1797)

Such business soon turns into a tourist industry. A good example is the
Massacre cave (Uamh Fhraing) in Eigg where up to 395 Macdonalds are said
to have been smoked to death by the Macleods at the end of the sixteenth
century. On the one hand there is the shock horror – but do come and see it
for yourselves!

> *The sight of the walls, still blackened by the smoke, and, above all, the*
> *quantity of human bones and skulls scattered on the ground, were for us too*
> *striking proofs of the truth of that horrid catastrophe; and the effect produced*
> *on us by the unexpected discovery of these human skulls, and the horror*
> *which momentarily overcame us, can be easier imagined than described.* (L.
> A. Necker de Saussure, *A Voyage to the Hebrides*, written in 1807)

On the other is macabre curiosity as visitors gather to carry off some grisly
trophy:

The floor, for about a hundred feet inwards from the narrow vestibule,
resembles that of a charnel-house. At almost every step we come upon heaps of
human bones grouped together . . . They are of a brownish, earthy hue, here
and there tinged with green; the skulls, with the exception of a few broken
fragments, have disappeared; for travellers in the Hebrides have of late years
been numerous and curious; and many a museum . . . exhibits, in a grinning
skull, its memorial of the Massacre at Eigg. We find, too, further marks of
visitors in the single bones separated from the heaps and scattered over the
area; but enough still remains to show, in the general disposition of the
remains, that the hapless islanders died under the walls in families, each little
group separated by a few feet from the others . . . And beneath every heap we
find, at the depth . . . of a few inches, the remains of the straw-bed upon
which the family had lain, largely mixed with the smaller bones of the human
frame, ribs and vertebrae, and hand and feet bones; occasionally, too, with
fragments of unglazed pottery, and various other implements of a rude
housewifery. (Hugh Miller, *The Cruise of the Betsey* (Written in 1845))

The cave became so notorious that the bones were eventually removed for
burial. Nevertheless a child's skull was still found in a corner only a few years
ago.

This type of tourism was satirised by Philip Johnstone in his poem *High*
Wood, about a First World War battlefield that has become a visitor
attraction:

> *Madame, please,*
> *You are requested kindly not to touch*
> *Or take away the Company's property*
> *As souvenirs; you'll find we have on sale*
> *A large variety, all guaranteed.*

At the other end of the skeletal scale, Monro specifically says that people from
other countries came to Lewis to search for pigmy bones. This particular
piece of traveller's lore may have been very ancient:

At the north poynt of Lewis there is a little ile, callit the Pigmies ile, with ane
little kirk in it of ther awn handey wark. Within this kirk the ancients of that
country of the Lewis says, that the saids pigmies has been eirded thair.
Maney men of divers countreys had delvit up dieplie the flure of the little
kirke, and I myself amanges the leave, and hes found in it, deepe under the
erthe, certain baines and round heads of wonderful little quantity, allegit to be
the baines of the said Pygmies, quhilk may be lykely, according to sundry
historys that we reid of the Pigmies. (D. Monro, *A Description of the*
Western Isles of Scotland, Birlinn, 1994)

(At the north point of Lewis there is a little isle, called the Pigmies isle, with a little kirk in it of their own handiwork. Within this kirk the old people of that country of the Lewis say, that the said pigmies have been buried there. Many men of various countries had dug up deeply the floor of the little kirk, and I myself amongst the rest, and have found in it, deep under the earth, certain bones and round heads of wonderful little quantity (size), alleged to be the bones of the said Pygmies, which may be likely, according to sundry histories that we read of the Pigmies.)

At the end of the sixteenth century we read: '*In this Ile thair is ane little Cove biggit in form of ane kirk, and is callit the Pygmies Kirk. It is sa little, that ane man may scairslie stand uprichtlie in it eftir he is gane in on his kneis. Thair is sum of the Pygmies banes thairinto as yit, of the quhilkis the thrie banes being measurit is not fullie twa inches lang.*' (Skene, *Celtic Scotland, 1577–1595*)

In 1630 Captain Dymes shed a little more light on the matter and suggested that the visitors were predominantly from Ireland:

> *Aboute a mile distant from this Chappell lyeth the Pygmeys Island w[hi]ch is a round high hill contening about one acre of land. This Ile is ioyned to the Leweis by a narrowe necke of land, w[hi]ch is in length about halfe the distance of a paire of Butts, wherein there is the walls of a Chappell to bee seene w[hi]ch is but 8 foote in length and 6 foote in breadth, the ground whereof hath bene often tymes digged vpp espetially by the Irish w[hi]ch come thither of purpose to gett the bones of those little people w[hi]ch they say were buryed there. At my beinge vpon the Ile I made search in the earth and found some of those bones, w[hi]ch are soe little that my beleife is scarce bigg enough to thinke them to bee the bones humane flesh.* (Captain Dymes, Description of Lewis, 1630, in W. C. Mackenzie, *History of the Outer Hebrides*

There is a unique early seventeenth-century map of Lewis and Harris in the National Library of Ireland (see Plate 4). It is tempting to link this with Captain Dymes's report which was once accompanied by both a map of the island and a plan of Stornoway. The map seems to be of Irish origin and near the Butt of Lewis there is a little island with the caption 'The Piggmes of Ness'. There are not many place-names on this map so it is interesting to see that, from an Irish perspective at least, the Pigmy's Isle was thought worthy of mention.

The same island appears in the Blaeu map of Lewis and Harris as *Ylen Dunibeg* which is a corrupt form of the Gaelic for 'Isle of the Little Men'. The name 'Pigmy's Isle' is just an anglicised version of this. In an article written in 1905, W.C. Mackenzie explored the pigmy traditions in the island and offered an ethnological approach to the problem. He felt that the discovery of small bones on 'Pigmy's Isle', and local traditions of 'little men', were independent of each other. To account for the latter he referred back to Irish mythology and its tales of giant and pigmy races.

Hence we have pigmies and giants to represent races who were shorter or taller than the race perpetuating the traditions.

The bones discovered on 'Pigmy's Isle' were most probably those of animals and birds – presumably the contents of a midden. However they fitted perfectly with visitor expectations and so the tradition was continued. We do not have to agree with all of Mackenzie's conclusions to find his general drift persuasive. In Lewis and Harris there were ancient folk memories of people of shorter stature. Irish visitors, with similar traditions of their own, were intrigued by these stories. The happy 'discovery' of small bones on a site associated with these 'little people' made the area more attractive to tourists. Much tourism, past and present, is based on such accidents.

Martin Martin writes in similar fashion of this island: '*The Island of Pigmies, or, as the natives call it, the Island of Little Men, is but of small extent. There has been many small bones dug out of the ground here, resembling those of human kind more than any other. This gave ground to a tradition which the natives have of a very low-statured people living once here, called Lusbirdan, i.e., pigmies.*' And of Colonsay: '*The other fort is called Dun-Evan: the natives have a tradition among them, of a very little generation of people, that lived once here, called Lusbirdan, the same with pigmies.*' (Martin Martin, *A Description of the Western Islands of Scotland.*)

Both in Ireland and Scotland there seem to have been ancient folk-myths of peoples large and small. These are then associated with particular places or islands where they made a last stand. Precisely similar stories concern the Vikings and the various places they were finally hunted down or vanquished (e.g. Fuday or Trotternish). The fact that the bones may actually have been of birds and animals in no way detracts from the strength of a former belief in little people.

Antiquities and Beregonium

An interest in antiquities is not new. People have always been interested in the monuments of the past. It is just that we now have the leisure and the resources to turn it into an industry. An early example of this nascent antiquarianism is Boece's probable reference to the two Glenelg brochs:

In ane vale of Ros ar twa housis, round in forme of ane bell; and ar saiffit to our dayis in memory of sum antiquiteis of our eldaris. (Boece in Hume Brown, *Scotland before 1700*)

(In a valley of Ross are two houses, round in form of a bell; and [they] are saved to our days in memory of some antiquities of our elders).

Although now in Inverness-shire the brochs in Glen Beag (Glenelg) are still amongst the most impressive in Scotland. What is intriguing about Boece's statement is the implication that they may have been deliberately preserved. This finds some support in local tradition as reported by Knox in 1786:

> *This place is famous for some remains of ancient fabrics, whose origin has baffled the enquiries of antiquarians. Two of these buildings appear in the form of circular ruins, of whose walls some feet still remain above ground. Two others are reduced to a heap of stones. They are placed in a line upon the banks of the river, on places which served for the purposes of observation, as well as defence . . . Perceiving that the country people were demolishing these buildings for the stones, I threatened to inform the laird of Macleod, to whom this country belongs, in order that every offender might be brought to punishment. Upon hearing this, an old man observed, that an ancient prophecy was now fulfilled; for it had been said, that 'whoever took a stone from those buildings, would meet with some terrible judgement, and never thrive thereafter.'* (J. Knox, *A Tour through the Highlands of Scotland*, 1786)

There were other antiquities not very carefully maintained by locals. Pennant writes of graveslabs on Iona which were covered in dung: '*With much difficulty, by virtue of fair words, and a bribe, prevail on one of these listless fellows to remove a great quantity of this dunghill; and by that means once more expose to light the tomb of the last prioress.*' (T. Pennant, *A Tour in Scotland and Voyage to the Hebrides*, 1772)

Different travellers had different interests. Pennant was fascinated by antiquities, Johnson much less so. He offers a good example of the once-you've-seen-one, you've-seen-them-all school of thought:

> *About three miles beyond Inverness, we saw, just by the road, a very complete specimen of what is called a Druid's temple. There was a double circle, one of very large, the other of smaller stones. Dr Johnson justly observed, that, 'to go and see one druidical temple is only to see that it is nothing, for there is neither art nor power in it; and seeing one is quite enough'.* (Boswell, *The Journal of a Tour to the Hebrides*, 1773)

Perhaps because the shortage of towns in the Highlands and Islands was felt to require some explanation, there were various stories about ancient but decayed cities. The mystical city of Beregonium was one such. Boece writes of Fergus, first king of the Scots, who brought law and justice among them:

> *Eftir this he beildit the castell of Berigone in Lochtquhabbir, quhilk standis in the west partis of Scotlannd, fornent the Ilis; quhair he exercit his lawis, that this pepill mycht be drawin thair the moir esely, for exercicioun of iustice.* (Boece, in Hume Brown, *Scotland before 1700*)

(After this he built the castle of Berigone in Lochaber, which stands in the west parts of Scotland, facing the Isles; where he exercised his laws, that this people might be drawn there the more easily, for execution of justice.)

Boece regarded Inverlochy as another important centre:

In the mouth of Lochtie wes ane riche toun namit Inverlochtie, quhair sum time wes gret change, be repair of uncouth marchandis; . . . Beyound Lochtie is the castell of Dunstafage, sum time namit Evonium. (Boece, in Hume Brown, *Scotland before 1700*)

(In the mouth of [the River] Lochy was a rich town named Inverlochy, where sometime [formerly] was great exchange [trade], by repair [resorting there] of uncouth [foreign] merchants; . . . Beyond Lochy is the castle of Dunstaffnage, sometime named Evonium.)

Boece's geographical knowledge of the west coast was hazy and he was undoubtedly muddled about the relative positions of Beregonium, Dunstaffnage and Inverlochy. A place called Rerigonium had appeared on Ptolemy's map of Scotland and early geographers expended a good deal of time and energy trying to locate it. It was probably by Loch Ryan in Galloway but, with the authority of Boece behind them, many tried to place it in the West Highlands. Nowell's large-scale map of Scotland (c.1565) put it at the head of Loch Awe under the name Bergomum. The notes appearing in *Macfarlane's Geographical Collections* locate it near the southern end of the Great Glen.

There was ane ancient castle builded whaire this Toircastle is, which was called Beragonium (Pont(?) in *Macfarlane's Geographical Collections*, vol II)

(Torcastle is an ancient castle next to the Caledonian Canal and lies north of Fort William).

Pont also draws attention to a vitrified fort just north of the Connel ferry across Loch Etive. It appears this was not yet claimed to be Beregonium:

At the Westend of this Countrey of Beandirlogh verie near the seasyde below the Mountaine there is a chappell called Killechallumchill in Beandirlogh one myll from the ferrie off Connell in Lorne. In this chappell toune there is ane high hill round and plaine about, and it is verie plaine above on the tope thereof. Ane Springand Water is on the one pairt therof And it is likelie to have been one strength or fort in ancient tymes which ancient men and woemen of that Countrey alledges that certane gyants or

*strong men hes bein the builders and Inhabitants theroff and there is one
kynd of graystone found in this toune, which when it is putt in the water, it
will not goe to the ground as other stones uses to doe, and such stones as
those are not to be had in anie pairt in these countries but in that chappell
toune called in English St. Columbs Chappell.* (Pont(?) in *Macfarlane's
Geographical Collections,* vol II)

This fort is certainly the vitrified fort at Dun Mac Sniachan (See RCAHMS
Argyll Vol 2, No 136) which, by the end of the eighteenth century, was
thought to be the site of Beregonium. Vitrified material has a pumice-like
quality which probably lies behind Pont's story that its stone will float. The
well lies on the SE side of the slope below the dun. Its status seems to have
made it a required item on a visitor's itinerary. In addition it had a place in the
Romantic pantheon as the site of the *Dun,* or fortress, of the sons of Uisneach,
famed in the story of Deirdre and Naisi.

Travellers found they had to disabuse themselves of any notion of another
Troy. Pennant took a practical line:

*A mile from Connel, near the shore, is Dun-mac-Sniochain, the ancient
Beregonium . . . The foundation of this city, as it is called, is attributed, by
apocryphal history, to Fergus II and was called the chief in Scotland for
many ages. It was at best such a city as Caesar found in our island at the time
of his invasion; an oppidum, or fortified town, placed in a thick wood,
surrounded with a rampart and fosse, a place of retreat from invaders.* (T.
Pennant, *A Tour in Scotland and Voyage to the Hebrides,* 1772)

However, Pennant was misled by the vitrified material of the fort into
thinking it was the remnant of a volcano. Knox also paid homage: '*On the
north side of Loch Etive stood the town of Beregonium, supposed to have been the
capital of the West Highlands. It seems, from certain mounds, excavations, and
other appearances, to have been a strong fortress, to prevent invasion, or to secure
a retreat, as occasions might require.*' (John Knox, *The Highlands and Hebrides
in 1786*)

E.D. Clarke visited the area in 1797 and gives us an idea of the attraction
felt towards this mystical ancient city:

*Having long felt a curiosity to visit the site of the ancient Beregonium, once
the capital of all Scotland, and being offered horses by Mr. Hugh Stevenson,
jun. we set out, in company with that gentleman, on the morning of the 16th
of August . . .*

*About two miles beyond the ferry is all that remains of Beregonium. When
I state what this all amounts to, few will deem it worth their while to explore
it, unless that local enthusiasm which Dr. Johnson deprecates the absence of,
upon 'any ground that has been dignified by wisdom, bravery, or virtue,'*

should lead them to a barren rock, without a vestige of human habitation . . .

The situation usually appropriated to Beregonium is a rock of slate, which rises, as it were, insulated in the middle of a plain, at the foot of lofty cliffs; and on this rock, I thought, but it might be conjecture, I could trace the circular basis of a fortress like those commonly attributed to the Danes. As I was employed in determining the traces of this edifice, a peasant from the plain below brought me a piece of pumice stone. Upon inquiry, I found that several fragments of the same nature were found at the bottom of the rock, but that they were all derived from one spot at the other end of the rock. Being conducted to the place, I found a mass of vitrified matter, upon a basis of slate, facing the west, on the summit of the rock. In this mass I observed a very extraordinary effect of fire upon a heap of stones, some of which were completely vitrified, and appeared covered with a glossy substance. Others like the substance found at the bottom of furnaces in the glass houses. Others, again, were reduced in part to pumice, but not entirely; the outside being pumice, and the interior part of the same stones less affected by fire. Others, again, remained in their original state, except being a little scorched on the outside. These probably owe their present appearance to artificial fire.

In the plain below the rock, are two causeways, which still bear among the natives the appellations of Meal-street and Market-street. That which is called Market-street is a mound or bank, like that of Romney Marsh, in Kent, and extends from the rock along the sea-shore, to the opposite cliffs. It appears to have been originally raised to prevent the incursions of the sea from the plain behind it, and has since received additional strength from the beach which has been thrown up against it. It is very probable, whatever might have been the original purport of its construction, that during the existence of Beregonium as a city, provisions were here exposed for sale, as it offered so fair a mart, in the immediate vicinity of those who came to the shore with their boats from the neighbouring country: and probably from this circumstance, which was a consequence and not a cause of its being erected, it obtained the appellation of Market-street.

In the plain behind this embankment, is one of those upright stones, often noticed by Mr. Pennant, and common to, all the Hebrides, the main land of Scotland, the Orkney isles, and the south-western counties of England, particularly those of Cornwall and Devonshire. Near this stone a number of human bones were lately discovered by the peasants in tilling the ground. A kind of coarse pavement was also found, not far from the same spot, but not mosaic; merely a rude layer of very irregular stones. A few years ago, in picking some stones from a neighbouring rock, one of the labourers found about half a dozen thin silver coins. I could not discover what afterward became of them; nor could any other account be obtained of the coins themselves, than merely what related to their original discovery.

When we look back to the remote periods in which the city of Beregonium must be supposed to have existed, we are not to wonder at the slight vestiges which now appear of a metropolis once so celebrated. It is highly probable, that a fortress, surrounded by huts, constituted all from which those vestiges are now to be derived.

At present, so destitute is the spot on which that metropolis is supposed to have been founded, that I could not contemplate the site of it without calling to mind the observation of a British nobleman, in Italy, whose remarks afforded no small degree of entertainment to those of his countrymen who resided with him in that country: 'When these antiquarians,' said he, 'explain the nature of a thing that is, I can listen to them with some degree of patience; but when they drag me about to shew where something has been, I can bear it no longer!' (E.D. Clarke, Journal, 1797)

Clarke plainly felt the need to explain to his readers that they must not let their disappointment at the meagreness of the site limit their imaginations – a sentiment aired by many others on visits to overgrown historical sites in the Highlands ever since. Equally we must pay tribute to his antiquarian enthusiasm which, like everything else he did, he tried to impart to others. He had also noticed a nearby standing stone – there is one to the north, and another just south of the dun.

Scottish waters

The properties of Scottish waters have long been renowned. Loch Lomond must have been famous from prehistoric times. In the Irish version of Nennius (and its later attachments) we find fabulous stories about Loch Lomond in the section on the wonders of the Island of Britain: '*The first wonder of the island of Britain is Loch Lemnon; there are sixty islands and sixty rocks in it, and sixty streams flow into it, and one stream out of it, that is the Leamain.*' (Todd, *The Irish Version of the Historia Britonum of Nennius*).

By the time of Geoffrey of Monmouth, writing about 1136, this had become:

This lake contains sixty islands and has sixty streams to feed it, yet only one of these streams flows down to the sea. On these islands one can make out sixty crags, which between them support exactly the same number of eagles' nests. The eagles used to flock together each year and foretell any prodigious event which was about to occur in the kingdom: this by a shrill-pitched scream which they emitted in concert. (Geoffrey of Monmouth, *History of the Kings of Britain*, p 219)

In the Gough Map of Britain these wonders, albeit placed by Loch Tay, have been refined to three: waves without wind, fish without fins and a floating island. The Gough Map is dated to about 1360 but the surveys on which its Scottish section is based may well have been conducted at the end of the previous century. (A floating island is also noted in Loch Loycha in Ireland by the thirteenth-century Norse author of *The King's Mirror*.) These three wonders then ran for centuries more:

Abone Renfrew, to the Occeane seis, lyis the Lennox, namit, be Ptolome, Lelgonia; in quhilk is ane gret loch namit Lochmond, xxiv milis of lenth, and viii milis of breid. Within this loch ar xxx Ilis, weil biggit with kirkis, templis, and housis: and in this loch ar thre notable thingis; fische swomand but ony fin; ane richt dangerus and storme wal, but ony wind; and ane Ile that fletis heir and thair as the wind servis. (Boece in Hume Brown, *Scotland before 1700*)

(Above Renfrew, to the Ocean seas, lies the Lennox, named, by Ptolemy, Lelgonia; in which is a great loch named Lomond, twenty-four miles of length, and eight miles of breadth. Within this loch are thirty isles, well built with kirks, temples, and houses: and in this loch are three notable things; fish swimming without any fins; a right dangerous and stormy wave without any wind; and an isle that floats here and there as the wind serves).

Loch Lomond does have an uncommon fish, the powan, but I do not see how it could be described as finless. Loch Lomond was not alone in having unusual properties. It was also thought wonderful that, despite its Northern location, Loch Ness did not freeze:

Heir the water of ye Ness flowis out of the loch of the same name, and baith haue this nature. that albeit the frost be nevir sa gret, thay freis neuir: bot gif ony frosin thing be put athir in the loch or in the river, it thowis fra hand. Quhairfor quhen horsmen cumis to Ennirness in a gret and horrible frost, afor they turne in to the lugeng, first in thay ryde into this riuer, to wasche thair horses, and to throw the pypes and schokles of yce, frosin vpon thame. (Dalrymple's translation in E. Cody (ed.), *Leslie's History of Scotland*, 1578)

(Here the water of the Ness flows out of the loch of the same name, and both have this nature – that albeit the frost be never so great, they freeze never: but if any frozen thing be put either in the loch or in the river, it thaws at once. Wherefore when horsemen come to Inverness in a great and horrible frost, before they turn in to the lodging, first in they ride into this river, to wash their horses, and to throw the pipes and shackles of ice, frozen upon them).

A great number of wells in the Highlands and Islands were revered for medicinal or religious reasons. Throughout the centuries they were visited by local people who came in search of cure or relief. Some were regarded as marvellous for other reasons. One natural process which drew particular attention was the way in which objects seemed to petrify or calcify in certain waters. Gerald of Wales writes:

> *There is a well in the far north of Ulster which is so cold that if logs of wood are left in it for seven years, they harden so as to become stones.*
> *There is in Norway also a well of the same kind, but its efficacy is the greater in as much as it is nearer to the frigid zone. Not only if wood, but if flax or a linen web be placed in it for a year, it becomes very hard stone . . .* (J. O'Meara, Gerald of Wales – The History and Topography of Ireland)

In the Norse work, *The King's Mirror*, written between 1217–1260, there is a section on the natural wonders of Ireland:

> *There is a lake in that country concerning the nature of which strange tales are told; it is called Logechag in the native speech. It is quite an extensive lake and has this property, that if you take a stick of the wood that some call holm and others holly but is called acrifolium [aquifolium] in Latin and fix it in the lake so that part of it is in the earth, a part in the water, and a part rising above, the part in the earth will turn into iron, the part in the water into stone, while that which stands out above will remain as before. But if you set any other sort of wood in the lake, its nature will not change.* (L.M. Larson, *The King's Mirror*)

We find something rather similar amongst Pont's(?) notes in *Macfarlane's Geographical Collections*. He is writing of Arnisdale in Glenelg:

> *On the south syde of this Countrie forgainst Knoidart there is a litle toune and a litle river running through the toune to the sea. And if anie man or woman will cast a tree in this water, all that is above the water will be a tree as it was affoir, and all that is under the water will be transformed in a stone als hard as anie other stone and this was tryed oftymes and anie tree that falls from the mountains into it is lykwayes transformit in a stone And this toune is called Arnistill in Glenelg.* (Pont(?) in *Macfarlane's Geographical Collections*, vol II)

Walker classed this as a fossil:

> *In Loch Huron [Hourn], opposite to Sky, there is a Species of Amiantus in vast Quantities. Sir Andrew Balfour and Sir Robert Sibbald in the last Century had Specimens of this Fossile from the same Place, but both of them*

acquiesced in the Traditional Opinion of the Natives of the Country, who all suppose it to be petrified Holly, a Wood which grows naturally in abundance upon the Banks of the River where it is found; though a genuine Amiantus, it has indeed a most exact Resemblance of petrified Wood, in its Colour and Structure, yet upon a narrow View of its Fibres, it is easy to discern, that they never have belonged to any Plant. (McKay, *Walker's Report on the Hebrides*, 1764 and 1771)

If Sibbald had a specimen from Loch Hourn I wonder if it originally came from Pont.

Water could also be used to prognosticate or foretell. The business of auguring the future is both ancient and universal, and many different media have been used. In the section on the wonders of Ireland in the Irish Nennius it is claimed that: '*There is a stone in a church in Ulster whose practice it is to shed blood three days previous to a plunder of the church.*' (Todd, *The Irish Version of the Historia Britonum of Nennius*).

This was the sort of thing that travellers reported – or had their attention drawn to. Pont(?) gives some corresponding examples for Scotland and it is interesting to see that in a Highland context the agency was liquid. In Barra, for instance:

And in this toune there is one springand fresh water Well. And the Inhabitants and ancient men and woemen both of men and woemen in this toune and of the Countrie especiallie one ancient man being of fyve or sexscoir zeares old doeth say that when appearance of Warrs wer to be in the Countrey of Barray That certaine drops of blood hath oftymes bein sein in this springand fresh Water Well. The Laird and Superior of this Countrey was called Rorie McNeill being ane verie ancient man of sexscore yeares old or therby did report this to be true. And also did report this to be true lykwayes whensoever appearance of peace wold be in the Countrie That certain litle bitts of Peitts wold be sein. (Pont(?) in *Macfarlane's Geographical Collections*, vol II)

Whereas near Loch Creran:

There is one fountaine springing out of the sand in the sea, of fresh water, not ane myll distant from the sanctuarie or holie Chappell in a toune called Ardnacloch which when anie in these pairts are sick, if the sick dieth, a dead worme is found in the bottome of the water or fountaine and if the sick shall recover a quick worme is found in it. (Pont(?) in Macfarlane's Geographical Collections, vol II)

Sometimes these marvels or curiosities are merely disguises for practical hygiene: '*There is in Connacht a well which has water that can be drunk only by men, but is pestilential to horses or cattle, or any other animals whatever that should taste it.'* (J. O'Meara, *Gerald of Wales – The History and Topography of Ireland.*)

Martin Martin writes of a large cave in the hill Ulweal in Harris: '*It hath two wells in it, one of which is excluded from dogs; for they say if a dog do but taste of the water, the well presently drieth up: and for this reason, all such as have occasion to lodge there, take care to tie their dogs, that they may not have access to the water. The other well is called the dogs-well, and is only drunk by them.'* (Martin Martin, *A Description of the Western Islands of Scotland.*)

If we strip away the mythic overlay it is plain that what we have here is sensible hygiene.

Finally of course water could be a threat. It is perhaps overdoing it to talk of an ancient folk-memory of the Flood but there was certainly an awareness of the dangers posed by the sea. In an Irish context, Gerald of Wales quotes the story about how Lough Neagh had risen and drowned former communities in its neighbourhood: '*There is some confirmation of this story in as much as fishermen of the lake clearly see under the waves in calm weather towers of churches, which, as is usual in that country, are tall, slender, and rounded. They frequently point them out to visitors who are amazed at the occurrence.'* (J. O'Meara, *Gerald of Wales – The History and Topography of Ireland.*)

Pont's(?) notes on Uist in Macfarlane's Geographical Collections have a similar theme. The machair-land on the west side of Uist was both created by, and always under threat from, the sea. Nevertheless there is something mythic about the following report:

Ancient men in that Countrey were reportand that there is much of the lands of Wist overwhelmed and destroyed with the sea, and the sand doeth flow with the winde and destroyes both the lands and hyds the houssis below the sand, and so the most pairt of the Countrie is overwhelmed with sand.

There was ane Ancient man in a toune in Wist called Killpettill and this old man said that he was sex or sevinscoir of years old and he did sie another church with the lands of the Parish wherein that church did stand. And these lands were more profitable fertill and pleasant then these that are in Wist now. And that his father and mother, his grandfather and Grandmother did see another parish Church which was destroyed with the sea long agoe. And that they did call that Church Kilmarchirmore The next was called Killpettill, And this Church wherin he doth dwell now into, was called Killmony which is now called Killpettill that is to say the Mure Church, because it lyeth next the Mures Mosses and Mountains And this Church is below the sands except foure or fyve foot length of the pinnacle of that church And the pairt of there houses which are nearest the seasyde for the Wind doth blow up the sand upon the lands and the churches were destroyed with the sea which were principall Churches of Ancient. Certaine of them will be seen when the sea ebbs in the summer tyme. And the Countrie people will take Lobsters out of the windowes of the Pinnacle of that which was first called Killpettill before it was destroyed with the sea. (Pont(?) in *Macfarlane's Geographical Collections*, vol II)

Monsters

Monsters were not confined to water:

> *It wes said be Schir Duncane Campbell to us, that out of Garloll, ane loch of Argyle, the yeir of God MDX yeris, come ane terrible beist, als mekil as ane grew-hound, futit lik ane ganar, and straik doun gret treis with the dint of hir tail; and slew thre men quhilkis wer at thair hountis with thre straikis of hir tail: and wer not the remanent huntaris clam up in strang aikis, thay had bene all slane in the samin maner. Eftir the slauchter of thir men, scho fled speidlie to the loch. Sindry prudent men belevit gret trubill to follow in Scotland, be appering of this beist; for scho was sene afore, and ay trubil following thairefter.* (Boece in Hume Brown, *Scotland before 1700*)

(It was said by Sir Duncan Campbell to us, that out of Gareloch, a loch of Argyll, the year of God 1510 years, came a terrible beast, as great as a greyhound, with feet like a gander, and struck down great trees with the blow of her tail; and slew three men which were at their hunts with three strokes of her tail: and had not the remaining hunters climbed up in strong oaks, they had been all slain in the same manner. After the slaughter of these men, she fled speedily to the loch. Sundry prudent men believed great trouble to follow in Scotland, by appearing of this beast; for she was seen before, and always trouble following thereafter).

The following story was related by Pont(?) and probably refers to the mythic destruction of a crannog in one of the small lochans on the west side of the Corran ferry in Ardgour.

> *Ardgoure next to Lochaquber on the eist syd of Loquhaber In this litle countrie of ancient there were certaine Inhabitants . . . And they did build ane house of timber in one litle Illand which was amongst Mosses next to the principall toune, which they hade in Ardgoure, And the saids Inhabitants having this Illand for ane strengh house to keep himself and the principall men of his kin and friends from their enemies. They being dwelling there for ane space, It fortuned on a tyme that ane monstrous beast being in that litle Logh, the most pairt of these Inhabitants being in this Illand It was overwhelmit and destroyed by that terrible and most fearfull Monstrous beast and so they all were perished and devoured.* (Pont(?), *Macfarlane's Geographical Collections*, vol II)

In the same text there are some later additions by those who transcribed and transmitted Pont's notes. One such apparently refers to adders on the River Arkaig. Some years ago I was lucky enough to see a migration of elvers up the River Morar. The water and surrounding rocks were literally black with slithery forms and it is easy to imagine how such a natural wonder could be exaggerated in the telling. Eels seem more likely than adders and their quantities could certainly upset the credulous.

> *In the water or river of Airgaik there was seen in the zeare 1620 yeirs. the fourteenth of August. the tennants and gentlemen of the Countrey being at the building of a bridge of timber on the said river, at the latter end of the making of the bridge, there appeared Innumerable Adders in this water of Airgaick Immediatlie efter the finitione of the said bridge, The gentlemen and tennants perceiving the Adders and all the water in such a pairt a litle above the bridge full of cruell and terrible beasts and certaine of the biggest of the adders did lope high above the water, and certaine others of them comeing to the land, did goe through the hadder and grass so fast that the whole Companie which did behold, were much affraied at this terrible and Marvelous sight. And at last they were forced to leave their work and depart from that place, which they did say, if there had bein such sight at the beginning of the work, they had never did it.* (Pont(?), *Macfarlane's Geographical Collections*, vol II)

True marvels

There were also what one might call true marvels; facts which were curious to the traveller because they were strange, antiquated or novel. One of the most frequently noted by travellers to the Highlands and Islands was the local method of making bread.

> *Lykwyse of [sheaves] of corne . . . breid wil thay make [quicker than would be thought. They do not thresh corn, but dry it on the stalk, by spreading the ears on the ground and burning away the straw and chaff] . . . quhen it is winnowit, thay grind it in a hand mil, quhilke properlie we call the queirnis, thaireftir thay sift it: frahand thay make breid aftir casting it upon the girdle, or than setting it til a stane, thay bake it at the harth, quhilke breid is nocht different far frome that breid, quhilke the ald fathers calles subcinericius, or bakne vnder the asse.* (Dalrymple's translation in E Cody (ed.), *Leslie's History of Scotland,* 1578)

(Likewise of [sheaves] of corn . . . bread will they make [quicker than would be thought. They do not thresh corn, but dry it on the stalk, by spreading the ears on the ground and burning away the straw and chaff] . . . when it is winnowed, they grind it in a hand mill, which properly we call the quern, thereafter they sift it: at once they make bread after casting it upon the girdle, or then setting it against a stone, they bake it at the hearth, which bread is not different far from that bread, which the old fathers call *subcinericius*, or baked under the ash.)

Cody, (Leslie's modern editor), notes that the reference is to Genesis XVIII. 6, which reads (in the Authorised Version): '*And Abraham hastened into the tent unto Sarah, and said, Make ready quickly three measures of fine meal, knead it, and make cakes upon the hearth.*'

Cody also states that the phrase 'upon the hearth' is a translation of 'subcinericii'.

Compared to the Lowlands there was a general absence of mills in the Highlands and Islands. There were sound economic reasons for this. It was expensive and risky moving your grain about by sea and most families would grind their corn as and when they required it. The most convenient method was by means of a hand quern. These were ubiquitous:

> there is no great rivers of fresh water in Barray but one litle Water in a toune called Quir, and there is a litle mill in that water and no more mills in all the Illand. Bot everie husbandman in the countrey hes ane Instrument in their houses called one Kewrne and the two stones doth lye on the house floore, and that place is made cleane (Pont(?) in *Macfarlane's Geographical Collections*, vol II)

> Their bread, for the most part, is of oat-meal, which, if thin and well baked upon broad irons or stones for that purpose, is palatable enough, and often brought to gentlemen's tables. But the vulgar are not so curious, for they only water the meal into a convenient consistence, and then making 'em into thick cakes, called bannocks, they set 'em before the fire to be hardened or toasted for their use. These people prepare the oats after this manner, – they take several sheaves, and setting fire to 'em consume the straw and chaff to ashes, which, after a convenient time, they blow away, then gathering up the grain sufficiently parched, they bruise it into meal. (Morer, 1689, in Hume Brown, *Early Travellers in Scotland*)

Martin Martin also describes the process of making graddan meal:

> The ancient way of dressing corn, which is yet used in several isles, is called graddan, from the Irish word grad, which signified quick. A woman sitting down takes a handful of corn, holding it by the stalks in her left hand, and then sets fire to the ears, which are presently in a flame. She has a stick in her right hand, which she manages very dexterously, beating off the grain at the very instant when the husk is quite burnt; for if she miss of that she must use

the kiln, but experience has taught them this art to perfection. The corn may be so dressed, winnowed, ground, and baked within an hour after reaping from the ground. The oat bread dressed as above is loosening, and that dressed in the kiln astringent, and of greater strength for labourers: but they love the graddan, as being more agreeable to their taste. This barbarous custom is much laid aside since the number of their mills increased. Captain Fairweather, master of an English vessel, having dropped anchor at Bernera of Glenelk over against Skye, saw two women at this employment, and wondering to see so much flame and smoke he came near, and finding that it was corn they burnt, he ran away in great haste telling the natives that he had seen two mad women very busy burning corn. The people came to see what the matter was, and laughed at the captain's mistake, though he was not a little surprised at the strangeness of a custom that he had never seen or heard of before. (Martin Martin, *A Description of the Western islands of Scotland,* c. 1695)

In some of the western islands (as well as in part of the Highlands), the people never rub out a greater quantity of oats than what is just necessary for seed against the following year; the rest they reserve in the sheaves, for their food; and as they have occasion, set fire to some of them, not only to dry the oats, which, for the most part, are wet, but to burn off the husk. Then, by winnowing, they separate, as well as they can, the sooty part from the grain; but as this cannot be done effectually, the 'bannack', or cake they make of it, is very black . . . This oatmeal is called 'graydon meal'. (Edmund Burt, *Letters from a Gentleman in the North of Scotland,* late 1720s)

Archibald Menzies describes the situation in Knoydart in 1768:

They retain the barbarous custom of burning their straw in making graddan meal. The parts they don't burn they use as thatch to their houses. They usually pull their corns by the roots, cut of a part of the straw at top, which is burnt to dry their grain. The method of doing it is this. Two women sit down, each having a small stick in their hands. They set the straw on fire and, by turning it nimbly with their sticks and putting on more straw with corn, they take care not to burn the grain. Then they separate the grain from the ashes, put it into a tub, where they rub it well with their hands & feet, and then winnow, clean & grind it in their querns, which are a kind of hand mills. From shearing their corns they will make bread in a few hours. (In V. Wills, *Reports on the Annexed Estates,* p 99)

Whilst mills had been present in some islands like Bute for hundreds of years, they only appeared in Arisaig from the mid-eighteenth century. Visitors were fascinated both by the process of hand-milling and by Biblical and classical comparisons. They could indulge in a little practical anthropology in their own country. Four years later Pennant described the milling process in Rum:

> *Notwithstanding this island has several streams, here is not a single mill; all the molinary operations are done at home: the corn is graddan'd, or burnt out of the ear, instead of being thrashed: this is performed two ways; first, by cutting off the ears, and drying them in a kiln, then setting fire to them on a floor, and picking out the grains, by this operation rendered as black as coal. The other method is more expeditious, for the whole sheaf is burnt, without the trouble of cutting off the ears: a most ruinous practice, as it destroys both thatch and manure, and on that account has been wisely prohibited in some of the islands. Graddaned corn was the parched corn of Holy Writ . . . The grinding was also performed by the same sort of machine the quern, in which two women were necessarily employed . . . I must observe too that the island lasses are as merry at their work of grinding the Graddan . . . as those of Greece were in the days of Aristophanes,*
> *Who warbled as they ground their parched corn.*
> *The quern or bra is made in some of the neighboring counties, in the mainland, and costs about fourteen shillings. This method of grinding is very tedious: for it employs two pairs of hands four hours to grind only a single bushel of corn. Instead of a hair sieve to sift the meal the inhabitants here have an ingenious substitute, a sheep's skin stretched round a hoop, and perforated with small holes made with a hot iron. They knead their bannock with water only, and bake or rather toast it, by laying it upright against a stone placed near the fire.* (Thomas Pennant, *A Tour in Scotland and Voyage to the Hebrides*, 1772)

The same was true of the outer isles:

> *They burn the straw of the sheaf, to make the oats dry for meal: and though the grain is black by the ashes, and the meal coloured, yet it is not unpleasant to the taste, and it is thought to be very wholesome food . . . Their cakes are made of barley meal, and toasted against a stone placed upright before a good fire; and sometimes, when either haste or hunger impels them, they are laid on the ashes, with more ashes above, to bake them more quickly.* (Buchanan, *Travels in the Western Hebrides from 1782 to 1790*)

Women washing

Another hardy perennial for the curious traveller was that of Scots women washing clothes. This features in accounts over several hundred years and was the subject of engravings and even twentieth-century postcards. It is comparable to the purely academic interest of Victorian ethnographers in naked African girls. It is of interest to us because of the references to Inverness.

In 1656–57 Richard Franck describes the bridge in Dumfries: '*where thrice in a week you shall rarely fail to see their maid-maukins dance corantos in tubs. So on every Sunday some as seldom miss to make their appearance on the stool of repentance.*' (Franck, *Northern Memoirs*)

In June 1677 Thomas Kirk visited Inverness: '*Over the river is a rotten wooden bridge, about ten or twelve pillars. Below this bridge are abundance of nasty women possing clothes with their feet, their clothes tucked up to the middle.*' (T. Kirk in Hume Brown (ed), *Tours in Scotland*)

Thomas Kirk was referring to the habit of women washing clothes in a river by pummelling them with their feet. To avoid their own clothes getting wet they would tuck them up and as a result attracted a gaggle of male admirers who were drawn by the sight of a bit of leg. Kirk gives his respectable version first. Two years later he published another version with more than a hint of the lascivious: '*Their banks and borders of these rivers (especially near their towns) are adorn'd with hardy amazons, though inverted, their valour being (chiefly) from the waste downwards, which parts they readily expose to all the dangers of a naked rencounter.*' (Thomas Kirk, 1679, in Hume Brown, *Early Travellers in Scotland*)

Burt saw something similar in Inverness fifty years later:

> *Before I leave the bridge, I shall take notice of one thing more, which is commonly to be seen by the sides of the river (and not only here, but in all the parts of Scotland where I have been), that is, women with their coats tucked up, stamping, in tubs, upon linen by this way of washing; and not only in summer, but in the hardest frosty weather, when their legs and feet are almost literally as red as blood with the cold; and often two of these wenches stamp in one tub, supporting themselves by their arms thrown over each other's shoulders.* (Edmund Burt, *Letters from a Gentleman in the North of Scotland*, late 1720s)

Burt's comments were supported by an engraving in his book. In 1746 an observer in Cumberland's army writes of the River Ness at Inverness:

> *To the Sides of this River, the Washerwomen come to wash their Linnen, and dry it upon the Stones or Grass adjacent. Their Method of Washing, is by treading it in a Tub with their naked Feet, and holding at the same Time their Petticoats up to their Middle, and with an unusual Motion, constantly turning round, they continue Day after Day, for they wash seldom, and a great deal at a Time, amongst the better Sort of Families; and those who are not worth a Tub, tread it in the River upon a large Stone under Water, for they very seldom use Soap. You'll see in a warm Morning, the River Edges lin'd with these Sort of Women that are Maid-servants, and frequently as*

many Soldiers admiring their Legs and Thighs, and particularly their Motion in treading. (A journey through Part of England and Scotland, 1746)

Whatever other changes history may bring, human nature doesn't change much!

Geographical lore

Although Pont can fairly claim to be the father of Scottish cartography it is interesting to find that his notes in *Macfarlane's Geographical Collections* make reference to geographical traditions that long predated him. For instance Ben Nevis was already supposed to be the highest mountain in Britain. It is, but presumably somebody had made some fairly sophisticated comparisons in former times.

> *There is one high or bigg mountaine on the Northeastsyde of that Countrie which is called Beaneves And this mountaine is the biggest and highest mountain in all that Countrey and it is said that this Mountaine is the biggest and highest in all Britaine.* (Pont(?) in *Macfarlane's Geographical Collections*, vol II)

Pont (13) is a delightful map of Mamore which gives a picture of Ben Nevis as easily the highest mountain in the area.

Similarly he reports a tradition that a place called Achadrom in the Great Glen was the mid-point of Scotland (length-wise):

> *And it is alleadgit be ancient men that this Achadron is the midst of Scotland in lenth. And there is one stone in a plaine ground in the stray which stands. and it is called the stone of the Ridge of Scotland And so the strath is named the mid part of Scotland.* (Pont(?) in *Macfarlane's Geographical Collections*, vol II)

There is no way of knowing how ancient these beliefs were but it is intriguing that Gerald of Wales reports a similar tradition about Meath in Ireland c. 1185.

> *The bounds of these divisions meet at a certain stone in Meath near the castle of Kilair (Killare). This stone is said to be the navel of Ireland, as it were, placed right in the middle of the land. Consequently that part of Ireland is called Meath, as being situated in the middle of the island.* (J. O'Meara, *Gerald of Wales – The History and Topography of Ireland*)

To make such claims, in either country, required a degree of travel, measurement, and mathematical calculation.

Similarly, it appears that important watersheds were known many years ago. Like Timothy Pont, Burt came across a remarkable piece of geographical lore concerning the stretch of the Great Glen between Loch Oich and Loch Lochy:

> *Here I must stop a little to acquaint you with a spot of ground which I take to be something remarkable. This I had passed over several times without observing anything extraordinary in it, and, perhaps, should never have taken notice of it, if it had not been pointed out to me by one of the natives.*
>
> *About the middle of the neck of land that divides the Lakes Oich and Lochy (which is but one mile), not far from the centre or the opening, there descends from the hills, on the south side, a burn, or rivulet, which, as it falls upon the plain, divides into two streams without any visible ridge to part them; and one of them runs through the Lakes Oich and Ness into the east sea, and the other takes the quite contrary course, and passes through Loch Lochy into the western ocean.* (Edmund Burt, *Letters from a Gentleman in the North of Scotland,* c. 1737)

Pennant comments on Tyndrum: '*The inn is seated the highest of any house in Scotland. The Tay runs east, and a few hundred yards further is a little lake, whose waters run west.*' (Pennant, *A Tour in Scotland 1769*)

Curios

There are also some stories which might be better described as curious rather than marvellous.

Gerald of Wales mentions a certain bell in Leinster which, unless exorcised and bound by chain each night, travels mysteriously back to the church of Saint Finian at Clonard in Meath, whence it came. Saint Finnan seems to have enjoyed similar powers in Scotland because comparable stories attach to the early Celtic bell still found on St Finnan's Isle in Loch Shiel. This always finds its way home again after any unauthorised migration. In mediaeval times a curse or protective legend was often more effective than a padlock and hasp to safeguard a precious relic, bell or book.

It is intriguing to find the same story attaching to Saint Ninian, (arguably the same as St Finnan):

> *On 21 July 1624, Cornelius Ward, Paul O'Neill, and Patrick Hegarty left Ireland and landed on the isle of Sanda, where they found a chapel dedicated to St Ninian which had a small cemetery attached to it; according to tradition, this cemetery was the resting place of fourteen saints, and it*

was said that any man or beast entering the burial place of the saints would die a sudden death or be stricken with a severe illness; it was said, too, that anything taken from the burial place would be miraculously restored. (Giblin, Irish Franciscan Mission to Scotland 1619–1646)

Strange noises off always send a chill up the spine: '*There is a valley in Aengus, in which shouting is heard every Monday night; Glen Ailbe is its name, and it is not known who makes the noise.*' (Todd, *The Irish Version of the Historia Britonum of Nennius*).

A mysterious voice is mentioned by Pont in his description of Islay: '*And there is one litle hill neare to the castle, which when the race and principall name of Clandonnalds of that house wer to decay. there was before that tyme wont to be heard in that place the voice of a womans lamentatione oftymes both in the Night and Day but especiallie in the Night.*' (Pont(?) in *Macfarlane's Geographical Collections*, vol II)

Another curiosity noted in the Highlands and Islands was a taboo on females in certain contexts. These too have Irish parallels since we find similar stories in the Irish Nennius and Gerald of Wales. The following Irish example comes from the thirteenth-century Norse text *The King's Mirror*:

> *In that same lake . . . called Logri, lies a little island named Inisclodran. Once there was a holy man named Diermicius who had a church on the isle near which he lived. Into this church and churchyard of which he is the patron no female creature is allowed to enter. All beasts are aware of this, for both birds and other animals which are without human reason avoid it as carefully as humans do. And no creature of the female sex ever ventures into that churchyard, nor could it enter if it tried.* (L. M. Larson, *The King's Mirror*)

We find similar taboos in the Highlands and Islands. In 1630 Captain Dymes writes of the chapel of 'St Mallonuy' in Lewis:

> *Within the Chappell there is a Sanctum Sanctorum w(hi)ch is soe holy in theire estimation that not anie of their weomen are sufferred to enter therein. Anie woman wth child dareth not to enter within the doores of the Chappell, but there are certaine places without where they goe to theire devotions.* (In W. C. Mackenzie, *History of the Outer Hebrides*, Appendix F)

Separation was not just in life. Martin Martin discusses the isle of Taransay which had two chapels, dedicated to Saints Tarran and Keith respectively:

> *There is an ancient tradition among the natives here, that a man must not be buried in St Tarran's, nor a woman in St Keith's, because otherwise the corpse would be found above ground the day after it is interred.* (Martin Martin, *A Description of the Western Islands of Scotland* c. 1695)

Pennant refers to a similar practice in Bute:

> *Descend to the ruin of old Kingarth Church. Two cemeteries belong to it, a higher and a lower: the last was allotted for the interment of females alone; because, in old times, certain women being employed to carry a quantity of holy earth, brought from Rome, lost some by the way, and so incurred this penalty for their negligence; that of being buried separated from the other sex.* (T. Pennant, *A Tour in Scotland and Voyage to the Hebrides*, 1772)

There was another taboo involving women and fish. Boece writes of Lewis:

> *In this Ile is bot ane reveir. It is said, gif ony woman waid throw this watter at the spring of the yeir, thair sall na salmond be sene for that yeir in the said watter: otherwayis, it sall abound in gret plente.* (Boece in Hume Brown, *Scotland before 1700*)

(In this Isle is but one river. It is said, if any woman wade through this water at the spring of the year, there shall no salmon be seen for that year in the said water: otherwise, it shall abound in great plenty).

Martin Martin specifically mentions the River Barvas in Lewis:

> *The natives in the village Barvas retain an ancient custom of sending a man very early to cross Barvas River, every first day of May, to prevent any female crossing it first; for that they say would hinder the salmon from coming into the river all the year round; they pretend to have learned this from a foreign sailor, who was shipwrecked upon that coast a long time ago. This observation they maintain to be true from experience.* (Martin Martin, *A Description of the Western Islands of Scotland* c. 1695)

The first day of May was the ancient Celtic festival of Beltane. Women have long had a mysterious association with salmon. Even today the most respectable angling journals can still carry some fairly extraordinary letters on the efficacy of female pheromones when catching salmon.

Johnson heard something similar on Skye; this time about herring:

> *It is held that the return of the laird to Dunvegan, after any considerable absence, produces a plentiful capture of herrings: and that, if any woman crosses the water to the opposite islands, the herrings will desert the coast . . . This tradition is not uniform. Some hold that no woman may pass, and others that none may pass but a Macleod.* (Johnson, *A Journey to the Western Islands of Scotland*, 1773)

Coda

I am normally a complete sceptic with regard to miracles but there is one ascribed to Abbot Baithine of Iona (c. 600) which deserves quotation because it demonstrates an endurance and stoicism more than ordinary:

> *And what is more difficult, at harvest-time when he was carrying to the stack a sheaf collected in his [one] hand, he meanwhile raised the other to the sky, and appealed to the Thunderer; and in his devotion did not remove the midges that settled on his face.* (Life of Baithine in Anderson's *Early Sources of Scottish History* pp 119–120)

Miracles by definition strain credulity, but this, if true, is truly wonderful.

Chapter 10

Sea travel

The Highlands and Islands were a maritime society. The western sea-board is heavily indented with sealochs. Here, and throughout the islands, communities occupied the more favoured agricultural sites in the bays or by the river-mouths. Between such communities sea travel was the norm. Of course there were settlements inland but again these were clustered along river-valleys or the major freshwater lochs. Some of the latter (such as Lochs Awe, Shiel and Morar) are so large that each hosted dozens of smaller settlements along their shores. Here again boat-transport was the norm.

The transport topology that held this maritime society together was built up over millennia. In prehistoric times boats were either dug-outs or made of skin. The Scottish and Pictish societies that occupied the west coast before the Vikings seem to have had impressive numbers of skin-built boats. About 800 AD the Vikings brought a new boat-building technology with them as they swept through the Hebrides. This set the pattern for the next millennium. Viking designs were adapted to suit Hebridean waters and the birlinn or West Highland Galley became the warrior and workhorse of the west coast. I have discussed these boats at length in *The West Highland Galley* and so here I wish to do no more than establish the premise.

Instead I am going to concentrate on the existence of a network or infrastructure rather than on the boats themselves. I have shown in Chapter 3 how much travel was sponsored by the church. The following quotations link some of the scanty and scattered pieces of evidence which indicate that there was indeed a system or topology – which travellers could utilise.

During the period of Viking domination there seems to have been a practice of exacting landing dues on new arrivals. This was just a variation on the customs dues exacted in the larger ports of Lowland Britain and Ireland. In the Hebrides such a system was more difficult to police. In Hrafn Svein-biornsson's saga there is a story about an enforced landing in the Hebrides. About 1202 Hrafn Sveinbiornsson was on board a merchant-ship with Gudmund, bishop-elect of Holar in Iceland, which was blown by contrary winds into the Hebrides.

They came into good harbourage, beside an island that is called Sand-ey . . . They lay beside the Hebrides, at anchor, for some nights. King Olaf ruled then over the Hebrides. The king's bailiff came to them there, and claimed from them land-dues, according as the laws of the Hebrides required; and told that they must pay twenty hundred wadmals [a unit of measurement for cloth], *because there were twenty Icelandic men in the ship. They refused to pay, because they thought they knew that they should have to pay as much again in Norway.*

There then followed a dispute with King Olaf himself in which the Icelanders showed their willingness to fight if need be. '*Then men went between them; and this was brought about, before it ended, that the bishop-elect [and Hrafn] paid six hundred wadmals.*' (Anderson, *Early Sources*, II, pp 358–360)

The 'King Olaf' in the story is Olaf the Black, born c. 1178, who was ruling Lewis and the Northern Hebrides while his brother Reginald was King of Man. Sanday is a common island name in the Hebrides but the Sanday by the isle of Canna is a likely candidate in this case because of its excellent harbour.

Hebrideans were heirs to the maritime societies of Scandinavia. They inherited the boat-building technology and wood-working skills. They also continued the assessment system that allowed such boats to be built and maintained. The Norse colonies in Scotland are precisely those where we find the land-assessment units of ouncelands and pennylands – units which underlay naval recruitment and taxation. Despite the popular image of the Vikings what we glimpse in Hebridean naval affairs is a highly organised and structured society. This was a society with systems of assessment and responsibility, with established customs and legal sanctions. For instance, one of the clauses in the Treaty of Perth in 1266, which returned the Hebrides to Scotland, dealt with the issue of shipwreck – a matter of the first concern in the stormy waters of the west:

If it happen (which God forbid!) that the men of the king of Norway suffer shipwreck in the kingdom or domain of the king of Scotland, or contrariwise, it shall be lawful for them, either in person or by others, freely and quietly to gather their ships, broken or shattered, along with all their goods, and to have them, to sell and to dispose of them, without any claim, as long as they have not abandoned them. And if anyone, contrary to this act of common agreement, seizes anything fraudulently or violently from these goods or ships, and is convicted thereof, let him be punished as a plunderer and breaker of the peace as he deserves. (G. Donaldson, *Scottish Historical Documents*)

A society with such a structured code of practice certainly does not sound lawless! They were also heirs to a very practical tradition of seafaring. The accumulated wisdom of this heritage was embodied in a Norse document called *The King's Mirror*, probably written in the 1240s. This sets out some commonsense guidelines:

Observe carefully how the sky is lighted, the course of the heavenly bodies, the grouping of the hours, and the points of the horizon. Learn also how to mark

the movements of the ocean and to discern how its turmoil ebbs and swells; for
that is knowledge which all must possess who wish to trade abroad . . .

   If you are preparing to carry on trade beyond the seas and you sail your
own ship, have it thoroughly coated with tar in the autumn and, if possible,
keep it tarred all winter. But if the ship is placed on timbers too late to be
coated in the autumn, tar it when spring opens and let it dry thoroughly
afterwards. Always buy shares in good vessels or in none at all. Keep your
ship attractive, for then capable men will join you and it will be well manned.
Be sure to have your ship ready when summer begins and do your traveling
while the season is best. Keep reliable tackle on shipboard at all times, and
never remain out at sea in late autumn, if you can avoid it. (L .M. Larson,
(transl.), *The King's Mirror*)

The weather in the Hebrides can be atrocious and later inhabitants were
equally realistic about the seasons favourable for sea voyages. The summer
was the time to travel in order to collect rent, pasture animals and cull seabirds
or seals. Pont(?) writes of the islands south-west of Barra:

And none can goe with scutts or boatts to those Sowthwest Illands but in those
tymes of the yeare such as Aprill and Summer and in the beginning of August.
The Master or Superior of these Illands hath in due payment from the
Inhabitants and tennants of the saids Illands for his dewtie. the half of ther
cornes butter cheese and all other comodities, which does Incres or grow to
them in the yeare, And hath ane officer or serjeant in everie Illand to uptake
the samen. The names of those Illands is called Watersa, Sandira, Pappa,
Mewla, and Bearnera. (Pont(?) in *Macfarlane's Geographical Collections*,
vol II)

and of North Uist:

There is ane Illand pertaining to the Superior and Lord of this Countrie
which is called Heysker and there is certaine Illands besyde that Illand in the
Main seas, And the Inhabitants of the Countrey doe meet and gather
themselves togidder once in the yeare upon ane certaine tyme in faire and
good weather and bring big trees and stafs in ther hands with them as
weapons to kill the selchis which doeth Innumerable conveen and gather to
that Illand at that tyme of the yeare. And so the men and the selchis doe fight
stronglie And there will be Innumerable selches slaine wherwith they loaden
ther boatts, which causes manie of them oftymes perish and droune in respect
that they loaden ther boatts with so manie selchis. (Pont(?) in *Macfarlane's*
Geographical Collections, vol II)

Since travelling could be so dangerous there were a number of charms,
superstitions and sea-taboos at work. There is a nice story about an early

colonist of Iceland in Olaf Tryggvi's son's Saga: '*Helgi the Lean went to Iceland with his wife and children. Helgi was called Christian, and yet was very mixed in his beliefs; he was baptized and professed faith in Christ, but he vowed to Thor for sea-journeys and difficult undertakings.*' (Anderson, *Early Sources*, I, p 343)

Christianity did well enough for ordinary occasions but sea-journeys required special measures!

Pont(?) writes of a chapel of 'Kilmoire' in Barra:

> *In this Chappell as the Inhabitants say that there is certaine earth within this Chappell which if anie man wold carrie the samen with him to the sea, And if the wind or stormie strong weather were cruell and vehement if he wold caste a litle of this earth into the sea it wold pacifie the wind and the sea wold grow calme immediatlie efter the casting the earth into the sea.* (Pont(?) in *Macfarlane's Geographical Collections*, vol II)

Certain harbours were regarded as particularly safe. The following quotation refers to Canna, Oigh-sgeir (a rock south-west of Canna), and Tiree. The implication is that if you couldn't land in one of these places then you couldn't land anywhere:

> *There is one litle Illand on the Southwest end or syde of this Illand called Haysgair nequissag. And when scutts boats or gallys cannot land in Cainna nor in Haysgair nor yet in Tiry The ancient Inhabitants and principall of these Countries do say that saids Gallies boats nor scutts can nowayes land neither in Scotland England nor yet in Ireland.* (Pont(?) in *Macfarlane's Geographical Collections*, vol II)

Sea travel was always a risky business and a large number of customs, superstitions and taboos built up over the years. Perhaps the most commonly observed practice was to make a sunwise circuit (*deiseil*) before setting off. This was by no means confined to travel by sea; it was regarded as an auspicious start for all manner of things, including burial! '*Some are very careful when they set out to sea that the boat be first rowed about sunways; and, if this be neglected, they are afraid their voyage may prove unfortunate.*' (Martin Martin, *A Description of the Western Islands of Scotland* c. 1695)

Martin Martin has a whole section on the customs to be observed when the Lewismen made their annual expedition to the Flannan Isles:

> *If any of their crew is a novice, and not versed in the customs of the place, he must be instructed perfectly in all the punctilioes observed here before landing; and to prevent inconveniences that they think may ensue upon the transgression of the least nicety observed here, every novice is always joined with another, that can instruct him all the time of their fowling: so all the boat's crew are matched in this manner. After their landing, they fasten the boat to*

the sides of a rock, and then fix a wooden ladder, by laying a stone at the foot of it, to prevent its falling into the sea; and when they are got up into the island, all of them uncover their heads, and make a turn sun-ways round, thanking God for their safety. The first injunction given after landing, is not to ease nature in that place where the boat lies, for that they reckon a crime of the highest nature, and of dangerous consequence to all their crew; for they have a great regard to that very piece of rock upon which they first set their feet, after escaping the danger of the ocean. (Martin Martin, *A Description of the Western Islands of Scotland* c. 1695)

And at the chapel dedicated to St Flannan:

When they are come within about 20 paces of the altar, they all strip themselves of their upper garments at once; and their upper clothes being laid upon a stone . . . all the crew pray three times before they begin fowling . . . Another rule is that it is absolutely unlawful to kill a fowl with a stone, for that they reckon a great barbarity, and directly contrary to ancient custom.

　　It is also unlawful to kill a fowl before they ascend by the ladder. It is absolutely unlawful to call the island of St Kilda . . . by its proper Irish name Hirt, but only the high country . . . There are several other things that must not be called by their common names, e.g. Visk, which in the language of the natives signifies Water, they call Burn; a Rock, which in their language is Creg, must here be called Cruey, i.e., hard; Shore in their language, expressed by Claddach, must here be called Vah, i.e., a Cave; Sour in their language as expressed Gort, but must be here called Gaire, i.e., Sharp; Slippery, which is expressed Bog, must be called Soft; and several other things to this purpose.

A peculiar feature of these taboos was the set of alternate names. This also applied to other islands such as Canna: '*The natives call this isle by the name Tarsin at sea.*' (Martin Martin, *A Description of the Western Islands of Scotland* c. 1695). And Eigg: '*The natives dare not call this isle by its ordinary name of Egg when they are at sea, but island Nim-Ban-More, i.e., the isle of big women.*' (Martin Martin, *A Description of the Western Islands of Scotland* c. 1695)

Tradition says, that of old the islands forming this parish [of the Small Isles], *had names sometimes given them different from those which they now bear : Thus Eigg was called Eillan nan Banmore, (the Island of the Great Women); Rum was called Rioghachd na Forraiste Fiadhaich, (the Kingdom of the Wild Forrest); Canna was called An t-eillan tarssuin, (the Island lying across); and Isle Muck, Tirr Chrainne, (the Sow's Island). But these may be supposed poetical names, given by the Gaelic bards; and the superstitious are said to have used them, and them only, when at sea, and bound for these islands.* (The Rev. Donald M'Lean, Old Statistical Account, 1794)

The Rev.C. M. Robertson explains the logic behind this: '*The intention of the use of those alternative names by the superstitious when at sea and bound for those islands was probably to conceal the destination from witches and other malign powers, which, with the illogic of superstition, were supposed to know the islands only by their true name.*' (The Rev. C. M. Robertson, *Topography and Traditions of Eigg*, 1898)

One could also take practical steps to keep the elements at bay. Martin Martin gives a Hebridean example of pouring oil on troubled waters:

> *The steward of Kilda, who lives in Pabbay, is accustomed in time of storm to tie a bundle of puddings made of the fat of sea fowl to the end of his cable, and lets it fall into the sea behind the rudder; this, he says, hinders the waves from breaking, and calms the sea; but the scent of the grease attracts the whales, which put the vessel in danger.* (Martin Martin, *A Description of the Western Islands of Scotland* c. 1695)

As well as a technique used in the Wells of Swinna in the Pentland Firth:

> *A little further to the south lies Swinna isle, remarkable only for a part of Pentland Firth lying to the west of it, called the Wells of Swinna. They are two whirlpools in the sea, which run about with such violence, that any vessel or boat coming within their reach, go always round until they sink. These wells are dangerous only when there is a dead calm; for if a boat be under sail with any wind, it is easy to go over them. If any boat be forced into these wells by the violence of the tide, the boat-men cast a barrel or an oar into the wells; and while it is swallowing it up, the sea continues calm, and gives the boat an opportunity to pass over.* (Martin Martin, *A Description of the Western Islands of Scotland* c. 1695)

Travelling together built a sense of common responsibility. A boat could only travel safely if the crew worked as a team. A sense of community and common endeavour might be reinforced by singing in unison. Edmund Burt discusses the role of the working songs used by women during harvest or when fulling cloth. He adds: '*And among numbers of men, employed in any work that requires strength and joint labour (as the launching of a large boat, or the like), they must have the piper to regulate their time, as well as whisky to keep up their spirits in the performance; for pay they often have little, or none at all.*' (Edmund Burt, *Letters from a Gentleman in the North of Scotland*, late 1720s)

One such song was the 'iorram' or rowing song which set the time for the oarsmen:

> *Our boat's crew were islanders (Skyemen) who gave us a species of marine music called in Erse (Iorrams). These songs when well composed are intended to regulate the stroke of the oars, and recalled to mind the custom of classical*

days. But in modern times, they are generally sung in couplets, the whole crew joining in the chorus at certain intervals, the notes are commonly long, the airs solemn and slow, rarely cheerful, it being impossible for the oars to keep quick time. The words generally have a religious turn, consonant to that of the people. (T. Pennant, *A Tour in Scotland and Voyage to the Hebrides* 1772)

Faujas de Saint Fond describes the effect of listening to iorrams on the way to Staffa:

The songs began and continued a long time. They consisted of monotonous recitatives, ending in choruses equally monotonous. A sort of dignity, mingled with plaintive and melancholy tones, was the chief characteristic of these songs. The oars, which always kept time with the singing, tended to make the monotony more complete. I became drowsy, and soon fell sound asleep. (Faujas de Saint Fond, *A journey through England and Scotland to the Hebrides in 1784*)

In 1786 John Knox was travelling along the coast of Sleat:

In this day's voyage, we observed a number of Highland boats, with four oars, and containing, generally, six or seven men. – They were returning from the fishery in Loch Urn [Hourn] to the south coast of Sky. The wind being contrary, these poor people were forced to labour at the oars from ten to twenty, or twenty-five miles, before they could reach their respective huts. They take the oars alternately, and refresh themselves now and then with water, though generally in a full sweat. They sing in chorus, observing a kind of time, with the movement of the oars. Though they kept close upon the shore, and at a considerable distance from our vessel, we heard the sound from almost every boat. Those who have the bagpipe, use that instrument, which has a pleasing effect upon the water, and makes these poor people forget their toils. (J. Knox, *A Tour through the Highlands of Scotland and the Hebride Isles in 1786*)

In 1796 Sarah Murray describes her trip from Morvern to Mull, by rowing boat, on a calm summer day: '*I requested the seamen to sing Gaelic songs, which they did the greatest part of the voyage. It is astonishing how much their songs animated them, particularly a chorus, that made them pull away with such velocity, that it was like flying more than rowing on the surface of the water.*' (S. Murray, *A Companion and Useful Guide to the Beauties of Scotland and the Hebrides*)

In this instance the Highlanders sang to please their employer, but the real purpose of such working songs was to establish a rhythm, relieve the tedium and ease the pain.

Today, travelling, and its difficulties, are the responsibility of the traveller, or the travel company they employ. Formerly there was a community responsibility. On some islands the boat was not just a huge economic asset, it was critical for the survival of the whole group. We see this in the procedure for securing the boat safely on St Kilda:

> *the birlin or boat is brought to the side of the rock, upon which all the inhabitants of both sexes are ready to join their united force to hale her through this rock, having for this end a rope fastened to the fore-part; a competent number of them are also employed on each side; both these are determined by a cryer, who is employed on purpose to warn them all at the same minute, and he ceases when he finds it convenient to give them a breathing.* (Martin Martin, *A Description of the Western Islands of Scotland* c. 1695)

This sense of communal endeavour was part of the structure of maritime communication along the west coast. From our individualistic point of view it is difficult to understand how a whole group was so closely bound by mutual dependence. Knox gives a sense of this in his description of launching a boat to pass from Coigach to Loch Inver in Assynt:

> *Our only difficulty in this voyage happened at the first setting out. The wind blew fresh from the sea, which sent in a high swell that rolled furiously along the beach, and dissolved in a cloud of white foam.*
>
> *Having dragged the boat to a proper station on the shore, it was resolved that Mr Mackenzie, the boatmen, and myself, should go on board before she was launched; that the people on shore, of whom there were a croud of men, women, and children, should be prepared to push the boat out, between the wave that had just passed, and that which was following, before it had time to break. – In effecting this, some of the people were almost up to their shoulders in water and foam, while those in the boat were straining every nerve to keep her out, by means of oars and poles. The tongues, the noise, and the bustle upon this occasion resembled, we may suppose, the confusion at Babylon; and this work, when the wind blows from certain points, is to be repeated upon the launch of every fishing boat; merely from the want of a small pier, a conveniency almost unknown in the Highlands, and which proves a great impediment to fisheries.* (J. Knox, *A Tour through the Highlands of Scotland*, 1786)

Tarberts

The Gaelic place-name *Tarbert* and the Norse place-name *Eid* both indicate a portage point where boats could be drawn across a narrow neck of land between two pieces of water. I have dealt with the political implications of this in *The West Highland Galley* so here I only wish to include some quotations about the effects on the transport network.

Adomnan's *Life of Columba* makes clear that dug-outs were being portaged from at least the sixth century: '*long hewn-out ships of pine and oak were being drawn over-land*' (Anderson, *Early Sources*, I, p 187.)

The Norse also favoured this practice, as shown by this extract from Magnus Bareleg's Saga: '*Kintyre is a great land, and better than the best island in the Hebrides, excepting Man. A narrow isthmus is between it and the mainland of Scotland; there long-ships are often drawn across.*' (Anderson, *Early Sources*, II, p 113)

The practice persisted throughout the Middle Ages:

> *Beyond Knapdale, Cantyre stretches to the south-west, and is the headland of the country opposite Ireland, from which it is divided by a narrow strait. It is longer than it is broad, and is joined to Knapdale by an isthmus of sand, scarcely a mile across, so low that the sailors often drag their vessels over it, in order to shorten their navigation.* (Buchanan in Hume Brown, *Scotland before 1700*)

Two centuries before the Crinan Canal was actually dug, farsighted men were contemplating such a project:

> *It is thought that with great charges this passage might be cutt so that boats might pass from the east seas to the West without going about the Mule of Kintyre, which were verie profitable for such as travell to the North Illands in regaird the Strait betwixt the Mule of Kintyre and the glenis of Ireland being but sixteen mylles makes the stream to runn with such force, that when the tyde turnes, altho a ship had twentie saills all full of wind, she shall not be able to go one myll against the tyde.* (Pont(?) in *Macfarlane's Geographical Collections*, vol II)

Burt makes a similar point about the Caledonian Canal. It was envisaged at least one hundred years before it was actually built.

Monipennie's *Briefe Description of Scotland* (1612) continues the theme with reference to Tarbert, Loch Fyne:

> *Kintyre is more long than broad, joyning to Knapdall by so narrow a throat, about one mile of bredth, which ground is sandy, and lyeth so plain and low, that marriners drawing along their vessels, as gallies and boats, through it, make their journey a great deale shorter than to passe about Kintyre, which is the common passage.* (Monipennie, *Scots Chronicles*)

Thomas Tucker discusses the trade between Glasgow and the Highlands in 1655:

The inhabitants . . . are traders and dealers: some for Ireland . . . some from France . . . some to Norway . . . and every one with theyr neighbours the Highlanders, who come hither from the isles and westerne parts; in summer by the Mul of Cantyre, and in winter by the Torban to the head of the Loquh Fyn, (which is a small neck of sandy land, over which they usually drawe theyr small boates into the Firth of Dunbarton,) and soe passe up in the Cluyde with pladding, dry hides, goate, kid, and deere skyns, which they sell, and purchase with theyr price such comodityes and provisions as they stand in neede of, from time to time. (T. Tucker in Hume Brown, *Early Travellers in Scotland*)

This practice continued until the latter part of the eighteenth century. In 1735 there was a complaint that portage damaged the road! Rev John Walker argued for a canal at Tarbert, Loch Fyne, to promote commerce between the Southern Hebrides and the Clyde. He claimed that: '*It is at present a frequent Practice with the Islanders, to draw their largest 6 Oar Boats, over the Isthmus, and to pay 3d a Horse Load, for carrying over their Goods, rather than venture to circumnavigate the Mule* [the Mull of Kintyre].' (In McKay, *Walker's Report on the Hebrides*, 1764 and 1771)

In 1772 Pennant writes: '*It is not very long since vessels of nine or ten tons were drawn by horses out of the west loch into that of the east, to avoid the dangers of the Mull of Cantyre, so dreaded and so little known was the navigation round the promontory.*' (T. Pennant, *A Tour in Scotland and Voyage to the Hebrides*, 1772)

Tarbert, Loch Fyne, was probably the most important portage point in Scotland but it was by no means the only one. There are several other *tarberts* in the West Highlands as well as examples of *eid* both on the west coast and in the Northern Isles. Portage was once an integral part of freight transport by boat.

John Knox writes of Tarbert, Harris: '*When the herrings are in West Loch Tarbat, the fishers on the east side drag their boats across the isthmus; and so vice versa when the herrings are on the opposite side.*' (J. Knox, *A Tour through the Highlands of Scotland*, 1786)

In a footnote he adds of Tarbert, Loch Fyne: '*Highlanders . . . still use the land passage, at the Tarbat, in very rough weather, or when there is a good fishery in Loch Fine.*' (J. Knox, *A Tour through the Highlands of Scotland*, 1786)

Ferries

Few could ever travel in their own boat. If you didn't own one, or your travel was distant, or partly overland, then you became dependent on ferries maintained by others. Many of these ferries probably owed their origin to the patronage of a local magnate or, occasionally, royalty. The following quotation refers to Queen Margaret's endowment of Queensferry, across the Firth of Forth, before 1093:

> *And since the church of St Andrews is frequented by the religious devotion of visitors from the peoples round about, she had built dwellings upon either shore of the sea that separates Lothian and Scotland; so that pilgrims and poor might turn aside there to rest, after the labour of the journey; and might find there ready everything that necessity might require for the restoration of the body. She appointed attendants for this purpose alone, to have always ready all that was needed for guests, and to wait upon them with great care. She provided for them also ships, to carry them across, both going and returning, without ever demanding any price for the passage from those who were to be taken over.* (Turgot, Life of Queen Margaret, in Anderson, *Early Sources II*)

There also seem to have been formal arrangements for crossing the River Spey from at least King Alexander III's time. According to a petition of 1305 these involved a royal subsidy:

> *On the petition of Duugal passager, that the King* [Edward I] *would give him aid to keep up two ferry boats on the Spee* [Spey], *as his charter from King Alexander bears.*
>
> Response – *Let him show the lieutenant and chamberlain his charter, and have help in its terms.* (Bain, *Calendar of Documents relating to Scotland*, vol IV)

The Highlands and Hebrides had a network of ferry crossings from time immemorial. Local families provided boats and ferry services in exchange for the tenure of an adjacent piece of ground. Unfortunately we only hear of these when they feature in official documents. In the Register of the Privy Council (Vol VIII), for example, we have a list of bonds given for the boats and currachs in Atholl on 16 July 1684. They included a little coble at Tulloch, a currach at Invergarry, a boat at Portnacraige and a ferry boat at Pitnacrie. The general shortage of documents on the west coast hampers our knowledge but the evidence we have for Argyll was most likely repeated throughout the area. Ferry crossings at strategic points such as Corran and Ballachulish (Loch Linnhe and Loch Leven), Kylerhea and Kyleakin (Skye) or at Fionnphort (Mull) for Iona must be very ancient.

The Pont(?) notes in Macfarlane's Geographical Collections mention ferries across Loch Fyne between Strachur and Portchregan; across Loch Awe at Sonachan; across Loch Leven at Ballachulish; across Loch Etive at Connel; across Loch Creran at Shian; between Appin and Lismore, and between Glenelg and Skye at Kylerhea:

there is one Keyle or ferrie one narrow part of the sea which runneth between Glenelg and Slait and there is abundance of fish slaine in that Logh and it is called Kilraa. (Pont(?) in *Macfarlane's Geographical Collections*, vol II)

(there is a Kyle or ferry – a narrow part of the sea which runs between Glenelg and Sleat [South Skye] and there is abundance of fish slain in that Loch and it is called Kylerhea.)

Pont's notes on Skye in the same volume mention: '*Item the ferry toun under Binscard called Scosa.*' (The ferry town beneath Beinn Sgairde is called Sconser.)
The following seventeenth-century sasines probably reflect landholding arrangements that had existed for centuries:

22 February 1654
Sasine of the 20 shilling land of Portsonachan on Lochawe . . . The property is situated between the streams called Altbane and Altinlepheane; and the grant includes the Lochawe ferry between the rivers Tetil and Beochlich, on the east shore, and the rivers Gannyvan and Awe, on the west shore.
(H. Campbell, *Argyll Sasines*, vol II, No 828)

22 May 1674
Sasine of the 2 merk land of Kill Catharine in Cowall . . . Reddendo: the maintenance of a boat of 4 oars near the said lands for the passage across Lochfyne.
(H. Campbell, *Argyll Sasines*, vol I, No 538)

Other seventeenth-century Argyllshire sasines refer to ferries at Dunoon, Portindornock, Strone-Kilmun, Stratheachaig, Portingapill (Row) and Row of Connell. Particular pieces of ground went with the job of ferryman and it is likely that the office was hereditary within certain families.

28 May 1621
Sasine given by Andrew, bishop of Argyll, to John Ure, of a house, garden and piece of land . . . and also of the office of ferryman between Dunoon and Clachestaine, of all of which it is understood that the said John Ure and his predecessors have been natives, tenants and occupiers these many years past . . . The property is in the town of Dunoon.
(H. Campbell, *Argyll Sasines*, vol 1, No 153)

Early ferry crossings could be quite nerve-wracking. Pont(?) writes of the ferry at Connel by Oban:

This ferrie called Gonnell when the sea aither ebbs or flows, cryes so vehementlie that it will be heard far off in sundrie parts, at the least one

myll or thereby, And when folks doeth goe over that ferrie, the boatt or scoutt
doeth goe up verie high and otherwhiles doun verie low, that these which are
in the boat, will think themselves likelie to be drowned in the sea, And the
cause thereof is that there are Connalls and rocks in that ferrie, And
especiallie those that are not acquaint with the ferrie, will be more affraid;
(Pont(?) in *Macfarlane's Geographical Collections*, vol II)

The word 'Connalls' derives from the Gaelic *conghail* which means tumultuous flood and is the origin of the place-name Connel near Oban. At Connel
the reference is to the Falls of Lora where a rock-sill causes rapids as the tide
falls. Pont(?) often uses it in the general sense of water-hazards caused by
shallows.
    Ferries did not formerly run on a regular basis; if you wished to cross and
the ferry was on the opposite side then you had to attract the ferryman's
attention. Shouting was a favoured method, as was fire, or even walking on a
particular spot. Martin Martin describes a ferry from Taransay:

> *This island is a mile distant from the main land of Harris, and when the*
> *inhabitants go from this island to Harris with a design to stay for any time,*
> *they agree with those that carry them over, on a particular motion of walking*
> *upon a certain piece of ground, unknown to every body but themselves, as a*
> *signal to bring them back.* (Martin Martin, *A Description of the Western*
> *Islands of Scotland* c. 1695)

This was only any use for a ferry between familiars, not strangers. Where the
kyle or strait was narrow, a shout might be sufficient: '*where the ferry-boat*
crosseth to Glenelg it is so narrow that one may call for the ferry-boat and be easily
heard on the other side.' (Martin Martin, *A Description of the Western Islands of*
Scotland c. 1695)
    Communications could always be established by beacon. Military assis-
tance was often summoned this way – or notice given. The report of the earl of
Argyll to the Privy Council of Scotland, November 1615, tells how men in
Kintyre helped the opposition by giving them warning. The earl of Argyll's
forces were trying to attack the rebels in Cara:

> *bot wer preventit by some of the Laird of Largie his servandis, quho persavit*
> *my Lord of Ergyle his forceis going towardis the ile quhair the rebellis wer,*
> *and set on grite baikynis to mak thame war* (Register of the Privy Council
> of Scotland, vol X, p758)

(but were prevented by some of the Laird of Largie's servants, who
perceived my Lord of Argyll's forces going towards the isle where the
rebels were, and set on great beacons to make them aware)

Exactly the same thing happened in Islay a few days later. The earl of Argyll was pursuing Sir James Macdonald, and his forces, who were in the Rhinns of Islay and the neighbouring islet of Orsay. Argyll:

> *maid ane onset on thame by sea, quhairin his Lordschipis men wer preventit by some who set on beikynis in the O of Yla, quhairby Sir James wes adverteist that my Lord his forces wer comeing on him.* (Register of the Privy Council of Scotland, vol X, p759)

> (made an onset on them by sea, wherein his Lordship's men were prevented by some who set on beacons in the O [Oa] of Islay, whereby Sir James was advertised that my Lord's forces were coming on him.)

Beacons were also a favoured means of attracting Hebridean soldiers to Northern Ireland.

Ferry crossings were always something of a risk. They became even more dangerous when animals were transported. Thomas Kirk writes of crossing the Cromarty Firth with a nervous horse.

> *Saturday 7th, we left Tayne, and about six miles from thence we came to a ferry of three miles, called Cromarty: it is an excellent harbour . . . Here is a very bad boat: we took in three horses (there being scarce room for them), and before we got a hundred yards from shore, they were ready to leap overboard, and overturn the boat. With much ado we got safe back to land again, and changed one of these horses for a soberer horse, and we were so foolhardy as to venture again. We had like all to have been cast away, and it was a great mercy that ever we came to land again.* (Kirk, Tour in Scotland 1677)

If the situation became really tricky there might be only one course of action that could save the boat from capsize. On 15 August 1595, Captain Anthony Deringe wrote to the English Privy Council from Chester that he had been driven back by a storm during his crossing to Ireland. Apparently they had: '*much ado to keep their horses' throats uncut.*' (Calendar of State Papers relating to Ireland, vol V)

Animals could be swum across narrow straits but for longer crossings they needed to be carried on a boat. Although we lack early records for the west coast, similar situations must surely have arisen.

The poverty of the area meant that Highland ferry-boats were not always as ship-shape as they should have been:

> *I came to a small river, where there was a ferry; for the water was too deep and rapid to pass the ford above. The boat was patched almost everywhere with rough pieces of boards, and the oars were kept in their places by small bands of twisted sticks.*

I could not but inquire its age, seeing it had so many marks of antiquity; and was told by the ferryman it had belonged to his father, and was above sixty years old . . . But in most places of the Highlands, where there is a boat (which is very rare), it is much worse than this, and not large enough to receive a horse; and therefore he is swum at the stern, while somebody holds up his head by a halter or bridle.

The horses swim very well at first setting out; but if the water be wide, in time they generally turn themselves on one of their sides, and patiently suffer themselves to be dragged along.

I remember one of these boats was so very much out of repair, we were forced to stand upon clods of turf to stop the leaks in her bottom, while we passed across the river. (Edmund Burt, *Letters from a Gentleman in the North of Scotland*, late 1720s)

Even accepting an invitation to go to dinner with a chief who lived near Inverness could be hazardous, and that was before you saw the food, of which Burt was also highly critical.

'*We set out early in the morning without guide or interpreter, and passed a pretty wide river, into the county of Ross, by a boat that we feared would fall to pieces in the passage.*' (Edmund Burt, *Letters from a Gentleman in the North of Scotland*, late 1720s)

In 1737 Duncan Forbes of Culloden travelled round parts of the duke of Argyll's Hebridean estate (Mull, Tiree and Coll). He had been taken in what was probably an eight-oared birlinn and gives us a rare factual account in a letter to the duke:

Your barge is a fine boat, her waste is so low for the convenience of rowing, that she is rather to watery for those stormy seas, one moveable plank to be put upon or taken from the waste as occasion might require, would make her more convenient where squales of wind are so frequent, and the waves run so high. We had an excellent steersman, and no accident did harm. In our voyage from Mull to the continent, the barge set upon a blind rock, but the wind being easy she got off next tide without any damage of consequence, and I proceeded in her next day to Fort-William, where I landed safe. (Appendix A.4, *Crofters Commission Report*, 1884)

Ferries were not always ideal. Pennant writes of a passage to Gigha: '*Embark in a rotten, leaky boat.*' (T. Pennant, *A Tour in Scotland and Voyage to the Hebrides*, 1772)

Sometimes the boarding arrangements were defective – as on his way to Golspie: '*Cross a very narrow inlet to a small bay at Porthbeg, or the little ferry, in a boat as dangerous as the last; for horses can neither get in or out without great risk, from the vast height of the sides and their want of slips.'* (Pennant, *A Tour in Scotland 1769*)

At other times they weren't even big enough to take the traveller's horse. He writes of the crossing from Glenelg to Skye at Kylerhea where cattle and horses had to swim: *This is the great pass into the island, but is destitute even of a horseferry.* (T. Pennant, *A Tour in Scotland and Voyage to the Hebrides,* 1772)

From the late eighteenth century we see signs of more formal arrangements. Pennant writes of Dunvegan, Skye: '*Adjacent is a village and the post office; for from hence a packet-boat, supported by subscription, sails every fortnight for the Long Island.*' (T. Pennant, *A Tour in Scotland and Voyage to the Hebrides,* 1772)

But even these were not for the faint-hearted. Knox writes of the fortnightly packet from Stornoway to Poolewe:

The vessel was small, and as I was afterwards informed, in a very improper state for going to sea, and ought to have been broke up long since. She is employed at certain seasons, in transporting cattle from Lewis to the Pool Ewe, which had rotted her timbers and bottom. She was at the same time in want of necessary tackling for a voyage of from forty to fifty miles, in a sea that lies open to the northern ocean. (J. Knox, *A Tour through the Highlands of Scotland,* 1786)

While Clarke took comfort from the fact that he hadn't heard of any fatal accidents:

Leaving Dunstaffage, we crossed the narrow mouth of Loch Etive; by what is called the Connel ferry. The tide rushes through this channel with such rapidity, that it sometimes forms a cascade of six feet. The ferry, in consequence, is frequently dangerous, and always requires the cautious management of an experienced boatman. The old pilot who conducted us over, with our horses, had attended the ferry upwards of sixty years, and the management of it has been in the same family, handed from father to son, for three hundred years. The mode by which we crossed it, reminded me of the rivers in Piedmont, the passage over which is exactly the same. The boat is launched from one side of the river, and intrusted to the torrent, which carries it with great rapidity down the stream, the men all the while tugging at the oars, till at last it reaches the opposite side, a considerable way lower down. By constant practice, the ferrymen are dexterous enough to reach generally the same point, where there is a sort of quay for landing; but this is not always the case, nor was it so when we crossed over. Sometimes the eddies are violent enough to turn the boat round, by which they lose the command of her, for a few seconds, and you are then hurried somewhat lower down the stream. Notwithstanding the perilous nature of the stream itself, the uncertainty of the old crazy boat they use, frequently thronged with passengers, and terrified

*horses, who betray great uneasiness in passing, – I heard of no instance in
which an accident had been fatal to anyone.* (E.D. Clarke, *Journal* 1797)

The quality of Highland ferries simply reflected the lack of capital available.
In an economy of scarce resources it was simply a matter of mending and
making do. Clarke visited the Highlands at a time when the tourist industry
was just beginning to take off. He noticed the recent and rapid changes in
Oban:

*It is impossible to leave Oban, without noticing the important consequences,
which have resulted to that place, from the talents and industry of a single
family, in the short period of twenty-six years. When the elder of two
brothers, Mr. Hugh Stevenson, arrived there, a single thatched hut, with
about five persons, constituted the whole of what has since, by their exertions,
risen to a populous and flourishing town. In the year 1791, a list of the
inhabitants was made by Mr. John Stevenson, at the request of the Duke of
Argyle, when they were found to amount to six hundred and fifty-nine souls.
And in the year 1797, their number had increased to seven hundred.* (E.D.
Clarke, *Journal* 1797)

The consequence of this new-found prosperity was that the money was now
available to provide facilities for the growing number of tourists:

*We found at Oban a very pleasant and commodious boat, neatly equipped
with sails, and mounting four oars, for the express purpose of conveying
passengers to the different islands and places in the neighbourhood. Having
agreed with the master of it to take us to Fort William, we took leave of our
cutter;* (E.D. Clarke, *Journal* 1797)

This was the time when there was a fever of interest in things Highland; when
boats carried poets and artists and musicians to islands such as Staffa. Tourist
demand has sustained such services ever since.

Boats had to be hired where was not an established ferry. Mrs Murray,
author of a *Companion and Useful Guide to the Beauties of Scotland*, describes a
boat she caught from Mull:

*It was a large flat bottomed boat, made on purpose to transport cattle and
sheep from one island to another. There was in it one division for beasts, one
for passengers, a hole to cook victuals in, and another hole for the people to lie
down in, which latter dark places I did not approach. The boat was
navigated by two south Morair men to whom it belonged, and we set sail
from Bunessain on the 21st of July 1802, at seven o'clock in the morning,
and steered for the island of Eigg.*

With wind and tide against them the boat had to steer for Coll instead. But:

> *all along the coast of Coll there are innumerable rocks in the sea, some to be seen, others concealed. The boatmen were unacquainted with the navigation, and began to be out of patience, and out of humour, declaring that if it became dark before they arrived at the Loch, at the head of which Coll's house is built, they would not venture into it, by reason of the numbers of rocks they had heard (for they were never there) lay scattered in it. We passed point after point, but no harbour appeared. The boatmen began to talk loud in Gaelic, and damn in English, for there is no such oath in the Gaelic language . . . The sea was dashing, the sails rattling, the sailors hollowing and shouting; in short, except in the gulf of Coire Vreaikain [Corryvreckan], it was the greatest bustle I ever was in.*

Mrs Murray now got into a small fishing-boat instead.

> *We had not been out of the large boat three minutes, before she struck upon a rock . . . happily however, the boat was quickly extricated from the rock, and soon after, to my great satisfaction, safely anchored.*

Accordingly Mrs Murray, who was a robust and practical traveller, issued the following advice to her readers:

> *All who navigate the sounds between island and island in the Hebrides, should be careful to have their crew well acquainted with the harbours and coasts of every island they propose to visit, for otherwise, should night from unavoidable delays surprise them, they run infinite risks of being lost.* (S. Murray, *Companion and Useful Guide to the Beauties of Scotland*)

James Hogg bears this out in his description of a journey from Irin, on the south side of Loch Ailort, to the north shore of Loch nan Uamh in 1804:

> *We at length reached the genteel house of Ewrin, where we were again entertained by Mr McEchern, who entreated us to stay all night, but perceiving that we wished to get forward, procured us a boat and crew to carry us over. The boat being small, and crouded, and the sea very rough, we were certainly in considerable danger; the waves often washing over her, threatened to suffocate us with brine; the man at the rudder however always bid us fear nothing, and, to encourage us, sung several Earse songs.*

John MacCulloch enjoyed himself with this colourful account of catching a ferry in Arisaig:

I had been directed to Sky by this route, as the best and the most commodious, and as there was, at Arasaik, the best of all possible ferry boats. But when the enquiry came to be made, nobody knew any thing about a ferry boat. There might be one, or not: if there was, it was uncertain if it would carry a horse; whether it was on this side of the water or the other; whether it would choose to go; whether there was a ferryman; whether the wind would allow it to go; whether the tide would suffer it. The Arasaik road had been made on account of the ferry, or the ferry on account of the road; and though a carriage ferry, and a horse ferry, there was no boat that could hold a carriage, and no horse had ever dared to cross. Furthermore, the ferry-boat, if there really was one, was two miles from Arasaik, somewhere, among some rocks; and there was no road to it, nor any pier. Lastly, I at length found a ferry-boat, a mile from the sea, as fit to carry a camelopardalis as a horse, and a ferry-boat man who could not speak English.

MacCulloch elaborates his tale with the rival claims of two ferryboats, the owner of one incapable (through drink), the owner of the other unwilling or missing. Moreover *'there was no one to navigate the vessel but the ferryman's wife, and she was employed in whipping her children.'*

His quest had started on the Sunday and concluded on the Tuesday when:

the men admitted me . . . with a promise to land me somewhere in Sky; if they did not change their minds. The horse did as he liked: it is good to conform to all events in this part of the world; and I was thus accommodated . . . with a passage to Sky, or elsewhere, in a ferry-boat over which I had no controul: in a ferry-boat which was not a ferry-boat, and which had no ferryman. All the arrangements were of the usual fashion; no floor, no rudder, no seat aft, oars patched and spliced and nailed, no rowlocks, a mast without stay, bolt, or haulyards; and all other things fitting, as the advertisements say.

My companions were soon tired of rowing, and, as usual, would set a sail. As it could not be hoisted, for want of haulyards, the yard was fastened to the mast, and thus it was all set up together, after much flapping and leeway. It was then found that there was neither tack nor sheet; besides which, three or four feet at the after leach were torn away. The holes in the sail were convenient; because they saved the trouble of reefing, in case of a squall . . . And then the boat began to go backwards. I did not care; it was a fine day and a long day, and an entertaining coast: they were good-natured fellows, and I was as well at sea as in Sky or Arasaik. (John MacCulloch, *The Highlands and Western Isles of Scotland*, 1824)

Lord Teignmouth was equally philosophical a few years later:

At Arisaig there is a ferry to Sky: a species of conveyance very different from that which the Southerns understand by such a mode of proceeding, and implying, in this instance, a transit of fifteen miles, – the delay in preparing the boat, which lies two miles distant from Arisaig, – the catching the boatmen, the clearing the coast, the management of intricate tides and conflicting winds, and the probability of a thorough ducking. (Lord Teignmouth, *Sketches of the Coasts and Islands of Scotland,* 1836)

Chapter 11

Roads

A lthough the north-west of Scotland was stereotypically regarded as a trackless waste this is probably a travesty of the real situation. Despite the primacy of sea travel for men and freight there had always been some overland communication. For hundreds, perhaps thousands of years, cattle, sheep and people had travelled between Highland pastures and Lowland markets. Passes had been crossed, fords found, ways worn, regular routes established. We might not characterize all these as roads but tracks or pathways they certainly were. They must have varied in quantity and quality throughout the vast area of the Highlands and Islands. In river valleys, along machair land, in gentler landscapes like Islay and Kintyre, routes may well have been more recognisable than in the harsher landscapes of Knoydart and Moidart. However, for these tracks to then become roads, for the bogs to be drained or bypassed, for the fords to be bridged, all this required capital – which is precisely what the Highlands lacked. The benefits of a costly road or bridge could never repay the outlay. Improvements were more likely to be small-scale and manageable within the resources available to the local community.

The first proper roads in the Highlands are normally associated with General Wade's work in the 1720s and 1730s. These were military roads, designed primarily for quick support of the Highland garrisons. In the early years of the nineteenth century there was another burst of government road-building under the auspices of the Commission for Roads and Bridges. This has been covered by A.R.B. Haldane in his book *New Ways through the Glens*. Nevertheless, although these were the first roads that we would entitle as such, we must also grant that there were recognised tracks and paths for centuries, perhaps millennia earlier. Many of these were worn by animals.

Anybody who walks in the Highlands will be familiar with the narrow paths made by sheep through the heather. In earlier times there would have been even more pronounced tracks worn by cattle. These were driven to market in the Lowlands for many hundreds of years. The droving trade reached its height in the period 1750–1850, (again covered by A.R.B. Haldane in his book *The Drove Roads of Scotland*), but stretches back into the mediaeval period. With all these hundreds of thousands of beasts travelling from the Highlands to Lowlands over many centuries there grew a network of recognised routes and tracks. These may not have been built, but they were certainly trodden.

Edmund Burt, author of *Letters from a Gentleman in the North of Scotland*, worked on Wade's new roads. His book is an invaluable source both for the new type of road and as evidence of a pre-existing network. He refused to grace the older tracks with the name *road*, preferring to refer to them as *ways*. He, like Pont before him, regarded them as downright dangerous in certain places:

And there is foure mylls from the head or bray of Glenaray, and the ferrie of Lochow called Portsoinghan And these foure mylls they are verie dangerous to travel or goe through this hill, which is called Monikleaganich, in tyme of evill stormie weather, in winter especiallie for it is ane high Mountaine. (Pont(?) in *Macfarlane's Geographical Collections*)

The former ways along those slopes were only paths worn by the feet of the Highlanders and their little garrons. They ran along upwards and downwards, one above another, in such a manner as was found most convenient at the first tracing them out. (Edmund Burt, *Letters from a Gentleman in the North of Scotland*, c. 1737)

And again:

The old ways (for roads I shall not call them) consisted chiefly of stony moors, bogs, rugged, rapid fords, declivity of hills, entangling woods, and giddy precipices. You will say this is a dreadful catalogue to be read to him that is about to take a Highland journey. (Edmund Burt, *Letters from a Gentleman in the North of Scotland*, c. 1737)

In describing the new roads made in the Great Glen, between Inverness and Fort William, Burt makes it clear that there was a previously existing line of communication which he calls the 'old way'. This 'made a considerable circuit' from Loch Ness before rejoining it at the south-west end. Thereafter 'the old ways, such as they were, ran along upon the sides of the hills' beside Lochs Oich and Lochy. Burt describes the old road running beside Loch Oich:

The dangers of this part of the old way began at the top of a steep ascent, of about fifty or sixty yards from the little plain that parts this lake and Loch Ness; and, not far from the summit, is a part they call The Maidens Leap . . . There the rocks project over the lake, and the path was so rugged and narrow that the Highlanders were obliged, for their safety, to hold by the rocks and shrubs as they passed, with the prospect of death beneath them.
This was not the only dangerous part, but for three miles together . . . it was nowhere safe, and in many places more difficult, and as dangerous, as at the entrance; for the rocks were so steep and uneven, that the passenger was

obliged to creep on his hands and knees. (Edmund Burt, *Letters from a Gentleman in the North of Scotland*, c. 1737)

Certainly such tracks were not suitable for wheeled vehicles or heavy loads: '*except along the sea coast and some new road, the ways are so rough and rocky that no wheel ever turned upon them since the formation of this globe;*' (Edmund Burt, Letters from a Gentleman in the North of Scotland, late 1720s)

And you needed a guide:

Set out with one servant and a guide; the latter, because no stranger (or even a native, unacquainted with the way) can venture among the hills without a conductor . . . In short, one might as well think of making a sea voyage without sun, moon, stars, or compass, as pretend to know which way to take, when lost among the hills and mountains. (Edmund Burt, *Letters from a Gentleman in the North of Scotland*, late 1720s)

Crossing bogs and mosses has always been a little unnerving. Burt describes how, on one of his journeys, he was guided across a quaking morass by a Highlander:

Our weight and the spring of motion, in many parts, caused a shaking all round about us, and the compression made the water rise through the sward, which was, in some parts, a kind of short flaggy grass, and in others a sort of mossy heath; but wherever any bushes grew, I knew, by experience of the peat-mosses I had gone over before, that it was not far to the bottom.

This rising of water made me conclude (for my guide was not intelligible to me) that we had nothing but a liquid under us, or, at most, something like a quicksand, and that the sward was only a little toughened by the entwining of the roots, and was supported, like ice, only by water, or something nearly as fluid. (Edmund Burt, *Letters from a Gentleman in the North of Scotland*, c. 1737)

In the event Burt refused to return the same way and, since reading his account, has enjoyed my full sympathy. It recalls similar experiences and there are few things as unnerving, for mortal men, as walking on water.

The evidence provided by Burt proves that there was indeed a network of 'ways' in Inverness-shire, even if he refused to grace them with the name 'roads'. F.S. Mackenna has researched the early roads in mid-Argyll through the Minutes of the Commissioners of Supply. These make it perfectly clear that there was also a whole network of recognised 'ways' through Argyll by the eighteenth century. Despite what Burt says about the opposition of some of the Inverness-shire lairds to the military roads, there was obviously local support for road-improvement in Argyll – from merchants, drovers and those taking goods to market. Local taxes or stents were raised to build stone bridges and improve the landing-places at ferry-terminals. There was demand for proper roads, new or wider bridges, improvements to quays, better access for animals when boarding boats and more punctual ferry services. In fact the concerns of the eighteenth century are almost exactly the same as ours today.

The road system in Argyll did not begin with General Wade and was already well-developed before the government's Commission for Roads and Bridges got underway in the early nineteenth century. Inverness-shire probably had a similar legacy of mediaeval 'ways' and tracks though the western part of the county may not have been able to match the improvements that took place in Argyll during the eighteenth century. However, we should also recognise the work of the Commissioners for Forfeited Estates who were responsible for many small-scale civil engineering projects over a period of nearly 40 years after the last Jacobite Rising in 1745.

In addition I suspect that many small-scale local improvements simply went unnoticed. Sean-achaidh in North Morar was abandoned after 1851 but not far away are the stone piers of an early bridge to carry locals across a burn which, in a downpour, quickly becomes dangerous. Above the nearby Loch an Nostarie there is a farm, abandoned before 1834, which has a paved ford across an adjacent burn. At Lochan Stole in the same area there is a set of stepping stones on the old track between Stoul and Bracara. (See Plate 8a). In 1841 these were two of the three biggest settlements in North Morar, and probably always had been. Such 'improvements' are now barely noticeable in the surrounding landscape. Many parts of the Highlands bear traces of earlier systems of communication which we no longer recognise.

Of course the road system of the Highlands could never bear comparison with that of Lowland Scotland. The terrain was harsher, capital was scarcer and returns were leaner. However we should not ascribe all Highland road-building to General Wade or the nineteenth-century Commission for Roads and Bridges. There were also small-scale native endeavours over many centuries, the roads made by statute labour, the enterprise shown in Argyll and the work of the Commissioners for Forfeited Estates. The result of the burst of road-building in the eighteenth century, whether military or civil, was a vastly improved communications system. This began to become evident on maps. In 1776 Taylor and Skinner published a book of road-maps of Scotland. Each sheet consisted of some three strips of road, a few of them to Highland destinations. We have maps to Bernera (Glenelg), Inverness, Fort William, Inveraray, Bonawe and Campbeltown. (See Plate 5b). The road to Campbeltown probably lay along the route which Edward Lhuyd took in 1699.

It is difficult to make generalisations about the state of the road network in the Highlands and Islands during the eighteenth century. At the beginning of the century there were probably very few roads anywhere. By the end of it there were plenty; but they varied greatly in quality, quantity and distribution. The following quotations give an idea of their range and variety.

The idea of roads was not unthinkable to Highlanders, just impractical. They only had to go to Iona to see an ancient roadway:

> *From this Place, to another Antient Building, which was a Nunnery, there runs a Causeway about 300 Paces in length, and about 15 Feet broad; intersected at right Angles by another of the same kind which runs from the Harbour, to what is judged to have been the antient Village of Sodor. This Causeway consists entirely of large Blocks of the same red Granite, of which the Cathedral is built, and have been very artfully wrought and compacted together.* (McKay, *Walker's Report on the Hebrides,* 1764 and 1771)

> *Advance . . . along a broad paved way, which is continued in a line from the nunnery to the cathedral: another branches from it to the Bay of Martyrs: and a third narrower than the others, points towards the hills.* (T. Pennant, *A Tour in Scotland and Voyage to the Hebrides,* 1772)

In Islay, Pennant found: '*the roads excellent*' and at Kingsburgh, Skye: '*a good horse road*' (T. Pennant, A Tour in Scotland and Voyage to the Hebrides, 1772)

But not all roads could take wheeled traffic. Johnson writes on setting off from Inverness: '*We were now to bid farewell to the luxury of travelling, and to enter a country upon which perhaps no wheel has ever rolled.*' While in Coll: '*The young laird has attempted what no islander perhaps ever thought on. He has begun a road capable of a wheel-carriage. He has carried it about a mile, and will continue it by annual elongation from his house to the harbour.*' (Johnson, *A Journey to the Western Islands of Scotland,* 1773)

On going from Armadale (Sleat) to Raasay, Johnson describes the contrast between the Isle of Skye and a country of road-signs and mileposts:

> *We were furnished therefore with horses and a guide. In the islands there are no roads, nor any marks by which a stranger may find his way. The horseman has always at his side a native of the place, who, by pursuing game, or tending cattle, or being often employed in messages or conduct, has learned where the ridge of the hill has breadth sufficient to allow a horse and his rider a passage, and where the moss or bog is hard enough to bear them. The bogs are avoided as toilsome at least, if not unsafe, and therefore the journey is made generally from precipice to precipice; from which if the eye ventures to look down, it sees below a gloomy cavity, whence the rush of water is sometimes heard.* (Johnson, *A Journey to the Western Islands of Scotland,* 1773)

Boswell also refers to the lack of waymarks on the route to Dunvegan in Skye: '*A guide, who had been sent with us from Kingsburgh, explored the way . . . by observing certain marks known only to the inhabitants'*; the lack of roads on Raasay: '*There are indeed no roads through the island, unless a few detached beaten tracks deserve that name;'* but their presence on Inch Kenneth, an island then leased by Sir Allan MacLean who had been in the army: '*As we walked up from the shore, Dr Johnson's heart was cheered by the sight of a road marked with cart-wheels, as on the main land; a thing which we had not seen for a long time.*' (Boswell, *The Journal of a Tour to the Hebrides*, 1773).

Finally, on being back on the mainland in a carriage:

> '*Our satisfaction of finding ourselves again in a comfortable carriage was very great. We had a pleasing conviction of the commodiousness of civiliza-tion, and heartily laughed at the ravings of those absurd visionaries who have attempted to persuade us of the superior advantages of a state of nature.*' (Boswell, *The Journal of a Tour to the Hebrides*, 1773)

Faujas de Saint Fond describes his journey from Aros to Torloisk on Mull in the company of two local guides:

> *We set out on our two little horses, with two persons to conduct us and bring them back, ignorant that our way lay across ravines, heaths, marshes and mountains, difficult of access, and without any trace of a road.*
>
> *Whilst day-light remained, we made good progress; our guides pushed forward with such speed as to outrun our horses, though these went at a good pace. Our two young Hebridians were well-made, light and indefatigable; they made nothing of streams, pools, bogs, or mountains; and I admired their courage, gaiety, and graceful figure. Their heads were decorated with a blue military bonnet, having a border of red, green, and white, and surmounted with one feather. They wore with grace a plaid, having squares of different colours, fastened to the right shoulder and folded over the left arm, with a waist-coat and jacket of the same stuff. Their thighs and legs were half naked, but the latter were covered with a coloured buskin, while a convenient kind of shoes completed this Roman dress. A poniard in the girdle gave them a military air, and a stick in the hand served to help them over the waters.*
>
> *Their eagerness to be useful to us made them doubly interesting. They never failed to go before to show us the way, returning however at intervals to caress and animate the horses, or to ask if we had need of their services.* (Faujas de Saint Fond, *A journey through England and Scotland to the Hebrides in 1784*)

Knox had a dim view of the success of road-making in Skye:

> *At this time the inhabitants of Sky were mostly engaged upon the roads in different parts of the island, under the inspection of the gentlemen and*

*tacksmen, and accompanied, each party, by the bagpiper . . . Yet, after all
these labours and inconveniences, no effectual roads, and much less effectual
bridges, can be made through these bogs and rocks, without the aid of the
military, and proper tools.* (J. Knox, *A Tour through the Highlands of
Scotland,* 1786)

Some parts of the Highlands remained inaccessible even at the end of the
eighteenth century. From Assynt, Pennant wanted to travel to the extreme
north-west of Scotland:

*It was our design, on leaving the ship, to have penetrated by land, as far as
the extremity of the island; but we were informed that the way was
impassable for horses, and that even a Highland foot-messenger must avoid
part of the hills by crossing an arm of the sea. Return the same road through a
variety of bog and hazardous rock, that nothing but our shoeless little steeds
could have carried us over.* (T. Pennant, *A Tour in Scotland and Voyage to
the Hebrides,* 1772)

Fourteen years later Knox entertained the same idea. He describes setting off
from Loch Broom in early October 1786 with the intention of going on foot to
Durness on the north coast and then across to Caithness.

*Many persons had painted in strong colours, the difficulty of performing this
journey at any season of the year, and much more so in October. They
represented the country from Assynt to Caithness as one continued wild or
desart, composed of almost impassable swamps and ridges of mountains,
where I would find few inhabitants, no seats of gentlemen, no roads, inns, or
conveniences of any kind except water. It was farther urged, that I would be
continually interrupted by arms of the sea, which it might be hazardous to
cross at that season in Highland boats; that the rivers might be swelled by
rains and rendered impassable; that the swamps would be covered with
water; that if, upon trial, I should find a journey through that country
impracticable . . . I would be obliged to return to Assynt, and cross the
country to the Dornoch Firth, itself a journey of great difficulty at all seasons,
and scarcely passable in winter.* (J. Knox, *A Tour through the Highlands of
Scotland,* 1786)

In the event he found the warnings fully justified. Having decided on the
above journey he writes of travelling between Scourie Bay and Loch
Laxford:

*Being furnished with a guide for Loch Laxford, we pushed on vigorously
towards that lake, where we might secure a lodging before night; when it
would be impossible to advance a hundred yards without danger from*

precipices or bogs. Even with daylight we found difficulty in getting forward. It is a country where no man, who cannot climb like a goat, and jump like a grasshopper, should attempt to travel, especially in the month of October. (J. Knox, *A Tour through the Highlands of Scotland,* 1786)

The Rev. J.L. Buchanan writes of NE Lewis and Uist:

This part of Lewis is passable for foot as well as horsemen. But in most places the least vestige of a track or path is not to be discerned: so that, what little intercourse takes place in this rugged island, is carried on by means of boats, on the rivers, lakes, and morasses when covered by water.

The whole west side of Uist, being plain and sandy, is extremely pleasant to ride through, but attended with danger to strangers and such as are overtaken by liquor, on account of fords over which the sea flows from east to west so rapidly, and which are at the same time of such extent, that an active horse or footman will hardly gain the further side, before the tide has filled up some one or other of the many small hollow channels of rivulets he has to cross. (Buchanan, *Travels in the Western Hebrides from 1782 to 1790*)

He reiterates this point when talking of lazybeds:

This renders the whole back settlements of Harris almost impassable, as a man meets constantly with feannags, and wide furrows to leap over. And indeed travelling through parts of Uist also is dangerous to strangers, because large white fields of dry sand, as far as the eye can reach, resembling new driven snow in whiteness, and driving across the paths, in so much that new footpaths are made daily, without any visible elevated objects to be directed by, one is generally bewildered. This is the case all over the immense plains of white sand left by the ebb, called fords, where the paths are always washed away, and no visible object to direct by. A stranger, on this account, without a guide, is almost sure of losing, not only his way, in going across these broad plains, but also his life. In the hills, and in the northern parts of Harris, there are pillars here and there erected, and stones placed on top of rocks, where travellers must make a stretch to pass through these zig-zag paths by their direction; otherwise the natives may lose their way, as well as strangers. It is, therefore, absolutely necessary to have skilful guides when travelling over either countries. (Buchanan, *Travels in the Western Hebrides from 1782 to 1790*)

He writes of the efforts of Alexander MacLeod of Rodel: '*He was also at much pains to begin roads through the country, as the first step towards improvements in any country like this, that lies in a state of nature.*' And of Mr Mackenzie in Lewis: '*Where the natural activity of the inhabitants is farther encouraged by the wise and liberal policy of Mr Mackenzie, in constructing roads, and by just regulations, leaving to the industrious the reward of their toil.'* (Buchanan, *Travels in the Western Hebrides from 1782 to 1790*)

But he recognises that certain inducements might speed your passage:

> *In passing to and from the islands, tobacco is necessary to a gentleman, if he wishes to avoid both delay and imposition. Here it deserves to be remarked, that though the gentlemen do squeeze subtenants themselves, yet they do not discourage, nay, some of the baser kind of masters encourage the poor oppressed creatures to make heavy charges on strangers; and I could produce instances when complaints were justly lodged against imposition. To prevent those gross charges, any knowing man will deal his tobacco liberally, and in that event, he is sure of a speedy and very cheap passage, or convoy, through the different isles.* (Buchanan, *Travels in the Western Hebrides from 1782 to 1790*)

However, wheeled transport was coming:

> *The road from Fort William to Fort Augustus, and all the way to Inverness, is excellent. Notwithstanding which, it cost us nine hours to get to Fort Augustus, which is only thirty miles. The only mode of conveyance was upon the shelties of the country, and these were such miserable, infirm, and aged animals, that it was painful to compel them to proceed. Travellers would do well to order a chaise for this purpose from Inverness. The expense is nearly the same, and if there is much baggage, such a plan would be more economical.* (E.D. Clarke, *Journal* 1797)

The military network was further enhanced by the work of the Commission for Roads and Bridges in the early nineteenth century. Their very first scheme was the Loch na Gaul road between Fort William and Arisaig (see Plate 8b). John MacCulloch thought well of it:

> *Every one who can find time or make it, should bestow a day on an excursion from Fort William to Arasaik. It is a beautiful ride of forty miles. As to the road itself, it is, like all the new ones which are so little used . . . more like a gravel walk in a garden, than a highway . . . It is a great pleasure, unquestionably, to see and to use such roads as these; but it would be much more pleasing to find them cut up, or, at least, marked by wheel tracks and hoof marks; that we might have the satisfaction of knowing that they were used, and that some interchange of something, if it was but that of ideas, was going on in this country . . .*

However he was also honest enough to realise the line of the road was not completely new and gave credit to its Highland ancestry:

it is impossible to give too much praise to the ingenuity which conducted this, as well as some other of these Highland roads . . . In many cases, the new roads have been traced, along, or very near to, the ancient cattle and country tracks . . . in many more, the distribution is due to the common Highlanders themselves, sometimes contractors, and sometimes overseers . . . I, for one, will lift up my voice . . . in defence of the talents and ingenuity of these Highland workmen: among the lowest of whom I have found such an eye for ground, and such a quick conception of its height, and distribution, and inclination . . . as even a general officer or a quarter-master might often envy. They are natural geographers . . .

These roads are, however, very treacherous, in spite of all the care bestowed on them: for, against torrents, it is often impossible to calculate, and, even when foreseen, they are sometimes not to be resisted . . . This very road was in perfect repair when I passed it first. When I returned in a few days, a foundation wall had slid away from a steep face of smooth rock, and the road was gone. (J. MacCulloch, *The Highlands and Western Isles of Scotland,* 1824)

MacCulloch was not the first to praise the Highlanders themselves. Fifty years earlier, Pennant had said something rather similar:

The roads are excellent; but from Fort William to Kinloch Leven, very injudiciously planned, often carried far about, and often so steep as to be scarce surmountable; whereas had the engineer followed the track used by the inhabitants, those inconveniences would have been avoided. (Pennant, *A Tour in Scotland 1769*)

Today most Highland communities clamour for new roads, or improvements to existing ones, but this enthusiasm did not exist everywhere in the eighteenth century. Burt gives a number of criticisms made by the Highlanders and their preference for the old ways: '*I make no doubt, the generality of the Highlanders will prefer the precipice to the gravel of the road and a greater number of steps.*' (Edmund Burt, *Letters from a Gentleman in the North of Scotland,* c. 1737)

The clan chiefs rightly feared that travel would weaken the bonds of clan society:

Those chiefs and other gentlemen complain, that thereby an easy passage is opened into their country for strangers, who, in time, by their suggestions of liberty, will destroy or weaken that attachment of their vassals which it is so necessary for them to support and preserve. (Edmund Burt, *Letters from a Gentleman in the North of Scotland,* c. 1737)

The attitude to new roads may have been different in Inverness-shire to Argyllshire. The latter county included more prosperous districts and was largely controlled by Campbell lairds who were more favourable to government. But the dislike voiced in Inverness-shire was not so irrational as it might seem. The new roads demanded changes of the Highlanders and these changes involved expense. For instance, both they and their animals now required shoes. Firstly let us glance at the animals.

Horses

The hardy Highland garrons were perfectly suited for their environment despite their comparatively small size:

> *Horses they have in plenty, and these show a great endurance both of work and cold. At St John* [Perth] *and Dundee a Highland Scot will bring down two hundred or three hundred horses, unbroken, that have never been mounted . . . They are brought up alongside of their dams in the forests and the cold, and are thus fitted to stand all severity of weather. They are of no great size, and are thus not fitted to carry a man in heavy armour to the wars, but a light-armed man may ride them at any speed where he will. More hardy horses of so small a size you shall nowhere find. In Scotland for the most part the horses are gelded, because their summer pasturing is in the open country, and this is attended by small expense; yet such a horse will travel further in a day, and for a longer time, than a horse that has not been gelded. He will do his ten or twelve leagues without food. Afterwards, while his master is eating his own victual, he puts his horse to pasture, and by the time he has had a sufficient meal he will find his horse fit to carry him further.* (John Major in Hume Brown, *Scotland before 1700*)

Burt also emphasised the utility of the Highland garron. Although they did carry people they were perhaps even more important as a pack animal:

> *These horses in miniature run wild among the mountains; some of them till they are eight or ten years old, which renders them exceedingly restive and stubborn . . . They are so small that a middle-sized man must keep his legs almost in lines parallel to their sides when carried over the stony ways; and it is almost incredible to those who have not seen it, how nimbly they skip with a heavy rider among the rocks and large moorstones, turning zigzag to such places that are passable. I think verily they all follow one another in the same irregular steps, because in those ways there appears some little smoothness, worn by their naked hoofs, which is not anywhere else to be seen.* (Edmund Burt, *Letters from a Gentleman in the North of Scotland*, late 1720s)

And he writes of their loads:

When a burden is to be carried on horseback they use two baskets, called 'creels', one on each side of the horse; and if the load be such as cannot be divided, they put it into one of them, and counterbalance it with stones in the other, so that one half of the horse's burden is – I cannot say unnecessary, because I do not see how they could do otherwise in the mountains. (Edmund Burt, *Letters from a Gentleman in the North of Scotland*, late 1720s)

Johnson writes of Skye:

Wheel carriages they have none, but make a frame of timber, which is drawn by one horse with the two points behind pressing on the ground. On this they sometimes drag home their sheaves, but often convey them home in a kind of open panier, or frame of sticks upon the horse's back. (Johnson, *A Journey to the Western Islands of Scotland*, 1773)

Boswell confirms this:

I observed today, that the common way of carrying home their grain here is in loads on horseback. They have also a few sleds, or cars, as we call them in Ayrshire, clumsily made, and rarely used. (Boswell, *The Journal of a Tour to the Hebrides*, 1773)

But in Harris the ground was too rough even for this: '*In the back settlement of Harris, men, women and children, must be constantly under the panniers, as no horse could be of much use there, where the men can hardly walk with their loads.*' (Buchanan, *Travels in the Western Hebrides from 1782 to 1790*)
    Riding a horse on a mountain track was not for the giddy or faint-hearted:

The side of the mountain below me was almost perpendicular; and the rest above, which seemed to reach the clouds, was exceedingly steep. The path which the Highlanders and their little horses had worn was scarcely two feet wide, but pretty smooth . . .
    It is a common thing for the natives to ride their horses over such little precipices; but for myself I never was upon the back of one of them; and, by the account some Highlanders have given me of them, I think I should never choose it in such places as I have been describing.

Because:

There is in some of those paths, at the very edge or extremity, a little mossy grass, and those shelties, being never shod, if they are ever so little footsore, they will, to favour their feet, creep to the very brink, which must certainly be very terrible to a stranger. (Edmund Burt, *Letters from a Gentleman in the North of Scotland,* late 1720s)

Pennant noticed exactly the same near the River Ranza in Arran: '*Ascend the steeps of the barren mountains, with precipices often on the one side of our path, of which our obstinate steeds preferred the very margin.*' But near Glen Docherty, Kinlochewe, he found cause to praise them: '*Ascended again. Arrive amidst strata of red and white marble, the way horrible, broken, steep and slippery; but our cautious steeds tried every step before they would venture to proceed.*' (T. Pennant, *A Tour in Scotland and Voyage to the Hebrides,* 1772)

Johnson confirmed that the tracks were very narrow: '*it is very disagreeable riding in Sky. The way is so narrow, one only at a time can travel, so it is quite unsocial; and you cannot indulge in meditation by yourself, because you must be always attending to the steps which your horse takes.*' (Boswell, *The Journal of a Tour to the Hebrides,* 1773)

As roads arrived so they introduced their own familiar problems. In 1806 the following situation vexed the heritors of Islay:

This Meeting being informed that Cart Drivers are very inattentive as to their Conduct upon the road with Carts – It is now recommended that all Travellers upon the road shall take to the Left in all situations, and that when a Traveller upon the road shall loose a shew of his horse, the Parochial Blacksmith shall be obliged to give preferrence to the Traveller, and any Driver not at the head of his horse when the Cart is upon the Road, shall be Fined at the Discretion of the Magistrate. (G. Smith, *The Book of Islay*)

Shoes

Numerous accounts bear out that most Highlanders spent most of their time barefoot. The Highland reluctance to wear shoes or trousers was founded on practical common sense. The Highlands were so wet, and so many fords had to be waded, that trews and shoes would be perpetually immersed in water. Since they could not easily be changed or dried they threatened the health of the wearer. It was only when travelling long distances, or crossing stony ground, or in winter, that the Highlanders required footwear. Even then, as both Elder and Burt pointed out, they drilled holes in their brogues to let the water out. Shoes were regarded as an expensive luxury and many preferred to give their feet liberty – particularly in the summer. Practice, prejudice and economy all compounded their conservatism.

The traditional Highland garment or belted plaid was well suited to the wet environment of the west. We have already seen how it was adopted by the Norwegian king, Magnus Bareleg, when he re-annexed the Western Isles in 1098. In this form of dress most of the leg was left bare and as a result became tanned and weathered. This was so characteristic of Highlanders that it earned them the nickname of redshanks or red-legs. John Elder gives us a description of this in a letter he wrote to Henry VIII in 1543 or 1544. He had been partly brought up in the Western Isles and knew the Highlands intimately:

Moreouer, wherfor they call ws in Scotland Reddshankes, and in your Graces dominion of England, roghe footide Scottis, Pleas it your Maiestie to vnderstande, that we of all people can tollerat, suffir, and away best with colde, for boithe somer and wyntir, (excepte whene the froest is mooste vehemonte,) goynge alwaies bair leggide and bair footide, our delite and pleasure is not onely in hwntynge of redd deir, wolfes, foxes, and graies, whereof we abounde, and haue great plentie, but also in rynninge, leapinge, swymmynge, shootynge, and thrawinge of dartis: therfor, in so moche as we vse and delite so to go alwaies, the tendir delicatt gentillmen of Scotland call ws Reddshankes. And agayne in wynter, when the froest is mooste vehement (as I haue saide) which we can not suffir bair footide, so weill as snow, whiche can neuer hurt ws whene it cummes to our girdills, we go a hwntynge, and after that we haue slayne redd deir, we flaye of the skyne, bey and bey, and settinge of our bair foote on the insyde thereof, for neide of cunnyge shoe-makers, by your Graces pardon, we play the swtters; compasinge and mesuringe so moche therof, as shall retche vp to our ancklers, pryckynge the vpper part thereof, also with holis, that the water may repas when it entres, and stretchide vp with a stronge thwange of the same, meitand aboue our saide ancklers, so, and pleas your noble Grace, we make our shoois: Therfor, we vsinge such maner of shoois, the roghe hairie syde outwart, in your Graces dominion of England, we be callit roghe footide Scottis. (John Elder, *Collectanea de Rebus Albanicis*)

(Moreover, wherefore they call us in Scotland 'Redshanks' [Redlegs], and in your Grace's dominion of England, rough-footed Scots, may it please your Majesty to understand, that we of all people can tolerate, suffer, and away best with cold, for both summer and winter, (except when the frost is most vehement,) going always bare legged and bare footed, our delight and pleasure is not only in hunting of red deer, wolves, foxes, and graies (heath-hens?), in which we abound, and have great plenty, but also in running, leaping, swimming, shooting, and throwing of darts: therefore, in so much as we use and delight so to go always, the tender delicate gentlemen of Scotland call us Redshanks. And again in winter, when the frost is most vehement (as I have said) which we cannot suffer bare footed, so well as snow, which can never hurt us when it comes to our girdles, we go a-hunting, and after that we have slain red deer, we flay off the skin, by and by, and setting of our bare foot on the inside thereof, for need of cunning shoemakers, by your

Grace's pardon, we play the cobblers; compassing and measuring so much thereof, as shall reach up to our ankles, pricking the upper part thereof, also with holes, that the water may repass when it enters, and stretched up with a strong thong of the same, meeting above our said ankles, so, and [may it] please your noble Grace, we make our shoes: Therefore, we using such manner of shoes, the rough hairy side outwards, in your Grace's dominion of England, we are called rough footed Scots.)

Since the Highland mercenaries in Ireland typically left the mid-leg bare they were often described as 'naked' Scots. In the Carew Manuscripts there is a list of the soldiers under the earl of Tyrone's command in 1598. Amongst these were '100 naked Scots with bows'.

In 1689 Morer writes of the Highlanders: '*They wear a sort of shooes, which they call brocks [brogues], like our pumps, without heels, of a very thin sole, and affording little security from the wet or stones, which is their main use and chiefly intended for.*' (Morer in Hume Brown, *Early Travellers in Scotland*)

When writing of the Scots in general, Morer comments on the cultural approval of going barefoot. This could be rationalised by an appeal to hardiness or machismo:

> *Their ordinary women go barefoot, especially in the summer. Yet the husbands have shoes, and therein seem unkind in letting their wives bear those hardships without partaking themselves. Their children fare no better when scarce able to go. But, what surprised me most, some of the better sort, lay and clergy, made their little ones go in the same manner, which I thought a piece of cruelty in them, that I imputed to the others poverty. But their apology was, the custom of the country, grounded on an ancient law, that no males were to use shoes till fourteen years of age, that so they might be hardened for the wars when their Prince had occasion for their service.*
> (Morer in Hume Brown, *Early Travellers in Scotland*)

Burt makes a similar comment to the effect that the children of gentry could only be distinguished from other youngsters by the fact that they spoke English. Johnson endorses this:

> *The numbers that go barefoot are still sufficient to shew that shoes may be spared: they are not yet considered as necessaries of life; for tall boys, not otherwise meanly dressed, run without them in the streets and in the islands; the sons of gentlemen pass several of their first years with naked feet.*
> (Johnson, *A Journey to the Western Islands of Scotland*, 1773)

Martin Martin, writing c. 1695, makes it clear that footwear was changing:

The shoes anciently wore were a piece of the hide of a deer, cow, or horse, with the hair on, being tied behind and before with a point of leather. The generality now wear shoes, having one thin sole only, and shaped after the right and left foot so that what is for one foot will not serve the other. (Martin Martin, *A Description of the Western Islands of Scotland* c. 1695)

But he also demonstrates that poverty was a great incentive to using whatever resources were available. Writing of St Kilda he states:

The women inhabiting this isle wear no shoes nor stockins in the summertime; the only and ordinary shoes they wear, are made of the necks of solan geese, which they cut above the eyes, the crown of the head serves for the heel, the whole skin being cut close at the breast, which end being sowed, the foot enter into it, as into a piece of narrow stockin; this shoe doth not wear above five days, and if the down side be next the ground, then not above three or four days; but, however, there is plenty of them; some thousands being catch'd, or, as they term it, stolen every March. (Martin Martin, *A Voyage to St Kilda*, 1698)

Whereas in Orkney: '*some wear a seal skin for shoes; which they do not sew, but only tie them about their feet with strings, and sometimes thongs of leather.*' (Martin Martin, *A Description of the Western Islands of Scotland* c. 1695)

Going barefoot was hard on the feet. So: '*When they are any way fatigued by travel, or otherwise, they fail not to bathe their feet in warm water, wherein red moss has been boiled, and rub them with it going to bed.* (Martin Martin, *A Description of the Western Islands of Scotland* c. 1695)

There was a certain cultural respectability attached to going barefoot. The real reasons may have been economic but they were rationalised away by an appeal to hardiness. It was not just a matter of manliness, it applied at least as much to women:

There is a laird's lady, about a mile from one of the Highland garrisons, who is often seen from the ramparts, on Sunday mornings, coming barefoot to the kirk, with her maid carrying the stockings and shoes after her. She stops at the foot of a certain rock, that serves her for a seat, not far from the hovel they call a church, and there she puts them on; and, in her return to the same place, she prepares to go home barefoot as she came. (Edmund Burt, *Letters from a Gentleman in the North of Scotland*, late 1720s)

In fact, even when they could afford shoes the Highlanders were not particularly egalitarian or gallant:

Not long ago, a French officer . . . met a Highland man with a good pair of brogues on his feet, and his wife marching bare foot after him. This indignity to the sex raised the Frenchman's anger to such a degree, that he leaped from his horse, and obliged the fellow to take off the shoes, and the woman to put them on. (Edmund Burt, *Letters from a Gentleman in the North of Scotland*, late 1720s)

By the way, they cut holes in their brogues, though new made, to let out the water, when they have far to go and rivers to pass: this they do to preserve their feet from galling. (Edmund Burt, *Letters from a Gentleman in the North of Scotland*, late 1720s)

When ordinary Highlanders travelled Burt claims they were often barefoot:

But some I have seen shod with a kind of pumps, made out of a raw cowhide, with the hair turned outward, which being ill-made, the wearer's foot looked something like those of a roughfooted hen or pigeon: these are called 'quarrants', and are not only offensive to the sight but intolerable to the smell of those who are near them. The stocking rises no higher than the thick of the calf, and from the middle of the thigh to the middle of the leg is a naked space, which being exposed to all weathers, becomes tanned and freckled. (Edmund Burt, *Letters from a Gentleman in the North of Scotland*, late 1720s)

In an article on ancient Highland dress in the *Transactions of the Iona Club*, Burt's term 'quarrant' is identified as 'cuaran' which is Gaelic for a shoe of untanned skin, commonly worn with the hairy side outward. The same article includes the following description of dress in Breadalbane before 1747: '*cuoranen, a laced shoe of skin, with the hairy side out, rather disused*'. (Transactions of the Iona Club, 1834, pp 50–1)

In 1769 Pennant says almost exactly the same thing: '*The stockings are short, and are tied below the knee. The cuoranen is a sort of laced shoe made of a skin with the hairy side out, but now seldom worn.*' (T. Pennant, *A Tour in Scotland 1769*)

While Johnson writes of Highland shoes:

In Sky I first observed the use of brogues, a kind of artless shoes, stitched with thongs so loosely, that though they defend the foot from stones, they do not exclude water. Brogues were formerly made of raw hides, with the hair inwards, and such are perhaps still used in rude and remote parts; but they are said not to last above two days. (Johnson, *A Journey to the Western Islands of Scotland*, 1773)

Their brogues (shoes) are made of cow or horse leather, and often of seal skins, that are commonly well tanned by the root of tormintile, which they dig out from the hillocks, and uncultivated lands, about the sea-side. This, properly pounded and prepared, without either lime or bark, is sufficient to make the hides pliant and fit for wearing. It answers their purpose much better than leather tanned with lime or bark, because they seldom grow hard or shrink when dried, even though wet all day; which is not the case with such as are burnt with lime. They never use tan-pits, but bind the hides fast with ropes, and hold them for several days in some remote solitary stream, until the hair begins to come off, of its own accord; and after that, the tormintile roots are applied for bark, as above described. (Buchanan, *Travels in the Western Hebrides from 1782 to 1790*)

So John Elder would have had no difficulty recognising Highlanders as 'Redshanks' even two centuries after his time.

Burt found that animals, as well as humans, now needed to be shod for the less forgiving surface of the new roads in the Highlands: '*The lowest class, who, many of them, at some times cannot compass a pair of shoes for themselves, they allege, that the gravel is intolerable to their naked feet; and the complaint has extended to their thin brogues.*'

As a result many Highlanders took wide detours to avoid using the new roads. Some of the English then accused the Highlanders of a stubborn refusal to use them simply because they were introduced by Englishmen! Burt, though, believed the Highlanders had a point. He asked: '*But why do the black cattle do the same thing? Certainly for the ease of their feet.*' (Edmund Burt, *Letters from a Gentleman in the North of Scotland*, c. 1737)

He discusses this in more detail in an analysis of whether or not the new roads were an unmixed blessing for the natives:

The middling order say the roads are to them an inconvenience, instead of being useful, as they have turned them out of their old ways; for their horses being never shod, the gravel would soon whet away their hoofs, so as to render them unserviceable: whereas the rocks and moorstones, though together they make a rough way, yet, considered separately, they are generally pretty smooth on the surface where they tread, and the heath is always easy to their feet. To this I have been inconsiderately asked, 'Why then do they not shoe their horses?'

This question is easily put, and costs nothing but a few various sounds. But where is the iron, the forge, the farrier, the people within a reasonable distance to maintain him? And lastly, where is the principal requisite – money? (Edmund Burt, *Letters from a Gentleman in the North of Scotland*, c. 1737)

(A.R.B. Haldane discusses the effect of the new roads on droving, and vice-versa, as well as the issue of shoeing cattle, in his book *The Drove Roads of Scotland*.)

Fords

Most people today have probably never used a ford, or even, despite St
Christopher, know what it is. Before bridges the only way to cross a river was
to wade across at a shallow point. Depending on the state of the river this
could involve considerable danger and even today climbers and walkers are
sometimes lost while attempting burns that have been transformed from
purling rills to raging torrents. The ford was always an important point in the
local landscape and many towns and villages have grown up around them.
The luxury of a bridge is relatively recent in many parts of Scotland.

Richard Franck writes of the dangers of river-crossings:

> *Theophilus: However, I'll remind you of our hazardous passage from
> Innerbrachy to the famous Ness, as at another time our personal hazard,
> when fording over Forres, and the rapid Trespey [Spey]; besides other great
> rivers and rivulets in our march, of very swift and violent motion; which we
> often discharg'd without the artifice of boats* (Franck, *Northern Memoirs*,
> 1656/7)

Burt describes watching some locals ford a Highland river after he had
gingerly crossed it himself on horseback:

> *The instant I had recovered the further side of the river, there appeared, near
> the water, six Highland men and a woman . . . Seeing they were preparing to
> wade, I stayed to observe them: first the men and the woman tucked up their
> petticoats, then they cast themselves into a rank, with the female in the
> middle, and laid their arms over one another's shoulders; and I saw they had
> placed the strongest toward the stream, as best able to resist the force of the
> torrent. In their passage, the large slippery stones, made some of them now
> and then lose their footing: and, on those occasions, the whole rank changed
> colour and countenance.*
>
> *I believe no painter ever remarked such strong impressions of fear and hope
> on a human face, with so many and sudden successions of those two opposite
> passions, as I observed among those poor people; but in the Highlands this is
> no uncommon thing.*
>
> *Perhaps you will ask, 'How does a single Highlander support himself
> against so great a force?' He bears himself up against the stream with a stick,
> which he always carries with him for that purpose.* (Edmund Burt, *Letters
> from a Gentleman in the North of Scotland*, late 1720s)

Important people could expect to be helped across difficult waters:

> *In one expedition, where I was well attended . . . there was a river in my way
> so dangerous that I was set upon the shoulders of four Highlanders, my horse*

not being to be trusted to in such roughness, depth, and rapidity; and I really thought sometimes we should all have gone together. In the same journey the shoulders of some of them were employed to ease the horses down from rock to rock; and all that long day I could make out but nine miles. This also was called a road. (Edmund Burt, *Letters from a Gentleman in the North of Scotland*, late 1720s)

It is clear from Burt's various descriptions that the small Highland garrons were more suited for crossing boggy ground but, by virtue of their size, the larger southern horses gave a greater sense of security when fording rivers.

River-crossings were very important during military operations. One of the important features in early maps of Scotland was where the bridges lay. Hardyng mentioned bridges at Stirling and Perth in his early fifteenth-century verse chronicle. In the sixteenth century Lily and Nowell included them on their maps. Even as late as March 1746 the absence of bridges hampered Cumberland's pursuit of the Jacobite forces. One of his army wrote: '*We have had such bad Weather lately, that it was impossible for an Army to live in the Field: and the Rivers being, by this means, impassible, has detained his Royal Highness the Duke, and Army.*' (*A journey through Part of England and Scotland*, 1746)

Whilst elsewhere he tells of fording the Deveron: '*From this Place to Bamff the Deveron obstructs our Way, which with great Difficulty and some Danger, I forded with my Horse.*' (*A journey through Part of England and Scotland*, 1746)

The same officer writes further of the River Spey and the folly of the Jacobite army in not making a stand there:

And as we approached the Spey, the Rebels made off with great Precipitation, excepting two or three, who had the Impudence to fire at some of our People, as they crossed that rapid broad River, which if they had stood, (it was thought,) might have defended that important Pass a long time, to our great loss; here being a very strong Current, and also deep. We were obliged to ford it with our Horses, and those who had none, waded it, the Rebels having broke all their Boats, which before were on purpose for the Use of Passengers; we lost two Women, and a Trooper, which were drowned: It was an odd sight to see the Women wade this strong rapid River, much above their Middles, holding up their Coats, and frequently giving way with the Stream, which it was a great Difficulty to withstand; they were also obliged to step with great Caution, for fear of the great Stones, which lye in every part of the Bottom. (*A journey through Part of England and Scotland*, 1746)

Pennant says much the same when writing of the River Spey near Castle Gordon:

The Duke of Cumberland passed this water at Beily church, near this place, when the channel was so deep as to take an officer, from whom I had the relation, and who was six feet four inches high, up to the breast. The opposite banks are very high and steep; so that, had not the rebels been providentially so infatuated as to neglect opposition, the passage must have been attended with considerable loss. (Pennant, *A Tour in Scotland 1769*)

Bonnie Prince Charlie also had to cope with some difficult fords in his long period as a fugitive after Culloden. On his return from the Hebrides in July 1746 he landed at Mallaig and eventually made his way south to Traigh in South Morar. To do so he had to cross the River Morar at the ford by Rhubana. This was where the river leaves the loch and although the latter has now been dammed, and is therefore higher than formerly, it would still have been a difficult and potentially dangerous crossing. Accordingly they stopped on the way: '*and procured a guide (the night being dark and the road bad) to shew them how to take the ford near Moran's house.*' (James Elphinston, 1749, in *Lyon in Mourning*)

The following description reinforces the point that those of high status might be carried across a ford, but the rest of the world had to wade:

In coming to the ford near Morar's house a comical adventure happened. Mr. MacKinnon desired the guide to be so kind as to take the poor sick young fellow (meaning the Prince) upon his back across the ford, as it was then pretty deep. 'The deel be on the back he comes,' says the guide, 'or any fellow of a servant like him. But I'll take you on my back, Sir, if you please, and carry you safely through the ford.' 'No, no, by no means,' said Mr. MacKinnon, 'if the lad must wade, I'll wade along with him and help him, lest any harm should happen to him.' Then John MacKinnon took hold of the Prince's arm and they went through the ford together. This adventure pleased Mr. MacKinnon very much, as it served to conceal the Prince more and more, for the guide had not the smallest suspicion that the sick lad was the Prince. (John Mackinnon, 1761, in *Lyon in Mourning*)

Bridges

Our first hard information about a bridge in the Highlands reminds us of the position of the church as a patron of civil engineering projects. Amongst the letters of Pope Clement VII we find:

16 October 1384
To all Christ's faithful. Indulgence of one year and forty days is granted to all who contribute towards the rebuilding of the bridge across the river Newdach in Cowal, Argyll diocese, which was swept away by floodwaters, causing those who now have to cross the river to be completely submerged and in great danger. (Papal Letters to Scotland of Clement VII, p 103)

What is significant about this document is the fact that there had existed a bridge previously and that the plaintiffs preferred a replacement bridge to the dangers of fording.

More evidence for early bridges in the Highlands comes from four place-names which contain the element *drochaid* (bridge). We have no way of knowing exactly how old these are but after each I have put in brackets the date of the earliest documentary reference I have found. They may of course be significantly earlier:

Ardnadhrogit (1510) – Mull
Kendrochit (1519) – parish of Inishail, near Dalmally
Kindrochid (1541) – Kilchoman, Islay
Coshandrochaid (1652) – North Knapdale

There is also the place-name Bruiland which occurs just beside the Claonaig water, not far from Skipness in North Kintyre. Unfortunately, since this is not named individually as a land-assessment unit I have found no early documentary reference to it. However it occurs in an area with a number of significant Norse names and may just possibly mean Bridge-land from Norse *bru* (bridge). (I do not think it has anything to do with the Borland or Bordland which appears on the Blaeu/Pont map of the area). There is also Brue by Barvas in Lewis.

Such early bridges were built without the benefit of modern techniques, materials and engineering knowledge. For quickness and convenience they may often have been built of wood rather than stone and not so securely anchored to river bed or bank. Flash floods could, and often did, carry them away. But we should not just presume that the Highlands were destitute of the knowledge, skills and resources to build bridges at all.

Jeffrey Stone has drawn attention to a handful of Highland bridges marked on the maps of Pont, Blaeu and Gordon. These include bridges by Kilmartin, Muckairn and Loch Ness on Pont's manuscript maps, as well as bridges over the Aros River in Mull, and by Kiloran, Colonsay, in Blaeu. Since Blaeu's work was based on Pont we know that these bridges, at least, were available to him c. 1590.

As we have seen earlier, a bridge was built over the River Arkaig in 1620: '*In the water or river of Airgaik . . . in the zeare 1620 yeirs the fourteenth of August. the tennants and gentlemen of the Countrey being at the building of a bridge of timber on the said river*' (*Macfarlane's Geographical Collections*, vol II).

In volume 17 of *Kist* (the magazine of the Natural History and Antiquarian Society of Mid-Argyll) there is a reference to, and sketch of, the old 'clapper' bridge at Achnamara in Knapdale. Apparently this dates to the late seventeenth century when the laird of Oib Greim upset the Kirk and was ordered to build a bridge over the Barnagad burn to help worshippers going to church. It appears that even after the Reformation the church was still a powerful patron of the traveller. There were formerly at least three other such bridges in the area and there are references to a Bridge of Douglas (south of Inveraray) as early as 1645.

Not all wooden bridges were terribly robust. Franck did not have a high opinion of one such at Inverness: *'for here you shall meet with a wooden bridg to convoy you over the rapid Ness; but certainly the weakest, in my opinion, that ever stradled over so strong a stream.* (R. Franck, *Northern Memoirs*, 1656/7)

Some seventy years later, Burt wrote more favourably of the same town:

> *The bridge is about eighty yards over, and a piece of good workmanship, consisting of seven arches, built with stone, and maintained by a toll of a 'bodle', or the sixth part of a penny for each foot-passenger with goods; a penny for a loaded horse, etc*

However he also makes it clear the extreme poverty of some meant that any toll was too high:

> *And here I cannot forbear to give you an instance of the extreme indigence of some of the country people, by assuring you, I have seen women with heavy loads, at a distance from the bridge (the water being low), wade over the large stones, which are made slippery by the sulphur, almost up to the middle, at the hazard of their lives, being desirous to save, or unable to pay, one single bodle.* (Edmund Burt, *Letters from a Gentleman in the North of Scotland*, late 1720s)

Burt gives numerous examples of the dangers of fording Highland rivers but also makes it clear that lack of resources prevented improvements in the transport infrastructure. There was insufficient capital for building roads and bridges, and, even if the landowners had raised the necessary money, their people were so poor that they could not afford the tolls necessary to maintain them. If we add to this the ferocity of the Highland weather which threatened each and every road or bridge, we can see there was little incentive to try and overcome the forces and obstacles of nature. Instead, the conservative rural economy of the Highlands adapted to its environment and was locked into a vicious circle. Perhaps because of its relative wealth and stability the lairds and people of Argyll attempted to break this cycle. Elsewhere in the north-west it was only overcome by intervention from outside; by the military roads built in the 1720s and 1730s under General Wade; by the Forfeited Estates Commissioners; or by the government-backed Commission for Roads and Bridges in the first decades of the nineteenth century.

Burt gives a clear indication of the home-made nature of some Highland bridges. On returning to Inverness at the end of one particular expedition he found that a small river had become impassable. He stopped to wait and after some time a party of merchants appeared on the other side of the water.

Within sight of the ford was a bridge, as they called it, made for the convenience of this place; it was composed of two small fir trees, not squared at all, laid, one beside the other, across a narrow part of the river, from rock to rock: there were gaps and intervals between those trees, and, beneath, a most tumultuous fall of water. Some of my merchants, bestriding the bridge, edged forwards, and moved the whisky vessels before them, but the others, afterwards, to my surprise, walked over this dangerous passage, and dragged their garrons through the torrent, while the poor little horses were almost drowned with the surge. (Edmund Burt, *Letters from a Gentleman in the North of Scotland*, late 1720s)

In 1769 Pennant describes the same, or similar, bridge at the upper falls of Foyers. His description is accompanied by an engraving.

About half a mile south of the first fall is another passing through a narrow chasm, whose sides it has undermined for a considerable way: over the gap is a true Alpine bridge of the bodies of trees covered with sods, from whose middle is an awful view of the water roaring beneath. (Pennant, *A Tour in Scotland 1769*)

Burt regarded the new bridges as the greatest boon to the Highlanders. It is difficult to argue with him. Highland burns and rivers can be extremely treacherous. '*But the last, and I think, the greatest conveniency, is the bridges, which prevent the dangers of the terrible fords . . . They are forty in number.*' (Edmund Burt, *Letters from a Gentleman in the North of Scotland*, c. 1737)

Finally, Burt makes interesting comments about why some Highlanders objected to the new bridges: '*That the bridges, in particular, will render the ordinary people effeminate, and less fit to pass the waters in other places where there are none.*' (Edmund Burt, *Letters from a Gentleman in the North of Scotland*, c. 1737)

This opinion probably came from the chiefs rather than the clansmen. It is easier to argue for this sort of manliness when you can cross a ford on someone else's shoulders. It is another example of the image some Highlanders entertained of themselves, and promoted for others.

Food and Lodging

Discomforts always loom large in travellers' accounts. I am sure a whole book could be written on this subject alone. Here I only want to feature one or two colourful accounts of cleanliness and hygiene – or the lack of them.

Butter was something that often exercised visitors. Franck writes: '*Then you must grant their butter but little better than grease we usually grease cartwheels withal; which nauseates my palat if but to think on't, or remember the hand that made it up.*' (R. Franck, *Northern Memoirs*, 1656/7)

Burt has a nice story of an English visitor faced with the hairs that were normally put into the churn to help butter coagulate:

> *an English gentleman, in his way hither, had some butter set before him in which were a great number of hairs; whereupon he called to the landlady, desiring she would bring him some butter upon one plate and the hairs upon another, and he would mix them himself.* (Edmund Burt, *Letters from a Gentleman in the North of Scotland*, late 1720s)

Thomas Kirk thought the meat in Scotland was so 'high' it could be the death of you! A Scottish cook could be relied upon to:

> *bring corruption to your table, only to mind men of mortality. Their meat is carrion when 'tis killed, but after it has been a fortnight a perfuming with the aromatick air, strained thro' the clammy trunks of flesh flies, then it passes the tryal of fire under the care of one of those exquisite artists, and is dish'd up in a sea of sweet Scotch butter, and so cover'd and served hot up to the table. O how happy is he that is placed next to it, with a privilege to uncover it, and receive the hot steams of this dainty dish, almost sufficient to cure all distempers.* (T. Kirk, 1679, in Hume Brown, *Early Travellers in Scotland*)

And the absence of culinary hygiene was a frequent theme:

> *I was one day greatly diverted with the grievous complaint of a neighbouring woman, of whom our cook had borrowed a pewter pudding pan . . . and when we had done with it, and she came for her dish, she was told, by the servants below stairs, that it should be cleaned, and then sent home.*
>
> *This the woman took to be such an intended injury to her pan, that she cried out, 'Lord! You'll wear it out!' and then came upstairs to make her complaint to us, which she did very earnestly.*
>
> *We perceived the jest, and gravely told her it was but reasonable and civil, since it was borrowed, to send it home clean. This did not at all content her, and she left us; but at the foot of the stairs, she peremptorily demanded her moveable; and when she found it had been scoured before it was used, she lost all patience, saying she had had it fifteen years, and it had never been scoured before; and she swore she would never lend it again to any of our country.* (Edmund Burt, *Letters from a Gentleman in the North of Scotland*, late 1720s)

James Hogg, the 'Ettrick Shepherd' writes of his lodgings at Kinlochailort in 1804:

When we arrived there the people were all in bed, but on rapping loudly at the door, the landlord, a big black, terrible-looking fellow, came stark naked, and let us in: he then lighted a candle, tied on his kilt, and asked how far we had come today. We told him from Harries. He stared us full in the faces, and perceiving that we were in our sober senses, answered only with a hem! as much as to say, I know how you should be believed. He then shewed us into a little damp room with an earthen floor and set before us what cheer he had in the house for supper, which consisted of cakes, milk, and rum, for what is very strange, he had no whisky. In this same apartment there were two heather beds without hangings, on one of which a woman and some children were lying. Mr W. was now in a terrible passion, and swore he would abandon that horrid place, and take shelter in the woods. The woman and children, however, slid away; the beds were made up with clean cloathes, and we were obliged to pass the night on them the best way we could.

Mr L. complained much in the morning of several rude engravings made on his body by the stubborn roots of the heather and Mr G.'s back was all tamboured work but I, by being forced to take to the bed which the family had left, got the advantage of a feather bed among the heath. (J. Hogg, Highland Tours)

Insect life

The Highlands, and Highland accommodation, have always rejoiced in a wide variety of insects – as well as ticks, lice, clegs, midges, flies and fleas. These can be very troublesome in a Highland summer. J. Stone describes how Pont 3 (a map of north-west Sutherland) has the following caption in Loch Stack:

all heir ar black flies in this wood . . . seene souking mens blood.

We do not know what, if any, insect repellent Pont might have used as he travelled around the Highlands on his surveys but we can feel for him. A few years later Taylor, the poet, describes his own experiences in characteristically humorous fashion:

at night I came to a lodging in the Laird of Eggels [Edzell's] land, where I lay at an Irish house, the folkes not being able to speake scarce any English, but I supped and went to bed, where I had not laine long, but I was enforced to rise; I was so stung with Irish musketaes, a creature that hath sixe legs, and lives like a monster altogether upon mans flesh; they doe inhabite and breed most upon sluttish houses, and this house was none of the cleanest: the beast is much like a louse in England, both in shape and nature; in a word, they were to me the A and the Z, the prologue and the epilogue, the first and the last that

I had in all my travels from Edenborough; and had not this Highland Irish house helped me at a pinch, I should have sworn that all Scotland had not been so kind as to have bestowed a louse upon me; but with a shift that I had, I shifted off my canibals, and was never more troubled with them. (J. Taylor, *The Pennyles Pilgrimage*, 1618)

Insect life is always a trial for the traveller, in any continent and at any time. Given his tribulations with a louse(?), it is surprising that Taylor does not mention midges but then he was always at pains to speak kindly of his hosts, only lapsing occasionally for the sake of humour. He had a happy disposition and seems to have thrown off his troubles as easily as his shirt.

Burt is seldom specific about insect infestation but he makes it clear that a bed might be shared with more than one kind of unwelcome companion:

My bed had clean sheets and blankets! but, which was best of all (though negative), I found no inconvenience from those troublesome companions with which most other huts abound. But the bare mention of them brings to my remembrance a passage between two officers of the army, the morning after a Highland night's lodging. One was taking off the slowest kind of the two, when the other cried out, 'Z . . . ds! What are you doing? Let us first secure the dragoons; we can take the foot at leisure.' (Edmund Burt, *Letters from a Gentleman in the North of Scotland*, late 1720s)

This military metaphor seems to have been long-lived. Knox writes of midges(?) at the mouth of Loch Hourn: '*With the help of a blanket, I made a shift to pass a night on board, accompanied by a whole corps of those nocturnal disturbers of the peace, called light infantry.*' (J Knox, *A Tour through the Highlands of Scotland*, 1786)

On another occasion Burt implies that self-interest debated with duty, obedience, and good manners, as to what the situation required:

The violent heat of the sun among the rocks, made my new companions (natives of the hovel) such voracious cannibals that I was obliged to lag behind, and set my servant to take vengeance on them for the plentiful repast they were making at my expense, and without my consent, and by which I was told they were become as red as blood. But I should have let you know, that when the table overnight was spread with such provisions as were carried with us, our chief man would needs have the lady of the house to grace the board; and it fell to my lot to sit next to her till I had loaded her plate, and bid her go and sup with her husband, for I foresaw the consequence of our conjunction. (Edmund Burt, *Letters from a Gentleman in the North of Scotland*, late 1720s)

He also had a close acquaintance with midges:

I have but one thing more to take notice of in relation to . . . [Fort Augustus], and that is, I have been sometimes vexed with a little plague (if I may use the expression), but do not you think I am too grave upon the subject; there are great swarms of little flies which the natives call 'mal-houlakins': 'houlack', they tell me, signifies, in the country language, a fly, and 'houlakin' is the diminutive of that name. These are so very small, that, separately, they are but just perceptible and that is all; and, being of a blackish colour, when a number of them settle upon the skin, they make it look as if it was dirty; there they soon bore with their little augers into the pores, and change the face from black to red.

They are only troublesome (I should say intolerable) in summer, when, there is a profound calm; for the least breath of wind immediately disperses them; and the only refuge from them is the house, into which I never knew them to enter. Sometimes, when I have been talking to any one, I have (though with the utmost self-denial) endured their stings to watch his face, and see how long they would suffer him to be quiet; but in three or four seconds, he has slapped his hand upon his face, and in great wrath cursed the little vermin: but I have found the same torment in some other parts of the Highlands where woods were at no great distance. (Edmund Burt, *Letters from a Gentleman in the North of Scotland*, c. 1737)

Bonnie Prince Charlie had first-hand experience of the Highland midge during the summer of 1746. The following passage describes a difficult night during his long months as a fugitive after Culloden:

The evening being very calm and warm, we greatly suffered by mitches, a species of litle creatures troublesome and numerous in the highlands; to preserve him from such troublesome guests, we wrapt him head and feet in his plead, and covered him with long heather that naturally grew about a bit hollow ground we laid him. After leaving him in that posture, he uttered several heavy sighes and groands. We planted ourselves about the best we coud. (John Macdonald of Borrodale, in G. Skene (ed.), *Narrative of Prince Charlie's escape*)

Cumberland's army also suffered. The following letter reflects on the insect life endured while staying by Fort Augustus: '*The Flies and Fleas were also as great a Plague to us in our Hutts, as I have seen them in some very hot Countries.*' (*A journey through Part of England and Scotland*, 1746)

Faujas de Saint Fond has a nice story about lice. He writes of friends who had been caught on Staffa by the weather and constrained to spend some time in a hut there:

The master of the cottage, his wife, and children lived in such a horrid state of filth that the place was as full of vermin as of wretchedness. Detachments of

*lice approached from all sides to pay their respects to the new lodgers, who
were soon infected with them. This was the most cruel of their torments, and
formed the object of an occupation which did not allow them a moment's
respite.*

*Their account brought to my remembrance a similar adventure which
happened in the same isle, and probably in the same house, to Sir Joseph
Banks, in the year 1772.*

*On leaving the hut next morning, he discovered that he was completely
covered with lice. He mentioned the circumstance to his host in terms of mild
reproach. But the latter, who was touched to the quick, perked himself up,
and assuming a tone of consequence, retorted haughtily and harshly that it
was Sir Joseph himself who had imported the lice into his island, and adding,
that he had better have left them behind him in England.* (Faujas de Saint
Fond, *A journey through England and Scotland to the Hebrides in 1784*)

Weather

No Highland traveller can help but notice the weather. Taylor, the poet,
perfectly describes the joys of climbing a Highland hill, even in high summer:

*The next day I travelled over an exceeding high mountaine . . . where I found
the valley very warme before I went up it; but when I came to the top of it, my
teeth beganne to dance in my head with cold . . . and withall, a most familiar
mist embraced me round, that I could not see thrice my length any way:
withall, it yeelded so friendly a deaw, that it did moysten thorow all my
clothes; where the old proverbe of a Scottish miste was verified, in wetting me
to the skinne. Up and downe, I thinke this hill is six miles, the way so uneven,
stony, and full of bogges, quagmires, and long heath, that a dogge with three
legs will out-runne a horse with foure.* (J. Taylor, *The Pennyles Pilgrimage*,
1618)

Burt further characterises the English view of Highland weather: '*they say, in
these northern parts, the year is composed of nine months winter and three months
bad weather.* (Edmund Burt, *Letters from a Gentleman in the North of Scotland*,
late 1720s)

And of the rain: '*At Fort William . . . I have heard the people talk as familiarly
of a shower (as they call it) of nine or ten weeks, as they would do of anything else
that was not out of the ordinary course.*' (Edmund Burt, *Letters from a Gentleman
in the North of Scotland*, c. 1737)

Burt makes it clear that the Highlanders did not attempt certain journeys if
they expected bad weather – although they, like the visitor, could always be
caught out in the event. He comments that the common compliment
addressed to him when travelling through the Highlands was to wish him

good weather: *'At mounting I received many compliments from my host; but the most earnest was, that common one of wishing me good weather. For, like the seafaring man, my safety depended upon it; especially at that season of the year.'* (Edmund Burt, *Letters from a Gentleman in the North of Scotland*, late 1720s)

A member of Cumberland's army writes of the Highland weather in the months following Culloden:

> *The Climate here was so excessive bad, that we had a Winter from the Beginning of July, and continued so all our Stay, continually raining, and cold Winds blowing, which occasioned great Numbers to fall sick daily, as well in their Minds, as Bodies; for it is a Rarity to see the Sun, but constantly black Skies, and rusty-looking, rocky Mountains, attended with misty Rains and cutting Winds, with violent Streams of Water rolling down from every Part of the Mountains, after hard Rains, and so filling the Rivers surprizingly soon.* (*A journey through Part of England and Scotland*, 1746)

Whilst MacCulloch wrote in a similar fashion of the island of Rum:

> *If it is not always bad weather in Rum, it cannot be good very often; since, on seven or eight occasions that I have passed it, there has been a storm, and on seven or eight more in which I have landed, it was never without the expectation of being turned into a cold fish. 'The bitter breathing winds with boist'rous blasts' seem to have set up their throne here, as at Loch Scavig: and the rains too. Like that place, it possesses a private winter of its own, even in what is here called summer.* (John MacCulloch, *The Highlands and Western Isles of Scotland*, Vol IV)

To a resident of the Highlands this will all sound familiar – to a visitor it will soon become familiar. Faujas de Saint Fond gave a French view:

> *Such is the life that is led in a country, where there is not a road nor a tree, where the mountains are covered only with heath, where it rains for eight months of the year, and where the sea, always in motion, seems to be in perpetual convulsions.* (Faujas de Saint Fond, *A journey through England and Scotland to the Hebrides in 1784*)

Keeping the visitors at bay

In mediaeval times the Gaelic-speaking world of the Highlands and Islands was robust enough, economically, demographically and militarily, to keep the culture of Lowland Scotland at bay. However this position has been steadily eroded for several hundred years. Economically the Highlands and Islands have become marginal. In demographic terms the balance has long since shifted in favour of the Lowlands, partly as a result of emigration and clearance. Militarily the issue was resolved at Culloden. The issue of how to keep an intrusive alien culture from swamping the indigenous forms has been fought on a thousand fronts over hundreds of years. How do you preserve local values when the dominant culture threatens to drown them, out of ignorance as often as hostility?

This battle is still being fought today over issues such as language, music, literature and Sunday working. But we can also see it in microcosm in early accounts of St Kilda. Standing almost symbolically for the health of Highland culture against external attack is the issue of the St Kilda cough. It was claimed that every time a visiting boat landed, the whole island went down with whatever noxious bug it had brought with it. This is a familiar theme in other parts of the world where imported disease and alcohol have been quite as effective as the white man in weakening native societies.

Martin Martin writes:

> they are seldom troubled with a cough, except at the steward's landing; which is no less rare, than firmly believed by the inhabitants of the adjacent isles.
>
> Those of St Kilda, upon the whole, gave me this following account, that they always contract a cough upon the steward's landing, and it proves a great deal more troublesome to them in the night-time, they then distilling a great deal of flegm; this indisposition continues for some ten, twelve or fourteen days.
>
> I told them plainly, that I thought all this notion of infection was but a mere fancy, and that, at least, it could not always hold; at which they seemed offended, saying, that never any, before the minister and my self, was heard doubt of the truth of it; which is plainly demonstrated upon the landing of every boat . . . but for confirmation of the whole, they appealed to the case of infants at the breast, who were likewise very subject to this cough, but could not be capable of affecting it, and therefore, in their opinion, they were infected by such as lodged in their houses. There were scarce young or old in the isle whom I did not examine particularly upon this head, and all agreed in the confirmation of it. They add farther, that when any foreign goods are brought thither, then the cough is of longer duration than otherwise. They remark, that if the fever has been among those of the steward's retinue, though before their arrival there, some of the inhabitants are infected with it . . . it was remarkable, that after this infected cough was over, we strangers, and the inhabitants of St Kilda, making up the number of about two hundred and fifty, though we had frequently assembled upon the occasion of divine service, yet neither young nor old amongst us all did so much as once cough more.

(Martin Martin, *A Voyage to St Kilda*, 1698)

A century later E.D. Clarke wrote:

It will be readily supposed that I neglected no inquiry respecting the remarkable circumstances which are related both by Martin and Macaulay, and reported all over the Western Islands, with regard to a cough the natives catch whenever strangers arrive upon their island. During the whole time I remained among them, I endeavoured by every possible means to ascertain the truth or falsehood of this extraordinary tale. The minister, Mr. Macleod, in answer to the first question I put to him, assured me, in the most solemn manner, that the circumstance was true. Both Mr. Maclean and myself examined and cross-examined, both his testimony and that of the natives themselves; and the result of our inquiry was, that a cold or cough, was annually communicated to all the inhabitants of St. Kilda; not from any vessel that might chance to arrive, but from the tacksman's boat alone, whose casual advent was not fixed for any stated period, but was a month sooner, or a month later, according as the weather proved favourable or unpropitious. A vessel from Norway visited St. Kilda this year, before the arrival of the tacksman, the crew of which mingled with the natives, but no cold or cough was communicated to them. The fact appeared now more marvellous than ever. That an effect so remarkable should be peculiar to the arrival of one particular boat, is hardly to be credited. Nevertheless, the fact is indisputable. The tacksman comes, and all the island catch a cough: other vessels arrive both before and after, and no such effect is produced. He had been gone only eight days when we arrived, and I saw several, both young and old afflicted with this malady to such a degree that it had nearly proved fatal to some of them. I was at first perfectly confounded with the evidence of my own senses. I felt that in relating it at my return, the tale would either become established as a fact, no longer to be doubted, or subject me to an imputation of the weakest credulity. I prosecuted my inquiry to greater extent, and with renewed vigilance; at length the light began to break forth, and the mystery was disclosed. I hope I shall be able to explain the real nature of this cough, by relating the true cause of its origin.

The young man whom I mentioned at my arrival upon the island, and whose attentions never left me during the time I remained there, had been married but a few days. They postpone their marriages till the arrival of the steward, and he expressed a wish that I had been present upon the occasion. 'Then,' said he, 'you would have seen the whole island dancing, and the whole island drunk.' And what did you find to get drunk with here? 'Whiskey! the steward always brings whiskey, and, when he comes, we dance and sing merrily.' And don't you dance during the rest of the year? 'Not so much; when the steward comes, we dance all night, and make a fine noise altogether.'

I applied to Mr. Macleod for farther information upon this subject, and was told that this was the reason of their postponing their marriages. The arrival of the tacksman, or as they call him, steward, is the jubilee of the year. He brings with him spirituous liquors, and a total change of diet; The return of this period is the only gleam of sunshine which cheers the long and gloomy night of their miseries. They hail his coming, they rejoice, they drink, they dance, their spirits are elevated, they become heated, they expose themselves to the humid influence of an atmosphere, constantly impregnated with fogs; their mode of diet is totally changed, and the consequence is very natural, that out of twenty-two families, the greatest part of them are afflicted with a violent cold and cough.

I expressed my sentiments on this subject to their minister, but nothing could alter his opinion. He admitted the truth of what I have stated with regard to the arrival of the tacksman; but remained bigotted to the old miraculous tale of the cough being taken from the smell of fresh air, which hangs upon the tacksman's clothes. Allowing for a moment the truth of so absurd a supposition, the tacksman, in that case, would not be the only person to communicate a smell of air, foreign to the olfactory nerves of the St. Kildians. The Norway vessel, which arrived before him, or our cutter which came after, would produce the same effect. I have no doubt whatever, in my own mind, respecting the real origin of the St. Kilda cough. Whether my readers will coincide in my opinion I know not; but, until I hear the circumstance otherwise rationally accounted for, I must attribute it to the alteration in manners and in diet, the intemperance and riot, which take place upon the arrival of the tacksman. It is true, many of the children in the island were afflicted with the same malady; from which I conclude, that the mothers who imprudently, or rather ignorantly, exposed themselves to the night air, heated by whiskey and dancing, exposed their children also.

In addition to the cause I have alleged for the St. Kilda cough, it is necessary also to mention the great heat of their little huts, filled with smoke and the fumes of peat; and when a number crowd into one of these to conduct a bride and bridegroom to their cell, they can have no occasion for the influence of whiskey, to increase the violent perspiration they are subject to, in consequence of confined air and dancing. (E.D. Clarke, *Journal 1797*)

Another issue which troubled many Hebrideans then, and the people of Lewis now, is the matter of Sunday working. Martin Martin writes of Captain Peters, a Dutchman who was in Borera. Apparently he '*built a cock-boat there on a Sunday, at which the natives were much offended.*' (Martin Martin, *A Description of the Western Islands of Scotland* c. 1695)

He writes of St Kilda where:

a company of French and Spaniards . . . lost their ship at Rokol in the year 1686, and came in, in a pinnace to St Kilda, where they were plentifully supplied with barly-bread, butter, cheese, solan geese, eggs, etc . . . The inhabitants acquainted me that the pinnace which carried the seamen from

Rokol was so very low, that the crew added a foot height of canvas round it all, and began to work at it upon Sunday, at which the inhabitants were astonished, and being highly dissatisfied, plucked the hatchets and other instruments out of their hands, and did not restore them till Monday morning. (Martin Martin, *A Voyage to St Kilda*, 1698)

Martin Martin also comments that the St Kildans had a poor view of Lowland visitors, not least because of the conduct of the crew of a Lowland vessel which dropped anchor there in 1696. As far as the St Kildans were concerned the Lowlanders were not Christians. The interpreter on the Lowland ship, who apparently spoke poor Gaelic, had not actually admitted this but, the St Kildans felt, their conduct demonstrated the fact. The Lowlanders had worked on a Sunday, paid poorly for some cows they had taken, and offered them money for their women. Martin relates:

the attempt made by them to ravish their women, a practice altogether unknown in St Kilda, where there has not been one instance of fornication or adultery for many ages before this time; I remember they told me, that the bribe offered for debauching the poor women, was a piece of broad money, than which there could be nothing less charming in a place where the inhabitants cannot distinguish a guinea from a sixpence. (Martin Martin, *A Voyage to St Kilda*, 1698)

Despite Martin's slightly ungallant ending to this story it is easy to see why small island communities would be wary of visiting boats. Visitors might not threaten their way of life but they could endanger their foodstocks or harm their women and children. For the future the St Kildans had decided to take precautions. One option was to throw stones at any attempting to land: '*They are resolved to make use of this for the future, to keep off the Lowlanders, against whom of late they have conceived prejudices.*' (Martin Martin, *A Voyage to St Kilda*, 1698)

The poor people of St Kilda were vainly struggling to keep the modern world at bay. In effect Martin Martin became their spokesperson to the outside world:

I must not omit acquainting the reader, that the account given of the seamens rudeness to the inhabitants, has created great prejudices in them against seamen in general; and though I endeavoured to bring them into some good opinion of them, it will not be, I hope, improper here to deliver the terms upon which the inhabitants are resolved to receive strangers, and no otherwise; they will not admit of any number exceeding ten, and those too must be unarmed, for else the inhabitants will oppose them with all their might; but if any number of them, not exceeding that abovesaid, come peaceably, and with good

designs, they may expect water and fire gratis, and what else the place
affords, at the easiest rates in the world. (Martin Martin, *A Voyage to St*
Kilda, 1698)

The St Kildans were naive to think they had any control, any more than any
other part of the Highlands and Islands. We can try to channel or regulate, but
need makes servants of us all.

Chapter 12

In the eye of the beholder

B eauty is, proverbially, in the eye of the beholder. To a degree this also holds for truth, or at least those truths presented us by travellers. When we have few, or no, other sources of information then it simply passes for truth, historical truth. This chapter represents a few of the earlier visions of the Highlands and Islands, of what was held to constitute their beauty. We can then compare these with our own ideals.

Pont's notes make it clear that he found some parts of the Highlands aesthetically pleasing. In his papers on Ross we find this verdict on Loch Ewe: '*All thir bounds is compas'd and hemd in with many hills but thois beautifull to look on, thair skirts being all adorned with wood even to the brink of the loch for the most part.*' (Pont in *Macfarlane's Geographical Collections*, vol II, p 540)

Franck introduces an oft-repeated theme – that the Highlands, in their state of nature, were somehow incomplete, unpolished by artificial improvement:

> *Theophilus*
> *For these Highlands, to my thinking, but represent a part of the creation left undrest: As some great and magnificent fabrick is erected, you know abundance of rubbish is left to remove; so I fancy those Highlands appear to me, because wanting ornament, and destitute of cultivation.* (Franck, *Northern Memoirs*, 1656/7)

While Martin Martin gives a Highland perspective on Arran: '*The hills are generally covered all over with heath, and produce a mixture of the erica-baccifera, catstail, and juniper, all which are very agreeable to the eye in summer.*' (Martin Martin, *A Description of the Western Islands of Scotland* c. 1695)

Burt was aware that he was breaking new ground in trying to give a description of the landscape of the Highlands and Islands:

> *Thus am I entering upon my most difficult task, for the customs and manners of the Highlanders will give me little trouble more than the transcribing; but as I believe I am the first who ever attempted a minute description of any such mountains I cannot but greatly doubt of my success herein.* (Edmund Burt, *Letters from a Gentleman in the North of Scotland*, late 1720s)

Travellers reflect their times and Burt was no different. His view of the Highlands was pretty utilitarian:

*I shall soon conclude this description of the outward appearance of the
mountains which I am already tired of, as a disagreeable subject, and I believe
you are so too: but, for your future ease in that particular, there is not much
variety in it, but gloomy spaces, different rocks, heath, and high and low.*

*To cast one's eye from an eminence toward a group of them, they appear
still one above another, fainter and fainter, according to the aerial perspective, and the whole of a dismal gloomy brown drawing upon a dirty purple;
and most of all disagreeable when the heath is in bloom.*

*Those ridges of the mountains that appear next to the ether – by their
rugged irregular lines, the heath and black rocks – are rendered extremely
harsh to the eye, by appearing close to that diaphanous body, without any
medium to soften the opposition; and the clearer the day, the more rude and
offensive they are to the sight; yet, in some few places, where any white crags
are atop, that harshness is something softened.*

*But of all the views, I think the most horrid is, to look at the hills from east
to west, or vice versa, for then the eye penetrates far among them, and sees
more particularly their stupendous bulk, frightful irregularity, and horrid
gloom, made yet more sombrous by the shades and faint reflections they
communicate one to another.* (Edmund Burt, *Letters from a Gentleman in
the North of Scotland,* late 1720s)

Burt's view was precisely opposite to what we would find beautiful today – the
heather in bloom, the jagged ridge of the Cuillins against a bright blue sky. But
to the eighteenth-century mind, nature was more frightful. They did not
control their environment as we do. They lived closer to it; the elements were
more of a threat. Burt makes this very specific:

*I have often heard it said by my countrymen, that they verily believed, if an
inhabitant of the south of England were to be brought blindfold into some
narrow, rocky hollow, enclosed with these horrid prospects, and there to have
his bandage taken off, he would be ready to die with fear, as thinking it
impossible he should ever get out to return to his native country.* (Edmund
Burt, *Letters from a Gentleman in the North of Scotland,* late 1720s)

Burt preferred the gentle, tutored, pastoral landscape of England: '*Now what
do you think of a poetical mountain, smooth and easy of ascent, clothed with a
verdant, flowery turf, where shepherds tend their flocks, sitting under the shade of
small poplars, etc.*' And he shares a reminiscence with his correspondent: '*How
have we been pleased with the easy ascent of an eminence, which almost
imperceptibly brought us to the beautiful prospects seen from its summit! What
a delightful variety of fields, and meadows of various tints of green, adorned with
trees and blooming hedges; and the whole embellished with woods, groves, waters,
flocks, herds, and magnificent seats of the happy . . . and every other rising ground
opening a new and lovely landscape!*'

But he recognised that Highlanders regarded their own hills as beautiful: *'And, certainly, it is the deformity of the hills that makes the natives conceive of their naked straths and glens, as of the most beautiful objects in nature.'*

Burt must have grown very fond of the mountains during his years in the Highlands. He admits, in a roundabout way, his bewitchment: *'but what is pretty strange, though very true (by what charm I know not), I have been well enough pleased to see them again, at my first entrance to them in my returns from England; and this has made my wonder cease that a native should be so fond of such a country.'* (Edmund Burt, *Letters from a Gentleman in the North of Scotland*, late 1720s)

We have another military commentator from the time of Culloden. Like Burt he delights less in natural than man-made landscapes. He writes of a march between Crieff and Perth: *'but now and then we had agreeable Firr Woods, which are mighty solitary and amusing, and are the only artificial Beauty of these Mountainous Places, being always planted very close and regular, and afford an entertaining Scene to a wearied Traveller.'* (*A journey through Part of England and Scotland*, 1746)

However, he was not averse to waterscapes. He says of the falls on the River Almond near Dunkeld: *'there's the most wonderful Cascade, caused by Rocks, that ever I saw: I believe it is near thirty Yards high, and is called the Rumbling Brig; for it makes a most surprizing Noise.'* (*A journey through Part of England and Scotland*, 1746)

And on the neighbourhood of the River Timel (Tummel):

> *From the woody Mountains here, run frequent Streams of the purest Water, which are obstructed now by the hard Frost, and make most romantick Winter-appearances, by the congealed Streams of Icicles, which hang pendulous over the rocky Banks of these Rivers. (A journey through Part of England and Scotland, 1746)*

He gives a more balanced appreciation of natural beauty on approaching Fort Augustus from the North:

> *We also meet with several small Rivers, (abounding more with Rocks than Water,) which together with the Woods and high Mountains, give great Variety and Entertainment to the solitary Traveller. (A journey through Part of England and Scotland, 1746)*

But in general terms he seems to have preferred the less harsh Highland landscapes. He writes of the River Deveron:

> *I thought it was the most pleasantly situated of any Place I had ever seen, and it gave me infinite Satisfaction to view it off a Mountain at a small Distance, when I stopped on my Horse a considerable Time to have the Pleasure of*

admiring so delightful a Place, and the serpentine Course of that charming River Deveron, on every Side, running through vast Valleys, lined with inaccessible Mountains, covered either by Snow or Clouds. (A journey through Part of England and Scotland, 1746)

By contrast he does not seem to have liked parts of the Great Glen so well. He gives an unusual justification for the games organised at Fort Augustus for the entertainment of Cumberland's army. Both sexes participated and some were rather scandalised by proceedings. But, he says,:

It was necessary to entertain Life in this Manner; otherwise, by the constant View of Mountains surrounding us, we should have been affected with hypochondriacal Melancholy. (A journey through Part of England and Scotland, 1746)

The influence of environment on mental health was recognised then as well as now. Several travellers comment on the effect of passing through some of the bleaker parts of the Highlands. Pennant writes on the barrenness in Ross-shire:

I never saw a country that seemed to have been so torn and convulsed: the shock, whenever it happened, shook off all that vegetates: among these aspiring heaps of barrenness, the sugar-loaf hill of Suil-bhein made a conspicuous figure: at their feet, the blackness of the moors by no means assisted to cheer our ideas. (T. Pennant, A Tour in Scotland and Voyage to the Hebrides, 1772)

And after climbing 'Beinn-a-Caillich' in Skye:

The prospect to the west was that of desolation itself; a savage series of rude mountains, discoloured, black and red, as if by the rage of fire. (T. Pennant, A Tour in Scotland and Voyage to the Hebrides, 1772)

Or crossing Rannoch:

Most of this long day's journey from the Black Mountain was truly melancholy, almost one continued scene of dusky moors, without arable land, trees, houses, or living creature, for numbers of miles. (Pennant, A Tour in Scotland 1769)

Johnson uses a journey across Skye in the evening gloom as a trigger to soliloquise on the susceptibilities of the mediaeval mind:

In travelling even thus almost without light thro' naked solitude, when there is a guide whose conduct may be trusted, a mind not naturally too much disposed to fear may preserve some degree of cheerfulness; but what must be the solitude of him who should be wandering, among the craggs and hollows, benighted, ignorant, and alone?

The fictions of the Gothick romances were not so remote from credibility as they are now thought. In the full prevalence of the feudal institution, when violence desolated the world, and every baron lived in a fortress, forests and castles were regularly succeeded by each other, and the adventurer might very suddenly pass from the gloom of woods, or the ruggedness of moors, to seats of plenty, gaiety, and magnificence. Whatever is imaged in the wildest tale, if giants, dragons, and enchantment be excepted, would be felt by him, who, wandering in the mountains without a guide, or upon the sea without a pilot, should be carried amidst his terror and uncertainty, to the hospitality and elegance of Raasay or Dunvegan. (Johnson, *A Journey to the Western Islands of Scotland, 1773*)

Faujas de Saint Fond comments on the road from Dalmally to Tyndrum:

The valley of Glenlochy, through which we passed, is pleasant in some places where skirted with hills which are covered with numerous flocks of sheep; but the mountains close in too much as one advances. The soil becomes marshy and sterile; the peat which is laid bare everywhere, gives a black colour to the face of the country, and a tint almost as sombre to the mind. (Faujas de Saint Fond, *A journey through England and Scotland to the Hebrides in 1784*)

On leaving Tyndrum he paints a contrast between a bleak and sterile mountainscape and the pastoral scenes of richer vales:

I left this place for Killin, by a road as dismal as it was monotonous. But what makes this route oppressively tiresome is, that it goes on thus for several leagues, between two ridges not far apart, covered with a black turf, on which nothing grows but short heather and some yellowish mosses, that distil the water, drop by drop, on all sides.

The mind soon takes on some of the same gloomy hue, and grows more and more melancholy as one proceeds; but the scene suddenly changes when one reaches the end of this kind of sombre gallery, the horizon then expands, and the fine valley of Glen Dochart opens into view.

Here limpid and copious streams, teeming with fish, glide in serpentine meanders, through the most smiling verdure, and form islets shaded with large trees. Charming rustic habitations now appear, together with numerous herds of cattle and sheep, while the young shepherds and shepherdesses who tend them make the air resound with their songs, and animate the delightful scene with their dances. (Faujas de Saint Fond, *A journey through England and Scotland to the Hebrides in 1784*)

Johnson was characteristically blunt on the uselessness of Highland hills:

They exhibit very little variety; being almost wholly covered with dark heath, and even that seems to be checked in its growth. What is not heath is nakedness, a little diversified by now and then a stream rushing down the steep. An eye accustomed to flowery pastures and waving harvests is astonished and repelled by this wide extent of hopeless sterility. The appearance is that of matter incapable of form or usefulness, dismissed by nature from her care and disinherited of her favours, left in its original elemental state, or quickened only with one sullen power of useless vegetation. (Johnson, *A Journey to the Western Islands of Scotland*, 1773)

He and Boswell don't seem to have been much interested in scenery:

He always said, that he was not come to Scotland to see fine places, of which there were enough in England; but wild objects – mountains, waterfalls, peculiar manners; in short, things which he had not seen before. I have a notion that he at no time has had much taste for rural beauties. I have myself very little. (Boswell, *The Journal of a Tour to the Hebrides*, 1773)

Fortunately Pennant enjoyed scenery – particularly if there was diversity. His text is littered with words like *pretty*, *picturesque* and *beautiful*. He writes of Dundonell:

We found ourselves seated in a spot equalized by few in picturesque and magnificent scenery. The banks of the river that rushes by the house is fringed with trees; and the course often interrupted by cascades. At a small distance the ground begins to rise: as we mount, the eye is entertained with new objects; the river rolling beneath the dark shade of alders, an extent of plain composed of fields bounded by groves; and as the walk advances, appears a deep and tremendous hollow, shagged with trees, and winding far amidst the hills. We are alarmed with the roar of invisible cataracts, long before their place is discovered; and find them precipitating themselves down narrow chasms of stupendous depths . . . They meander for miles amidst the mountains, and are the age-worn work of water, branch off into every glen, hid with trees of various species . . . Besides these darksome waters, multitudes of others precipitate themselves in full view down the steep sides of the adjacent hills; and create for several hundreds of feet a series of most magnificent falls.
Above rises a magnificent hill, which as far as the sight can reach is clothed with birch and pines, the shelter of stags, roes and black game.
To the west is a view where the awful, or rather the horrible predominates. A chain of rocky mountains, some conoid, but united by links of a height equal to most in North Britain, with sides dark, deep, and precipitous, with summits broken, sharp, serrated, and spiring into all terrific forms; with

snowy glaciers lodged in the deep-shaded apertures. (T. Pennant, *A Tour in Scotland and Voyage to the Hebrides*, 1772)

And of Loch Hourn:

The scenery that surrounds the whole of this lake has an Alpine wildness and magnificence; the hills of an enormous height, and for the most part clothed with extensive forests of oak and birch, often to the very summits. In many places are extensive tracts of open space, verdant, and only varied with a few trees scattered over them: amidst the thickest woods aspire vast grey rocks, a noble contrast! Nor are the lofty headlands a less embellishment; for through the trees that wave on their summit, is an awful sight of sky, and spiring summits of vast mountains. (T. Pennant, *A Tour in Scotland and Voyage to the Hebrides*, 1772)

And of Scottish lochs in general:

North Britain may well boast of its waters; for so short a ride as thirty miles presents the traveller with the view of four most magnificent pieces. Loch Aw, Loch Fine, Loch Long, and Loch Lomond. Two indeed are of salt water; but, by their narrowness, give the idea of freshwater lakes. It is an idle observation of travellers, that seeing one is the same with seeing all of these superb waters; for almost every one I visited has its proper character. ((Pennant, *A Tour in Scotland 1769*)

Knox waxed lyrical over Loch Broom:

Having arrived at the edge of the mountains on the north side, where the road is carried almost perpendicularly from the summits, the view of Loch Broom, and a track of champaign country at the head of it, with two winding streams falling into the loch from opposite directions, afford one of the finest landscapes in nature. (J. Knox, *A Tour through the Highlands of Scotland*, 1786)

Scotland's scenery is justly famous, but today we can admire it without being distracted by poverty and degradation. We are just as likely to see these in the great cities as in the Highlands. But it was not always so. The Rev. John Lane Buchanan made some fair points about the extent to which early visitors were shielded from the worst sights in the Highlands:

Although the Western Hebrides lie beyond the route pursued by the most distinguished travellers from the south, who have published accounts of their travels and voyages (Mr Pennant, Dr Johnson and Captain Newte) several gentlemen have visited most of those remote Islands, with a view of acquiring such local knowledge as might enable them to employ the people in a fishing trade, or other industry; though none of them ever touched on the horrid islands of Harris. But the want of time and there not being able to converse with the common people, who know no other language than the Celtic and who alone could, or would point out their grievances in their native colours, the benevolent purpose of those gentlemen was, in a great measure frustrated. The tacksmen, with whom they conversed, and their own factors, had an interest in concealing some truths, the knowledge of which might have equally benefited the independent freeholders, and the great body of the labouring people. (Buchanan, *Travels in the Western Hebrides from 1782 to 1790*)

Many early travellers ferreted about after rocks or antiquities or natural history. Buchanan held radical views on agrarian reform and had little sympathy for those who did not share his social and economic agenda. He wrote of a recent visit by Prince William Henry:

And as the Prince performed a more extensive voyage in those parts, than our common travelling antiquarians, and botanists, so he was more curious and minute, and perhaps, more judicious in his enquiries, which he did not so much relate to insects, shells, feathers, and druidical remains, and those whirligigs of Nature, that so much attracted the attention of a certain Welsh traveller [Pennant], as to the civil and political state of society, the domestic situation of the people, and the state of the useful or mechanic arts. (Buchanan, *Travels in the Western Hebrides from 1782 to 1790*)

Buchanan had a personal axe to grind against local tacksmen but he offers persuasive arguments as to how visitors, in this case a missionary clergyman, could be misled as to real conditions in the Hebrides:

Let us suppose such a visitant arrived in any of the islands – Harris, for example: – He is most hospitably entertained by the minister, and the tacksman of Luskintire, caressed, humoured, cajoled, and flattered with all manner of adulation. He passes on to some other isle with letters of introduction from these gentlemen to their friends, who treat him in the same manner; and so on, with letters from them to the lairds, ministers, and tacksmen of some other island. He is kept in a constant round of entertainment, I had almost said, of dissipation. He lives with those in easy and affluent circumstances: he hears their tale, and theirs only: sees only the fair face of things: and, instead of exploring and feeling for the religious neglect, and civil oppression of the great body of the people, returns home, highly delighted with his jaunt and reception; and is even apt to represent the poor, miserable Aebudae as the fortunate islands, in the Atlantic Ocean, spoken of by the ancients, although their exact geographical situation had never before been determined. (Buchanan, *Travels in the Western Hebrides from 1782 to 1790*)

Poverty, though, cannot be long hid, and Buchanan underestimated some of the early travellers. They may not have responded to the issues that he raised but they were certainly aware of them. Burt writes of Inverness: '*Here are four or five fairs in the year, when the Highlanders bring their commodities to market: but, good God! You could not conceive there was such misery in this island.*' (Edmund Burt, *Letters from a Gentleman in the North of Scotland*, late 1720s)

Pennant comments ironically on the Highlands since Culloden: '*The halcyon days are near at hand: oppression will beget depopulation; and depopulation will give us a dear-bought tranquillity.*' (T. Pennant, *A Tour in Scotland and Voyage to the Hebrides*, 1772)

As he finished his voyage he wrote:

Thus ended this voyage of amusement, successful and satisfactory in every part, unless where embittered with reflections on the sufferings of my fellow-creatures. Gratitude forbids my silence respecting the kind reception I universally met with; or the active zeal of every one to facilitate my pursuits. (T. Pennant, *A Tour in Scotland and Voyage to the Hebrides*, 1772)

In fact, these 'reflections on the sufferings of my fellow-creatures' prompted him to moralise. He uses an unexpected literary device to end his section on the north-west Highlands. He conjures a dream figure, an archetypal Highland chief whom he dates, obliquely, to 1545. Using this spectre he paints an elaborate sketch of a benign, if occasionally violent, patriarchal society. Chiefs spent their rents locally, fostered their clans, protected their people. He then moves on to contrast this with the present situation in the Highlands:

The mighty chieftains, the brave and disinterested heroes of old times, by a most violent and surprising transformation, at once sunk into the rapacious landlords; determined to compensate the loss of power, with the increase of revenue; to exchange the warm affections of their people for sordid trash. Their visits, to those of their forefathers, are like the surveys of a cruel land-jobber, attended by a set of quick-sighted vultures, skilled in pointing out the most exquisite methods of oppression, or to instruct them in the art of exhausting their purses of sums to be wasted in distant lands. (T. Pennant, *A Tour in Scotland and Voyage to the Hebrides*, 1772)

Johnson gives similar comments about poverty not giving pleasure: '*Of these islands it must be confessed, that they have not many allurements, but to the mere lover of naked nature. The inhabitants are thin, provisions are scarce, and desolation and penury give little pleasure.*' (Johnson, *A Journey to the Western Islands of Scotland*, 1773)

When visiting Boswell's father, Johnson was called on by some neighbouring gentlemen: '*One of them asked Dr Johnson how he liked the Highlands. The question seemed to irritate him, for he answered, 'How, sir, can you ask me what obliges me to speak unfavourably of a country where I have been hospitably entertained? Who can like the Highlands? – I like the inhabitants very well.'* (Boswell, *The Journal of a Tour to the Hebrides*, 1773)

There was nothing wrong with Pennant's analysis of his present, but we can question his conservative premise in conjuring the picture of the patriarchal, mediaeval Highland chief. This myth had been spun by Boece, Leslie, Taylor and many others. But there are different ways of looking at the mediaeval Highlands. Yes, there was social cohesion, but primarily within the clan. Rival clans and families were guilty of ruthless oppression. The Macleans evicted the Macmasters from Ardgour. The Macdonalds were foes of the Campbells for centuries. The Macleans were one-time friends and allies of the Campbells, until their bitter dispute in the latter part of the seventeenth century. The family of Glengarry usurped Knoydart from a branch of the Clanranald c. 1613. In the course of the next two centuries there was an almost biological quality in the way they established cadet branches in the principal farms of Knoydart.

Whatever we may think of Pennant's picture of this conservative Highland archetype there is no doubt he had great sympathy for Highlanders in their current predicament. Through his 'ancient native' he throws up a range of options for the future improvement of the Highlands. These include fishing, weaving, and employment in the army and navy. He ends with an appeal to the present Highland lairds not to oppress their people:

> *Leave them (if you will do no more) but the bare power of existence in their native country, and they will not envy you your new luxuries. Waste your hours in the lap of dissipation . . . and sport in the bower of bliss. Cover your tables with delicacies, at the expense of your famished clans. Think not of the wretches, at those seasons, lest your appetite for the hors d'oeuvres be palled, and you feel a momentary remorse for deaths occasioned by ye, ye thoughtless deserters of your people! With all my failings, I exult in innocence of such crimes; and felicitate myself on my aerial state, capable of withdrawing from the sight of miseries I cannot alleviate, and of oppressions I cannot prevent.*
> (T. Pennant, *A Tour in Scotland and Voyage to the Hebrides*, 1772)

In a passage like this Pennant does not appear so very different from Boece. Their myth has now become ours. We may differ on what exactly was to blame for the death of Highland culture – government repression, absentee landlords, sheep, rents, tacksmen, the lack of tacksmen; but many accept the premise that there was some ideal, benign, patriarchal precedent. I doubt it. I think it is largely a projection of these travellers, historians, poets and bards. I take a Hobbesian view. Highland society produced poetry, music, song and sculpture of great beauty. But for most Highlanders, in most centuries, life was probably nasty, brutish and short.

Climbing hills

Since so many visitors come now to climb, I give some precedents: On climbing Ben Nevis – simply because it was there?

> *Some English officers took it in their fancy to go to the top, but could not attain it for bogs and huge perpendicular rocks; and when they were got as high as they could go, they found a vast change in the quality of the air, saw nothing but the tops of other mountains, and altogether a prospect of one tremendous heath, with here and there some spots of crags and snow.* (Edmund Burt, *Letters from a Gentleman in the North of Scotland*, late 1720s)

Walker climbed Askival, the highest peak in Rum. On ascending Beinn-an-oir, in Jura, Pennant wrote:

> *Gain the top, and find our fatigues fully recompensed by the grandeur of the prospect from this sublime spot . . . On the summit are several lofty cairns, not the work of devotion, but of idle herds, or curious travellers . . . The other paps are seen very distinctly; each inferior in height to this, but all of the same figure, perfectly mamillary. Mr Banks and his friends mounted that to the south, and found the height to be two thousand three hundred and fifty-nine feet.* (T. Pennant, *A Tour in Scotland and Voyage to the Hebrides*, 1772)

The presence of cairns begs the question of who raised them and when. The suggestion of idle shepherds is not persuasive.

Faujas de Saint Fond had set off to climb Ben More in Mull but abandoned the attempt before reaching the summit. He wrote:

> *In my journeys among the High Alps I never found so much difficulty as here. Almost impenetrable heather, above a soil saturated with water, covers the lower ground, the middle and the summit of the mountain.*

Disenchanted, he states rather petulantly:

> *Upon the whole, the mountain of Ben More, notwithstanding its height, and a kind of resemblance which it has at a distance to Mount Vesuvius, does not repay the trouble of ascending it.* (Faujas de Saint Fond, *A journey through England and Scotland to the Hebrides in 1784*)

While Knox plainly admits the natives were fitter: '*In climbing the mountains of the Highlands, I often remarked the superior strength and agility of the natives, to my own. I have frequently been glad to sit down, all in sweat, when my friends were scarcely sensible of fatigue.*' (J Knox, *A Tour through the Highlands of Scotland*, 1786)

When in Rome . . .

One of the most intriguing aspects of travel literature is how traveller and host react to each other. Each side comes to the meeting with a great deal of psychological and emotional baggage. Some travellers are tolerant, easy-going and open-minded. Others wear their prejudices like a suit of armour. The same could be said of their hosts. One area in which differences become acutely exposed is language. We have already seen this in the context of church benefices. Another is dress which we have seen in the context of hunting. The irony is that although the distinctive form of Highland dress was banned after Culloden it actually survived to become the marketing man's stereotype of Scottish garb. Across the globe the kilt and bagpipes are regarded as quintessentially Scottish. By contrast, although Gaelic has never been banned, except in school, it has been far more successfully hounded out by hostile forces.

Taylor seems to have been a sympathetic traveller, quite prepared to leave his own cultural baggage behind him and adapt to the customs and mores of the Highlands. In effect he disarmed his hosts by kindness. Other travellers then, and since, have not always been so understanding. By contrast Thomas Kirk writes in 1679:

> *The Lowland language may be well enough understood by an English man, but the Highlanders have a peculiar lingue to themselves, which they call Erst* [Erse=Gaelic], *unknown to most of the Lowland men, except only in those places that border on them, where they can speak both. Yet these people are so currish, that if a stranger enquire the way in English, they will certainly answer in Erst, and find no other language than what is inforc'd from them with a cudgel.* (T. Kirk in Hume Brown, *Early Travellers in Scotland*)

These two approaches, Taylor's and Kirk's, point up a contrast in attitudes that is timeless. They could be repeated in almost any country, in any century, and for any imperial language. Unfortunately there are still many people who, when abroad, and finding their words not understood, think that the only solution is to repeat them more loudly.

When two cultures collide there is often hostility. One of the beneficial effects of travel, and the literature of travel, is that this is increasingly overtaken by humour. Because it reflects the preconceptions of the visitor such humour as we find in early travel literature is often at the expense of the local society.

Humour

Walker writes of Skye: '*so ignorant are the People of these green Crops, that old Macdonald of Kingsbury, having once raised a Field of Pease, gave out in order to save them from Depredation, that it was a poisonous Plant he had sown, to kill the Foxes.*' (McKay, *Walker's Report on the Hebrides*, 1764 and 1771)
Pennant comments on cairns on the south-west side of Iona:

> *a vast tract near this place was covered with heaps of stones, of unequal sizes: these, as is said, were the penances of monks who were to raise heaps of dimensions equal to their crimes: and to judge by some, it is no breach of charity to think there were among them enormous sinners.* (T. Pennant, *A Tour in Scotland and Voyage to the Hebrides*, 1772)

Boswell states that Johnson, who was scathing about the lack of trees in Scotland,: '*carried in his hand a large English oak stick.*' Unfortunately this went missing during their travels. Boswell writes: '*I could not persuade him out of a suspicion that it had been stolen. 'No, no, my friend,' said he, 'it is not to be expected that any man in Mull, who has got it, will part with it. Consider, sir, the value of such a piece of timber here!*' (Boswell, *The Journal of a Tour to the Hebrides*, 1773)
Towards the end of their trip Johnson met Maclean of Lochbuy in Mull: '*Lochbuy, where we found a true Highland laird, rough and haughty, and tenacious of his dignity; who, hearing my name, inquired whether I was of the Johnstons of Glencoe, or of Ardnamurchan.*' (Johnson, *A Journey to the Western Islands of Scotland*, 1773)
Edward Daniel Clarke gives a rather different version of this story:

> *But Dr. J. has not thought proper to represent accurately the conversation that passed between them. I suppose his pride was too much hurt to permit so strict an adherence to candour; since, I believe, no one will suspect him of a wish to soften any harsh features in the characteristics of the natives with whom he conversed. Loch Buy, according to the usual custom among the Highlanders, demanded the name of his guest; and upon being informed that it was Johnson, inquired 'Which of the Johnston's? of Glencoe or Ardnamurchan?' – 'Neither!' replied the Doctor, somewhat piqued by the question, and not a little sulky with the fatigue he had encountered during the day's journey. 'Neither!' rejoined the Laird, with all the native roughness of a genuine Highlander, 'then you must be a bastard'.* (E.D. Clarke, *Journal*, 1797)

Clarke, though, enjoyed Johnson. He understood and appreciated his humour where others took offence. In 1791, six years before his own trip to the Hebrides, Clarke cited Johnson's legendary address to a Highland crow: '*What, have wings, and stay here?*'

In the case of Faujas de Saint Fond the humour derives less from the wit than the situation. Faujas had just spent a constructive and enjoyable day collecting rock-specimens near Oban:

I supped with much pleasure, and sleep soon making my eyes heavy, I gladly went to bed; it was hard, but clean, and fatigue made it into down.

But one can hardly enjoy every happiness at once in this vile world. Will it be believed that music of a kind new to me, but very terrible to my ears, disturbed the repose I so much needed? I had scarcely lain down when a cursed piper came and placed himself under my window. He waited upon me every evening in the passage of the inn, to regale me with an air; he then established himself in front of the house. There was no way of making him stop, and he went on to play this noisy instrument until eleven o'clock, with the wish to be agreeable to me, and to do me a kind of honour, of which I in vain endeavoured to convince him I was unworthy.

On the day of our arrival, this man came before our lodging, walking to and fro with equal steps, and a bold and martial expression of face, deafening us with perpetual repetitions of the most unharmonious sounds, without any air or meaning. At first we took him to be a kind of madman, who earned his livelihood in this way; but Patrick Fraser assured us, that not only was this good Highlander in his senses, but that he had the reputation of being an excellent musician of the Highland school; that his principal intention in playing on this instrument before us was to show his joy at our arrival in a country so seldom visited by foreigners. Touched by this hospitable motive, I was prodigal in my applause, and begged of him to accept some shillings, which he at first refused, and seemed only to receive that he might not displease me. He never played but the same air, if I may give that name to a kind of composition unintelligible to foreigners, but which brings to the recollection of the Highlanders and Hebridians historical events which have the greatest interest for them. As the piper had seen my companions set off, he persuaded himself that I remained behind to hear his music: and thinking, that his concerts would be most agreeable to me in the silence of the night, he continued his serenade under my window till eleven or twelve o'clock. Nothing could induce him to desist. I rose one evening with impatience, and not being able to make myself understood by speech, I took him by the hand to lead him to a distance. He returned immediately, however, as one who disputes a point of politeness, giving me to understand by his gestures, that he was not at all tired, and that he would play all night to please me; and he kept his word. Next day I forced him to accept again a small present, and made signs to him that I did not wish to hear him any more; but he was not to be outdone in civility. That very evening he returned, and made his pipe resound until midnight, playing constantly the same air. (Faujas de Saint Fond, *A journey through England and Scotland to the Hebrides in 1784*)

Tourist guides

Tourism produces its own literature and in the context of the Highlands and Islands this starts to appear from about 1770. Franck, Burt and other earlier visitors had described the difficulties of travelling in the Highlands but they had been writing for the sake of a public elsewhere, not for prospective tourists.

Johnson and Boswell were aware of such literature and its style. On visiting Inch Keith, in the Firth of Forth, Boswell wrote:

Dr Johnson afterwards bade me try to write a description of our discovering Inch Keith, in the usual style of travellers, describing fully every particular; stating the grounds on which we concluded that it must have once been inhabited, and introducing many sage reflections; and we should see how a thing might be covered in words, so as to induce people to come and survey it. (Boswell, *The Journal of a Tour to the Hebrides*, 1773)

Pennant must have been aware of the growing interest in visiting the Highlands, or at least the more accessible parts of it, when he refers to: '*the route which travellers must take, who make what I call the petit tour of Scotland.*' (Pennant, *A Tour in Scotland 1769*)

He then gives the latter part of it, in a footnote, as Taymouth, Killin, Tyndrum, Glenorchy, Inveraray, Luss, Dumbarton, Glasgow, Stirling, Edinburgh: '*A tract unparalleled, for the variety, and frequency of fine and magnificent scenery.*' (Pennant, *A Tour in Scotland 1769*)

At the time there was a tremendous international interest in things Highland – not least because of the fame, or notoriety, of MacPherson's Ossianic poetry. The claims of fine scenery were helped by a succession of geologists and naturalists. The former included Faujas de Saint Fond (1784) and Edward Daniel Clarke (1797), who were succeeded, a generation or two later, by John MacCulloch and Hugh Miller. The route to the islands soon became a well-trod path. Faujas de Saint Fond writes of his reception by the Duke of Argyll at Inveraray Castle in 1784:

They did not fail to enquire the object of our journey to a country so little visited as this remote part of Scotland; but they were not at all surprised when they heard that our purpose was to go to the Isle of Staffa, with its Cave of Fingal, which had now a great reputation in the country. (Faujas de Saint Fond, *A journey through England and Scotland to the Hebrides in 1784*)

A characteristic of tourist literature – that literature produced consciously for other travellers – was its instructional nature. Phrases such as 'The visitor should . . .', indicate the purpose and market. Johnson and Boswell may have avoided it, Pennant steered a middle course but Sarah Murray positively adopted it.

Of Iona:

> *The traveller must not neglect to ascend the hill of Dun-ii; from whose summit is a most picturesque view of the long chain of little islands, neighbours to this; of the long low isles of Col and Tir-I to the west; and the vast height of Rum and Skie to the north.* (T. Pennant, *A Tour in Scotland and Voyage to the Hebrides*, 1772)

Faujas de Saint Fond, writing for other geologists who visited Torloisk in Mull:

> *The traveller should not omit visiting . . . a quarry, out of which all the stones of his buildings have been taken. Here several lavas may be found which are worthy of attention.* (Faujas de Saint Fond, *A journey through England and Scotland to the Hebrides in 1784*)

While Mrs Murray's *Companion and Useful Guide to the Beauties of Scotland, and the Hebrides* etc., contains the following Advertisement to the Reader:

> *This Guide points out to the Traveller what is worth noticing in his Tour, with the distances from place to place; mentions the Inns on the road, whether good or bad; also what state the Roads are in; and informs him of those fit for a carriage, and those where it cannot go, with safety. In these respects, the present work differs from any other Publication of the kind: for no writer of Tours has hitherto taken the trouble of ascertaining what may be seen, worthy of notice, in the course of a Traveller's journey: and it very often happens that he passes within a mile, or less, of very great Natural Beauties, without either knowing or having heard of them; and the country people seldom or ever name to strangers what they think nothing of; because, seeing them every day, they regard them not as objects of admiration.* (Mrs Murray, *Companion and Useful Guide to the Beauties of Scotland*)

We are now recognisably on modern ground.

Select Bibliography

This is not an exhaustive bibliography. It is intended as a guide to further reading for those who become sufficiently interested to pursue their own research.

In this book I have followed the convention of referring to the 'Old' and 'New' Statistical Accounts. Technically the former was not 'old'.

For E. D. Clarke see under Otter.

A Journey through Part of England and Scotland by a Volunteer, London, 1747

Accounts of the Lord High Treasurer of Scotland, 1473–1566, T. Dickson & Sir J. Balfour Paul, (eds), 1877–1916

Anderson, A. O. *Early Sources of Scottish History*, vols 1–2, Stamford, 1990

Anderson, A. O. *Scottish Annals from English Chroniclers*, Stamford, 1991

Anderson, J. *An Account of the present state of the Hebrides and western coasts of Scotland*, Edinburgh, 1785

The Auchinleck Chronicle, Edinburgh, 1819

Bliss, W. and Twemlow, J. (eds), *Calendar of Entries in the Papal Registers, Papal Letters*, vol 4 (1362–1404), London, 1902.

Blundell, O., *Catholic Highlands of Scotland*, Edinburgh, 1917

Broderick, G., *Chronicles of the Kings of Man and the Isles*, Douglas, 1995

David Bruce (Manuscript), Hardwicke Papers, Vol 99, British Library

Buchan, Rev. A., *A Description of St Kilda 1773*, Glasgow, 1818

Buchanan, J. L., *Travels in the Western Hebrides from 1782 to 1790*, Skye, 1997

Burns, C. (ed.), *Papal Letters to Scotland of Clement VII of Avignon 1378–1394*, Scottish History Society, Edinburgh, 1976

Calendar of Documents relating to Scotland, Bain et al. (eds), Edinburgh, 1881–8

Calendar of State Papers – Carew, Brewer & Bullen (eds), London, 1867

Calendar of State Papers Ireland, Hamilton et al. (eds), London, 1877

Calendar of State Papers relating to Scotland, Boyd et al. (eds), Edinburgh, 1898–1952

Cameron, A. *Reliquiae Celticae*, vols. 1–2, Inverness, 1892–94

Campbell, H. *Argyll Sasines*, Edinburgh, 1933–34

Campbell, J. L. and Thomson, D. *Edward Lhuyd in the Scottish Highlands 1699–1700*, Oxford, 1963

Chronicles of the Frasers, Wardlaw Manuscript, Scottish History Society, Edinburgh, 1905

Cody, E. (ed.), *Leslie's History of Scotland*, Scottish Text Society, Edinburgh, 1884–5.

Collectanea de Rebus Albanicis, Edinburgh, 1847

Craigie, W. A. (ed.), *The Asloan Manuscript*, Edinburgh, 1923

Craven, J. B. *Journals of the Episcopal Visitations of the Right Rev. Robert Forbes*, London, 1923

Craven, J. B. *Records of the Dioceses of Argyll and the Isles 1560–1860*, Kirkwall, 1907

Daniell, W. *A Voyage round Great Britain*, London, 1814–25

Donaldson, G. *Scottish Historical Documents*, Edinburgh, 1970

Dunlop, A. I. (ed.), *Calendar of Scottish Supplications to Rome 1423–1428*, Scottish History Society, Edinburgh, 1956

Dunlop, A. I. (ed.), *Calendar of Scottish Supplications to Rome 1428–1432*, Scottish History Society, Edinburgh, 1970

Extracts from the Records of the Burgh of Stirling, 1519–1666, Glasgow, 1887

Forbes, Revd R. *The Lyon in Mourning*, Scottish History Society, Edinburgh, 1895–97

Franck, R. *Northern Memoirs*, Edinburgh, 1821.

Geikie, A. (ed.), B. Faujas de Saint Fond, *A journey through England and Scotland to the Hebrides in 1784*, Glasgow, 1907

Giblin, C. *The 'Acta' of Propaganda Archives and the Scottish Mission, 1623–1670*, in The Innes Review Vol 5, No 1, 1954.

Giblin, C. *Irish Franciscan Mission to Scotland 1619–1646*, Dublin, 1964

Gunther, R. T. *Life and Letters of Edward Lhwyd* (Early Science at Oxford Series, Vol XIV), Oxford, 1945.

Haldane, A. R. B. *New Ways through the Glens*, Newton Abbot, 1973

Haldane, A. R. B. *The Drove Roads of Scotland*, Newton Abbot, 1973

Hayes-McCoy, G. A., *Scots Mercenary Forces in Ireland*, Dublin, 1996

Highland Papers, vols I-IV, Scottish History Society, Edinburgh, 1914–34

Hogg, J. *Highland Tours*, Hawick, 1981

Hughes, J. and Ramson, W. S. *Poetry of the Stewart Court*, Canberra, 1982

Hume Brown, P. (ed.), *Early Travellers in Scotland*, Edinburgh, 1891

Hume Brown, P. (ed.), *Scotland before 1700*, Edinburgh, 1893

Hume Brown, P. (ed.), *Tours in Scotland 1677 and 1681 by Thomas Kirk and Ralph Thoresby*, Edinburgh 1892

The Innes Review, John S. Burns and Sons, Glasgow

Knox, J. *A Tour through the Highlands of Scotland and the Hebride Isles in 1786*, London, 1787.

Lang, A. *The Highlands of Scotland in 1750*, London, 1898.

Larson, L. M. *The King's Mirror, (Speculum Regale – Konungs Skuggsja)*, New York, 1917

Letters and Papers of the Reign of Henry VIII, vol XXI, Pt I, Gairdner & Brodie (eds), London, 1908

Alexander Lindsay – A rutter of the Scottish seas, National Maritime Museum Monograph 44, London, 1980

Lindsay, E. R. and Cameron, A. I. (eds), *Calendar of Scottish Supplications to Rome 1418–1422*, Scottish History Society, Edinburgh, 1934

MacCulloch, J. *The Highlands and Western Isles of Scotland*, 1824

Macdonald, F. *Irish Priests in the Highlands*, in The Innes Review, vol LXVI, I, 1995.

McGurk, F. (ed.), *Papal Letters to Scotland of Benedict XIII of Avignon 1394–1419*, Scottish History Society, Edinburgh, 1976

McKay, M. M. (ed.), *The Rev Dr John Walker's Report on the Hebrides of 1764 and 1771*, Edinburgh, 1980

Mackenna, F. S., *Kist* (The Magazine of the Antiquarian and Natural History Society of Mid-Argyll) No's 17 & 18, 1979

Mackenzie, W. C. *The Highlands and Isles of Scotland*, Edinburgh, 1937

Mackenzie, W. C. *History of the Outer Hebrides*, Paisley, 1903

Mackenzie, W. C. *Notes on the Pigmies Isle*, in Proceedings of the Society of Antiquaries of Scotland, vol 39, Edinburgh, 1905.

Martin, Martin, *A Description of the Western Islands of Scotland*, Birlinn, 1994 (also includes Donald Monro's description)

Megaw, B. *Norseman and Native in the Kingdom of the Isles*, in Scottish Studies, Vol 20, 1976

Miller, H. *The Cruise of the Betsey* (written in 1845), Edinburgh, 1897

Mitchell A. (ed.), *Macfarlane's Geographical Collections, Vol II*, Scottish History Society, Edinburgh, 1907

Monipennie, J. *Scots Chronicles*, Edinburgh, 1818.

Monro, D. *A Description of the Western Isles of Scotland*, [included with Martin Martin], Birlinn, 1994

Monsen, E. (ed.), *Heimskringla or the Lives of the Norse Kings by Snorre Sturlason*, Cambridge, 1932

Muller, Max *Lectures on the Science of Language*, London, 1880

Munro, R. W. (ed), *Monro's Western Isles of Scotland*, Edinburgh, 1961

Murray, S. *A Companion and Useful Guide to the Beauties of Scotland and the Hebrides*, London, 1810

O'Meara, J. J. (trans), *Gerald of Wales – The History and Topography of Ireland*, Penguin, 1982

Origines Parochiales Scotiae, Edinburgh, 1851

Otter, Revd W. *The Life and Remains of Edward Daniel Clarke*, 2nd edition, London, 1825

Pelham, R. A. *The Gough Map*, in Early Maps of Great Britain, Geographical Journal, vol 81, 1923

Pennant, T. *A Tour in Scotland and Voyage to the Hebrides 1772*, Edinburgh, 1998

Pennant, T. *A Tour in Scotland 1769*, Edinburgh, 2000

Poole, R. L. *The Scottish Islands in the Diocese of Sodor*, Scottish Historical Review, vol 8, 1911

Pursemaster's Accounts, Scottish History Society, Miscellany X, Edinburgh, 1965

Raine, J. (ed.), *Reginaldi Monachi Dunelmensis Libellus*, Surtees Society, London, 1835

Ramsay, L. (ed.), *The Stent Book and Acts of the Balliary of Islay, 1718–1843*, Edinburgh, 1890

Reeves, W. (ed) *Life of Saint Columba*, Edinburgh, 1874

Register of the Privy Council of Scotland, J. Hill Burton & D. Masson (eds), Edinburgh, 1877–1970

Registrum Magni Sigilli Regum Scottorum, J. M. Thomson (ed.), Edinburgh, 1984

Rixson, D. *The Small Isles*, Edinburgh, 2001

Rixson, D. *The West Highland Galley*, Edinburgh, 1998

Robertson, Revd C. M. Topography and Traditions of Eigg, in *Transactions of the Gaelic Society of Inverness*, vol XXII, 1897–8

Rotuli Scotiae, D. MacPherson, et al. (eds), London, 1814–19

Necker de Saussure, L. A. *A Voyage to the Hebrides*, London, 1822

Scotichronicon by Walter Bower, D. E. R. Watt et al. (eds), Aberdeen, 1987–1998

Skene, G. (ed.), *Narrative of Prince Charlie's escape*, Blackwood's Magazine, vol 114, 1873

Skene, W. F. *John of Fordun's Chronicle of the Scottish Nation*, Llanerch, 1993

Skene, W. F. *Celtic Scotland*, Edinburgh, 1880

Smith, G. G. (ed.), *The Book of Islay*, 1895

Somers, R. *Letters from the Highlands*, Inverness, 1977

Stone, J. *Illustrated Maps of Scotland*, Studio Editions, London, 1991

Stone, J. The Depiction of Routeways and Bridges by Timothy Pont, in *Northern Scotland*, vol 23, 2003.

Stone, J. *The Pont Manuscript Maps of Scotland*, Map Collector Publications, Tring, 1989

Taylor, J. *The Pennyles Pilgrimage*, London, 1618

Teignmouth, Lord, *Sketches of the Coasts and Islands of Scotland*, London, 1836

Thomson, D. *An Introduction to Gaelic Poetry*, London, 1977

Thorpe, L. (transl.), *Geoffrey of Monmouth, The History of the Kings of Britain*, Harmondsworth, 1966

Tocher 36–7, Journal of the School of Scottish Studies, Edinburgh, 1981–2

Todd, J. H. (ed & transl.), *The Irish version of the Historia Britonum of Nennius*, Dublin, 1848

Twemlow, J. A. (ed.), *Calendar of Papal Letters*, vol IX, London, 1912

Vaughan, R. *The Illustrated Chronicles of Matthew Paris*, Stroud, 1993

Waghenaer, L. *Speculum Nauticum*, Leyden, 1586

Wills, V. (ed.), *Reports on the Annexed Estates*, Edinburgh, 1973